FACTBOOK OF
THE 20ᵀᴴ
CENTURY

FACTBOOK OF
THE 20TH
CENTURY

Galley Press

Author
George Beal

Editor
John Grisewood

Copyright © 1985 by
Grisewood & Dempsey Ltd.
Published in this edition by Galley
Press, an imprint of W.H. Smith and
Son Limited, Registered No.
237811 England. Trading as
W H Smith Distributors,
St John's House, East Street,
Leicester, LE1 6NE

Revised and updated 1989

ISBN 0861360842

Printed and bound in Italy
by Vallardi Industrie Grafiche, Milan.

Contents

Events of the Century	10
Countries of the World	65
Politics and International Affairs	82
Science, Technology and Medicine	122
Transport and Exploration	143
The Arts of the Century	163
The World of Sport	206
Religion and Philosophy	214
The World of Business	216
Nobel Prizewinners	221
Index	228

Cross References

Throughout this book the names of certain people and events are printed in small capital letters (DREYFUS or OCTOBER REVOLUTION, for example). This indicates that these subjects have entries of their own. The pages of these will be found by referring to the index.

Events of the Century

1900 7 Feb: Labour Representation Committee founded in Britain (LABOUR PARTY).
28 Feb: BOER WAR. Ladysmith is relieved by General Buller.
13 March: General Roberts captures Bloemfontein.
17 May: Mafeking is relieved.
20 May to 28 Oct: The IInd Olympic Games are held at Paris.
24 May: Britain annexes the Orange Free State, which becomes the Orange River Colony.
12 June: German Navy Law provides for massive increase in sea power; starts arms race with Britain.
13 June - 14 Aug: Boxer Rebellion. Nationalist forces in China (Boxers) rebel and besiege foreign legations. Rebellion suppressed by international forces.
2 July: The first Zeppelin makes a trial flight.
25 Oct: Transvaal is annexed by Britain.

1901 1 Jan: The Commonwealth of Australia is born.
22 Jan: Queen Victoria dies. EDWARD VII becomes King of England.
J.P. Morgan founds the United States Steel Corporation.

1902 30 Jan: Anglo-Japanese alliance concluded.
31 May: Treaty of Vereeniging ends Boer War.
19 Dec: British, German and Italian fleets seize Venezuelan navy to force payment of debts.

1903 15 March: British conquest of Northern Nigeria is completed.
May: Scandal about appalling labour conditions in Congo Free State.
20 July: Following the death of Pope Leo XIII, Giuseppe Sarto is elected as PIUS X.
Oct: Women's Social and Political Union formed in Britain by suffragette Mrs Emmeline PANKHURST.
3 Nov: Panama becomes independent of Colombia.
Nov: Meeting in London of Russian Social Democratic party. It splits into Mensheviks (moderates) and Bolsheviks (extremists).
17 Dec: Orville and Wilbur WRIGHT, at Kitty Hawk, USA, make the world's first flight by a heavier-than-air machine.
Krupps Works at Essen founded.

Suffragettes—militant campaigners for votes for women—celebrating the release of two of their members from Holloway Prison, London.

1904 4 Feb: RUSSO-JAPANESE WAR begins.
8 April: *Entente cordiale* (friendly understanding) between Britain and France.
4 May: Work begins on the Panama Canal.
1 July to 23 Nov: The IIIrd Olympic Games are held at St Louis, USA.
7 Sept: British explorer Sir Francis Younghusband leads expedition to Lhasa, Tibet, and treaty with Tibet is signed, opening up country to western trade.
2 Nov: The British newspaper *The Daily Mirror* is founded by Alfred Harmsworth.
8 Nov: Theodore ROOSEVELT Republican, is re-elected as president of USA.
The Subway (underground rail-way) opens in Broadway, New York.

1905 1 Jan: Port Arthur falls to Japan in Russo-Japanese war.
22 Jan: Massacre in St Petersburg in Russia, known as 'Bloody Sunday'.
27 May: Destruction of Russian fleet by Admiral Togo at battle of Tsushima.
28 June: In Russia, sailors aboard the battleship *Potemkin* mutiny.
5 Sept: Treaty of Portsmouth, USA, ends Russo-Japanese war.
31 March: Moroccan crisis between France and Germany.
26 Oct: Union of Sweden and Norway ends.
30 Oct: The Russian Tsar agrees, by the 'October Manifesto' to grant civil liberties and elections.
18 Nov: Prince Carl of Denmark chosen to become King Haakon VII of Norway.
5 Dec: Liberal government in Britain, with Henry Campbell-Bannerman as prime minister.

In 1905 the Russian fleet was surprisingly and humiliatingly defeated by the Japanese at Tsushima.

22 Dec.- 1 Jan: In Russia, an insurrection of workers in Moscow.

1906 12 Jan: Liberal landslide in British general election. First Labour MPs returned. LABOUR PARTY formed.

16 Jan. - April: International meeting at Algeciras to discuss Morocco, at which French rights were recognized.

10 Feb: Britain's first modern battleship, HMS *Dreadnought,* is launched.

18 April: San Francisco is destroyed by earthquake and fire.

22 April to 2 May: The 10th Anniversary Olympic Games are held at Athens.

10 May: Russian *Duma* (parliament) meets for the first time, but is dissolved.

17 May: Simplon tunnel, Switzerland, is opened for railway.

12 July: Alfred DREYFUS, French army officer, is retried and found innocent.

1907 15 June - 18 Oct: Second Peace Conference at the Hague. Arms limitation opposed by Germany.

16 June: Second Duma is dismissed in Russia. A third more conservative Duma lasts until 1912.

July: The Triple Alliance of the Central Powers: Germany, Austria-Hungary and Italy is renewed for three years.

31 Aug: *Triple Entente* set up between Britain, France and Russia, in opposition to the Central Powers.

26 Sept: New Zealand becomes a dominion.

16 Nov: Oklahoma is admitted as the 46th state of the USA.

1908 8 April: In Britain, ASQUITH becomes prime minister.

27 April to 31 Oct: The IVth Olympic Games are held in London.

23 June: In Persia, Shah Mohammed Ali overturns the constitution of December, 1906.

6 July: The Young Turk movement stages a revolution in Turkey.

20 Aug: The Congo Free State (previously a personal possession of Leopold II of the Belgians) becomes a colony under the name Belgian Congo.

5 Oct: Bulgaria declares independence from Turkey. Ferdinand I becomes Tsar of Bulgaria.

6 Oct: Austria annexes Bosnia and Herzegovina.

7 Oct: Crete revolts against Turkey and proclaims union with Greece.

3 Nov: William Howard Taft, Republican, is elected 27th president of the USA.

Robert BADEN-POWELL founds the Boy Scouts.

Launching of the liners *Lusitania* and *Mauretania.*

Harvey Crippen, the wife-poisoner, and Ethel Le Neve (disguised as a boy) being arrested aboard ship in 1910 as they tried to escape across the Atlantic.

1909 6 April: Robert Peary, American explorer, reaches the North Pole, after seven trips to the Arctic.
27 April: The Sultan of Turkey, Abdul Hamid II, is overthrown by Young Turks and succeeded by Mohammed V.
25 July: BLÉRIOT makes the first cross-channel flight in a heavier-than-air machine.
17 Dec: In Belgium, Leopold II dies and is succeeded by Albert I.
In the USA, Henry FORD begins 'assembly line' production of cheap motor-cars, producing the Model T.

1910 1 Feb: Labour exchanges are established in Britain.
6 May: In Britain, EDWARD VII dies. GEORGE V succeeds.
1 July: The Union of South Africa is formed with dominion status.
22 Aug: Japan annexes Korea.
4 Oct: King Manuel II of Portugal flees to England; Portugal becomes a republic.
23 Nov: The American wife poisoner, Hawley Harvey Crippen, is executed.
Militant activities by the British suffragette movement.
Opening of Manhattan Bridge, New York.
The 11th edition of the *Encyclopaedia Britannica* is published.

1911 25 May: Revolution in Mexico. President Diaz is overthrown.
1 July: Crisis between France and Germany over Agadir, Morocco. Germany sends a gunboat, but withdraws claims.
10 Aug: The Parliament Act reduces the power of the House of Lords.
5 Nov: Italy declares war on Turkey and takes Tripoli and Cyrenaica.
15 Dec: Roald AMUNDSEN, Norwegian explorer, reaches the South Pole.
30 Dec: SUN YAT-SEN becomes president of China, after leading a revolution.

The *Mona Lisa* painting by Leonardo da Vinci, is stolen from the Louvre in Paris.

1912 6 Jan: New Mexico becomes the 47th state of the USA.
18 Jan: R.F. SCOTT's last expedition; reaches South Pole.
12 Feb: The Manchu dynasty is overthrown and China becomes a republic.
14 Feb: Arizona becomes the 48th state of the USA.
26 Feb. - 1 March: Strike of coal-miners in Britain.
30 March: French protectorate established in Morocco; Spanish zone defined by agreement.
4 April: In Tibet, a Chinese republic is proclaimed.
15 April: The White Star liner *Titanic* sinks on her maiden voyage, with a loss of 1513 lives.
5 May to 22 July: The Vth Olympic Games are held in Stockholm, and are timed electrically.
15 July: British National Health Insurance Act comes into force.
8 Oct: First BALKAN WAR. Bulgaria, Greece, Serbia and Montenegro unite against Turkey.
18 Oct: Italo-Turkish war ends, when Tripoli and Cyrenaica are ceded to Italy.
The Royal Flying Corps is started.
The 'Piltdown Man' skull is found, but 40 years later (21st Nov., 1953) is declared to be a hoax.

1913 30 Jan: The Irish Home Rule Bill rejected by the House of Lords. Threat of civil war in Ireland. Ulster Volunteers (private Protestant army) formed in opposition to Home Rule.
4 March: Woodrow WILSON is inaugurated as 28th president of the USA.
30 May: First Balkan war ends (Treaty of London). Balkan states victorious; new state of Albania created.

30 June: Second BALKAN WAR. Serbia, Greece, Romania and Turkey unite against Bulgaria.
10 Aug: Balkan war ends (Treaty of Bucharest) and Bulgaria is defeated.
14 Dec: Crete is officially taken over by Greece.

The Woolworth Building in New York, designed by Cass Gilbert, is completed.

The fox-trot comes into fashion.

John D. ROCKEFELLER founds the Rockefeller Institute.

Federal income tax is introduced in the USA.

1914 25 May: The British House of Commons passes the Irish Home Rule Act. Provides for separate Parliament in Ireland, with some MPs at Westminster.
28 June: The Archduke Franz Ferdinand and his wife are assassinated at Sarajevo by a Bosnian student.
WORLD WAR I begins. Allied powers are Great Britain, France, Russia, Italy and the USA. The Central powers are Germany, Austria-Hungary and Turkey.
28 June: Austria invades Serbia.
15 Aug: Panama Canal opens officially to traffic.
20 Aug: Pope Pius X dies.

26 Aug: Battle of Tannenburg. Russians defeated by German forces.
1 Sept: In Russia, St Petersburg becomes 'Petrograd'
3 Sept: Cardinal Giacomo della Chiesa becomes Pope BENEDICT XV.
5 - 12 Sept: First Battle of the Marne. Allies halt German advance on Paris.
9 - 12 Sept: Battle of the Masurian lakes. Russians retreat from East Prussia.
15 Sept: Operation of the Irish Home Rule Bill is suspended until after the war.
16 Sept: Three British cruisers are sunk by one U-Boat.
30 Oct. - 21 Nov: Battle of Ypres. Germans fail to reach Channel ports. Trench warfare on Western and Eastern fronts until the end of war.
1 Nov: At the Battle of Coronel (off Chile), two German cruisers sink two British cruisers.
5 Nov: Britain annexes Cyprus (occupied since June, 1878).
8 Nov: German squadron off Falkland Islands is destroyed.
17 Dec: British protectorate over Egypt proclaimed.

Currency notes for £1 and 10 shillings issued in Britain.

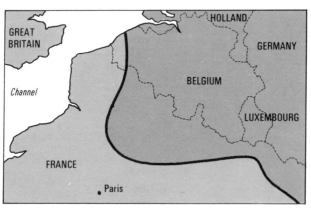

By the end of the first year of the First World War, the Western Front had settled into a long line from the Belgian coast to the Swiss border. With only very small changes, this was to remain the shape of the front for the next four years.

1915 4 Feb: Naval blockade of Germany announced by Britain.

18 Feb: Germany begins submarine blockade of Britain.

11 March: British blockade of Germany starts to operate.

22 April - 25 May: Second Battle of Ypres. Poison gas used for the first time by Germany on the Western Front.

23 April: Rupert BROOKE, English poet, dies.

25 April: Allied forces land on Gallipoli Peninsula, Turkey, but fail to win control of Dardanelles straits.

1 May: German submarines sink the US ship *Gulflight.*

7 May: Cunard liner *Lusitania* is sunk by German U-boat. 1198 lives lost, including 124 Americans. This brings the US close to war with Germany.

26 May: British Coalition government formed under H.H. ASQUITH.

1 June: The first Zeppelin air raid on London.

7 June: Zeppelin destroyed in raid over Britain.

September: Battles of Artois, Champagne and Loos. British and French offensive fails.

11 Oct: Edith Cavell is executed by the Germans in Brussels.

15 Oct: Bulgaria joins the Central powers.

23 Oct: W.G. Grace, English cricketer, dies.

12 Nov: Britain annexes the Gilbert and Ellice Islands.

3 Dec: Marshal Joffre becomes the French commander-in-chief.

16 Dec: General Haig becomes British commander-in-chief in France and Flanders.

Albert EINSTEIN publishes his *General Theory of Relativity.*

In Britain, Women's Institutes are founded.

1916 27 Jan: In Berlin, the Communist party 'Spartacus' is formed.

29 Jan: First Zeppelin air raid on Paris.

9th Feb: British military service act (conscription) comes into force.

21 Feb. - 16 Dec: Battle of Verdun; German offensive on Western Front (February to July).

24 April: Easter rising in Ireland; suppressed after one week.

21 May: Summer Time (daylight saving) is begun in Britain.

31 May: Battle of Jutland: the only major naval battle between Britain and Germany.

2 June: Second battle of Ypres.

4 June: Brusilov offensive on the Eastern Front. Russian attack led by General Brusilov fails.

5 June: Lord KITCHENER drowns when warship HMS *Hampshire* strikes a mine.

1 July - 8 Nov: Battle of the Somme. British and French offensive. Over one million killed. 30th Aug: Paul von HINDENBURG becomes chief of general staff in Germany.

15 Sept: First use of tanks by Britain on the Western Front.

7 Nov: Woodrow Wilson, Democrat, is re-elected president of the USA.

21 Nov: Franz Josef of Austria dies. His grand-nephew becomes Charles I.

29 Nov: Von Hindenburg becomes German commander-in-chief on the Western Front.

7 Dec: In Britain, H.H. Asquith resigns and David Lloyd George becomes prime minister.

Food rationed in Germany.

1917 4 - 14 March: Revolution in Russia.

11 March: British capture Baghdad from Turkey.

16 March: In Russia, Tsar Nicholas II abdicates, and provisional government takes over.

6 April: United States declares war on Germany.

9 April: Battle of Arras until 14 April.

10 April: Vimy Ridge taken by Canadian forces.

15 May: Henri PÉTAIN becomes French commander-in-chief.

19 June: All German titles and names are renounced by the British royal family, who adopt the name Windsor.

24 June: In Russia, the Black Sea fleet mutinies.

26 June: First American forces arrive in France.

19 July - 2 Aug: Mutinies in the German navy.

22 July: Alexander KERENSKY becomes Russian prime minister.

31 July - 10 Nov: Third Battle of Ypres (Passchendaele): minor British offensive on Western Front.

July: The Allies execute Mata Hari as a spy.

15 Sept: Russia is proclaimed a republic by Alexander Kerensky.

24 Oct: Battle of Caporetto: Italy is defeated by the Austrians.

2 Nov: In the Balfour Declaration, Britain announces support for a Jewish state in Palestine.

5 Nov: American troops under General Pershing go into action for the first time on the Western Front.

7 Nov: (Russian Old Style Calendar 26th Oct.) OCTOBER REVOLUTION. The Bolsheviks under Lenin seize power from Kerensky in Russia.

20 Nov: At Cambrai, British tanks take part in first major battle.

20 Nov: Ukrainian republic declared.

5 Dec: Russia signs an armistice with Germany.

9 Dec: British forces capture Jerusalem.

The bobbed hair style sweeps the USA and Great Britain.

Russia, 1917. Peasants mobbing a train. The interruption of traffic and communications caused enormous problems to the already overstretched Russian administration.

1918 6 Feb: British Act of Parliament grants votes for women (aged 30 and over).
3 March: Russia withdraws from the war having signed the Treaty of Brest-Litovsk with Germany.
21 March: Second Battle of the Somme. Germans launch offensive.
23 March: Germans shell Paris from a distance of 75 miles.
23 March: Lithuania proclaims her independence.
1 April: Formation of the Royal Air Force, replacing the Royal Flying Corps.
9 April: Latvia proclaims her independence.
22 - 23 April: British naval raid on Zeebrugge.
1 - 10 May: British naval raid on Ostend.
15 July - 4 Aug: Second Battle of the Marne.
16 July: Tsar Nicholas and all Russian royal family murdered.
2 Aug: Last German offensive fails.
20 Aug: British offensive on Western Front.
4 Sept: Germans retreat to Siegfried Line.
17 Oct: Yugoslav republic established.
24 Oct: Italian victory at Vittorio Veneto. Austria-Hungary surrenders.
30 Oct: Czechoslovakian republic proclaimed.
Austria becomes a republic.
Allies sign Armistices with Turkey (30 Oct.); Austria Hungary (3 Nov.).
3 Nov: German fleet mutinies at Kiel.
6 Nov: Republic of Poland proclaimed.
9 Nov: Republic proclaimed in Bavaria.
9 Nov: Revolution in Germany. Kaiser WILHELM II abdicates.
11 Nov: Germany signs an armistice. End of World War I.

12 Nov: Emperor Karl of Austria-Hungary abdicates. Austria becomes a republic.
1 Dec: Iceland becomes independent.
4 Dec: The Kingdom of Serbs, Croats and Slovenes (Yugoslavia) is proclaimed in Belgrade.
In the USA, daylight saving is introduced.
First Chicago-New York airmail. Flying time 10 hours 5 minutes.
In the USA, Missouri is the last state to ratify the school attendance law.

1919 5 Jan: National Socialist Party formed in Germany. Communist (Spartacist) rising in Berlin until crushed on 11 Jan.
18 Jan: Peace Conference in Paris.
21 Jan: Dail Eireann meets in Dublin.
25 Jan: Founding of the League of Nations.
January: Paderewski becomes prime minister of Poland (until November, 1919).
11 Feb: German republican government takes office.
23 Feb: MUSSOLINI founds the Fascist Party in Italy.
March: Severe influenza epidemic in Britain.
13 April: Amritsar massacre. British fire on nationalist rioters in India.
14 June: First direct flight across Atlantic by J.W. ALCOCK and A. WHITTEN BROWN.
21 June: Germans scuttle their fleet at Scapa Flow.
28 June: Germany signs the Peace Treaty at Versailles. Alsace-Lorraine to be returned to France. German colonies to be under mandate: German East Africa to Britain and German South-West Africa to South Africa.
12 Sept: Gabriele D'ANNUNZIO leads an unofficial Italian army and seizes Fiume from Yugoslavia.

22 Sept: Steel strike in the USA until January, 1920.

28 Nov: Lady ASTOR becomes the first woman to sit as an MP in the British House of Commons.

10 Dec: Ross Smith flies from London to Australia in 135 hours.

1920 10 Jan: The League of Nations meets for the first time.

16 Jan: Prohibition comes into force in the USA. The US Senate votes against joining the League of Nations.

2 Feb: Estonia declares her independence of Russia.

10 Feb: Northern Ireland votes to accept the Home Rule Bill.

1 March: Austria becomes a kingdom once more, under the regency of Admiral HORTHY.

19th March: The US Senate rejects the Versailles Treaty.

20 April to 12 Sept: After a break of 8 years, the VIIth Olympic Games are held, in Antwerp, Belgium. The VIth Games were due to be held in Berlin in 1916, but were cancelled owing to World War I.

8 July: Britain takes over the East African Protectorate as Kenya Colony.

10 Aug: Treaty of Sèvres signed between the Allies and Turkey, but opposed by Turkish nationalists under Mustafa Kemal (ATATÜRK).

26 Aug: Under the 19th Amendment, women receive the vote in the United States.

27 Oct: The League of Nations moves to headquarters in Geneva.

2 Nov: Warren G. Harding, Republican, becomes 29th President of the USA.

The first broadcasting station (KDKA) in the USA opens at East Pittsburgh.

23 Dec: Northern and Southern Ireland each to have its own parliament, under Government of Ireland Act.

1921 1 March: Ruanda, East Africa, is ceded to Britain.

31 March: British coal-miners go on strike.

19 April: Government of Ireland Act comes into force. Northern Ireland is separate from the Irish Free State.

24 May: The British Legion is founded.

12 Nov: The Washington Conference on Disarmament begins, and continues until 6 Feb. 1922.

13 Nov: Pacific Treaty signed between the USA, the British Empire, France and Japan.

29 Nov: The same nations sign the Washington treaty to limit naval armaments.

Capital punishment is abolished in Sweden.

Mackenzie KING becomes prime minister of Canada.

Australia wins the Ashes.

The Ku Klux Klan is active in southern USA.

1922 6 Feb: Cardinal Achille Ratti elected Pope PIUS XI.

21 Feb: Egypt becomes independent after British protectorate ends.

16 March: Britain recognizes Kingdom of Egypt under Fuad I.

11 Sept: British mandate in Palestine begins.

28 Sept: MUSSOLINI marches on Rome and forms the Fascist government (30th Sept.)

14 Nov: The British Broadcasting Company (BBC) makes its first broadcast from the 2LO station at Marconi House.

Nov: The tomb of Tutankhamen is discovered by Lord Carnarvon and Howard Carter at Luxor, Egypt.

6 Dec: Official proclamation of the Irish Free State.

Insulin is prepared by Canadian scientists, and used for the first time.

The American cocktail becomes popular.

Above: 'Bright Young things' of the 20s. Centre: The mask of Tutankhamen whose tomb was discovered in 1922. Right: Kemal Ataturk who was elected the first president of the Turkish republic in 1923.

1923 1 Jan: The Union of Socialist Soviet Republics is established.
11 Jan: French and Belgian troops occupy the Ruhr, after Germany fails to pay reparations.
15 April: The first public sound-on-film performance is shown at the Rialto Theater, New York.
10 July: Non-fascist parties in Italy are dissolved.
2 Aug: President Harding of the USA dies and is succeeded by Calvin Coolidge as 30th President.
13 Aug: Mustapha Kemal [ATATÜRK] is elected as President of Turkey.
14 Sept: Miguel Primo de Rivera becames dictator of Spain.
11 Oct: Due to enormous inflation, the value of the German mark falls to be equivalent to 10,000,000,000 to the British pound, and 4,000,000,000 to the US dollar.

8 Nov: Adolf HITLER attempts a *coup d'état* in Munich to overthrow the Bavarian government, but fails and is imprisoned.
In the USA, *Time* magazine is issued.
Nevada and Montana are the first states to introduce the old age pension.
The Gregorian calendar is introduced in the USSR.
First birth control clinics in the USA (NY).
Col. Jacob Schick patents the electric razor.
Martial law is declared in Oklahoma to protect people and property from the Klu Klux Klan.

1924 21 Jan: Vladimir LENIN dies and is succeeded by Joseph STALIN.
The Chinese Nationalist government meets at Canton, and admits Communists to its ranks.
23 Jan: Ramsay MacDONALD forms the first Labour government in Britain.
25 Jan. to 4 Feb: First Winter Olympics are held at Chamonix, France.
9 March: Italy annexes Fiume.

24 March: Greece becomes a republic.

4 May: Nationalists and Communists win many seats in the German Reichstag elections.

4 May to 27 July: VIIIth Olympic Games are held in Paris.

10 June: Giacomo Matteotti, Italian Socialist deputy, is murdered by Fascists.

9th Oct: The Labour government falls in Britain.

29 Oct: Conservatives win British general election with 413 seats against Labour's 151 and the Liberals' 40.

4 Nov: Calvin Coolidge, Republican, wins US presidential election.

6 Nov: Stanley BALDWIN becomes British prime minister.

24 Dec: Albania becomes a republic.

The New Zealand 'All Blacks' rugby team make an undefeated tour of Britain.

The Ford Motor Company produce their 10 millionth car.

Mah-jongg becomes a world craze.

1925 1 Jan: Norway's capital city's name is changed from Christiania to Oslo.

5 Jan: The first woman governor in the USA is Mrs Nellie Tayloe Ross, of Wyoming.

25 April: Hindenburg becomes President of Germany.

1 May: Cyprus becomes a British Crown Colony.

31 July: The Unemployment Insurance Act is passed in Britain.

5 Oct: (until 16th Oct). The Locarno Conference meets and the great powers guarantee frontiers and agree to put disputes to arbitration.

In the USA, *The New Yorker* magazine is founded.

The Charleston is a fashionable dance.

The Chrysler Corporation is founded.

New Madison Square Garden, New York, is opened.

1926 8 Jan: Ibn Saud becomes King of Hejaz, and changes name of country to Saudi Arabia.

26 Jan: John Logie BAIRD demonstrates television in London.

1 May (until 19th Nov.). British coal-miners go on strike.

4 May (until 12th May): General Strike in Britain.

10 Nov: Vincent Massey becomes the first Canadian minister to Washington, USA.

1927 1 Jan: The British Broadcasting Company becomes the British Broadcasting Corporation.

9 May: Parliament House, Canberra, Australia, is opened.

20 - 21 May: Charles A. LINDBERGH flies from New York to Paris in 37 hours.

6 Oct: The first talking feature film - *The Jazz Singer* - is shown in New York.

1928 7 May: The age for women voters in Britain is reduced from 30 to 21.

17 May to 12 Aug: The IXth Olympic Games are held in Amsterdam.

1 Sept: Albania is declared a kingdom, and Zogu I becomes king.

6 Oct: CHIANG KAI-SHEK becomes president of China.

3 Nov: Turkey abolishes the use of the Arabic alphabet, and adopts the Roman.

6 Nov: Herbert HOOVER, Republican, is elected 31st President of the USA.

1929 5 Jan: King Alexander of Yugoslavia establishes himself as dictator.

31 Jan: Leon TROTSKY is expelled from Russia.

11 Feb: Lateran Treaty establishes an independent Vatican state.

14 Feb: St Valentine's Day massacre: six notorious Chicago gangsters are machine-gunned to death by a rival gang.

3 Oct: Official name of Kingdom of

Serbs, Croats and Slovenes is changed to Yugoslavia.

28 Oct: 'Black Friday' - the US Stock Exchange in New York collapses with the beginning of the world economic crisis, known as the Great Depression.

Richard BYRD flies over the North Pole.

The German airship *Graf Zeppelin* makes a world flight.

The 14th edition of *Encyclopaedia Britannica* is issued.

1930 8 March: Mahatma GANDHI starts a civil disobedience campaign in India.

18 March: The planet Pluto is discovered by the American Clyde Tombaugh.

3 April: Ras Tafari becomes Emperor HAILE SELASSIE of Abyssinia (Ethiopia).

22 April: London Conference meets and the great powers agree on limitations on submarines and aircraft carriers.

24 May: Amy JOHNSON, British aviator, completes her solo flight from London to Australia in 19½ days.

14 Sept: In German elections, Socialists and Communists win more seats, but National Socialists (Nazis) gain 107 seats.

7 Oct: The British airship R101 crashes near Beauvais, France with much loss of life.

30 Oct: Treaty of friendship between Turkey and Greece.

Donald Bradman scores 334 for Australia in the Leeds Test Match.

1931 14 April: In Spain, King Alfonso flees and revolutionary provisional government set up.

24 Aug: In Britain, after large budget deficit, Government resigns. Ramsay MacDonald forms National Government, and the Labour party expels him.

15 Sept: British naval force mutinies at Invergordon over pay.

Crowds gather outside the New York Stock Exchange on 28 October, 1929 the day of the Wall Street Crash and the beginning of the world economic crisis known as the Great Depression.

27 Oct: The all-party National Government wins 558 seats in British election, the opposition only 56.

9 Dec: Spain becomes a republic.

11 Dec: The Statute of Westminster defines the status of Britain and the Dominions.

Building of Rockefeller Center, New York, is begun.

The north face of the Matterhorn is climbed for the first time, by Franz and Toni Schmid.

Al ('Scarface') Capone, gangster, is jailed for income tax evasion.

Mrs Hattie T. Caraway (Dem., Arkansas) is the first woman to be elected to the US Senate.

The Bata Shoe company of Czechoslovakia produces 75,000 pairs daily.

1932 2 Jan: Having occupied Manchuria, the Japanese set up a puppet republic of Manchukuo.

4 Jan: In India, the Indian National Congress is declared illegal, and GANDHI is arrested.

28 Jan: Japan occupies Shanghai.

2 Feb. (until July): Sixty countries attend the Geneva Disarmament Conference.

1 March: The LINDBERGH baby is kidnapped.

9 March: Eamon DE VALERA becomes president of Ireland.

10 April: Hindenburg re-elected German president with 19 million votes. HITLER receives 13 million.

24 April: Nazis win seats in large German cities.

1 May: President Doumer of France is assassinated.

5 July: Oliveira SALAZAR becomes virtual dictator of Portugal at head of a fascist regime.

30 July to 14 Aug: Xth Olympic Games are held in Los Angeles.

29 Oct: The French liner *Normandie* is launched.

31 July: In Reichstag elections in Germany, Nazis win 230 seats, but not an overall majority.

8 Nov: F.D. ROOSEVELT, Democrat, wins election in the USA, and becomes 32nd president.

Oswald MOSLEY founds the British Union of Fascists.

In the Netherlands, the Zuider Zee drainage project is completed.

Sydney Harbour Bridge is opened.

The Shakespeare Memorial Theatre, designed by Miss E. Scott, at Stratford-upon-Avon, is opened.

A famine occurs in the USSR.

The expression 'New Deal' is used by F.D. Roosevelt.

1933 30 Jan: Adolf HITLER becomes Chancellor of Germany, being appointed by President Paul von HINDENBURG.

27 Feb: Burning of the German Reichstag, or parliament. Hitler calls it a Communist plot, and suspends civil liberties.

6 - 9 March: US banks close.

7 March: Parliamentary government in Austria is suspended by the Chancellor, DOLLFUSS.

23 March: Adolf Hitler becomes dictator of Germany.

1 April: Persecution of Jews begins in Germany.

2 May: German trades unions are forbidden.

28 May: Nazis win elections in Danzig, a free city.

12 June to 27 July: World Economic Conference fails to reach agreement.

14 Oct: Germany quits the League of Nations.

12 Nov: In new elections, Nazis receive 92 per cent of votes.

5 Dec: Prohibition is repealed in the USA.

21 Dec: Newfoundland reverts to the position of a crown colony.

1934 1 Feb: The Austrian Chancellor, Dollfuss, dissolves all parties except his own Fatherland Front.

9 Feb: Balkan Pact signed by Romania, Greece, Yugoslavia and Turkey.

12 - 13 Feb: General strike in France.

24 March: US Act declares that the Philippines will be independent from 1945.

26 March: In Britain, driving tests are introduced.

28 May: The Dionne quintuplets (Cecile, Yvonne, Annette and Emilie) are born.

30 June: The Nazis stage a blood purge in their own party. Von Schleicher, Roehm and others are executed in the 'Night of the Long Knives'.

25 July: In an attempted coup by Nazis in Austria, the Chancellor, Engelbert DOLLFUSS, is murdered.

30 July: Kurt Schuschnigg is appointed Austrian Chancellor.

2 Aug: Paul von HINDENBURG, President of Germany, dies, aged 87.

16 Aug: The American explorer, William Beebe descends 3,028 feet (1922.5 metres) in his bathysphere into the ocean near Bermuda.

19 Aug: Plebiscite in Germany gives sole power to Adolf Hitler as *Führer* (leader).

26 Sept: The liner *Queen Mary* is launched.

9 Oct: King Alexander of Yugoslavia and Louis Barthou, French foreign minister, assassinated at Marseilles by a Croatian terrorist.

1 Dec: Sergei Kirov, associate of Josef STALIN, is assassinated, and Communist party in Russia is purged.

1935 13 Jan: Plebiscite in the Saar indicates desire to join Germany.

15 - 17 Jan: Zinoviev and others in Russia convicted of treason.

7 March: The Saar is incorporated into Germany.

16 March: Hitler renounces the Treaty of Versailles.

29 May: The French liner *Normandie* leaves Le Havre on her maiden voyage to New York, via Southampton.

2 Aug: Government of India Act is passed by British parliament; sets up provincial councils.

15 Sept: In Germany, Nuremberg laws passed, outlawing Jews, and making the Swastika the official flag of the country.

2 Oct: Italy invades Abyssinia (Ethiopia).

3 Nov: George II returns to Greece and the country becomes a monarchy once again.

15 Nov: Commonwealth of the Philippines inaugurated.

Persia officially changes its name to Iran.

The publisher Allen Lane launches the paperback series Penguin Books.

Silver Jubilee of King George V. Celebrations in the United Kingdom and in the Empire.

Bank of Canada founded.

The rumba is a fashionable dance.

1936 20 Jan: George V dies, and EDWARD VIII accedes to the throne.

6 to 16 Feb: IVth Winter Oympics are held at Garmisch-partenkirchen, Germany.

7 March: Germany occupies the Rhineland in violation of the Treaty of Versailles.

9 May: After Italy takes Addis Ababa, the Abyssinian war ends, and Italy annexes the country.

A fashion-plate of the 1930s.

18 July: In Spain, an army revolt under Emilio Mola and Francisco FRANCO begins Civil War.

1 to 16 Aug: XIth Olympic Games are held in Berlin.

1 Nov: After meeting in Berlin, the Rome-Berlin Axis is set up.

2 Nov: In Britain, the BBC begins a regular television service from Alexandra Palace, London.

3 Nov: F.D. ROOSEVELT Democrat, is re-elected as President of the USA.

18 Nov: Germany and Italy support the government of Franco in Spain.

10 Dec: Following a crisis after King EDWARD VIII states his intention of rying Mrs Wallis Simpson, a divorcee, he abdicates, and becomes Duke of Windsor.

11 Dec: GEORGE VI succeeds to the British throne.

In Britain, the first BUTLIN holiday camp is opened at Skegness.

1937 23 Jan: On trial in Moscow, Karl Radek and other leaders are accused.

26 April: German planes bomb Guernica in Spain.

1 May: Roosevelt signs the US Neutrality Act.

31 May: German naval units bombard Almeria in Spain.

17 - 21 Nov: Lord Halifax visits Adolf Hitler, marking beginning of British policy of appeasement.

29 Dec: The Irish Free State becomes Eire.

The British newspaper *Morning Post* closes, and is merged with *The Daily Telegraph.*

The first jet engine is built by Frank WHITTLE.

In the USA, Wallace H. CAROTHERS patents nylon.

The Lincoln Tunnel is opened between New York and New Jersey.

The Golden Gate Bridge, San Francisco, opens.

1938 20 Feb: Anthony EDEN resigns in protest at Chamberlain's policies.

2 - 15 March: Soviet leaders are put on trial.

11 March: German troops enter Austria.

13 March: Austria is declared to be part of the German Reich (the *Anschluss*).

23 April: Sudeten Germans (in Czechoslovakia) demand complete self-government.

4 May: The first president of Eire is Douglas Hyde, a Protestant.

19 - 20 May: Crisis over Czechoslovakia after demands by Hitler.

15 Sept: Neville Chamberlain visits Hitler at Berchtesgaden over Czech crisis.

27 Sept: Hitler states his intention to annex Sudetenland.

27 Sept: The liner *Queen Elizabeth* is launched.

29 Sept: Munich Conference, attended by Chamberlain, Daladier of France, Hitler and Mussolini. It is agreed to transfer Sudetenland to Germany, but Czech frontier to be guaranteed.

10 Oct: Germany occupies Sudetenland.

The ball-point pen is invented by Lázlo BIRÓ.

The British magazine *Picture Post* is launched by Edward Hulton.

In the USA, 32,000 people die in car accidents.

1939 26 Jan: In Spain, Franco, with aid from Italy, takes Barcelona.

27 Feb: Britain and France recognize the Franco government in Spain.

15 March: Hitler's troops occupy Czechoslovakia (Bohemia and Moravia).

16 March: Slovakia is placed under German 'protection', and Hungary annexes Ruthenia (both part of Czechoslovakia).

21 March: Germany seizes Memel from Lithuania.

28 March: Madrid surrenders to

Franco, and the Spanish Civil war ends.

31 March: Britain and France agree to support Poland if invaded by Hitler.

1 April: The US recognizes the Franco government in Spain.

7 April: Italy invades Albania.

30 April: The New York World's Fair opens in the USA.

20 May: Pan American airlines open regular flights between the USA and Europe.

23 May: British parliament agrees a plan for the independence of Palestine by 1949. This is denounced by Arabs and Jews.

23 May: The British decoration, the George Cross is started.

23 Aug: The USSR and Germany conclude a non-agression pact.

23 Aug: John Cobb, British motorist, drives at 368.85 mph (592 kph) at Bonneville Salt Flats, Utah, USA.

31 Aug: Women and children are evacuated from London.

1 Sept: German invades Poland and seizes Danzig free city. Start of WORLD WAR II.

3 Sept: Britain and France declare war on Germany.

17 Sept: The USSR invades Poland from the east.

30 Sept: Germany and the USSR sign a pact agreeing on partition of Poland.

30 Sept: British Expeditionary Force of 158,000 men sent to France.

8 Oct: Western Poland is made part of the German Reich.

30 Nov: The USSR invades Finland.

13 - 17 Dec: Battle of the River Plate, when the German battleship *Graf Spee* is scuttled off Montevideo.

The US Supreme Court rules that sitdown strikes are illegal.

Igor Sikorsky builds the first successful helicopter.

Malcolm Campbell sets up a wat-erspeed record of 368.86 mph (593.62 kph).

Nylon stockings first appear.

1940 8 Jan: First World War II rationing in Britain: bacon, butter and sugar.

12 March: Finland signs peace treaty with the USSR, making territorial concessions.

9 April: Germany invades Norway and Denmark.

7 May: Neville CHAMBERLAIN resigns and Winston CHURCHILL, as prime minister, forms National government.

10 May: Germany invades the Netherlands, Belgium and Luxembourg.

10 May: The Local Defence Volunteers (LDV) later called the Home Guard, formed in Britain.

14 May: The Netherlands army surrenders to German forces.

17 May: Germany invades France.

27 May - 3 June: 300,000 men of British and Allied forces are evacuated from Dunkirk.

The German Fuhrer, Hitler, with Britain's appeasing prime minister, Neville Chamberlain, 1938.

28 May: Belgium surrenders to Germany.

10 June: Italy declares war on Britain and France.

4 June: Paris is entered by German forces.

22 June: France surrenders, concluding an armistice with Germany.

3 July: The Royal Navy sinks the French fleets at Oran and other ports in North Africa.

10 - 21 July: 90 German bombers are shot down over Britain. Beginning of the Battle of Britain.

23 July: The 'Blitz' begins with an all-night raid on London.

20 Aug: Leon TROTSKY is assassinated in Mexico.

3 Sept: The USA sends destroyers to Britain, in return for the leasing of bases in Newfoundland and the Caribbean. (Lend-Lease).

23 Sept: The George Cross is instituted by King George VI.

2 Oct: The liner *Empress of Britain*, bound for Canada with refugees, is sunk.

13 - 21 Oct: Heavy air raids on London.

5 Nov: President Roosevelt is re-elected for a third term.

9 Dec: Under General Wavell, the Eighth Army opens offensive in North Africa.

The song *Lili Marlene* is popular in Germany.

1941 7 March: British troops invade Abyssinia (Ethiopia).

11 March: The Lend-Lease Bill is signed in the USA.

31 March: Germany starts a counter-offensive in North Africa.

11 April: Major German 'blitz' on Coventry, England.

10 May: During London's heaviest air raid, the House of Commons is destroyed.

20 May: Germany invades Crete.

22 June: Germany invades the USSR.

22 June: Finland invades Karelia (lost to the USSR in March, 1940).

27 July: Japanese forces land in Indo-China.

11 Aug: Churchill and Roosevelt sign the Atlantic Charter.

16 Oct: German forces advance to within 60 miles (96 kilometres) of Moscow.

27 Nov: The USSR, under Marshal Timoshenko, launch a counteroffensive, forcing a German retreat.

7 Dec: The Japanese bomb Pearl Harbour, Hawaii and Malaya.

8 Dec: Britain and the USA declare war on Japan.

17 Dec: In North Africa, German troops, led by Rommel, retreat.

25 Dec: Hong Kong surrenders to Japan.

1942 10 Jan: Japanese invade the Dutch East Indies.

11 Jan: Japanese conquer Kuala Lumpur, in Malaya.

16 April: Malta is awarded the George Cross after suffering continuing bombardment by German aircraft.

19 Jan: Japanese invade Burma.

15 Feb: Singapore surrenders to the Japanese.

28 Feb: Japanese land at Java.

6 June: Nazis burn village of Lidice in Bohemia as a reprisal for the killing of Heydrich.

21 June: Rommel takes Tobruk in North Africa.

25 June: RAF makes a 1000 bomber raid on Bremen.

28 June: The Eighth Army retreats to El Alamein.

7 Aug: US forces land on Guadalcanal.

13 Sept: German attack on Stalingrad begins.

23 Oct: The Eighth Army, under General MONTGOMERY, attacks Rommel at the Battle of El Alamein.

Oct: In North America, the Alaska Highway is opened.

Women at war. Workers assemble a barrage balloon. Above right: The Japanese attack on Pearl Harbor brought the United States into the World War II.

8 Nov: Under General EISENHOWER, Allied forces land in French North Africa.

19 Nov: The USSR counter-attacks at Stalingrad and surround Germans.

24 Dec: French Admiral DARLAN assassinated in Algiers.

Sugar rationing in the USA.

Enrico Fermi splits the atom.

The first electronic computer is built.

Magnetic recording tape is invented.

1943 14 - 24 Jan: Churchill and Roosevelt meet at Casablanca to discuss strategy.

15 Jan: Japanese are driven off Guadalcanal.

30 Jan: Soviet troops eliminate the German army south-west of Stalingrad.

10 Feb: The Eighth Army sweeps across North Africa, and reaches Tunisia.

6 April: British and US armies link up after Rommel's retreat.

12 May: The German army in North Africa surrenders.

29 June: US forces land in New Guinea, and raid the Solomon Islands.

26 July: The Italian dictator Benito Mussolini is dismissed from office.

3 Sept: The Allies invade Italy, landing at Salerno. The Italian government surrenders.

13 Oct: Italy declares war on Germany.

1944 20 Jan: RAF drops 2300 tons of bombs on Berlin.

22 Jan: Allies land at Nettuno and Anzio in Italy.

27 Jan: Leningrad relieved by Soviet forces.

6 March: US Air Force begins daylight bombing attacks on Berlin.

4 June: The Fifth Army enters Rome.

6 June: 'D-Day'. The Allies land in Normandy, Northern France; the Germans retreat.

13 June: The first flying-bomb is dropped on London.

20 July: Von Stauffenberg attempts to assassinate Hitler, but fails and is arrested.

25 Aug: Allied troops enter Paris.
30 Aug: Soviet troops enter Bucharest, Romania.
5 Sept: Brussels liberated by the Allies.
8 Sept: The first V-2 rocket lands in Britain.
8 Sept: First non-stop flight from London to Canada completed.
29 Sept: Soviet troops invade Yugoslavia.
19 Oct: US forces land in the Philippines.
23 Oct: The Soviet army advances through Hungary.
25 Oct: Japanese navy is defeated at the battle of Leyte Gulf.
7 Nov: Roosevelt is re-elected president for a fourth term.

1945 17 Jan: The Soviet army takes Warsaw.
4 - 11 Feb: At Yalta, Churchill, Roosevelt and Stalin meet to discuss the unconditional surrender of Germany.
5 Feb: Under General MacARTHUR, US troops enter Manila, in the Philippines.

2 March: In Burma, the British 14th Army enters Mandalay.
12 April: President Roosevelt dies and is succeeded by Harry S. TRUMAN as 33rd President of the USA.
20 April: Soviet troops enter Berlin.
28 April: Benito Mussolini is assassinated by Italian partisans.
30 April: Adolf Hitler commits suicide in Berlin.
7 May: General Jodl surrenders to General Eisenhower.
8 May: General von Keitel surrenders to Marshal ZHUKOV, the Soviet commander.
With the end of the war in Europe, this is called 'V.E. Day.'
16 July. The first atomic bomb is detonated in New Mexico, USA.
17 July - 2 Aug: The Potsdam Conference meets to settle the occupation of Germany.
26 July: In the British general election Labour wins with 412 seats against Conservatives 213 and Liberals 12.
6 Aug: US bombers drop an atomic bomb on Hiroshima, Japan.

British troops land on a Normandy beach on D-Day—6 June 1944—at the start of the liberation of France.

The USSR declares war on Japan.
9 Aug: US bombers drop an atomic bomb on Nagasaki, Japan.
14 Aug: Japan surrenders, ending WORLD WAR II.
28 Aug: US forces land in Japan.
11 Oct: Fighting breaks in China between Nationalists under CHIANG KAI-SHEK and Communists under MAO TSE-TUNG.
24 Oct: The United Nations come into existence.
20 Nov: Trial of Nazi war criminals opens at Nuremberg.
Women's suffrage becomes law in France.
'Bepop' comes into fashion.

1946 10 Jan: First UN Assembly opens in London.
1 Feb: Trygve LIE, a Norwegian Socialist, elected Secretary-General of the United Nations.
14 Feb: Bank of England is nationalized.
5 March: Churchill makes a speech at Fulton, in the USA, warning western countries to beware of the USSR, referring to an 'Iron Curtain' across Europe.
18 April: The League of Nations is dissolved.
9 May: King Victor Emmanuel II of Italy abdicates; succeeded by Umberto II. A referendum is held which narrowly votes for a republic.
28 June: Enrico de Nicola becomes the first president of the republic of Italy.
21 July: Bread rationing in Britain because of world shortage of wheat.
30 Sept: At the Nuremberg trials, von RIBBENTROP, GOERING, and other Nazis are sentenced to death. Goering commits suicide.
Xerography is invented by Chester CARLSON.
Women in Italy given the right to vote.

1947 1 Jan: The coal industry of Britain is nationalized.

7 Feb: Britain proposes that Palestine is divided into Arab and Jewish zones but both sides reject the plan.
5 June: In a speech in the USA, George MARSHALL asks for a European recovery programme (Marshall Aid).
15 Aug: India becomes independent, and is partitioned. Pandit NEHRU becomes prime minister of (Hindu) India, and Liaquat Ali Khan of (Islamic) Pakistan.
5 Oct: The Communist Information Bureau (Cominform) is set up to aid European Communist parties.
14 Oct: First supersonic air flight (670 mph; 1078 kph) by Charles Yeager in California.
20 Nov: Princess Elizabeth marries Philip Mountbatten, Duke of Edinburgh.
29 Nov: The UN proposes a plan for the partition of Palestine.
17 Dec: In New York, a blizzard results of 27 inches of snow.
30 Dec: King Michael of Romania abdicates.
Britain's John Cobb sets up a world ground speed record of 394.197 mph (634.4 kph).
The New Look female fashion is in vogue.
Thor HEYERDAHL sails on raft from Peru to Polynesia in 101 days to prove prehistoric immigration.

1948 1 Jan: British railways are nationalized.
4 Jan: Burma becomes an independent republic outside the Commonwealth.
20 Jan: GANDHI is assassinated by a Hindu fanatic.
4 Feb: Ceylon becomes a self-governing dominion.
25 Feb: A Communist coup in Czechoslovakia results in proclamation of a People's republic.
14 May: British mandate in Palestine ends. A Jewish provisional government formed for 'Israel'.

26 May: South Africa elects Nationalist government with *apartheid* policy.

24 June: The USSR stops road and rail communication between Berlin and the west. Western powers supply zone by airlift.

29 July to 14 Aug: XIVth Olympic Games are held in London. The XIIth and XIIIth, due in 1940 and 1944, were not held, due to World War II.

15 Aug: Republic of Korea proclaimed.

1 Sept: North China People's republic formed by Communists.

4 Sept: Queen WILHELMINA of the Netherlands abdicates.

6 Sept: JULIANA becomes Queen of the Netherlands.

9 Sept: A Communist republic is set up in North Korea.

17 Sept: Jewish terrorists in Palestine assassinate Count Folke BERNADOTTE, U.N. mediator.

2 Nov: Harry S. Truman is re-elected as president of the USA.

7 Nov: Charles DE GAULLE's party gains many seats in French election.

14 Nov. CHARLES, Prince of Wales, is born.

1949 18 Jan: COMECON formed in Moscow.

31 March: Newfoundland joins Canada as the tenth province of the Dominion.

4 April: NATO treaty signed in Washington.

5 May: COUNCIL OF EUROPE set up in London.

11 May: Siam changes its name to Thailand.

12 May: The blockade by the USSR of Berlin is lifted.

23 May: The Federal Republic of Germany comes into being.

23 May: Communist armies drive the Chinese Nationalists off mainland China.

2 June: Transjordan is renamed as Jordan.

14 June: The State of Vietnam is set up, with strong opposition from the Communists.

30 Sept: After 277,264 flights, the Berlin airlift ends.

1 Oct: Communist government set up in Peking under Mao Tse Tung.

7 Oct: The German Democratic Republic is set up in Eastern Germany.

24 Nov: British iron and steel industries are nationalized.

26 Nov: India becomes a federal republic within the COMMONWEALTH.

The USSR explodes an atomic bomb in tests.

1950 8 March: The USSR claims to be the possessor of the atomic bomb.

25 June: The KOREAN WAR starts when North Korean forces invade South Korea.

8 July: Douglas MacARTHUR is appointed commander of UN forces in Korea.

22 July: After six years in exile, King Leopold returns to Belgium.

1 Aug: Leopold abdicates in favour of Baudouin.

15 Sept: UN forces land in Korea.

21 Oct: Chinese forces occupy Tibet.

1951 1 Jan: Chinese and North Koreans advance through UN lines and capture Seoul.

11 April: President Truman relieves General MacArthur of command in Far East.

18 April: France, West Germany, Italy, Belgium, Luxembourg and the Netherlands sign the treaty setting up a coal and steel community.

23 June: British diplomats Guy Burgess and Donald Maclean flee to the USSR.

20 July: King ABDULLAH of Jordan assassinated in Jerusalem.

8 Sept: Peace treaty is signed by Japan and representatives of 49 powers.

16 Oct: Liaquat Ali Khan, prime minister of Pakistan, assassinated.

25 Oct: In British general election, Conservatives win 321 seats against the 295 for Labour, 6 for Liberals and 3 others.

Colour TV is introduced in the USA.

Julius and Ethel Rosenberg are sentenced to death for espionage against the USA.

1952 6 Feb: In Britain, King GEORGE VI dies, and Queen ELIZABETH II accedes to the throne.

27 - 31 May: European Defence Treaty signed in Paris.

19 July to 3 Aug: XVth Olympic Games are held at Helsinki, Finland.

23 July: General Neguib seizes power in Egypt.

11 Aug: HUSSEIN proclaimed king of Jordan.

Oct: Britain makes her first atomic bomb tests in Monte Bello Islands, Australia.

20 Oct: In Kenya, a state of emergency is declared owing to disturbances by the terrorist organization, Mau Mau.

4 Nov: Dwight D. EISENHOWER is elected as 34th president of the USA.

6 Nov: First hydrogen bomb exploded by USA at Eniwetok Atoll, in the Pacific.

The coronation of Queen Elizabeth II in June 1953 was a scene of glorious pageantry attended by rulers of many countries.

1953 1 Jan: The Maldive Islands become a republic.

10 Jan: The Iron and Steel Community meets for the first time.

14 Jan: Marshal TITO is elected first President of the Yugoslav republic.

5 March: Josef STALIN dies at age of 73.

6 March: Malenkov succeeds Stalin as Chairman of the Council of Ministers in the USSR.

24 March: In Britain, Queen Mary dies.

7 April: Dag HAMMARSKJÖLD of Sweden is elected SecretaryGeneral of the UN.

8 April: In Kenya Jomo KENYATTA and five others are convicted of being involved with Mau Mau.

29 May: Edmund HILLARY and Norkey Tenzing climb Mount Everest.

2 June: Coronation of Queen ELIZABETH II in Westminster Abbey.

17 June: In East Berlin, a rising takes place against the Communist government.

18 June: Republic proclaimed in Egypt, and General Neguib becomes president.

27 July: Korean war ends after an armistice is signed at Panmunjom.

29 Aug: The USSR explodes a hydrogen bomb.

12 Sept: Nikita KHRUSHCHEV becomes first secretary of the Central Committee of the Communist party in the USSR.

21 Nov: 'Piltdown Man' (discovered in 1912) is proved to have been a forgery (by W. Le Gros Clark and others at the British Museum [Natural History]).

23 Dec: Lavrenty BERIA, former Soviet minister for internal affairs, and six others are executed for high treason.

1954 1 March: The USA explodes a hydrogen bomb at Bikini Atoll in the Pacific.

31 March: The USSR offers to join NATO.

18 April: After seizing power, Colonel NASSER becomes prime minister and military governor of Egypt.

21 April: The US Air Force flies a French battalion to Vietnam to defend that country against the Vietminh at Dien Bien Phu in North Vietnam.

27 April: Georgi Malenkov becomes premier of the USSR.

6 May: British athlete Roger BANNISTER runs the mile in less than four minutes (59.4 secs).

7 May: Dien Bien Phu falls to the Vietminh (Communists).

27 June: The first atomic power station is opened at Obninsk, near Moscow.

20 July: An armistice in Indo-China is signed. Vietnam is divided; the north under Communist rule, and the south supported by Great Britain and the USA.

3 Aug: First VTOL aircraft 'The Flying Bedstead' is flown in Britain.

8 Sept: South East Asia Defence Treaty (SEATO) signed to prevent spread of Communism through South-East Asia.

23 Oct: Britain, France, the USA and the USSR agree to end of occupation of Germany.

14 Dec: Disturbances and riots in Cyprus and Greece over the ENOSIS (union with Greece) issue.

In Britain, Gordon RICHARDS is the first professional jockey to be knighted.

A desert locust plague in Morocco; $14 million citrus crop is destroyed.

1955 8 Feb: In the USSR, Malenkov resigns and is succeeded by N.A. Bulganin.

5 April: Churchill resigns as prime minister in Britain, and is succeeded by Anthony EDEN.

9 May: West Germany becomes a member of NATO.

15 May: Britain, France, the USA and the USSR sign the Vienna Treaty restoring Austria as an independent nation.

8 Aug: Conference at Geneva held to discuss peaceful uses of atomic energy.

22 Sept: Commercial television begins in Britain.

8 Oct: In the USA, the aircraft-carrier Saratoga (59,600 tonnes) is launched. It is the world's most powerful warship.

3 Nov: Cocos Islands are transferred to Australia.

5 Nov: The new Vienna Opera House is opened.

26 Nov: The USSR claims to have exploded a hydrogen bomb of 'unprecedented force'.

26 Nov: Following terrorist activities by EOKA, Greek Cypriot organiza-

tion in Cyprus, the governor, John Harding, declares a state of emergency.

1956 12 Feb: The missing diplomats, Burgess and Maclean, appear in Moscow and make a statement.

14 Feb: Nikita Khrushchev, at Communist Party Conference, denounces the policies of Stalin.

16 Feb: The British Parliament votes to end the death penalty.

9 March: In Cyprus, Archbishop MAKARIOS is deported to the Seychelles.

20 March: France recognizes the independence of Tunisia.

23 March: Sudan becomes an independent republic.

7 April: The Cominform is dissolved.

18 April: Prince Rainier III of Monaco marries Grace KELLY, American film actress.

3 May: A new range of mountains is discovered in Antarctica, with two peaks of over 13,000 feet (3000 metres).

2 June: In Britain, third class is abolished on trains, and renamed second-class.

23 June: Colonel NASSER elected President of Egypt.

28 June: In riots in Poznan, Poland, tanks are called out, and 38 people die, with 270 wounded.

26 July: Colonel Nasser seizes the Suez Canal.

26 July: The 29,083-tonne Italian liner *Andrea Doria* sinks after colliding with the 11,644-tonne Swedish liner *Stockholm*.

22 Aug: John Harding, governor of Cyprus, offers surrender terms to EOKA, but they are refused.

10 Sept: Nasser rejects proposals for Suez Canal.

17 Oct: First large scale nuclear power station opens at Calder Hall, Cumberland, England.

23 Oct: Demonstrations in Hungary call for democratic government and

Soviet tanks in the streets of Budapest. Hungary's attempt to leave the Soviet bloc in 1956 was ruthlessly suppressed by the Red Army.

the withdrawal of Soviet troops.

24 Oct: Soviet troops intervene in Hungary.

31 Oct: British and French troops bomb Egyptian airfields in Suez War.

2 Nov: Hungarian government appeals to UN against Soviet invasion.

4 Nov: Soviet troops attack Budapest.

6 Nov: Eisenhower is re-elected as president of the USA.

7 Nov: Britain and France cease fire in Egypt.

8 Nov: UN demand that the USSR withdraws from Hungary, but the uprising there is crushed.

22 Nov. to 8 Dec: XVIth Olympic Games are held in Melbourne, Australia.

1957 9 Jan: In Britain, Anthony EDEN resigns as Prime Minister.

10 Jan: In Britain, Harold MACMILLAN becomes Prime Minister.

12 Feb: In the USA, it is announced that Borazon, a material harder than diamonds, has been made.

6 March: The colony of the Gold Coast, now styled Ghana, becomes independent within the Commonwealth of Nations.

25 March: Treaty of Rome is signed by the 'Six': Belgium, France, West Germany, Italy, Luxembourg and the Netherlands, beginning the Common Market.

15 May: Britain explodes British nuclear bomb in Central Pacific.

31 Aug: Malaysia becomes independent.

21 Sept: King Haakon VII of Norway dies, and Crown Prince Olaf succeeds.

4 Oct: Soviet space satellite, *Sputnik 1*, launched.

3 Nov: The USSR launches *Sputnik 2*, carrying an Eskimo dog.

1958 13 Jan: The American newspaper *Daily Worker* ceases publication.

31 Jan: The USA launches *Explorer 1*, its first space satellite.

1 Feb: Egypt and Syria form the United Arab Republic.

6 Feb: Seven members of the British football team Manchester United are among 21 people killed in an air crash at Munich, West Germany.

4 March: The US nuclear submarine *Nautilus* travels under the North Polar ice-cap.

11 March: In the USA, unemployment reaches the total of 5,200,000.

27 March: Khrushchev becomes chairman of the Council of Ministers in the USSR.

April: The first stereo disc records are sold in the USA. (In Britain, May).

13 May: In Algeria, rioting by French settlers leads to the French army seizing power.

29 May: General DE GAULLE is voted into power in France.

10 July: First parking meters installed in London (625 in all).

14 July: In Iraq, King Faisal II is assassinated. Country is proclaimed a republic under Abdul Kassem.

24 July: In Britain, the first Life Peerages are announced.

26 July: Prince Charles becomes Prince of Wales.

27 Aug: The USSR launches *Sputnik 3*, carrying two dogs.

28 Oct: Cardinal Roncalli is elected as Pope JOHN XXIII.

21 Dec: Charles de Gaulle is elected president of the French Fifth Republic.

In the USA, tension mounts as desegregation of schools is attempted in the South.

In Hungary, Imre Nagy, former president, is executed after a secret trial.

1959 1 Jan: The president of Cuba, Batista is overthrown and flees to the Dominican Republic.

2 Jan: The USSR launches lunar rocket *Luna 1*.

3 Jan: Alaska becomes the 49th State of the USA.

16 Feb: Fidel CASTRO becomes prime minister of Cuba.

19 Feb: Prince Andrew born; the first birth to a reigning monarch in Britain since 1857.

26 June: The St Lawrence Seaway in North America is opened by Queen Elizabeth II and President Eisenhower.

6 July: The Saar becomes part of West Germany.

25 July: British hovercraft crosses the English Channel in two hours.

21 Aug: Hawaii becomes the 50th state of the USA.

25 Sept: S.W.R.D. Bandaranaike, prime minister of Ceylon (Sri Lanka), assassinated.

4 Oct: Soviet lunar satellite *Luna 3* photographs the Moon.

17 Nov: De Beers diamond firm in South Africa announce that synthetic diamonds had been made.

20 - 29 Nov: The European Free

Trade Association (EFTA) is set up, consisting of Great Britain, Norway, Portugal, Switzerland, Austria, Denmark and Sweden.
In Kenya, L.S.B. LEAKEY finds the skull of 'Nutcracker Man'.
In Britain, the first section of the M1 motorway is opened.

1960 23rd Jan: The bathyscaphe *Trieste*, designed by Professor Piccard, descends to the deepest-known part of the ocean (35,800 feet; 11,000 metres) in the Pacific.
13 Feb: France explodes an atomic bomb in the Sahara.
2 May: In the USA, Caryl Chessman, rapist, is executed in San Quentin prison after 12 years of appeals.
6 May: Princess Margaret marries Antony Armstrong-Jones in Westminster Abbey.
7 May: Leonid BREZHNEV becomes president of the USSR.
11 May: The liner *France* is launched at St. Nazaire, the French shipyard.
30 June: The Belgian Congo becomes independent as the Congo Republic.
7 July: The USSR shoots down a US aircraft over the Barents sea.
11 July: Moise Tshombe, prime minister of the Congolese province of Katanga, declares independence.
16 Aug: Cyprus becomes an independent republic with Archbishop Makarios as president.
25 Aug to 11 Sept: XVIIth Olympic Games are held in Rome.
25 Sept: The first atomic-powered aircraft carrier, the US *Enterprise* is launched in the USA.
1 Oct: Nigeria becomes an independent republic within the Commonwealth.
18 Oct: The British newspaper *News Chronicle* is merged with the *Daily Mail* and the London evening newspaper the *Star* is merged with *The Evening News*.
21 Oct: Britain's first nuclear-powered submarine, HMS *Dreadnought* is launched.
8 Nov: In the USA, John F. KENNEDY, Democrat, is elected as 35th President, the first Roman Catholic and the youngest president so far.
In Africa, the following countries became independent: Cameroons (1st Jan.); Togo (27th April); Madagascar (26th June); British Somaliland, joining Somalia (27th June); Belgian Congo (30th June); Dahomey, Niger, Upper Volta, Gabon, Ivory Coast, Chad, Central Africa, and the French Congo (August); Nigeria (1st Oct); Mauritania (28th Nov.).

MAURITANIA — MOROCCO
Tunisia
Western Sahara
ALGERIA
LIBYA
EGYPT
MALI
NIGER
CHAD
SUDAN
SOMALI DEM. REP.
NIGERIA
Central African Rep
ETHIOPIA
Cameroon
GABON
ZAIRE
Uganda
KENYA
TANZANIA
ANGOLA
ZAMBIA
MOZAMBIQUE
Madagascy Rep
NAMIBIA
REP OF SOUTH AFRICA
ZIMBABWE
BOTSWANA

☐ INDEPENDENT IN 1950
☐ INDEPENDENT AFTER 1950

1 Senegal
2 Gambia
3 Guinea-Bissau
4 Guinea
5 Sierra Leone
6 Liberia

7 Ivory Coast
8 Upper Volta
9 Ghana
10 Togo

11 Benin
12 Equatorial Guinea
13 Rwanda

14 Burundi
15 Malawi
16 Lesotho
17 Swaziland

The Berlin Wall was built in 1961 to prevent East Berliners who disliked living under Communist rule crossing to West Berlin.

1961 12 April: Major Yuri GAGARIN is the first man to travel in space, after circling the earth in a Soviet rocket.
17 April: 1400 Cuban exiles in the USA landed in the Bay of Pigs, Cuba, in an attempt to overthrow CASTRO. The attempt fails.
21 April: A French army revolt under General Challe starts in Algeria.
27 April: Sierra Leone becomes independent within the Commonwealth.
28 May: The Orient Express train, Paris-Bucharest, ceases after 78 years.
31 May: South Africa becomes a republic and leaves the Commonwealth.
10 Aug: Britain applies for membership of the EEC (Common Market).
17 - 18 Aug: East Germany erects the Berlin Wall.
18 Sept: Dag HAMMARSKJÖLD killed in air crash over Congo.
1 Oct: The British trust territory of Southern Cameroons joins with the French Cameroons to form the republic of Cameroon.
10 Oct: A volcano believed to have been extinct erupts on Tristan da Cunha and the inhabitants are evacuated.

9 Dec: Tanganyika becomes independent within the Commonwealth.
In Britain, farthings are no longer legal tender.
Adolf Eichmann, Nazi war criminal, is found guilty in a Jerusalem trial.

1962 1 Jan: Western Samoa becomes independent.
1 July: In Africa, Ruanda and Burundi become independent.
3 July: France proclaims the independence of Algeria.
1 Aug: Jamaica becomes independent within the Commonwealth.
31 Aug: Trinidad and Tobago become independent within the Commonwealth.
9 Oct: Uganda becomes independent within the Commonwealth.
22 Oct: President Kennedy announces that the USSR has installed missiles in Cuba.
24 Oct: The USA blockades Cuba.
2 Nov: President Kennedy announces that the USSR is dismantling the missile sites in Cuba.
20 Nov: After the USSR agrees to withdraw bombers from Cuba, USA lifts blockade.
30 Nov: U Thant, Burmese diplomat, elected Secretary-General of the UN.

1963 19 Feb: The USSR agrees to withdraw troops from Cuba.

30 June: Cardinal Montini is elected as Pope PAUL VI.

5 Aug: Nuclear test ban treaty is signed by Britain, USA and the USSR.

8 Aug: The Great Train Robbery. A Glasgow-London mail train is robbed of a total of £2,500,000 ($3,250,000).

1 Nov: In an army coup in South Vietnam, the president, Ngo Dinh Diem, is assassinated.

22 Nov: President John F. KENNEDY is assassinated in Dallas by Lee Harvey Oswald. Lyndon B. JOHNSON becomes 36th President.

10 Dec: Zanzibar becomes independent within the Commonwealth.

1964 11 Feb: Fighting breaks out at Limassol, Cyprus, between Greeks and Turks.

6 March: King Paul I of the Hellenes dies, and is succeeded by Constantine II.

27 March: UN peace force takes over in Cyprus.

27 April: The new state of Tanzania comes into being after Tanganyika and Zanzibar unite.

2 July: In the USA, President Johnson signs the Civil Rights Act.

6 July: Nyasaland, renamed as Malawi, becomes independent within the Commonwealth.

2 Aug: After an American destroyer is attacked off North Vietnam, US aircraft attack North Vietnam bases.

8 Aug: Turkish planes attack Cyprus.

2 Sept: Indonesian forces land in Malaya.

21 Sept: Malta becomes independent within the Commonwealth.

10 to 24 Oct: XVIIIth Olympic Games are held in Tokyo.

15 Oct: KHRUSHCHEV is replaced as first secretary of the Communist Party by Leonid BREZHNEV, and as

prime minister by Alexei KOSYGIN.

24 Oct: Northern Rhodesia, renamed as Zambia, becomes an independent republic within the Commonwealth.

2 Nov: Lyndon B. JOHNSON is re-elected as president of the USA.

12th Dec: Kenya becomes a republic within the Commonwealth.

In the USA, race riots break out in Harlem, New York, as a reaction to Civil Rights laws.

1965 24 Jan: Sir Winston CHURCHILL dies in London, aged 90.

7 Feb: US aircraft bomb North Vietnam after attacks by the North Vietnamese on American areas in the South.

18 Feb: The Gambia becomes independent within the Commonwealth.

8th March: The USA 'lands 3500 marines in South Vietnam.

4 April: North Vietnam aircraft shoot down US jets.

1 Sept: Pakistani troops cross into Kashmir over cease-fire line.

6 Sept: India invades West Pakistan.

4 Oct: Pope PAUL VI sets foot in New York. He is the first Pope to visit America.

9 Nov: A new Act abolishes the Death Penalty in Britain.

11 Nov: Rhodesia declares herself to be independent. Britain replies that this is illegal.

26 Nov: The first French satellite is launched into orbit in the Sahara.

9 Dec: Nikolai Podgorny becomes President of the Soviet Union in place of Anastas Mikoyan.

In the USA, President Johnson signs legislation on Medicare and war on poverty.

Entire areas of north-eastern USA and parts of Canada lose electric power. Blackout affects 30 million; increase in birthrate 9 months later.

Ed MURROW, journalist, dies.

MALCOLM X, black leader, is shot.

1966 10 Jan: Harold WILSON, the British prime minister, arrives in Lagos for a conference on Rhodesia with Commonwealth prime ministers.

17 Jan: After a military coup in Nigeria, a new military governor, Maj.Gen. Ironsi, takes over.

17 Jan: After a US air collision, a hydrogen bomb is lost over Spain. It is later (7th April) recovered off the Palomares.

10 March: Crown Princess Beatrix of the Netherlands is married to Claus von Amsberg.

23 March: The Archbishop of Canterbury visits Rome and meets the Pope; the first official meeting between the Anglican and Roman Catholic churches for 400 years.

30 April: A regular Hovercraft service begins between Calais and Ramsgate.

6 July: Malawi, independent since 1964, becomes a republic.

30 July: England wins the World Football Cup at Wembley.

1 Aug: After a military coup, Maj. Gen Ironsi is captured, and Lt.Col. Gowon takes control of the government in Nigeria.

6 Sept: Dr Verwoerd, South African prime minister, is assassinated in Cape Town.

8 Sept: In Britain, the Severn Bridge is opened.

15 Sept: Britain's first Polaris submarine HMS *Resolution* is launched.

30 Sept: Bechuanaland becomes independent as the republic of Botswana.

4 Oct: Basutoland becomes independent as the Kingdom of Lesotho.

18 Oct: After a report which found that Timothy Evans, hanged in 1950 for the murder of his daughter, was probably not guilty, Evans is granted a posthumous free pardon.

21 Oct: A huge coal-tip at Aberfan, Glamorgan, in Wales avalanches, engulfing a school, a row of cottages and a farm, and killing 124 people, including 116 children.

23 Oct: George Blake, serving a 42 year sentence for espionage, escapes from Wormwood Scrubs prison in London.

30 Nov: Dr Kurt-Georg Kiesinger becomes West German chancellor in succession to Dr Ludwig Erhard.

12 Dec: Francis Chichester arrives at Sydney after a solo voyage of 13,000 miles (20,900 km) in 107 days.

Floods ravage Northern Italy; art treasures are damaged in Florence and Venice.

Mini skirts are in fashion.

The New York *Herald Tribune* ceases publication.

The Salvation Army celebrates its centenary.

The *Times* of London changes its format; it has news on the front page.

The Swedish newspaper *Stockholm Tidende* ceases publication.

The Red Guards demonstrate in China.

Roman Catholics are no longer required to abstain from meat on Fridays.

Race riots in Newark and Detroit, USA.

1967 4 Jan: Donald CAMPBELL is killed in the *Bluebird* speedboat on Coniston Water, in the Lake District, England.

24 Feb: Army officers in Sierra Leone seize power.

30 May: Eastern Nigeria declares itself independent as the Republic of Biafra.

5 June: Fighting breaks out between Israel and the Arab states. (The Six Day War).

7 June: Israeli forces capture Jerusalem and other areas in Egypt and Jordan.

10 June: Crown Princess Margrethe

of Denmark marries Count Henri de Monpezat.

17 June: China explodes a hydrogen bomb.

7 July: Fighting breaks out between Nigerian federal troops and men from the breakaway province of Biafra.

25 Aug: The leader of the American Nazi party, George Rockwell, is shot dead.

3 Sept: Sweden changes its rule of the road from left to right.

10 Sept: Gibraltar votes overwhelmingly to stay British: 12,138 votes for British rule and 44 for Spanish rule.

20 Sept: The Cunard liner *Queen Elizabeth II* is launched.

21 Oct: The Israeli destroyer *Eilat* is sunk by Egyptian missiles.

24 Oct: Israeli artillery destroys a petrol refinery at Port Suez.

26 Oct: The Shah of Iran and his Queen are crowned in Teheran.

29 Oct: The international exhibition EXPO-67 is opened in Montreal.

8 Nov: Britain's first local radio station, Radio Leicester, goes on the air.

24 Nov: U Thant, UN SecretaryGeneral, says that Greece and Turkey are 'on the brink of war' over Cyprus.

27 Nov: General de Gaulle says he is not prepared at present to negotiate the entry of Britain into the Common Market.

30 Nov: The Federation of South Arabia becomes the independent People's Republic of South Yemen.

1 Dec: The Isaac Newton telescope, largest in Western Europe, is inaugurated at the Royal Greenwich Observatory.

3 Dec: The first human heart transplant is carried out successfully in Cape Town.

11 Dec: The prototype of the supersonic airliner Concorde is shown for

Above: War in Vietnam. A Vietcong (Communist) village is set alight by South Vietnamese troops. Below: Mini-skirted girls of the 'Swinging Sixties'.

the first time in Toulouse, France.

17 Dec: Harold Holt, prime minister of Australia, is drowned while swimming.

17 Dec: Alec Rose arrives at Melbourne in his ketch *Lively Lady* after a solo voyage from Portsmouth of five months.

21 Dec: The patient who received a new heart in Cape Town dies from lung failure.

Lake Point Tower, Chicago, USA, 645 feet high (197 metres), becomes the world's tallest reinforced concrete apartment block.

1968 23 Jan: The American intelligence ship *Pueblo*, with 82 crew members, is seized by North Korean forces.

26 Jan: In Britain, the National Provincial and Westminster banks merge to form the National Westminster Bank.

31 Jan: After heavy fighting with Vietcong forces, martial law is proclaimed throughout Vietnam.

4 Feb: The world's largest hovercraft (165 tonnes) is launched at Cowes, England.

12 March: Mauritius becomes independent.

22 March: Antonin Novotny, president of Czechoslovakia is succeeded by General Ludvik Svoboda.

27 March: Yuri GAGARIN, Soviet cosmonaut, is killed in an aircraft accident.

4 April: Martin Luther KING US civil rights leader, is assassinated in Memphis, Tennessee.

5 April: The Cunard liner *Queen Elizabeth* is sold to an American syndicate for £3,230,000 ($4,200,000).

20 April: Pierre TRUDEAU becomes prime minister of Canada.

23 April: In Britain, two decimal coins are issued, but will be used as shilling and two shilling pieces until decimalization in 1971.

6 May: Spain closes the border between Spain and Gibraltar to all but Spaniards.

10 May: Violent clashes between students and police in Paris.

19 May: More than two million workers are on strike in France.

22 May: French strikers are estimated to total nine million.

5 June: Robert KENNEDY, US senator, is shot (dies 25 hours later).

17 June: The first British heart transplant patient dies.

18 July: James Earl Ray (alias Ramon George Sneyd) is extradited to the US for complicity in the murder of Martin Luther King.

23 July: An Israeli Boeing 707 en route from Rome to Tel Aviv, is hijacked to Algeria.

Demonstrators marching to the Arc de Triomphe during the Paris students' strike in 1968

31 July: The cross-Channel Hovercraft service is inaugurated.

20 Aug: Soviet and other Warsaw Pact countries send troops into Czechoslovakia.

27 Aug: Princess Marina, Duchess of Kent, dies, aged 61.

31 Aug: An earthquake in Iran results in the loss of over 20,000 lives.

6 Sept: Swaziland becomes an independent member of the Commonwealth.

26 Sept: Dr SALAZAR of Portugal is succeeded as prime minister by Dr Marcello Caetano.

12 to 27 Oct: The XIXth Olympic Games are held in Mexico City, Mexico.

31 Oct: President Johnson orders a total halt to US bombing of North Vietnam.

3 Nov: Severe storms and floods in Northern Italy result in more than 100 deaths.

5 Nov: Richard NIXON is elected 37th President of the USA with a narrow majority.

19 Nov: The Cunard liner *Queen Elizabeth 2* makes her first voyage.

23rd Dec: In North Korea, 82 crew members of the ship *Pueblo*, seized in January, are released.

26 Dec: An Isaeli Boeing 707 is attacked in Athens by two Arab gunmen, killing one passenger.

28 Dec: In an Israeli commando raid on Beirut airport, 13 Lebanese aircraft are destroyed.

In Egypt, the Aswan Dam is completed.

King Olav V of Norway pays a state visit to Washington, USA.

1969 27 Jan: In Iraq, 14 men, most of them Jewish, are publicly hanged on charges of spying for Israel.

18 Feb: At Zurich, an Israeli aircraft is attacked by four Arab nationalists, injuring six passengers. One Arab is killed.

5 March: In West Germany, Dr Gustav Heinemann becomes president in succession to Dr Lubke.

19 March: British parachute troops take over the Caribbean island of Anguilla.

25 March: President Ayub Khan of Pakistan resigns, and Gen. Yahya Khan, army C.-in.-C., takes over, proclaiming martial law.

28 March: General Dwight D. EISENHOWER dies.

17 April: In Czechoslovakia, Alexander DUBCEK is replaced by Dr Gustav Husak as first secretary of the Communist party.

22 April: Robin Knox-Johnston sails into Falmouth, England in his ketch *Suhaili* after a 312 day non-stop voyage.

28 April: General DE GAULLE resigns as President of France.

25 May: In Sudan, a military junta seizes power.

30 May: The British Trans-Arctic Expedition completes the first surface crossing of the frozen Arctic Ocean; 3,620 miles (5826 km) in 464 days.

2 June: The US destroyer *Frank E. Evans* is cut in two after colliding with the Australian aircraft-carrier *Melbourne* in the South China sea. Over 70 American sailors are missing.

8 June: President Nixon announces that 25,000 US troops would be withdrawn from Vietnam by the end of August.

15 June: Georges POMPIDOU becomes president of France.

20 June: A referendum in Rhodesia overwhelmingly approves Ian Smith's plan for a republic with segregation-style constitution.

1 July: Prince CHARLES is invested with the insignia of Prince of Wales at Caernarvon Castle.

21 July: After landing on the Moon in the Apollo 11 spacecraft, Neil

ARMSTRONG becomes the first man to walk on its surface.

31 July: Pope PAUL VI visits Uganda; the first time a Pope has visited Africa.

4 Aug: Violent rioting between Protestants and Catholics in North Ireland results in shops set on fire in Belfast.

14 Aug: British troops are moved to Northern Ireland to restore order.

21 Aug: In Vietnam, Australian Warrant Officer Rayene Stewart Simpson is awarded the VC for two acts of bravery.

29 Aug: Arab guerillas hijack a TWA aircraft in flight from Rome to Tel Aviv and force it to land at Damascus.

1 Sept: In Libya, army officers seize power, deposing King Idris.

3 Sept: HO CHI MINH, president of North Vietnam, dies, aged 79.

4 Sept: In Rio de Janeiro, the US Ambassador to Brazil, Charles Burke Elbrick, is kidnapped by terrorists.

7 Sept: Mr Elbrick is set free in exchange for the release of 15 political prisoners in Brazil.

8 Sept: In Vietnam, Australian Warrant Officer Keith Payne is awarded the VC for devotion to duty.

12 Sept: President Nixon orders the resumption of bombing raids on North Vietnam, after they were suspended for 36 hours.

16 Sept: President Nixon announces that another 35,000 US troops will be withdrawn from Vietnam by mid-December.

24 Sept: Ton Duc Thang becomes president of North Vietnam.

12 Oct: In Belfast, parachute troops are flown in after rioting causes the deaths of a policeman and two civilians.

15 Oct: In the US, demonstrations are staged to protest against the Vietnam war.

21 Oct: Willy BRANDT is elected as chancellor of West Germany.

31 Oct: An American marine hijacks a TWA Boeing 707 in California and forces it to fly to Rome.

24 Nov: Lieut. William Calley, a US platoon commander at My Lai, Vietnam, is to be court-martialled on charges of murdering 109 Vietnamese.

3 Dec: *The Temptation of Eve*, a painting by Hans Baldung, a 16th century German artist, previously valued at £20 ($25), is sold at Sotheby's, London, for £224,000 ($290,000).

Mrs Golda MEIR becomes Israel's fourth Prime Minister.

1970 11 Jan: Owerri, the provincial capital of Biafra, is captured by Nigerian forces.

12 Jan: The Biafran army surrenders, bringing to an end the civil war which began in May, 1967.

23 Feb: Guyana becomes a republic within the Commonwealth.

2 March: Rhodesia declares itself to be a republic.

15 March: The exhibition EXPO 70 opens at Osaka, Japan.

16 March: The complete *New English Bible* is published. The New Testament was published in 1961.

18 March: Prince Norodom Sihanouk head of State in Cambodia, is deposed by right-wing leaders.

19 March: The heads of state of East and West Germany meet for the first time in 20 years.

3 April: In Korea, a Japanese Boeing 727 is hijacked by nine Japanese, and flies to Pyongyang. 103 passengers are released after 78 hours.

5 April: In Guatemala, the West German ambassador is found murdered after having been kidnapped by left-wing rebels five days earlier.

8 April: Israeli fighter-bombers attack an Egyptian village, killing 30 children and a teacher.

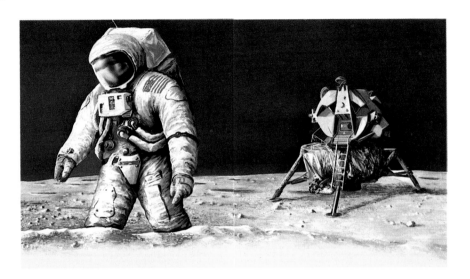

Astronauts exploring the Moon. The first astronauts on the Moon were Neil Armstrong and Edwin Aldrin in 1969.

20 April: President Nixon announces that 150,000 more US troops will be withdrawn from Vietnam.

22 April: Dr Eric Williams, prime minister of Trinidad, asks Britain's help to control Black Power rioters.

31 May: In an earthquake in Peru, an estimated 70,000 people lose their lives.

18 June: The Conservative party win the British General Election, with 330 seats, against 287 seats for Labour and 6 for the Liberals. Edward HEATH becomes prime minister.

29 June: In Cambodia, US troops complete their withdrawal.

9 July: The Bank of England issues £20 banknotes. Previous £20 notes were withdrawn in 1945.

12 July: Thor HEYERDAHL and a crew of seven cross the Atlantic in the papyrus craft *Ra-2* in 57 days, reaching Bridgetown, Barbados from Morocco.

19 July: Brunel's iron ship, S.S. *Great Britain* is brought back to England from the Falkland Islands.

25 Aug: Middle East peace talks open in New York.

6 Sept: Four aircraft are hijacked by Arabs in Western Europe. A Swissair DC-8 and a Trans-World 707 are forced to fly to Jordan; a Pan American jumbo is blown up in Cairo, and an El Al 707 hijacking fails after a terrorist is shot dead.

9 Sept: A BOAC VC10 aircraft en route from Bombay to London is hijacked over the Persian Gulf, forced to land and refuel at Beirut, and then is sent to Jordan to join the other two plans already held hostage.

28 Sept: Gamal Abdel NASSER, president of the United Arab Republic (Egypt), dies aged 52.

10 Oct: Fiji becomes independent within the Commonwealth.

17 Oct: Anwar al-SADAT becomes president of the United Arab Republic (Egypt).

9 Nov: Charles DE GAULLE, French statesman, dies, aged 79.

13 Nov: In East Pakistan, a cyclone and tidal waves cause the death of more than 500,000 people.

27 Nov: Pope PAUL VI arrives at Manila airport for a three-day visit. An attempt is made on his life, but the Pope is unharmed.

27 Nov: Velasquez's portrait of Juan de Pareja is sold at Sotheby's, London, for a record £2,310,000 ($3,000,000).

7 Dec: The Swiss ambassador to Brazil is kidnapped by terrorists who demand the release of 70 prisoners.

14 Dec: Field Marshal Viscount SLIM dies, aged 79.

20 Dec: In Poland, Wladyslaw Gomulka, first secretary of the Communist Party resigns, and is succeeded by Edward Gierek.

20 Dec: In Poland, unconfirmed reports are that 300 people have been killed during clashes between police and demonstrators in Gdansk.

In Canada, Pierre TRUDEAU invokes the War Measures Act after the murder of Quebec minister Pierre Laporte by the Quebec Liberation Front.

Salvador Allende is elected president of Chile.

1971 8 Jan: In Uruguay, the British ambassador, Geoffrey Jackson, is kidnapped by guerrillas.

16 Jan: The Swiss ambassador to Brazil is freed after 70 political prisoners are released.

25 Jan: In Uganda, the president, Milton Obote, is deposed after a military coup by Maj.Gen. Idi AMIN who seizes control.

15 Feb: Britain changes over to decimal currency. New bronze 2p, 1p and $\frac{1}{2}$p coins are issued.

26 Feb: In Belfast, two policemen are killed by machine-gun fire.

10 March: In Northern Ireland, three young Scottish soldiers are found shot in a lane near Belfast.

26 March: Civil war breaks out in East Pakistan after Sheikh Mujibur Rahman declares the province to be independent.

28 March: Reports from East Pakistan state that Sheikh Mujibur is captured and that 7000 people have been killed.

29 March: In Georgia, USA, Lieut. William Calley is found guilty of murdering 22 civilians at My Lai, Vietnam, and receives a life sentence.

21 April: François Duvalier, (Papa Doc), Haitian dicator, dies, aged 64.

11 May: The British newspaper Daily Sketch appears for the last time and is merged with the Daily Mail, which has changed from broadsheet to tabloid format.

24 June: In Britain, the Mersey Tunnel is opened.

30 June: The Soviet spacecraft Soyuz 11 returns to Earth but the three cosmonauts are found dead in their seats.

2 July: The Erskine bridge over the river Clyde in Scotland is opened.

9 Aug: Over 300 IRA suspects are arrested in Northern Ireland. 17 civilians are killed in street battles.

14 Aug: Bahrain becomes independent.

9 Sept: In Uruguay, the British ambassador is released by guerrillas.

24 Sept: Britain expels 90 Soviet diplomats and officials.

29 Sept: A bomb explodes in a Belfast public house with the loss of two lives.

1 Oct: A soldier is shot dead in Belfast, making a total of 23 soldiers killed this year in Northern Ireland.

8 Oct: The USSR expels four diplo-

British soldiers in Northern Ireland have since 1970 had the task of trying to prevent outbreaks of violence between the Roman Catholics and Protestants. Here a lorry burns as troops move in during riots in Belfast's Falls Road area.

mats and a businessman, and bans a further 13 from entering.

25 Oct: The United Nations General Assembly votes to expel Taiwan from the UN and to admit China.

28 Oct: The House of Commons votes in favour of Britain joining the Common Market, with a majority of 112.

4 Dec: India is on a war footing after fighting occurs on the western frontier with Pakistan.

6 Dec: India recognizes Bangladesh (East Pakistan) as an independent republic.

8 Dec: Indian troops are within 30 miles of Dacca, East Pakistan.

16 Dec: All East Pakistani forces surrender to India.

20 Dec: In Pakistan, Zulfikar Ali Bhutto becomes president in place of Yahya Khan.

21 Dec: Dr Kurt WALDHEIM of Austria becomes UN SecretaryGeneral.

24 Dec: Giovanni Leone becomes President of Italy.

In Switzerland, women are granted the right to vote.

The Church of England and the Roman Catholic Church end a dispute dating back 400 years. They agree on a definition as to the essential meaning of the Eucharist.

In the USA, the 26th Amendment to the Consitution is ratified, allowing 18-yearolds to vote.

In Bengal, a cyclone and tidal wave result in the deaths of some 10,000 people.

1972 4 Jan: Rose Heilbron is the first woman to sit as a judge at the Old Bailey in London.

5 Jan: The Congregational Church in England and Wales and the Presbyterian Church of England vote to form a United Reformed Church.

12 Jan: Sheikh Mujibur becomes prime minister of Bangladesh (formerly East Pakistan).

14 Jan: King Frederik IX of Denmark dies, aged 72.

15 Jan: Princess Margrethe becomes Queen of Denmark.

30 Jan: In Northern Ireland, 13 civilians are shot dead by troops in Londonderry after a civil rights procession turned into a riot.

30 Jan: Pakistan leaves the Commonwealth after Britain, Australia and New Zealand recognize the independence of Bangladesh.

30 Jan: King Mahendra of Nepal dies aged 51.

9 Feb: Due to the month-long miners' strike, the British Government declares a state of emergency.

28 Feb: The British miners return to work after accepting a wage increase agreement.

1 March: In Turkey, a 14-year-old schoolboy, Timothy Davey, is jailed for more than six years and fined for attempting to sell hashish.

16 March: Fog on the British M1 motorway results in 9 deaths and 50 people injured.

24 March: It is announced that direct rule from Westminster is to be imposed on Northern Ireland.

30 April: The *Brighton Belle* train makes its last journey from Victoria to Brighton.

15 May: Governor George Wallace of Alabama is shot and wounded, resulting in permanent paralysis.

18 May: After a bomb threat aboard the *Queen Elizabeth 2*, bomb experts are parachuted aboard, but find nothing.

22 May: Ceylon changes its name to Sri Lanka and becomes a republic.

28 May: The Duke of Windsor dies in Paris, aged 77.

1 June: Iraq nationalizes the Iraq Petroleum Company.

26 June: A total of 87 British soldiers have now died while serving in Northern Ireland.

16 July: During the previous week, 33 people in Northern Ireland have been killed.

26 Aug. to 10 Sept: The XXth Olympic Games are held in Munich, West Germany.

28 Aug: While taking part in an air race, Prince William of Gloucester and his co-pilot are killed when their plane crashes after take-off near Wolverhampton.

5 Sept: At the Olympic Village in Munich, Arab terrorists break in and murder two members of the Olympic team. Nine others are held hostage. Later, the terrorists are ambushed by German police; all nine hostages are killed, plus a German policeman and five Arab terrorists. Three terrorists are captured.

8 Sept: Israeli jets attack guerrilla bases in Palestine in retaliation for the Olympic attack.

18 Sept: In Uganda, General AMIN starts to expel 8000 Asians.

25 Sept: In a referendum, Norway votes against joining the Common Market.

2 Oct: Denmark's referendum votes in favour of joining the Common Market.

10 Oct: Sir John BETJEMAN becomes Britain's Poet Laureate.

29 Oct: A German aircraft is hijacked over Turkey; Germany releases three Arab terrorists held since 5th Sept.

7 Nov: Richard NIXON is reelected as president of the USA.
11 Nov: The P. & O. liner *Spirit of London* begins her maiden voyage.
25 Nov: In New Zealand, the Labour party has a landslide win.
28 Nov: The 100th British soldier dies in Northern Ireland.
2 Dec: In Australia, the Labour Party wins the general election.
8 Dec: Seven hijackers are killed in an Ethiopian aircraft.
10 Dec: In Buenos Aires, British businessman Ronald Grove is kidnapped.
23 Dec: In Managua, Nicaragua, more than 10,000 people die in an earthquake.

During the year, 467 people are killed in Northern Ireland, of whom 103 are soldiers and 14 policemen.

In the USA, police in the District of Columbia arrest five men outside the Democratic party National Headquarters in the Watergate complex.

Kwame NKRUMAH, former leader in Ghana, dies.

1973 1 Jan: Britain, Denmark and Ireland join the Common Market.
27 Jan: A Vietnam ceasefire comes into force. In the following 60 days, remaining US forces will be withdrawn and all American prisoners-of-war will be returned.
2 Feb: After three more young men are killed in Belfast, the total deaths in Northern Ireland since the emergency began in 1969 rises to 701.
9 Feb: Britain and East Germany establish diplomatic relations.
12 Feb: The first American POWs from North Vietnam are flown out.
21 Feb: A Libyan Boeing 727 is forced down in the Sinai desert by Israeli fighters, with the loss of 104 lives.

The headquarters of the European Economic Community (the EEC or Common Market) in Brussels, Belgium. In January 1973 the original six countries of the community were joined by Denmark, Great Britain and Ireland.

1 March: Palestinian guerrillas storm the Saudi Arabian embassy in Khartoum, holding five diplomats hostage.

2 March: At the Saudi Arabian embassy, terrorists murder the American ambassador, his chargé d'affaires, and the Belgian chargé d'affaires.

26 March: Women are allowed on the floor of the London Stock Exchange for the first time.

9 April: Arab terrorists attempt to hijack an Israeli plane at Nicosia. One Arab is killed and seven are captured.

18 May: Near Iceland, following a dispute between Iceland and Britain over cod fishing, three Royal Navy frigates begin patrolling.

26 May: An Icelandic gunboat shells and holes a British trawler.

1 June: In Greece, the monarchy is abolished, and George Papadopoulos becomes the first president of the republic.

22 June: Applications by West and East Germany to join UN are accepted.

25 June: Erskine Childers becomes president of Ireland, succeeding Eamon DE VALERA.

4 July: Eight soldiers, four warders and 21 prisoners are injured during a riot at Maze Prison, Northern Ireland.

18 July: In the French Alps, 43 Belgian tourists are killed when their coach plunges from a mountain road into a river.

20 July: A Japanese Boeing 747 with 123 passengers and 22 crew is hijacked over Holland and forced to fly to Dubai. Later, at Benghazi, the plane is blown up by the hijackers. A girl hijacker is killed by a grenade explosion, but all passengers and crew escape.

21 July: France explodes a nuclear device at Maruroa Atoll.

11 Sept: A military junta takes over in Chile after President Allende is deposed.

11 Sept: During a riot at a gold mine near Johannesburg, 11 African miners are shot and killed.

15 Sept: King Gustaf Adolf of Sweden dies; he is succeeded by Carl Gustaf, his grandson, who becomes King Carl XVI Gustav.

23 Sept: General Juan PERÓN is elected as president of Argentina.

8 Oct: Britain's first legal commercial radio station, LBC (London Broadcasting Company) starts transmitting.

10 Oct: After being fined $10,000 for income tax evasion, and being placed on probation for three years, Spiro Agnew resigns as US Vice-President.

12 Oct: In the US, Gerald FORD is nominated Vice-President by Richard NIXON.

19 Oct: In Spain, over 200 people die in floods in the Granada, Murcia, and Almeria provinces.

20 Oct: The new Sydney Opera House opens.

31 Oct: Three Provisional IRA leaders are snatched from Mountjoy Prison, Dublin, in a hijacked helicopter.

11 Nov: Israel and Egypt sign a cease-fire.

13 Nov: Iceland agrees a plan to end the 'cod war' with Britain.

14 Nov: Princess Anne and Captain Mark Phillips are married in Westminster Abbey.

25 Nov: In Greece, President Papadoloulos is deposed and succeeded by General Phaidon Gizikis.

13 Dec: Edward HEATH, the Prime Minister, announces severe restrictions on the use of electricity after industrial action by miners, power engineers and train drivers. A three-day working week is imposed.

17 Dec: At Rome airport, Arab

guerrillas, armed with machine guns, kill 32 people, hijack a Lufthansa aircraft, and fly to Kuwait. Crew and hostages are released, and the five guerrillas surrender.

The five defendants in the Watergate affair in the USA plead guilty. The Watergate committee attempts to implicate President Nixon.

The US devalues the dollar for the second time in two years.

East and West Germany establish diplomatic relations.

Salvador Allende, the overthrown president of Chile, is alleged to have committed suicide.

1974 26 Jan: In Australia, Brisbane is cut off after torrential rains and a cyclone cause flooding. Five people die and 8000 are homeless.

1 Feb: Ronald Biggs, who escaped from London's Wandsworth prison in 1965 is arrested in Rio de Janeiro, but extradition is refused. Biggs was serving 30 years for his part in the Great Train Robbery.

7 Feb: Grenada becomes independent.

13 Feb: Alexander SOLZHENITSYN, Soviet author and Nobel prizewinner, is expelled from USSR and deprived of his citizenship.

28 Feb: The British General Election results in no overall majority for any party, the seats being divided: Labour 301, Conservatives 296, Liberals 14, others 9.

1 March: Seven of President Nixon's former advisers are indicted on charges of conspiracy to obstruct investigations into the Watergate scandal.

3 March: In the world's worst air disaster, a Turkish DC-10 crashes

The Sydney Opera House—a glorious fantasy of modern architecture—was designed by the Danish architect Utzon.

after take off from Orly airport in Paris, with the loss of 346 lives.

3 March: A British Airways VC10 en route from Bombay to London, is hijacked by Arab terrorists after leaving Beirut. At Amsterdam, all passengers and crew are saved and the terrorists are arrested after setting fire to the plane.

4 March: In Britain, Edward HEATH resigns as Prime Minister, and Harold WILSON forms a Labour Government.

1 April: Boundary changes are made in England and Wales which affect nearly all counties. Rutland disappears, but four new counties are created: Avon, Cleveland, Humberside and Cumbria.

2 April: Georges POMPIDOU, French President, dies aged 62.

25 April: In Portugal, a military junta deposes the government, president and prime minister.

18 May: India explodes her first nuclear bomb.

1 July: General Juan PERÓN, president of Argentina, dies, aged 78. He is succeeded by his wife, Maria Estela Perón.

15 July: In Cyprus, Archbishop MAKARIOS is deposed as president in a coup by Greek officers of the Cyprus National Guard. Nicos Sampson is installed as president.

20 July: Turkish forces invade Cyprus.

22 July: Greece and Turkey agree to a cease-fire in Cyprus.

23 July: Nicos Sampson is replaced as President of Cyprus by Glafkos Clerides. 2000 British and foreign residents and tourists are evacuated by Royal Navy ships and helicopters.

27 July: In the US, a Judiciary Committee votes to impeach President Nixon for obstructing justice in the Watergate affair.

30 July: Great Britain, Greece and Turkey sign an interim peace agreement on Cyprus.

8 Aug: Richard NIXON resigns as president of the USA.

9 Aug: Vice-President Gerald FORD is sworn in as 38th president of the USA. He is the first man not to have been elected by ballot to the vice-presidency or presidency.

19 Aug: In Cyprus, the US Ambassador, Rodger Paul Davies, and his secretary are shot dead by Greek-Cypriot demonstrators.

31 Aug: Norman Kirk, New Zealand Prime Minister, dies aged 51.

8 Sept: President Ford grants a full pardon to Richard Nixon for offences he might have committed while in office.

12 Sept: In Ethiopia, Emperor HAILE SELASSIE is deposed.

21 Sept: In Honduras, floods caused by hurricanes result in the deaths of more than 8000 people.

30 Sept: In Portugal, General Antonio Spinola resigns and is succeeded as president by General Francisco Costa Gomes.

10 Oct: In the British General Election, Labour is returned with an overall majority of three.

17 Nov: Erskine Childers, president of Ireland, dies aged 68.

22 Nov: A British Airways VC10 is hijacked at Dubai and forced by four Arab terrorists to fly to Tunis. The crew is released after seven Palestinians are freed from jails in Cairo and the Hague.

13 Dec: Malta becomes a republic within the Commonwealth.

24 Dec: British Labour MP John Stonehouse, who disappeared from Miami in November, is detained by immigration authorities in Melbourne, Australia.

1975 1 Jan: In the USA, former Attorney-General John Mitchell, and former President Nixon's aides H.R. Haldeman and John Ehrlichman are found guilty of conspiracy to obstruct justice.

21 Feb: In the USA, those convicted of conspiracy in the Watergate cover-up are sentenced to a minimum of 30 months and a maximum of 8 years imprisonment.

28 Feb: In West Germany, Peter Lorenz, Opposition Leader, is kidnapped by anarchists, who demand the release of five other anarchists in prison.

5 March: Palestinian guerrillas· raid a hotel at Tel Aviv, taking 30 hostages. Israeli troops storm the hotel, killing seven of eight terrorists, with the loss of 11 other lives.

25 March: In Saudi Arabia, King Faisal is assassinated by his 'mentally de-ranged' nephew, and Crown Prince Khalid ibn Abdul Aziz succeeds to the throne.

30 March: North Vietnamese forces capture the port of Da Nang. Ships attempt to rescue more than a million refugees.

17 April: In Cambodia, the civil war ends after the capital, Phnom Penh, surrenders to Khmer Rouge forces.

25 April: In Stockholm, the West German embassy is blown up by terrorists.

25 April: Portugal holds its first free elections for 50 years, and the three main non-Communist parties win a large majority.

30 April: The South Vietnamese government surrenders unconditionally to the Vietcong.

1 June: In Rhodesia (Zimbabwe), police shoot dead 13 Africans when a crowd of 2000 riot in Salisbury.

25 June: Mozambique becomes independent of Portugal.

18 July: John Stonehouse, former Labour minister, returns to Britain to face 21 charges of fraud, forgery and conspiracy.

29 July: In Nigeria, a military coup deposes General Gowon.

Watergate floods the press.

15 Aug: In Bangladesh, Sheikh Mujibur Rahman is deposed and later killed in a military coup. Khandakar Mushtaque Ahmed is sworn in as president.

6 Sept: In Turkey, a massive earthquake centred on Lice results in nearly 3000 deaths.

22 Sept: In San Francisco, a woman is arrested after trying to shoot President Ford.

10 Nov: The independence of Angola from Portugal is proclaimed, but three different liberation factions are fighting for control.

11 Nov: In Australia, the Governor-General, Sir John Kerr dismisses the Labour prime minister, Gough Whitlam.

11 Nov: After four men are killed in Northern Ireland, the total number of civilians killed since troubles began in 1969 amount to 1000.

20 Nov: General FRANCO, Spanish Head of State, dies, aged 82.

25 Nov: Surinam becomes an independent republic.

27 Nov: King JUAN CARLOS I accedes to the throne of Spain.

29 Nov: British racing driver Graham HILL, piloting a light plane, dies with five others after a crash in thick

fog at Elstree, north of London.

2 Dec: In the Netherlands, Dutch East Indies immigrants hijack a train, killing the driver and two passengers and holding captive 50 others.

4 Dec: In the Netherlands, another group of East Indies immigrants seize the Indonesian Consulate.

6 Dec: In London, four IRA gunmen barricade themselves into a private sitting-room, holding the occupants hostage.

12 Dec: The IRA gunmen surrender and free their hostages.

13 Dec: In Australia, the Liberal-Country party led by Malcolm Fraser, has a landslide victory over Gough Whitlam's Labour party.

14 Dec: The terrorists on the train in the Netherlands surrender and the hostages are freed.

19 Dec: The siege in the Indonesian Consulate in Amsterdam ends when the terrorists surrender and free their hostages.

21 Dec: Palestinian guerrillas in Vienna seize 70 hostages at a meeting of OPEC ministers.

22 Dec: The guerrillas demand to be flown out with the hostages is agreed by the Austrians. Later the hostages are freed and the terrorists surrender in Algiers.

The Suez Canal is reopened. It was closed in 1967.

1976 8 Jan: CHOU EN-LAI, prime minister of China, dies, aged 78.

18 Jan: Two survivors of the Norwegian supertanker *Berge Istra* are picked up by a Japanese fishing boat. No other trace is found of the other 30 members of crew or of the tanker, which disappeared on 29 December, 1975.

28 Jan: 100 British mercenaries fly to Angola to join the FNLA forces.

1 Feb: In Avignon, France, 119 Picasso paintings are stolen.

2 Feb: The National Exhibition

Centre in Birmingham, England, is opened.

4 Feb: In Guatemala, an earthquake devastates the country, and over 22,000 people are dead.

8 Feb: 14 British mercenaries are executed by a firing squad in Angola.

12 Feb: An IRA prisoner at Wakefield prison, England, dies after hunger-striking for 61 days.

24 March: In Argentina, a military junta seizes power, deposing the president, Maria Estela Perón.

5 April: Mr Callaghan becomes prime minister of Great Britain.

25 April: The British Post Office makes its last collection on a Sunday.

1 June: Britain and Iceland sign an agreement to end the 'cod' war.

17 June: During three days of rioting in African townships in South Africa, 176 people die and 1000 are injured.

27 June: General Antonio Ramalho Eanes is elected president of Portugal.

28 June: In Angola, four mercenaries (3 British, 1 American) are sentenced to death, and nine others receive long terms of imprisonment.

3 July: Israeli troops, using three aircraft, raid Entebbe airport, Uganda, and free more than 100 hostages held after an Air France airbus is hijacked there by Palestinian guerrillas. 31 lives are lost (3 hostages, 1 Israeli, 20 Ugandan soldiers, 7 hijackers), and 11 Ugandan aircraft are destroyed.

4 July. Celebrations are held throughout the USA to mark the country's bicentenary.

7 July: In Britain, David Steel becomes leader of the Liberal party.

10 July: In Angola, the four mercenaries are executed by firing squad.

10 July: After an explosion at a chemical plant at Seveso, Italy, a

7km radius area is contaminated by the poison gas, dioxin.

6 Aug: John Stonehouse, Labour MP for Walsall North, is found guilty of theft and conspiracy and sentenced to seven years imprisonment.

17 Aug: In the Philippines, a severe earthquake followed by tidal waves results in the loss of more than 3000 lives.

9 Sept: MAO TSE-TUNG (Mao Zedong) chairman of the Chinese Communist party for 40 years, dies, aged 82.

19 Sept: In Sweden, the Social Democratic party is defeated. The Party had been in office for 44 years.

6 Oct: Seni Pramoj, prime minister of Thailand, is deposed in a military coup, and Admiral Sangad Chalawoyo assumes power.

25 Oct: In London, the National Theatre is officially opened.

2 Nov: Jimmy CARTER, Democrat, is elected 39th president of the USA.

24 Nov: In Turkey, the province of Van is devasted by a severe earthquake; and 3700 people lose their lives.

17 Dec: In London, the longest-running play, *The Mousetrap*, reaches its 10,000th performance.

Riots occur in Soweto African township against compulsory learning of Afrikaans.

India raises the minimum age of marriage: men, from 18 to 21; and women from 15 to 18.

1977 3 Feb: In Ethiopia, the head of state, Brig.Gen. Teferi Bante, and six others, are executed by the military council.

27 March: In the world's worst air disaster to date, a Pan Am jumbo jet collides with a KLM jumbo jet at Tenerife, with the loss of 576 lives.

29 April: Hawker Siddeley, British Aircraft Corporation and Scottish Aviation combine to form the British Aerospace Corporation.

18 May: A sale at Mentmore Towers, home of the Earl of Rosebery begins. At the end of the sale, a total of $8,307,000 is realized.

22 May: The Orient Express arrives in Istanbul for the last time, having begun in Paris in 1883.

7 June: Queen Elizabeth II and the Duke of Edinburgh attend a thanksgiving service at St Paul's to celebrate her Silver Jubilee.

11 June: Dutch troops attack a train in northern Holland, held by South Moluccan terrorists. Two hostages and six hijackers were killed.

15 June: In the first general election in Spain for 40 years, Señor Saurez's Democratic Centre party wins.

5 July: In Pakistan, Mr Bhutto, the prime minister, is deposed, and martial law is declared.

5 Sept: In Cologne, West Germany, terrorists ambush a car, killing four and kidnapping Dr Hanns-Martin

A roadblock during the riots at the South African township of Soweto in June 1976.

Schleyer, president of the West German Employers' Federation. He is later found dead.

26 Sept: Laker Skytrains start a regular service between London's Gatwick and New York at low fares.

9th Oct: In Scotland, public houses serve alcoholic drinks on a Sunday, for the first time in 100 years.

18 Oct: West German commandos storm a hijacked Lufthansa plane at Mogadishu, Somalia, killing three of four terrorists, and freeing hostages.

20 Nov: President SADAT of Egypt is the first Arab leader to visit Israel.

24 Nov: In Greece, an archaeologist confirms that a tomb found is that of Philip II of Macedon, father of Alexander the Great. Philip was assassinated in 336 BC.

4 Dec: In the Central African Empire, Jean Bedel Bokassa crowns himself emperor.

16 Dec: In London, the Piccadilly line tube is extended from Hatton Cross to London Airport

In East Africa, Ethiopia invades Somalia.

The UN imposes mandatory arms embargo on South Africa.

President Sadat of Egypt visits Israel.

In Britain, the 'punk' era starts, with aggressive music and fashions soon to follow.

1978 19 Feb: In Cyprus, Egyptian commandos storm a hijacked DC-8 at Larnaca Airport. All hostages are released, but 15 commandos are killed by Greek Cypriot national guardsmen.

5 March: Ethiopian forces, supported by Russians and Cubans, retake the town of Ogaden, seized by Somalia in September. Fighting has continued since.

11 March: Palestinian terrorists land on the Israel coast near Tel Aviv. Thirty-two Israelis are killed and over 70 injured. Nine terrorists are killed and 2 taken prisoner.

15 March: In retaliation for the terrorist raid, Israeli forces invade southern Lebanon and destroy five Palestinian bases.

16 March: Aldo Moro, five times prime minister of Italy, is kidnapped in Rome by terrorists. His five bodyguards are shot dead.

18 April: A Panama treaty with the USA agrees that the control of the canal will revert to Panama by the year 2000.

20 April: A South Korean Boeing 707, 1000 miles off course, is fired at by a Soviet fighter aircraft and forced to land at Murmansk. Two passengers are killed and 13 others injured.

9 May: The body of Aldo Moro, kidnapped on 16 March, is found in a car in Rome.

10 May: It is announced that Princess Margaret and the Earl of Snowdon are seeking a divorce.

19 May: French troops parachute into Zaire to rescue 2000 Europeans held hostage by rebels. 100 Europeans are found to have been massacred.

20 May: Five terrorists and two policemen are killed at Orly Airport, Paris after terrorists fired at passengers boarding an Israeli plane.

15 June: King HUSSEIN of Jordan marries Elizabeth Halaby, a 26-year-old American, who becomes Queen Nur.

6 Aug: Pope PAUL VI dies.

10 Aug: The American Chrysler car firm announces that it is selling its European manufacturing operations to the French Peugeot-Citroën group.

22 Aug: Jomo KENYATTA, president of Kenya, dies in Mombasa, aged 84.

26 Aug: Cardinal Albino Luciani is elected Pope and is to be known as JOHN PAUL I.

3 Sept: An Air Rhodesia Viscount is shot down by Joshua Nkomo's Patriotic Front. It crashes near Lake Kariba, with the loss of 38 lives. Of the 18 survivors, 10 are shot dead by Nationalist guerrillas.

5 Sept: In India, the Jumna river bursts its banks, and 10,000 lives are estimated to have been lost in the floods.

8 Sept: In Iran, martial law is imposed by the shah in Teheran after demonstrations against his regime, after 58 die in the rioting.

28 Sept: After only 33 days as Pope, JOHN PAUL I dies.

1 Oct: Tuvalu, in the Pacific, becomes an independent state.

16 Oct: Cardinal Karol Wojtyla, Archbishop of Cracow, Poland, is elected pope and takes the name JOHN PAUL II. He is the first non-Italian pope for 400 years.

2 Nov: In Britain, a new newspaper, the *Daily Star*, is published by Express Newspapers.

3 Nov: The Caribbean island of Dominica becomes an independent republic.

5 Nov: In Iran, there is fierce fighting in Teheran. The prime minister, Sharif-Emami, resigns.

20 Nov: In Guyana, 912 bodies of members of the People's Temple religious sect are found, all believed to have committed suicide.

8 Dec: Mrs Golda Meir, a former prime minister of Israel, dies in Jerusalem aged 80.

27 Dec: Spain becomes a democracy after 40 years of dictatorship.

The USA establishes diplomatic relations with Communist China.

1979 7 Jan: Vietnamese-led rebel forces capture Phnom Penh, capital of Democratic Kampuchea (Cambodia).

16 Jan: The shah of Iran and Empress Farah flee to Aswan in Egypt.

Mao Zedong (1893–1976) chairman of China's Communist Party, united his country in 1949 and became a hero.

Anwar el Sadat of Egypt (right) and Menachem Begin were jointly awarded the Nobel Peace Prize in 1978 for their efforts to establish a lasting peace between their countries.

28 Jan: Violent rioting occurs in Teheran.

1 Feb: After 14 years in exile, the Ayatollah KHOMEINI returns to Iran.

6 Feb: Pakistan's Supreme Court rules that the former prime minister, Zulfikar Ali Bhutto, should be hanged for conspiring to murder an opponent.

12 Feb: An Air Rhodesia Viscount airliner is brought down by missiles fired by nationalist guerrillas, with the loss of 59 lives.

15 Feb: In Iran, four Iranian army generals are executed by firing squad, and two members of the shah's government are executed on the following day.

26 March: In Washington, President SADAT of Egypt and Mr Begin of Israel sign a peace treaty.

April: The Ayatollah Khomeini declares Iran an Islamic republic.

4 April: Zulfikar Ali Bhutto is hanged in Rawalpindi, despite pleas from world leaders.

11 April: Kampala, capital of Uganda, is captured by Tanzanian forces, who depose General Idi AMIN.

22 April: Tanzanian forces capture Jinja, 50 miles (80 km) from Kampala.

3 May: In the British General Election, the Conservatives win with a majority of 43 over all other parties.

4 May: Mrs Margaret THATCHER becomes Britain's first woman Prime Minister.

29 May: Bishop Abel Muzorewa is sworn in as the first black prime minister of Zimbabwe-Rhodesia.

1 June: Rhodesia becomes the State of Zimbabwe-Rhodesia.

7 June: The first elections are held for the European Parliament.

12 June: Bryan Allen, an American, makes the first man-powered flight across the English Channel, pedalling his *Gossamer Albatross* from Folkestone to Cap Gris Nez in 2 hours 50 minutes.

12 July: The Gilbert Islands becomes independent as the republic of Kiribati.

11 Aug: In Gujarat, India, a dam at Morvi bursts, resulting in thousands of lives lost.

27 Aug: British Admiral of the Fleet Earl MOUNTBATTEN, his 14-year-old grandson, Nicholas, and 15-year-old boatman Paul Maxwell are killed when an IRA bomb explodes in their boat in Sligo Bay, Ireland. Three others are seriously injured, while 82-year-old Lady Brabourne dies the next day.

30 Aug: In Ireland, Francis McGirl and Thomas McMahon are charged in Dublin with the murder of Earl Mountbatten.

1 Oct: The USA hands back to Panama control of the Canal Zone.

26 Oct: President Park of South Korea is shot accidentally at a dinner party.

4 Nov: Iranian students storm the US embassy in Teheran, taking over 60 hostages and demanding that the Shah be returned for trial.

11 Nov: In Canada, 200,000 people are evacuated from the town of Mississauga after a freight train jumps the rails and chemicals burst into flames.

15 Nov: In the British House of Commons, the prime minister names Sir Anthony Blunt, a former officer in the security services, as the 'fourth man' in the defection of Burgess and Maclean in 1951.

21 Nov: Demonstrators attack the US embassy in Islamabad, Pakistan, and four people are killed.

3 Dec: At a rock concert given at the Cincinnati Coliseum, Ohio, by the British group *The Who*, 11 young people are crushed to death and 28 seriously injured.

12 Dec: Lord Soames arrives in Salisbury as the new British gover-

nor of Southern Rhodesia. The 14-year-old rebellion ends.

18 Dec: In California, Stanley Barrett is the first man to break the sound barrier on land, after his rocket car reaches a speed of 739.666 mph (1190.35 kph).

27 Dec: President Hafizullah of Afghanistan is deposed and executed after a coup strongly backed by Soviet troops.

1980 8 Jan: President CARTER describes the Soviet invasion of Afghanistan as the greatest threat to peace since World War II.

9 Jan: In Saudi Arabia, 63 people are beheaded for attacking the Grand Mosque in Mecca during November last.

31 Jan: In Guatemala City, police storm the Spanish embassy after it has been taken over by extremists, with the loss of 39 lives.

22 Feb: In Kabul, Afghanistan, martial law is imposed after violent anti-Soviet demonstrations.

27 Feb: In Bogotá, Colombia. left-wing guerrillas seize the embassy of the Dominican Republic, and take 60 people hostage, including 14 ambassadors.

11 March: Robert MUGABE becomes prime minister of Zimbabwe and forms his cabinet.

30 March: At the funeral Mass for Archbishop Romero in San Salvador (assassinated 24 March), shooting breaks out, and 39 people are killed.

2 April: In Bristol, England, black youths riot after a raid on a club in the St Paul's district.

5 April: The world's rarest stamp, the 1c black on magenta British Guiana of 1856, is sold in New York for $850,000 (£500,000 approx.).

18 April: Rhodesia becomes independent as the Republic of Zimbabwe.

25 April: President Carter makes an announcement on an attempt to

Pope John Paul II blesses children at Knock Shrine in Ireland, 1980.

Iranian women dressed in traditional chador marching past the US embassy in Teheran.

rescue the hostages in Teheran the previous day. This had to be abandoned after the mechanical failure of three helicopters. Eight American servicemen die when a helicopter collides with a plane in Iran.

27 April: The siege in the Dominican embassy ends when 16 guerrillas are flown to Havana with 11 diplomats, who are then released.

30 April: After the abdication of her mother, Queen JULIANA, Princess Beatrix becomes Queen of the Netherlands.

30 April: In London, six armed men take over the Iranian embassy, holding 26 people hostage. They threaten to blow up the embassy if 91 prisoners in Iran are not released.

4 May: President TITO of Yugo-slavia dies, aged 87.

5 May: A team from the Special Air Service Regiment storms the Iranian embassy, rescuing the hostages. Four terrorists die, another dies later, and one is captured.

8 May: The World Health Organization declares formally that smallpox has been eradicated.

27 July: The former shah of Iran dies in a Cairo military hospital, aged 60.

30 July: The Anglo-French condominium of the New Hébrides in the Pacific becomes independent as the Republic of Vanuatu.

2 Aug: In Italy, a bomb explosion demolishes much of Bologna railway station, with the loss of 76 lives and with 200 people injured.

21 Aug: A Soviet nuclear submarine catches fire, with the loss of nine lives. It refuses help from a Japanese rescue team.

5 Sept: In Switzerland, the world's longest road tunnel opens, running over ten miles (16 km) under the St. Gotthard range.

22 Sept: Iraqi aircraft attack Iranian

bases after fighting for some weeks has taken place on the Iran-Iraq borders.

23 Sept: Iranian planes attack the petro-chemical complex at Zubayr, Iraq, and four Britons and three Americans are killed.

26 Sept: In Munich, neo-Nazis plant a bomb at a beer festival, with the loss of 12 lives and 200 injured people.

4 Nov· Ronald REAGAN wins the US presidential election in a landslide, and the Republicans win control of the Senate for the first time for 26 years.

10 Nov: In Britain, Michael Foot becomes leader of the Labour Party.

4th Dec: The prime minister of Portugal, Dr Francisco da Carneiro, is killed after a light aircraft crashes at Lisbon, with the loss of six other lives.

8 Dec: John LENNON, a member of the BEATLES pop group, is shot dead in New York.

10 Dec: In the first elections in Uganda for 18 years, Dr Milton Obote is declared the winner.

31 Dec: In Kenya, at the Norfolk Hotel, Nairobi, a bomb explosion results in the death of 15 people.

In Poland, the trades unions form the Solidarity movement.

1981 1 Jan: Greece becomes the 10th member of the Common Market.

20 Jan: Ronald REAGAN is sworn in as the 40th President of the USA.

20 Jan: The American hostages, 50 men and 2 women, are flown out of Iran, after spending 444 days in captivity.

25 Jan: British Labour MPs David Owen and William Rodgers, together with Mrs Shirley Williams and Roy Jenkins announce the setting up of a Council for Social Democracy.

23 Feb: In Spain, 200 civil guards led by Lt.Col. Tejero Molina, storm

Signing the Rhodesia cease-fire agreement in December 1979. In 1980 Rhodesia became Zimbabwe with Robert Mugabe as its first black prime minister.

the lower house of the parliament in Madrid and hold 350 deputies hostage in an attempt to overthrow the government. They later surrender and the leaders are arrested.

26 March: In Britain, the new Social Democratic Party is officially launched.

30 March: President Reagan is shot and wounded outside the Hilton Hotel, Washington.

5 May: In the Maze prison, Belfast, Northern Ireland, Robert Sands dies on the 66th day of his hunger strike. Riots break out in Belfast.

10 May: In France, François MITTERAND, Socialist, is elected president of France, defeating Valéry GISCARD D'ESTAING.

13 May: Pope JOHN PAUL II is shot and seriously injured in St Peter's Square, Rome, by a Turkish terrorist, Mehmet Ali Agca.

22 May: In Britain, Peter William Sutcliffe (the Yorkshire Ripper) is found guilty of the murder of thirteen women, and the attempted murder of seven others. He is sentenced to life imprisonment.

24 June: In Britain, the new Humber suspension bridge is opened to traffic. It has the longest single-span in the world.

28 June: In Teheran, a bomb destroys the headquarters of the Islamic Republican party. Head of the Supreme Court Ayatollah Beheshti and four Cabinet Ministers are among 72 people killed.

5 July: In the Toxteth area of Liverpool, mobs of youths riot for the second night running.

29 July: The Prince of Wales marries Lady Diana Spencer.

21 Sept: Belize becomes independent. This is the last British colony on the continental mainland of America to do so.

6 Oct: President Anwar SADAT of Egypt is assassinated in Cairo. Three other people are also killed, and 27 injured.

14 Oct: Vice-President Hosni Mubarak of Egypt becomes president.

1 Nov: Antigua becomes independent.

5 Dec: Elizabeth Canham, a British theology teacher is ordained priest in the USA. She is the first British woman to become a priest.

11 Dec: Javier Perez de Cuellar, a Peruvian diplomat, becomes UN Secretary-General, succeeding Dr Kurt WALDHEIM.

31 Dec: In Ghana, after a military coup, President Hilla Liman is deposed by Flight Lieut. Jerry Rawlings.

In China, the 'Gang of Four' is sentenced to death.

1982 5 Jan: Public donations to the Penlee lifeboat disaster fund amount to

£2,000,000 ($2,600,000), all to be shared by the families of the lost men.

20 Jan: In Madrid, a girl dies after consuming contaminated cooking oil. Similar oil has previously caused the deaths of 250 people in Spain.

17 Feb: In Zimbabwe, Robert MU-GABE, prime minister, dismisses Joshua Nkomo from the Government, after caches of arms are found on farms owned by him.

23 Feb: Greenland, a Danish territory with home rule, votes to leave the Common Market.

23 March: In Guatemala, a group of army officers overthrow the government.

24 March: In Bangladesh, the Army chief of staff, Lieut.Gen. Hossain Mohammed Ershad seizes power, deposes President Abdus Sattar, and imposes martial law.

29 March: A bomb explodes on a train travelling from Paris to Toulouse, resulting in the deaths of five people and injuries to 10 more.

2 April: Argentine forces invade and take control of the Falkland Islands. (FALKLANDS WAR).

3 April: The UN Security Council votes in favour of the withdrawal of Argentine forces from the Falklands.

4 April: South Georgia, a dependency of the Falklands, is seized by Argentine forces.

7 April: Britain declares a 200-mile war zone around the Falkland Islands.

17 April: The capital of Zimbabwe is renamed Harare (formerly Salisbury).

25 April: Royal Marines land from helicopters and recapture South Georgia. There are no casualties.

25 April: Israel withdraws from the Sinai Peninsula after 15 years of occupation.

2 May: A British submarine torpedoes and severely damages the Argentine cruiser General Belgrano. Of the crew of 1042, there are 800 survivors.

21 May: The British frigate, HMS Ardent, is hit by Argentine rockets and sinks, with the loss of 22 lives.

24 May: HMS Antelope, another frigate, sinks after being hit by a bomb during an Argentine air raid. Eight lives are lost.

25 May: The destroyer HMS Coventry, and the Cunard container ship Atlantic Conveyor are destroyed by Exocet missiles. 32 lives are lost.

28 May: Pope JOHN PAUL II begins a six-day visit to Britain, the first ever made by a pope to the country.

30 May: Spain joins NATO.

13 June: King Khalid of Saudi Arabia dies, aged 69, and is succeeded by his brother, Prince Fahd.

15 June: Maj.Gen. Jeremy Moore, commander of the British land forces on the Falklands, accepts the surrender of the Argentine forces, led by Maj. Gen. Menendez.

17 June: In Argentina, Gen. Leopoldo Galtieri is ousted as president, and Gen. Alfredo Saint Jean is appointed interim president.

20 July: A car-bomb explodes in Hyde Park, London, killing two soldiers riding back to barracks, and injuring 20 more soldiers and civilians. Two hours later, a bomb explodes under the bandstand at Regent's Park, where the Royal Green Jackets are giving a lunchtime concert. Six bandsmen are killed and there are 30 other civilian and military casualties. Two more soldiers die later. The IRA admit responsibility.

9 Aug: In Paris, six people die when terrorists open fire in Jewish restaurant.

21 Aug: The world's longest reigning monarch, King Sobhuza II of Swaziland, dies aged 83. He as-

cended the throne in 1921. On 3 Oct. 1982, Prince Makhosemivo, aged 11, is chosen to succeed him.

7 Sept: Floods in the Shansi province of China result in 764 people dead, 5,000 injured, and 200,000 homeless.

14 Sept: Princess Grace of Monaco (Grace KELLY) dies from injuries in a car crash the day before.

17 Sept: Hundreds of Palestinian civilians are massacred by Christian Phalangist militia in refugee camps in West Beirut. The area was occupied by the Israeli army.

19 Sept: In Sweden, the Social Democrats win in the general election.

1 Oct: Helmut Kohl becomes Chancellor of West Germany.

11 Oct: Henry VIII's warship *Mary Rose*, which sank off Portsmouth in 1545 with the loss of nearly all her 700 crew, is raised in the Solent.

16 Oct: In Japan, 94 miners are killed by methane gas in a mine in northern Japan.

10 Nov: Leonid BREZHNEV, Soviet leader for the previous 18 years, dies aged 75.

2 Dec: In the Salt Lake City, USA, surgeons remove the heart of a 61-year-old man and replace it with a permanent artificial one.

12 Dec: At RAF Greenham Common in Berkshire, England, 30,000 women form a human chain around the perimeter in protest against the siting there in 1983 of 96 American Cruise missiles.

1983 5 Feb: Klaus Barbie, a Nazi war criminal, is flown to France to face charges after being expelled from Bolivia.

8 Feb: *Shergar*, the 1981 Derby winner and one of the world's most valuable race horses, is stolen by an armed gang from the Aga Khan's stud farm in Co. Kildare, Ireland.

16 Feb: Bush fires rage in south-east Australia; at least 71 are dead.

20 Feb: In the Indian state of Assam, election riots cause the deaths of between 800 and 1000 people.

3 March: Devastating floods occur in South Australia.

5 March: In Australia, the Liberal party, led by Malcolm Fraser, loses the election to the Labour party, led by Bob Hawke.

5 April: In France, 47 Soviet diplomats and officials are expelled, accused of spying.

18 April: In Beirut, the US embassy is badly damaged by a car bomb explosion which kills 47.

21 April: In Britain, a £1 coin is put into circulation for the first time.

24 April: Austrian chancellor Dr Bruno Kreisky resigns after 13 years in office.

1 May: Police break up demonstrations in 20 Polish cities.

6 May: West German government pronounces the so-called Hitler diaries published in *Stern* magazine to be forgeries.

19 May: Missing barrels of dioxin from the chemical plant at Seveso, are found in southern France.

9 June: In the British General Election, the Conservatives are returned with an increased majority.

16 June: Yuri Vladimirovich Andropov is elected president of the USSR.

6 Sept: The USSR admits shooting down a South Korean aircraft which entered Soviet air space on 31 Aug. This was to 'stop the flight' after the aircraft 'tried to evade pursuit'.

22 Sept: In France, a world speed record for passenger trains is set up, covering the journey from Paris to Lyons in two hours at an average speed of 132 mph (212 kph).

2 Oct: Neil Kinnock is elected leader of the British Labour Party.

5 Oct: Lech Walesa, leader of the Polish trade union Solidarity, is

Shergar, *the 1981 Derby winner, was stolen by an armed gang from the Aga Khan's stud farm in Ireland.*

awarded the Nobel Peace Prize.

19 Oct: The prime minister of Grenada and three other ministers are shot dead by troops.

23 Oct: 300 US and French troops are killed in Beirut by 'suicide' bomb attacks by terrorists.

25 Oct: US troops and forces from six Caribbean countries invade Grenada.

30 Oct: In the Argentine elections, a civilian government is chosen for the first time in a decade.

3 Nov: President Reagan announces that US troops will withdraw from Grenada, having achieved their objectives.

4 Nov. A truck loaded with explosives explodes at Israeli HQ in Tyre, Lebanon, killing 39 people.

15 Nov: Turkish Cypriots declare their sector in Cyprus to be independent, but only Turkey recognizes this.

17 Dec: Six people are killed and 91 injured after a bomb explodes in a car outside Harrods store in London

1984 1 Jan: After a bloodless coup, Maj.-Gen. Buhari becomes ruler of Nigeria.

9 Feb: Mr Andropov, secretary-general of the Soviet Communist party, dies.

13 Feb: Konstantin Chernenko is named the new secretary-general of the Soviet Communist party.

9 March: In Britain, the National Union of Mineworkers begins an indefinite strike.

11 Apr: Mr Chernenko is declared president of the USSR.

17 Apr: In London, Libyans open fire from their People's Bureau in St James's Square, and WPC Yvonne Fletcher is killed.

20 Apr: It is announced that Britain is to hand over Hong Kong to China in 1997.

6 June: In India, troops seize the Golden Temple at Amritsar,

5 July: A former Nigerian minister, Umaru Dikko, is found drugged in a crate at Stansted airport, England.

9 July: In Britain, York Minster is badly damaged by fire caused by lightning.

19 July: In the USA, a police marksman shoots a man dead after he has shot 21 people in a California border town.

28 July: The XXIIIrd Olympic Games open in Los Angeles, USA.

25 Aug: A French cargo ship, the *Mont Louis*, carrying nuclear material, sinks after a collision with a German ferry off the Belgian coast.

31 Oct: In India, Mrs Indira Gandhi is assassinated by her Sikh bodyguards.

7 Nov: Ronald Reagan wins the US election

3 Dec: In Bhopal, India, 500 people are killed after a toxic gas leak at the Union Carbide pesticide plant.

29 Dec: The Congress Party, led by Rajiv Gandhi, wins a landslide victory in the Indian general election.

1985 20 Jan: Ronald Reagan is sworn in for a second term as President of the United States.

5 Feb: Spain lifts travel restrictions to and from Gibraltar.

28 Feb: IRA kill nine policemen in a mortar attack in Newry, Northern Ireland.

3 March: Britain's coal strike ends after almost a year.

10 March: Soviet leader Konstantin Chernenko dies and is succeeded by Mikhail Gorbachev.

6 April: President Nimeiry of the Sudan is overthrown by the army, Sudan, like neighbouring Ethiopia, is in the grip of drought and famine.

10 May: Sikh extremists kill more than 70 people in terrorist attacks in India, mainly in the capital Delhi.

2 July: Eduard Shevardnadze succeeds Andrei Gromyko as Soviet foreign minister.

10 July: French agents sink Greenpeace vessel *Rainbow Warrior* in Auckland harbour, New Zealand.

27 July: Coup in Uganda deposes President Milton Obote.

7 Oct: Palestinian terrorists hijack the Italian cruise liner *Achille Lauro* in the Mediterranean. One American passenger is shot dead. The terrorists surrender and are being flown secretly to Tunisia when US jets intercept and force down the Egyptian plane carrying them.

6 Nov: General Wojciech Jaruzelski is chosen as Poland's new head of state.

15 Nov: The Anglo-Irish agreement is signed at Hillsborough, Co. Down. The accord between the British and Irish governments over future consultation procedures is denounced by Unionists as a step towards unification.

19 Nov: Reagan–Gorbachev summit meeting in Geneva; the first US–USSR heads of state meeting in six years and the beginning of a new period of better relations between the two super-powers.

1986 1 Jan: Spain and Portugal become the 11th and 12th members of the

Members of Poland's independent trade unions 'Solidarity' demonstrating outside a court in Warsaw.

European Community.

28 Jan: Seven astronauts are killed when the US space shuttle *Challenger* explodes shortly after take-off from Cape Canaveral, Florida.

7 Feb: After a turbulent election, Mrs Corazon Aquino is declared President of the Philippines, replacing Ferdinand Marcos.

7 Feb: Haiti ousts its dictator Jean-Claude Duvalier who flees to France.

14 April: US jets bomb Libya in retaliation for Libya's alleged support of terrorism.

24 April: Kurt Waldheim, UN Secretary-General 1972–81, is barred from entering the USA because of his alleged complicity in Nazi war crimes.

28 April: The accident at the Chernobyl nuclear power plant in the USSR causes massive radiation leaks over a wide area. Local people are evacuated and the wrecked plant sealed in concrete for ever.

8 June: Waldheim is elected President of Austria.

5 Aug: Commonwealth leaders meeting in London disagree over question of trade sanctions against South Africa. Mrs Thatcher opposes the general wish to see such sanctions.

10 Oct: Javier Perz de Cuellar is re-elected for a second five-year term as UN Secretary General.

19 Oct: Samora Machel, President of

Mozambique, dies in a plane crash.

6 Nov: John and Michael Walker are jailed in USA on charges of having passed secrets to the USSR.

23 Dec: *Voyager* aircraft, an ultra-lightweight design carrying Dick Rutan and Jeana Yeager of the USA completes a nine-day, non-stop flight around the world.

1987 20 Jan: Terry Waite, the Archbishop of Canterbury's envoy, negotiating in Lebanon for release of foreign hostages, is himself taken hostage.

13 Feb: China and Portugal agree for the return of Portuguese-ruled Macao to China in 1999.

17 Feb: Fianna Fail forms the new government after Irish elections. On 10 March Charles Haughey succeeds Garret Fitzgerald as *Taioseach* (prime minister).

17 May: USS *Stark* is hit by missiles while on patrol in the Persian Gulf.

11 June: Margaret Thatcher and the Conservatives win the British general election. The Conservatives win 375 seats, Labour 229, the Alliance 22, and others 24.

31 July: Violence in Mecca leads to the deaths of 400 Iranian Muslim pilgrims. Iran accuses Saudi Arabian police of shooting Iranians.

24 Sept: The New South Wales court of appeal upholds a supreme court ruling refusing to grant the British government a banning injunction on the controversial book *Spycatcher* by Peter Wright. The book is banned in Britain.

11 Nov: 11 people are killed and 60 injured by an IRA bomb attack on a Remembrance Day service at Enniskillen, Northern Ireland.

18 Nov: Iran-*contra* report by US Senate is critical of the Reagan administration.

8 Dec: USA and USSR sign treaty to eliminate intermediate range nuclear missiles.

1988 26 Jan: Australia celebrates bicen-tennial of the arrival of the first fleet from England.

6 March: Three IRA members are shot dead by security forces in Gibraltar while allegedly planning a bomb attack.

2 May: 116 member states of the World Health Organization meeting in Geneva express concern at the increase in reported AIDS cases.

7 May: Cricketer Graeme Hick of Worcestershire scores 405 not out against Somerset – the second highest score in a county championship match.

8 May: President Mitterand is re-elected in France for a second seven-year term.

11 May: Kim Philby, who spied for the USSR for 28 years until fleeing from Britain in 1963, dies in the USSR, aged 76.

26 May: Vietnam announces its troops are to withdraw from Kampuchea.

23 June: Ne Win resigns as leader of Burma after 26 years. Civil unrest follows.

18 July: US Navy cruiser *Vincennes* accidentally shoots down an Iranian airliner in the Persian Gulf. All 290 people on board the plane are killed.

18 July: Iran accepts ceasefire agreement to end the Iran–Iraq war.

1 Sept: Ceasefire in Afghanistan, Soviet forces speed up their withdrawal.

18 Sept: The XXIVth Olympic Games open in Seoul, South Korea. Despite fears about security, the Games pass off peacefully. Matt Biondi of the USA is the biggest individual medal-winner with seven (five gold, one silver, one bronze). Ben Johnson, Canadian sprinter, is stripped of his 100-metre gold medal for taking illegal drugs.

2 Oct: Chilean voters reject General Pinochet in a referendum, but he refuses to stand down.

8 Nov: George Bush is elected President of the United States.

Countries of the World

AFGHANISTAN Republic of Asia. Area 250,000 sq.m. (650,000 sq.km.). Pop. 15,000,000. Cap. Kabul.

ALBANIA Republic of Europe in the Balkans. Area 11,000 sq.m. (28,500 sq.km.). Pop. 3,100,000. Cap. Tirana.

ALGERIA Republic of North Africa. Area 919,600 sq.m. (2,382,000 sq.km.). Pop. 23,500,000. Cap. Algiers.

ANDORRA Tiny country of the Pyrenees: sovereignty divided between France and the Spanish Bishop of Urgel. Area 175 sq.m. (453 sq.km.). Pop. 48,000. Cap. Andorra la Vella.

ANGOLA Republic of west-central Africa. Area 481,000 sq.m. (1,247,000 sq.km.). Pop. 8,000,000 Cap. Luanda.

ANGUILLA British colony of the Leeward Islands, West Indies. Area 35 sq.m. (90 sq.km.). Pop. 7000. Cap. The Valley.

ANTIGUA and BARBUDA British Associated State of the West Indies. Area 170 sq.m. (440 sq.km.). Pop. 100,000. Cap. St John's.

ARGENTINA Republic of South America. Area 1,068,360 sq.m. (2,766,890 sq.km.). Pop. 31,500.000. Cap. Buenos Aires.

ASCENSION Island in the South Atlantic, a dependency of St Helena. Area 34 sq.m. (88 sq.km.). Pop. 1000. Cap. Georgetown.

AUSTRALIA An independent member of the Commonwealth occupying the whole of the continent of Australia and outlying islands. Area 2,968,000 sq.m. (7,686,800 sq.km.). Pop. 16,200,000. Cap. Canberra.

AUSTRIA Republic of Central Europe. Area 32,376 sq.m. (83,850 sq.km.). Pop. 7,600,000. Cap. Vienna.

BAHAMAS An independent member of the Commonwealth in the West Atlantic. Area 5380 sq.m. (14,000 sq.km.). Pop. 200,000. Cap. Nassau.

BAHRAIN Group of islands forming a State in the Persian Gulf. Area 240 sq.m. (622 sq.km.). Pop. 467,000. Cap. Manama.

BANGLADESH Republic in the deltas of the Ganges and Brahmaputra, South East Asia. A member of the Commonwealth. Area 55,600 sq.m. (144,000 sq.km.). Pop. 107,000,000. Cap. Dacca.

BARBADOS An independent member of the Commonwealth in the West Indies. Area 166 sq.m. (430 sq.km.). Pop. 300,000. Cap. Bridgetown.

BELGIUM Kingdom of Northern Europe. Area 11,800 sq.m. (30,500 sq.km.). Pop. 9,940,000. Cap. Brussels.

BELIZE State on the east coast of Central America, a member of the Commonwealth. Area 8860 sq.m. (22,960 sq.km.). Pop. 200,000. Cap. Belmopan.

BENIN Republic on the Gulf of Guinea, West Africa. Area 43,480 sq.m. (112,600 sq.km.). Pop. 4,300,000. Cap. Porto Novo.

BERMUDA British dependent territory in the West Atlantic. Area 20 sq.m. (53 sq.km.). Pop. 62,000. Cap. Hamilton.

BHUTAN Kingdom of the Himalayas. Area 18,000 sq.m. (47,000 sq.km.). Pop. 1,500,000. Cap. Thimphu.

BOLIVIA Republic of South America. Area 424,000 sq.m. (1,093,500 sq.km.). Pop. 6,500,000.

THE COMMONWEALTH OF AUSTRALIA

State or Territory	Area sq.m.	sq.km.	Pop.	Cap.
Capital Territory	939	2,432	245,600	Canberra
New South Wales	309,450	801,428	5,405,000	Sydney
Northern Territory	520,308	1,347,519	139,000	Darwin
Queensland	667,036	1,727,522	2,505,000	Brisbane
South Australia	380,091	984,377	1,353,000	Adelaide
Tasmania	26,385	68,322	437,300	Hobart
Victoria	87,889	227,618	4,076,000	Melbourne
Western Australia	975,973	2,527,621	1,383,000	Perth

65

Greenland

Alaska
(USA)

ICELAND

CANADA

IRELAND UNIT
KING

PORTUGAL

SPAIN

MOROCCO

ALG

TROPIC OF CANCER

MEXICO

BAHAMAS

CUBA

PUERTO RICO
DOMINICA
ST LUCIA

MAURITANIA MA

CAPE
VERDE
ISLANDS

46 53 54 55
48 56 57
50 52
47 VENEZUELA
49 51 58 59 60
COLOMBIA

26
27 29 3
28
30 31

IVORY COAST GHANA

EQUATOR

ECUADOR

PERU

BRAZIL

BOLIVIA

TROPIC OF CAPRICORN

PARAGUAY

URUGUAY

ARGENTINA

Falkland Islands

1 DENMARK	11 YUGOSLAVIA	21 YEMEN
2 NETHERLANDS	12 ALBANIA	22 BHUTAN
3 BELGIUM	13 CYPRUS	23 BANGLADESH
4 LUXEMBOURG	14 LEBANON	24 KAMPUCHEA
5 W. GERMANY	15 ISRAEL	25 TUNISIA
6 E. GERMANY	16 SYRIA	26 SENEGAL
7 SWITZERLAND	17 JORDAN	27 GAMBIA
8 AUSTRIA	18 KUWAIT	28 GUINEA-BISSAU
9 CZECHOSLOVAKIA	19 BAHRAIN	29 GUINEA
10 HUNGARY	20 UNITED ARAB EMIRATES	30 SIERRA LEONE

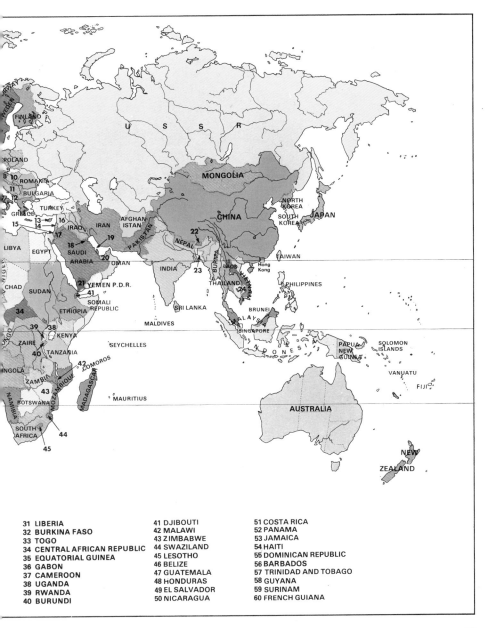

31 LIBERIA	41 DJIBOUTI	51 COSTA RICA
32 BURKINA FASO	42 MALAWI	52 PANAMA
33 TOGO	43 ZIMBABWE	53 JAMAICA
34 CENTRAL AFRICAN REPUBLIC	44 SWAZILAND	54 HAITI
35 EQUATORIAL GUINEA	45 LESOTHO	55 DOMINICAN REPUBLIC
36 GABON	46 BELIZE	56 BARBADOS
37 CAMEROON	47 GUATEMALA	57 TRINIDAD AND TOBAGO
38 UGANDA	48 HONDURAS	58 GUYANA
39 RWANDA	49 EL SALVADOR	59 SURINAM
40 BURUNDI	50 NICARAGUA	60 FRENCH GUIANA

BOTSWANA Republic of Southern Africa, a member of the Commonwealth. Formerly Bechuanaland Protectorate. Area 232,000 sq.m. (600,400 sq.km.). Pop. 1,200,000. Cap. Gaborone.

BRAZIL Republic, largest country of South America. Area 3,286,670 sq.m. (8,512,000 sq.km.). Pop. 141,500,000. Cap. Brasilia.

BRUNEI Sultanate on north-west coast of Borneo. A member of the Commonwealth. Area 2230 sq.m. (5,760 sq.km.). Pop. 248,000. Cap. Bandar Seri Begawan.

BULGARIA Republic of Europe in the Balkans. Area 42,855 sq.m. (11,000 sq.km.). Pop. 9,000,000. Cap. Sofia.

BURKINA FASO (formerly Upper Volta) Republic of West Africa. Area 105,900 sq.m. (274,200 sq.km.). Pop. 7,300,000. Cap. Ouagadougou.

BURMA Republic of South East Asia. Area 261,230 sq.m. (676,500 sq.km.). Pop. 38,800,000. Cap. Rangoon.

BURUNDI Republic of Central Africa. Formerly the Belgian territory Ruanda-Urundi. Area 10,750 sq.m. (27,800 sq.km.). Pop. 5,000,000. Cap. Bujumbura.

CAMEROON Republic of West Africa. Area 183,580 sq.m. (475,450 sq.km.). Pop. 10,300,000. Cap. Yaoundé.

CANADA Independent member of the Commonwealth in the north of North America. Area 3,852,000 sq.m. (9,976,000 sq.km.). Pop. 25,900,000. Cap. Ottawa.

CAPE VERDE Republic, a number of islands in the North Atlantic, about 300 miles off West Africa. Area 1560 sq.m. (4030 sq.km.). Pop. 300,000. Cap. Praia.

CAYMAN ISLANDS British colony, a number of islands in the West Indies. Area 100 sq.m. (260 sq.km.). Pop. 11,000. Cap. George Town.

CENTRAL AFRICAN REPUBLIC Republic of Equatorial Africa within the French Community. Area 240,550 sq.m. (622,984 sq.km.). Pop. 2,700,000. Cap. Bangui.

CHAD Republic of Equatorial Africa within the French Community. Area 496,000 sq.m. (1,284,000 sq.km.). Pop. 4,600,000. Cap. N'djamena.

CHILE Republic of South America. Area 292,274 sq.m. (757,000 sq.km.). Pop. 12,400,000. Cap. Santiago.

CHINA (People's Republic) Republic of South East Asia. Area 3,706,000 sq.m. (9,597,000 sq.km.). Pop. 1,063,000,000. Cap. Beijing.

CHRISTMAS ISLAND Australian territory in the Indian Ocean. Area 52 sq.m. (135 sq.km.). Pop. 3200. Cap. Flying Fish Cove.

COCOS (KEELING) ISLANDS Australian territory in the Indian Ocean. Area $5\frac{1}{2}$ sq.m. (14 sq.km.). Pop. 500. Cap. Bantam Village.

COLUMBIA Republic of South America. Area 440,000 sq.m. (1,139,000 sq.km.). Pop. 29,900,00 Cap. Bogotá.

COMOROS Island republic off Mozambique, in Africa. Area 838 sq.m. (2170 sq.km.). Pop. 400,000. Cap. Moroni.

CONGO A republic of Equatorial Africa within the

CANADIAN PROVINCES AND TERRITORIES

Province or Territory	Area sq.m.	sq.km.	Pop.	Cap.
Alberta	255,300	661,187	2,400,000	Edmonton
British Columbia	366,240	948,560	2,830,000	Victoria
Manitoba	251,014	650,089	1,050,000	Winnipeg
New Brunswick	28,356	73,437	707,000	Fredericton
Newfoundland	156,194	404,518	577,000	St John's
Northwest Territory	1,304,978	3,379,693	49,000	Yellowknife
Nova Scotia	1,426	55,491	860,000	Halifax
Ontario	412,606	1,068,586	8,820,000	Toronto
Prince Edward Island	2,184	5,567	124,000	Charlottetown
Quebec	594,894	1,540,685	6,520,000	Quebec
Saskatchewan	251,795	651,902	993,000	Regina
Yukon Territory	207,088	536,326	23,000	Whitehorse

French Community. Area 132,000 sq.m. (342,000 sq.km.). Pop. 2,100,000. Cap. Brazzaville.

COOK ISLANDS Self-governing territory of New Zealand in the South Pacific. Area 90 sq.m. (234 sq.km.). Pop. 18,000. Cap. Avarua.

COSTA RICA Republic of Central America. Area 19,600 sq.m. (50,700 sq.km.). Pop. 2,800,000. Cap. San José.

CUBA Republic of the West Indies. Area 44,220 sq.m. (114,550 sq.km.). Pop. 10,400,000. Cap. Havana.

CYPRUS Island republic in the Mediterranean, at the moment divided after Turkish forces occupied the North in 1974. A member of the Commonwealth. Area 3600 sq.m. (9250 sq.km.). Pop. 700,000. Cap. Nicosia. The Turkish occupied area, proclaimed as the 'Turkish Cypriot Federated State' is 40% of the total.

CZECHOSLOVAKIA Republic of Central Europe. Area 50,000 sq.m. (128,000 sq.km.). Pop. 15,600,000. Cap. Prague.

DENMARK Kingdom of Northern Europe. Area 17,400 sq.m. (45,000 sq.km.). Pop. 5,175,000. Cap. Copenhagen.

DJIBOUTI Republic of north-east Africa within the French Community, on the Red Sea. Area 8500 sq.m. (22,000 sq.km.). Pop. 300,000. Cap. Djibouti.

DOMINICA Republic within the Commonwealth in the Windward Islands, West Indies. Area 290 sq.m. (751 sq.km.). Pop. 100,000. Cap. Roseau.

DOMINICAN REPUBLIC Republic of the West Indies, occupying the eastern two-thirds of the island of Hispaniola. Area 18,800 sq.m. (49,000 sq.km.). Pop. 6,500,000. Cap. Santo Domingo.

ECUADOR Republic of South America. Area 109,500 sq.m. (283,600 sq.km.). Pop. 10,000,000. Cap. Quito.

EGYPT Arab republic of north-east Africa. Area 387,000 sq.m. (1,000,000 sq.km.). Pop. 52,000,000. Cap. Cairo.

EL SALVADOR Republic of Central America. Area 8000 sq.m. (21,000 sq.km.). Pop. 5,300,000. Cap. San Salvador.

EQUATORIAL GUINEA Republic of West Africa. Area 10,800 sq.m. (28,000 sq.km.). Pop. 300,000. Cap. Malabo.

ETHIOPIA Republic of north-east Africa. Area 472,000 sq.m. (1,222,000 sq.km.). Pop. 46,000,000. Cap. Addis Ababa.

FALKLAND ISLANDS British colony in the South Atlantic. Area 4700 sq.m. (12,200 sq.km.). Pop. 2000. Cap. Stanley.

FIJI An independent member of the Commonwealth in south-west Pacific. Area 7050 sq.m. (18,300 sq.km.). Pop. 700,000. Cap. Suva.

FINLAND Republic of north-east Europe. Area 130,000 sq.m. (337,000 sq.km.). Pop. 5,000,000. Cap. Helsinki.

FRANCE Republic of Western Europe. Area 213,000 sq.m. (547,000 sq.km.). Pop. 55,600,000. Cap. Paris.

FRENCH GUIANA A French overseas department in north-east South America. Area 35,000 sq.m. (91,000 sq.km.). Pop. 78,000. Cap. Cayenne.

FRENCH POLYNESIA A French overseas department in the Eastern Pacific. Area 1550 sq.m. (4000 sq.km.). Pop. 200,000. Cap. Papeete.

GABON Republic of Equatorial Africa within the French Community. Area 103,000 sq.m. (268,000 sq.km.). Pop. 1,200,000. Cap. Libreville.

GAMBIA A republic within the Commonwealth in West Africa. Area 4300 sq.m. (11,300 sq.km.). Pop. 800,000. Cap. Banjul.

GERMAN DEMOCRATIC REPUBLIC Republic of Eastern Europe. Area 41,800, sq.m. (108,000 sq.km.). Pop. 16,700,000. Cap. East Berlin.

GERMANY, FEDERAL REPUBLIC OF Republic of Western Europe. Area 96,000 sq.m. (248,600 sq.km.). Pop. 61,000,000. Cap. Bonn.

GHANA Republic of West Africa, a member of the Commonwealth. Area 92,000 sq.m. (239,000 sq.km.). Pop. 14,000,000. Cap. Accra.

GIBRALTAR British colony at the entrance to the Mediterranean. Area $2\frac{1}{2}$ sq.m. (6.5 sq.km.). Pop. 31,000. Cap. Gibraltar.

GREECE Republic of south-east Europe. Area 51,000 sq.m. (132,000 sq.km.). Pop. 10,000,000. Cap. Athens.

GREENLAND A self-governing county of Denmark in the North Atlantic. Area 840,000 sq.m. (2,176,000 sq.km.). Pop. 50,000. Cap. Godthaab.

GRENADA An independent country within the Commonwealth, located in the West Indies, one of the Windward Islands. Area 133 sq.m. (344 sq.km.). Pop. 113,000. Cap. St. George's.

GUADELOUPE A French overseas department in the West Indies. Area 688 sq.m. (1780 sq.km.). Pop. 332,000. Cap. Basse-Terre.

GUAM A territory of the United States in the Marianas archipelago in the North Pacific. Area 212

sq.m. (549 sq.km.). Pop 106,000. Cap. Agana.
GUATEMALA Republic of Central America. Area 42,000 sq.m. (108,900 sq.km.). Pop. 8,400,000. Cap. Guatemala City.
GUINEA Republic of West Africa. Area 95,000 sq.m. (246,000 sq.km.). Pop. 6,400,000. Cap. Conakry.
GUINEA-BISSAU Republic of West Africa. Area 14,000 sq.m. (36,000 sq.km.). Pop. 900,000. Cap. Bissau.
GUYANA Republic of north-east South America, a member of the Commonwealth. Area 83,000 sq.m. (215,000 sq.km.). Pop. 800,000. Cap. Georgetown.
HAITI Republic of the West Indies, occupying the western third of the island of Hispanioloa. Area 10,700 sq.m. (28,000 sq.km.). Pop. 6,200,000 Cap. Port-au-Prince.
HONDURAS Republic of Central America. Area 43,000 sq.m. (112,000 sq.km.). Pop. 4,700,000. Cap. Tegucigalpa.
HONG KONG British colony on the south-east coast of China. Area 403 sq.m. (1045 sq.km.). Pop. 5,600,000. Cap. Victoria.
HUNGARY Republic of Central Europe. Area 36,000 sq.m. (93,000 sq.km.). Pop. 10,600,000. Cap. Budapest.
ICELAND Island republic of the North Atlantic. Area 40,000 sq.m. (103,000 sq.km.). Pop. 234,000. Cap. Reykjavik.
INDIA Republic of south-east Asia, a member of the Commonwealth. Area 1,270,000 sq.m. (3,287,600 sq.km.). Pop. 800,500,000. Cap. Delhi.
INDONESIA Island republic of south-east Asia. Area 782,700 sq.m. (2,027,000 sq.km.). Pop. 175,000,000. Cap. Jakarta.
IRAN Republic of south-west Asia. Area 636,000 sq.m. (1,648,000 sq.km.). Pop. 50,400,000. Cap. Tehran.
IRAQ Republic of south-west Asia. Area 168,000 sq.m. (435,000 sq.km.). Pop. 17,000,000. Cap. Baghdad.
IRELAND, REPUBLIC OF Republic of Northern Europe. Area 27,000 sq.m. (70,200 sq.km.). Pop. 3,500,000. Cap. Dublin.
ISRAEL Republic of the Middle East. Area 8000 sq.m. (20,700 sq.km.). Pop. 4,400,000. Cap. Jerusalem.
ITALY Republic of Southern Europe. Area 116,000 sq.m. (301,000 sq.km.). Pop. 57,500,000. Cap. Rome.

IVORY COAST (CÔTE D'IVOIRE) Republic of West Africa. Area 124,000 sq.m. (322,500 sq.km.). Pop. 10,800,000. Cap. Abidjan.
JAMAICA An independent member of the Commonwealth in the West Indies. Area 4,200 sq.m. (11,000 sq.km.). Pop. 2,500,000. Cap. Kingston.
JAPAN An island country and constitutional monarchy of the Far East. Area 143,800 sq.m. (372,300 sq.km.). Pop. 122,300,000. Cap. Tokyo.
JORDAN Kingdom of the Middle East. Area 37,700 sq.m. (97,740 sq.km.). Pop. 3,700,00. Cap. Amman.
KAMPUCHEA Republic of south-east Asia. Area 70,000 sq.m. (181,000 sq.km.). Pop. 6,500,000. Cap. Phnom Penh.
KENYA Republic of East Africa, a member of the Commonwealth. Area 225,000 sq.m. (582,700 sq.km.). Pop. 22,400,000. Cap. Nairobi.
KIRIBATI Island republic of the Central Pacific, a member of the Commonwealth. Area 360 sq.m. (930 sq.km.). Pop. 62,000. Cap. Tarawa.
KOREA, NORTH Republic of the Far East. Area 46,500 sq.m. (120,500 sq.km.). Pop. 21,400,000 Cap. Pyongyang.
KOREA, SOUTH Republic of the Far East. Area 38,000 sq.m. (98,000 sq.km.). Pop. 42,200,000 Cap. Seoul.
KUWAIT An Emirate on the Persian Gulf. Area 6,900 sq.m. (17,800 sq.km.). Pop. 2,000,000. Cap. Kuwait.
LAOS A republic of south-east Asia. Area 91,400 sq.m. (236,800 sq.km.). Pop. 3,800,000. Cap. Vientiane.
LEBANON Republic of the Middle East. Area 4000 sq.m. (10,400 sq.km.). Pop. 3,400,000. Cap. Beirut.
LESOTHO Kingdom of Southern Africa. Area 11,700 sq.m. (30,360 sq.km.). Pop. 1,600,000. Cap. Maseru.
LIBERIA Republic of West Africa. Area 43,000 sq.m. (111,370 sq.km.). Pop. 2,400,000 Cap. Monrovia.
LIBYA Republic of North Africa. Area 680,000 sq.m. (1,760,000 sq.km.). Pop. 3,800,000. Cap. Tripoli.
LIECHTENSTEIN A principality of Western Europe. Area 62 sq.m. (157 sq.km.). Pop. 28,000. Cap. Vaduz.
LUXEMBOURG A Grand Duchy of Western Europe. Area 1000 sq.m. (2600 sq.km.). Pop. 400,000. Cap. Luxembourg.

The two cities of Buda and Pest came together as Budapest, capital of Hungary. Between them runs the river Danube.

MACAO An overseas territory of Portugal on the south-east coast of China. Area 6 sq.m. (16 sq.km.). Pop. 330,000. Cap. Macao.

MADAGASCAR An island republic 250 miles east of Africa. Area 226,700 sq.m. (587,000 sq.km.). Pop. 10,600,000. Cap. Antananariva.

MALAWI. Republic of Southern Africa. Area 45,800 sq.m. (118,500 sq.km.). Pop. 7,404,000. Cap. Lilongwe.

MALAYSIA An independent state of south-east Asia. A member of the Commonwealth. Area 127,300 sq.m. (330,000 sq.km.). Pop. 16,100,000. Cap. Kuala Lumpur.

MALDIVES An island republic of the Indian Ocean, with about 2000 islands. A member of the Commonwealth. Area 115 sq.m. (300 sq.km.). Pop. 200,000. Cap. Malé.

MALI Republic of north-west Africa. Area 479,000 sq.m. (1,240,000 sq.km.). Pop. 8,400,000. Cap. Bamako.

MALTA An island republic of the Mediterranean, a member of the Commonwealth. Area 122 sq.m. (316 sq.km.). Pop. 400,000. Cap. Valetta.

MARTINIQUE A French overseas department in the West Indies. Area 426 sq.m. (1100 sq.km.). Pop. 326,000. Cap. Fort-de-France.

MAURITANIA A republic of north-west Africa. Area 400,000 sq.m. (1,030,700 sq.km.). Pop. 2,000,000. Cap. Nouakchott.

MAURITIUS An independent state in the Indian Ocean, made up of two main islands. A member of the Commonwealth. Area 790 sq.m. (2050 sq.km.). Pop. 1,100,000. Cap. Port Louis.

MAYOTTE A French territory, an island in the Comoro Archipelago. Area 145 sq.m. (374 sq.km.). Pop. 32,000. Cap. Dzaoudzi.

MEXICO Republic of North America. Area 761,000 sq.m. (1,970,000 sq.km.). Pop. 82,000,000. Cap. Mexico City.

MONACO A principality on the Mediterranean coast, in south-east France. Area 467 acres (1.8 sq.km.). Pop. 28,000. Cap. Monaco.

MONGOLIA Republic of central Asia. Area 604,300 sq.m. (1,565,000 sq.km.). Pop. 2,000,000. Cap. Ulan Bator.

MONTSERRAT British colony in the Leeward Islands, West Indies. Area 38 sq.m. (98 sq.km.). Pop. 12,000. Cap. Plymouth.

MOROCCO A monarchy of north-west Africa. Area 172,400 sq.m. (446,500 sq.km.). Pop. 24,400,000. Cap. Rabat.

MOZAMBIQUE Republic of south-east Africa. Area 302,000 sq.m. (783,000 sq.km.). Pop. 14,700,000. Cap. Maputo.

NAMIBIA A disputed territory of south-west Africa known to the Republic of South Africa as South West Africa. A mandate was granted to South Africa in 1920 by the League of Nations, but the

United Nations and South Africa have been unable to reach agreement on its present status. Area 318,000 sq.m. (824,000 sq.km.). Pop. 1,300,000. Cap. Windhoek.

NAURU An island republic in the Western Pacific, with special relations with the Commonwealth. Area 8 sq.m. (21 sq.km.). Pop. 8000. Cap. Nauru.

NEPAL A monarchy of the Himalayas between China and India. Area 54,000 sq.m. (140,800 sq.km.). Pop. 17,800,000. Cap. Katmandu.

NETHERLANDS Kingdom of Western Europe. Area 15,800 sq.m. (40,800 sq.km.). Pop. 14,600,000. Cap. Amsterdam.

NETHERLANDS ANTILLES Two groups of Dutch islands in the Caribbean, with full internal autonomy. Area 370 sq.m. (960 sq.km.). Pop. 273,000. Cap. Willemstad, on Curaçao.

NEW ZEALAND An independent member of the Commonwealth in the south-west Pacific. Area 103,700 sq.m. (268,600 sq.km.). Pop. 3,400,000. Cap. Wellington.

NICARAGUA Republic of Central America. Area 50,000 sq.m. (130,000 sq.km.). Pop. 3,500,000. Cap. Managua.

NIGER Republic of West Africa. Area 489,000 sq.m. (1,267,000 sq.km.). Pop. 7,000,000. Cap. Niamey.

NIGERIA Republic of West Africa. Area 356,700 sq.m. (923,800 sq.km.). Pop. 108,700.000. Cap. Lagos (Abuja).

NIUE A self-governing territory of New Zealand in the Cook Islands, South Pacific. Area 100 sq.m. (260 sq.km.). Pop. 4000. Cap. Alofi.

NORFOLK ISLAND An Australian territory in the south-west Pacific. Area 14 sq.m. (36 sq.km.). Cap. 2000. Cap. Kingstown.

NORWAY Kingdom of Northern Europe. Area 125,000 sq.m. (324,000 sq.km.). Pop. 4,200,000. Cap. Oslo.

OMAN A sultanate at the eastern end of the Arabian peninsula. Area 82,000 sq.m. (212,400 sq.km.). Pop. 1,300,000. Cap. Muscat.

PACIFIC ISLANDS TRUST TERRITORY Group of islands, including the Marianas, Caroline and Marshall Island, governed by the United States. Area 687 sq.m. (1,780 sq.km.). Pop. 149,000. Cap. Saipan.

PAKISTAN Republic of Southern Asia. Area 310,400 sq.m. (804,000 sq.km.). Pop. 104,700,000. Cap. Islamabad.

PANAMA Republic of Central America. Area 29,000 sq.m. (75,700 sq.km.). Pop. 2,300,000. Cap. Panama.

PAPUA NEW GUINEA An independent state within the Commonwealth in the south-west Pacific. Area 178,200 sq.m. (461,700 sq.km.). Pop. 3,600,000. Cap. Port Moresby.

PARAGUAY Republic of South America. Area 157,000 sq.m. (406,700 sq.km.). Pop. 4,300,000. Cap. Asunción.

PERU Republic of western South America. Area 496,000 sq.m. (1,285,200 sq.km.). Pop. 20,800,000. Cap. Lima.

PHILIPPINES Republic of south-east Asia. Area 116,000 sq.m. (330,000 sq.km.). Pop. 62,000,000. Cap. Manila.

PITCAIRN ISLAND British colony in the South Pacific. Area 2 sq.m. (5 sq.km.). Pop. 63. Cap. Adamstown.

POLAND Republic of Eastern Europe. Area 120,700 sq.m. (312,700 sq.km.). Pop. 37,800,000. Cap. Warsaw.

PORTUGAL Republic of Western Europe. Area 35,500 sq.m. (92,000 sq.km.). Pop. 10,400,000. Cap. Lisbon.

PUERTO RICO A United States self-governing Commonwealth in the West Indies. Area 3435 sq.m. (8900 sq.km.). Pop. 3,300,000. Cap. San Juan.

QATAR An Emirate, a peninsula in the Persian Gulf. Area 4000 sq.m. (11,000 sq.km.). Pop. 300,000. Cap. Doha.

REUNION A French overseas department in the Indian Ocean. Area 969 sq.m. (2,500 sq.km.). Pop. 546,000. Cap. St Denis.

ROMANIA Republic of Eastern Europe. Area 91,700 sq.m. (237,500 sq.km.). Pop. 22,900,000. Cap. Bucharest.

RWANDA Republic of Central Africa. Area 100,000 sq.m. (26,400 sq.km.). Pop. 6,800,000. Cap. Kigali.

ST HELENA British colony, including the island of Ascension and the four islands of Tristan da Cunha, in the South Atlantic. St Helena area: 47 sq.m. (122 sq.km.). Pop. 5200. Cap. Jamestown.

ST KITTS-NEVIS A State in the Leeward Islands of the West Indies, associated with the Commonwealth. Area 100 sq.m. (260 sq.km.). Pop. 50,000. Cap. Basseterre.

ST LUCIA An independent state within the Commonwealth; one of the Windward Islands in the

West Indies. Area 238 sq.m. (616 sq.km.). Pop. 110,000. Cap. Castries.

ST PIERRE AND MIQUELON A French overseas department, eight islands off Newfoundland, Canada. Area 93 sq.m. (242 sq.km.). Pop. 6000. Cap. St Pierre.

ST VINCENT AND THE GRENADINES An independent member of the Commonwealth in the Windward Islands, West Indies. Area 150 sq.m. (388 sq.km.). Pop. 100,000. Cap. Kingstown.

SAMOA, AMERICAN Group of eight islands in the South Pacific, governed by the United States. Area 76 sq.m. (197 sq.km.). Pop. 35,000. Cap. Pago Pago.

SAMOA, WESTERN An independent state, a member of the Commonwealth, in the Pacific. Area 1090 sq.m. (2900 sq.km.). Pop. 200,000. Cap. Apia.

SAN MARINO Republic in the Apennines, Italy. Area 24 sq.m. (61 sq.km.). Pop. 23,000. Cap. San Marino.

SÃO TOMÉ AND PRINCIPE Island republic in the Gulf of Guinea, Africa. Area 372 sq.m. (964 sq.km.). Pop. 110,000. Cap. São Tomé.

SAUDI ARABIA Kingdom occupying most of the Arabian peninsula. Area 830,000 sq.m. (2,150,000 sq.km.). Pop. 14,800,000. Cap. Riyadh.

SENEGAL Republic of West Africa. Area 76,000 sq.m. (196,000 sq.km.). Pop. 7,100,000. Cap. Dakar.

SEYCHELLES Island republic of the Indian Ocean, a member of the Commonwealth. Area 108 sq.m. (280 sq.km.). Pop. 100,000. Cap. Victoria.

SIERRA LEONE Republic of West Africa, an independent member of the Commonwealth. Area 27,700 sq.m. (71,700 sq.km.). Pop. 3,900,000. Cap. Freetown.

SINGAPORE Island republic off the Malay peninsula, a member of the Commonwealth. Area 224 sq.m. (580 sq.km.). Pop. 2,600,000. Cap. Singapore.

SOLOMON ISLANDS An independent state, a member of the Commonwealth, in the south-west Pacific. Area 11,000 sq.m. (28,500 sq.km.). Pop. 300,000. Cap. Honiara, on Guadalcanal.

SOMALI REPUBLIC Republic of Africa, facing Aden. Area 246,000 sq.m. (637,700 sq.km.). Pop. 7,700,000. Cap. Mogadishu.

SOUTH AFRICA Republic of Southern Africa. Area 471,500 sq.m. (1,221,000 sq.km.). Pop. 34,400,000. Cap. Cape Town (seat of Legislature); Pretoria (seat of Government).

SPAIN Kingdom of Western Europe. Area 195,000

sq.m. (504,700 sq.km.). Pop. 39,000,000. Cap. Madrid.

SRI LANKA Republic of South Asia, a member of the Commonwealth. Area 25,000 sq.m. (65,600 sq.km.). Pop. 16,400,000. Cap. Colombo.

SUDAN Republic of north-east Africa. Area 967,500 sq.m. (2,506,000 sq.km.). Pop. 23,500,000. Cap. Khartoum.

SURINAM Republic of north-east South America. Area 63,000 sq.m. (163,300 sq.km.). Pop. 404,000. Cap. Paramaribo.

SWAZILAND Kingdom of southern Africa, a member of the Commonwealth. Area 6,700 sq.m. (17,400 sq.km.). Pop. 700,000. Cap. Mbabane.

SWEDEN Kingdom of Northern Europe. Area 173,700 sq.m. (450,000 sq.km.). Pop. 8,400,000. Cap. Stockholm.

SWITZERLAND Republic of Western Europe. Area 16,000 sq.m. (41,000 sq.km.). Pop. 6,600,000. Cap. Berne.

SYRIA Republic of the Middle East. Area 71,500 sq.m. (185,000 sq.km.). Pop. 11,400,000. Cap. Damascus.

TAIWAN (Republic of China). Nationalist republic, lying off the Chinese mainland. Area 14,000 sq.m. (36,000 sq.km.). Pop. 19,700,000. Cap. Taipei.

TANZANIA Republic of East Africa, a member of the Commonwealth. Area 365,000 sq.m. (945,000 sq.km.). Pop. 23,600,000. Cap. Dodoma.

THAILAND Kingdom of south east Asia. Area 198,500 sq.m. (514,000 sq.km.). Pop. 53,700,000. Cap. Bangkok.

TOGO Republic of West Africa. Area 21,600 sq.m. (56,000 sq.km.). Pop. 3,200,000. Cap. Lome.

TONGA Island kingdom in the South Pacific within the Commonwealth. Area 270 sq.m. (700 sq.km.). Pop. 107,000. Cap. Nuku'alofa.

TRINIDAD AND TOBAGO Island Republic of the West Indies within the Commonwealth. Area 2000 sq.m. (5000 sq.km.). Pop. 1,300,000. Cap. Port-of-Spain.

TRISDAN DA CUNHA Island in the South Atlantic, a dependency of St Helena. Area 38 sq.m. (98 sq.km.). Pop. 320. Cap. Edinburgh.

TUNISIA Republic of North Africa. Area 63,000 sq.m. (163 sq.km.). Pop. 7,700,000. Cap. Tunis.

TURKEY Republic, partly in Europe and partly in Asia. Area 301,400 sq.m. (780,600 sq.km.). Pop. 51,500,000. Cap. Ankara.

PROVINCES OF SOUTH AFRICA

	Area sq.m.	sq.km.	Population 1980	Seat of Government
Cape Province	278,395	721,001	5,091,000	Cape Town
Natal	33,580	86,967	5,722,215	Pietermaritzburg
Transvaal	109,627	283,917	8,351,000	Pretoria
Orange Free State	49,869	129,152	1,932,000	Bloemfontein

THE BLACK HOMELANDS

[South Africa claims that these are independent, but this is not recognised by the United Nations]

Homeland	Area sq.m.	sq.km.	Pop.	People	Cap.	Independence
Bophuthatswana	14,670	37,994	1,736,000	Tswana	Mmabatho	1977
Ciskei	–	–	675,000	Xhosa	Zwelitsha	1981
Transkei	14,250	36,900	2,400,000	Xhosa	Umtata	1976
Venda	2,510	6,500	400,000	Venda	–	1979

The following are stated to be self-governing, but not yet independent, with main peoples indicated in brackets:

Basotho-Qwaqwa (South Sotho)   Lebowa (Pedi)
Gazankulu (Shangaan)   Ndebele (Ndebele)
Kwazulu (Zulu)   Swazi (Swazi)

REPUBLICS OF THE USSR

	Area sq.m.	sq.km.	Pop.	Cap.
Armenia	11,540	30,000	3,317,000	Yerevan
Azerbaijan	33,400	87,000	6,614,000	Baku
Belorussia	80,000	208,000	9,942,000	Minsk
Estonia	17,300	45,000	1,530,000	Tallin
Georgia	27,700	70,000	5,200,000	Tbilisi
Kazakhstan	1,102,300	2,717,000	15,840,000	Alma-Ata
Kirgizia	76,150	198,000	3,970,000	Frunze
Latvia	24,600	64,000	2,605,000	Riga
Lithuania	25,000	65,000	3,600,000	Vilnius
Moldavia	13,000	34,000	4,100,000	Kishinev
Russian SFSR	6,569,000	17,075,000	143,090,000	Moscow
Tadzhikistan	54,600	143,000	4,500,000	Dushanbe
Turkmenistan	188,450	488,100	3,000,000	Ashkhabad
Ukraine	231,000	604,000	50,900,000	Kiev
Uzbekistan	153,400	447,000	18,000,000	Tashkent

A carnival on the small West Indian island of Trinidad. Trinidad has developed a distinctive culture characterized by calypso and steel band, and the limbo dance.

TURKS AND CAICOS ISLANDS British colony in the Caribbean. Area 166 sq.m. (430 sq.km.). Pop. 7200. Cap. Cockburn Town.

TUVALU An independent member of the Commonwealth, a group of islands in the South Pacific. Area 3 sq.m. (8 sq.km.). Pop. 8000. Cap. Fongafale or Funafuti.

UGANDA Republic of equatorial Africa. A member of the Commonwealth. Area 91,000 sq.m. (236,000 sq.km.). Pop. 16,000,000. Cap. Kampala.

UNION OF SOVIET SOCIALIST REPUBLICS Usually abbreviated to USSR, this is the world's largest nation, and occupies territory stretching from Europe to Asia. Total area 8,650,000 sq.m. (22,402,200 sq.km.). Pop. 285,000,000. Cap. Moscow.

UNITED ARAB EMIRATES. A federation of seven emirates, formerly the British-protected Trucial States, in the Persian Gulf. They are: Abu Dhabi, Ajman, Dubai, Fujairah, Ras al Khaimah,

Sharjah and Umm al Qaiwain. Area 32,300 sq.m. (83,600 sq.km.). Pop. 1,500,000. Cap. Abu Dhabi.

UNITED KINGDOM Kingdom of north-west Europe. Area 94,232 sq.m. (244,046 sq.km.). Pop. 56,900,000. Cap. London. The United Kingdom consists of the following:

England Kingdom; Area 50,336 sq.m. (130,363 sq.km.). Pop. 47,000,000. Cap. London.

Scotland Kingdom; Area 30,416 sq.m. (78,772 sq.km.). Pop. 5,200,000. Cap. Edinburgh.

Wales Principality; Area 8,017 sq.m. (20,763 sq.km.). Pop. 2,840,000. Cap. Cardiff.

Northern Ireland; Area 5,463 sq.m. (14,148 sq.km.). Pop. 1,600,000. Cap. Belfast.

Isle of Man; Area 227 sq.m. (588 sq.km.). Pop. 62,000. Cap. Douglas.

Channel Islands; Group of islands off north-west coast of France. Area 75 sq.m. (195 sq.km.). Pop. 140,000. The islands are: Jersey Area 45 sq.m. (116 sq.km.). Pop. 73,000. Cap. St Helier. Guernsey Area

$24\frac{1}{2}$ sq.m. (63 sq.km.). Dependencies Alderney 3 sq.m. (8 sq.km.), Sark 2 sq.m. (5 sq.km.), Herm 320 acres (130 hectares), Brechou 74 acres (30 hectares), Jethou 44 acres (18 hectares), Lithou 38 acres (15 hectares). Total pop. 140,000. Cap. St Peter Port.

UNITED STATES OF AMERICA Federal republic of North America. Area 3,615,319 sq.m. (9,363,123 sq.km.). Pop. 226,505,000. Cap. Washing, District of Columbia.

UPPER VOLTA *Burkina Faso*

URUGUAY Republic of South America. Area 68,000 sq.m. (176,200 sq.km.). Pop. 3,100,000. Cap. Montevideo.

VANUATU Island republic in the south-west Pacific, a member of the Commonwealth. Area 5700 sq.m. (14,800 sq.km.). Pop. 200,000. Cap. Port Vila.

VATICAN CITY State in north-west Rome, Italy, in which is located the government of the Roman Catholic Church, headed by the Pope. Area 108.7 acres (44 hectares). Pop. 1000.

VENEZUELA Republic of South America. Area 352,000 sq.m. (912,000 sq.km.). Pop. 18,300,000. Cap. Caracas.

VIETNAM Republic of south-east Asia. Area 127,250 sq.m. (330,000 sq.km.). Pop. 62,200,000. Cap. Hanoi.

VIRGIN ISLANDS (British) Group of 36 islands in the West Indies. Area 59 sq.m. (153 sq.km.). Pop. 11,500. Cap. Road Town.

VIRGIN ISLANDS (US) A territory near Puerto Rico in the West Indies. Area 133 sq.m. (344 sq.km.). Pop. 119,000. Cap. Charlotte Amalie.

WALLIS AND FUTUNA ISLANDS A French overseas territory in the south-west Pacific. Area 77 sq.m. (200 sq.km.). Pop. 9000. Cap. Mata-Utu.

WESTERN SAHARA A North African territory

THE STATES OF THE USA

State	Area sq.m.	sq.km.	Pop.	Cap.
Alabama	51,612	133,667	3,890,000	Montgomery
Alaska	586,444	1,518,800	400,500	Juneau
Arizona	113,915	295,023	2,718,000	Phoenix
Arkansas	53,107	137,539	2,285,000	Little Rock
California	158,702	411,013	23,668,500	Sacramento
Colorado	104,253	269,998	2,889,000	Denver
Connecticut	5,009	12,973	3,107,500	Hartford
Delaware	2,057	5,328	595,000	Dover
Florida	58,563	151,670	9,740,000	Tallahassee
Georgia	58,879	152,488	5,464,265	Atlanta
Hawaii	6,450	16,705	965,000	Honolulu
Idaho	83,562	216,412	944,000	Boise
Illinois	56,403	146,075	11,418,500	Springfield
Indiana	36,293	93,993	5,490,000	Indianapolis
Iowa	56,293	145,790	2,913,000	Des Moines
Kansas	82,269	213,063	2,363,000	Topeka
Kentucky	40,397	104,623	3,661,433	Frankfort
Louisiana	48,526	125,674	4,204,000	Baton Rouge
Maine	33,127	86,026	1,124,600	Augusta
Maryland	10,577	27,394	4,216,446	Annapolis
Massachusetts	8,258	21,386	5,737,037	Boston
Michigan	58,219	150,779	9,258,000	Lansing
Minnesota	84,073	217,735	4,077,000	St.Paul

facing the Atlantic. At the moment disputed between Morocco and the local POLISARIO organization seeking independence. Area 102,700 sq.m. (266,000 sq.km.). Pop. 76,000. Cap. El Aiun.

WESTERN SAMOA An independent state in the South Pacific and a member of the Commonwealth. Area 1095 sq.m. (2842 sq.km.). Pop. 200,000. Cap. Apia.

YEMEN ARAB REPUBLIC A country in the south-west of the Arabian peninsula. Area 75,300 sq.m. (195,000 sq.km.). Pop. 6,500,000. Cap. San'a.

YEMEN PEOPLE'S DEMOCRATIC REPUBLIC A country in the South Arabian peninsula. Area 128,600 sq.m. (333,000 sq.km.). Pop. 2,400,000. Cap. Aden.

YUGOSLAVIA A federal republic on the Adriatic. Area 98,800 sq.m. (255,800 sq.km.). Pop. 23,400,000. Cap. Belgrade.

ZAIRE Republic of west-central Africa. Area 905,600 sq.m. (2,345,400 sq.km.). Pop. 31,900,000. Cap. Kinshasa.

ZAMBIA A land-locked republic in south-central Africa. A member of the Commonwealth. Area 290,600 sq.m. (752,600 sq.km.). Pop. 7,200,000. Cap. Lusaka.

ZIMBABWE Republic of Southern Africa (the former Rhodesia). A member of the Commonwealth. Area 150,800 sq.m. (390,600 sq.km.). Pop. 9,500,000. Cap. Harare.

Mississippi	47,719	123,584	2,520,638	Jackson
Missouri	69,690	180,486	4,917,500	Jefferson City
Montana	147,146	381,086	786,700	Helena
Nebraska	77,231	200,017	1,570,000	Lincoln
Nevada	110,546	286,297	800,000	Carson City
New Hampshire	9,304	24,097	920,600	Concord
New Jersey	7,836	20,295	7,364,000	Trenton
New Mexico	121,672	315,113	1,300,000	Santa Fe
New York	49,579	128,401	17,557,000	Albany
North Carolina	52,589	136,197	5,874,500	Raleigh
North Dakota	70,669	183,022	653,000	Bismarck
Ohio	41,224	106,765	10,798,000	Columbus
Oklahoma	69,923	181,089	3,025,266	Oklahoma City
Oregon	96,986	251,180	2,632,663	Salem
Pennsylvania	45,336	117,412	11,867,000	Harrisburg
Rhode Island	1,214	3,144	947,000	Providence
South Carolina	31,057	80,432	3,120,000	Columbia
South Dakota	77,051	199,551	690,000	Pierre
Tennessee	42,246	109,411	4,591,000	Nashville
Texas	267,353	692,402	14,228,000	Austin
Utah	84,920	219,931	1,461,037	Salt Lake City
Vermont	9,609	24,887	511,456	Montpelier
Virginia	40,819	105,716	5,346,000	Richmond
Washington	68,196	176,617	4,130,000	Olympia
West Virginia	24,183	62,629	1,949,644	Charlestown
Wisconsin	56,157	145,438	4,705,000	Madison
Wyoming	97,919	253,596	470,816	Cheyenne

Right: Manhattan, city of glass and steel
skyscrapers. Below: A traditional village in
Zambia. Although six out of every ten
Zambians live in rural areas and depend
on farming for a living, copper is the
nation's most valuable source of wealth.

INTERNATIONAL ORGANIZATIONS

THE UNITED NATIONS This came into being on 24th October, 1945, (now celebrated as United Nations Day). Fifty Allied Nations signed the Charter, other countries joining later. The headquarters of the Organization is in Manhattan, New York City. *The Six Main Organs of the U.N. are:*
THE GENERAL ASSEMBLY This consists of all the members, each of which can have five representatives, but only one vote. The General Assembly meets once a year. The work of the Assembly is done by committees: (1) Political and Security; (2) Special Political; (3) Economic and Financial; (4) Social, Humanitarian and Cultural; (5) Trusteeship; (6) Administrative and Budgetary; and (7) Legal.

The symbol of the United Nations, a map of the world inside olive branches, for peace.

THE SECURITY COUNCIL This consists of 15 members, each with one vote. Five - China, France, USSR, the UK, and the USA are permanent members, the other ten being elected for two-year periods. The Council is responsible for peace and security.
THE ECONOMIC AND SOCIAL COUNCIL Responsible to the General Assembly for economic, social, cultural, educational, health and related matters.
TRUSTEESHIP COUNCIL Responsible for administering Trust Territories.
INTERNATIONAL COURT OF JUSTICE The main judicial organ of the U.N. It consists of 15 judges, all of different nationalities, and is based at the Hague.
THE SECRETARIAT Consists of the Secretary-General, a Director-General and the staffs.
UNITED NATIONS AGENCIES Food and Agricultural Organization (FAO); International Monetary Fund (FUND); General Agreement on Tariffs and Trade (GATT); International Atomic Energy Authority (IAEA); International Civil Avia-

tion Authority (ICAO); International Development Association (IDA); International Finance Corporation (IFC); International Labour Organization (ILO); Inter-Governmental Maritime Consultative Organization (IMCO); International Telecommunication Union (ITU); United Nations Educational, Scientific, and Cultural Organisation (UNESCO); Office of the U.N. High Commissioner for Refugees (UNHCR); U.N. Children's Fund (UNICEF); Universal Postal Union (UPU); International Bank for Reconstruction and Development (WORLD BANK); World Health Organization (WHO) World Meteorological Organization (WMO).

* * * * *

THE COMMONWEALTH The Commonwealth of Nations is a voluntary association of independent states. The Head of the Commonwealth is HM Queen Elizabeth II. Present members of the Commonwealth (with date of independence in parenthesis) are: Antigua & Barbuda (1981), Australia (1901), Bahamas (1973), Bangladesh:

(from Pakistan, 1971), Barbados (1966), Belize (1981), Botswana (1966), Brunei (1984), Canada (1931), Cyprus (1960), Dominica (1978), Fiji (1970), The Gambia (1965), Ghana (1957), Great Britain, Grenada (1974), Guyana (1966), India (1947), Jamaica (1962), Kenya (1963), Kiribati (1979), Lesotho (1966), Malawi (1964), Malaysia (1957), Maldives (1965), Malta (1964), Mauritius (1968), Nauru (1968), New Zealand (1907), Nigeria (1960), Papua New Guinea (1975), St Kitts-Nevis (1983), St Lucia (1979), St Vincent (1979), Seychelles (1976), Sierra Leone (1961), Singapore (1965), Solomon Islands (1978), Sri Lanka (1948), Swaziland (1968), Tanzania (1961), Tonga (1970), Trinidad & Tobago (1962), Tuvalu (1978), Uganda (1962), Vanuatu (1980), Western Samoa (1962), Zambia (1964), Zimbabwe (1980). Former members of the Commonwealth, who have now left, are: Irish Republic, South Africa and Pakistan.

EUROPEAN COMMUNITY (COMMON MARKET): This began in 1958 when France, Germany, Italy, Belgium, Luxembourg and the Netherlands, having pooled their coal and steel industries, signed a treaty in Rome to form a customs and economic union. The original countries were joined in 1973 by Denmark, the Irish Republic and the United Kingdom. In 1981 Greece joined the EC, followed in 1986 by Spain and Portugal. *The European Parliament* held its first direct elections in 1979. The 434 seats are divided as follows: France, Italy, West Germany and the United Kingdom: 81 each; Spain: 60; the Netherlands: 25; Belgium, Greece and Portugal: 24; Denmark: 16; Irish Republic: 15 and Luxembourg: 6. It meets in Luxembourg.

Other Organizations within EC are The Commission, in Brussels, The Council of Ministers in Brussels, the European Court of Justice in Luxembourg, and the European Investment Bank in Luxembourg.

OTHER INTERNATIONAL ORGANIZATIONS

ASSOCIATION OF SOUTH EAST ASIAN NATIONS (ASEAN): to accelerate the economic growth, social progress and cultural development, the promotion of collaboration and mutual assistance in matters of common interest, and the continuing stability of the South East Asian region. Members: Indonesia, Malaysia, the Philippines and Thailand.

ANZUS A mutual defence treaty, signed in 1951 by Australia, New Zealand and the USA.

ARAB LEAGUE The League of Arab states was formed in 1945 to unite, re-create and reintegrate the Arab community. Members include Algeria, Bahrain, Djibouti, Iraq, Jordan, Kuwait, Lebanon, Libya, Mauritania, Morocco, Oman, Palestine, Qatar, Saudi Arabia, Somalia, Sudan, Syria, Tunisia, the United Arab Emirates, Arab Republic of Yemen, and the Democratic Republic of Yemen.

CARIBBEAN COMMUNITY AND COMMON MARKET (CARICOM) To co-ordinate foreign policy, to provide common services and co-operation in functional matters such as health, education and culture, communications and industrial relations. Members: Antigua & Barbuda, Barbados, Belize, Dominica, Grenada, Guyana, Jamaica, Montserrat, St Kitts-Nevis, St Lucia, St Vincent, and Trinidad & Tobago. The Bahamas has a special relationship with CARICOM.

COUNCIL FOR MUTUAL ECONOMIC ASSISTANCE Usually abbreviated to CO-MECON, this is a kind of Eastern European version of the EEC. The members are: Bulgaria, Cuba, Czechoslovakia, East Germany, Hungary, Mongolia, Poland, Romania and the USSR. Yugoslavia is an associate member. The headquarters is in Moscow.

COUNCIL OF EUROPE Founded in 1949, this was set up to safeguard European heritage. Member states are: Austria, Belgium, Cyprus, Denmark, France, West Germany, Greece, Iceland, Irish Republic, Italy, Liechtenstein, Luxembourg, Malta, the Netherlands, Norway, Portugal, Spain, Sweden, Switzerland, Turkey and the United Kingdom. The Parliamentary Assembly meets twice a year, having 170 members chosen by member states.

EUROPEAN FREE TRADE ASSOCIATION (EFTA) To promote economic expansion, to ensure fair trading and competition, to avoid disparity in supply of raw materials and to contribute to harmonious development and expansion of world trade. Members: Austria, Iceland, Norway, Portugal, Sweden, Switzerland. Associate member: Finland. Members of EFTA have a special relationship with the EEC.

NORTH ATLANTIC TREATY ORGANIZATION (NATO) Formed in 1949, this is a defence organization of Western nations. Present members are: Belgium, Canada, Denmark, France, West Germany, Greece, Iceland, Italy, Luxembourg, the Netherlands, Norway, Portugal, Spain, Turkey, the United Kingdom and the United States of America.

ORGANIZATION OF AMERICAN STATES (OAS) To foster mutual under-standing and co-operation among nations of the western hemisphere. Members: Antigua & Barbuda, Argentina, Bahamas, Barbados, Bolivia, Brazil, Chile, Colombia, Costa Rica, Cuba, Dominica, Dominican Republic, Ecuador, El Salvador, Grenada, Guatemala, Haiti, Honduras, Jamaica, Mexico, Nicaragua, Panama, Peru, St Lucia, St Vincent, Surinam, Trinidad and Tobago, the United States, Uruguay and Venezuela.

ORGANIZATION OF AFRICAN UNITY (OAU) To further African unity and solidarity, to co-ordinate political, economic, social and defence policies; to eliminate colonialism in Africa. There are 32 members.

ORGANIZATION FOR ECONOMIC CO-OPERATION AND DEVELOPMENT (OECD) This was formed in 1961, and the member countries are Australia, Austria, Belgium, Canada, Denmark, West Germany, Finland, France, Greece, Iceland, Irish Republic, Italy, Japan, Luxembourg, the Netherlands, New Zealand, Norway, Portugal, Spain, Sweden, Switzerland, Turkey, United Kingdom and USA. Yugoslavia has a special status.

ORGANIZATION OF THE PETROLEUM EXPORTING COUNTRIES (OPEC) To unify abd co-ordinate the petroleum policies of members and determine the best means of protecting their interests. Members: Algeria, Ecuador, Gabon, Indonesia, Iran, Iraq, Kuwait, Libya, Nigeria, Qatar, Saudi Arabia, United Arab Emirates and Venezuela.

WARSAW PACT: A defence treaty, signed in 1955, of Eastern European countries. Members are Albania, Bulgaria, Czechoslovakia, East Germany, Hungary, Poland, Romania, and the USSR.

International Affairs

AFRIKANERS. The word *Afrikaner* is used to describe those people in South Africa who speak the Afrikaans language, and who are descended from the Dutch settlers of the 17th and 18th centuries. To these were added small numbers of French Huguenots and Germans who arrived later. English-speaking colonists often referred to them as *Boers*, an Afrikaans word meaning 'farmers'.

APARTHEID. This is an Afrikaans word meaning 'separate development'. It originated in South Africa, being used to describe the policy of keeping the white population segregated from the non-white people, that is, those who are black, Asian or of mixed race. The word first came into use around 1949, when it was employed by the South African Nationalist party in their declared political programme. As part of this policy, modern South African governments have set apart 'Black Homelands', which are areas where black people are allowed a measure of self-government. So far, four areas have been declared to be independent: Bophuthatswana, Ciskei, Transkei, and Venda. All lie geographically within the borders of South Africa.

CHRISTIAN DEMOCRATS. An attempt to apply Christian ideas and principles to politics. Following the anti-clerical ideas of the 19th century, the Roman Catholic church fostered the idea of having progressive parties with a Christian bias. Some Christian Democratic parties are Protestant, rather than Roman Catholic.

COMMUNISM. An extreme and more radical form of Socialism, based on the writings of Karl Marx (1818-83), who founded his Communist League in 1847. With Friedrich Engels (1820-95), a fellow German, Marx wrote and published the Communist Manifesto in 1848. Marx believed that Communism would follow Socialism, the compelling and repressive forces of the state having 'withered away'. In a Communist society, all goods would be publicly owned, to be distributed by the state 'from each according to his ability, to each according to his means.' Capitalism would give way to Socialism.

Various Marxist parties were set up in a number of countries, but it was not until 1917 that any was able to take office as a government. This followed the seizure of power in Russia by LENIN, when revolutionary Marxist Socialists (known as Bolsheviks), overthrew the moderate Socialist government of KERENSKY.

True Communism has not yet been achieved. The Russian Communists claim that the present system, a Socialist one, will eventually give way to a Communist state.

Since the end of World War II, a number of other countries have followed the example of the Soviet Union (Russia), and set up similar political systems. Such countries are Albania, Bulgaria, China, Cuba, Czechoslovakia, East Germany, Hungary, Poland, Ròmania and Yugoslavia. More recently, there have been Communist-type regimes in North Korea and Vietnam. The character of each one varies considerably, from the severe, orthodox government of Albania to the more liberally minded Yugoslavian version - sometimes called 'Communism with a smiling face'.

CONSERVATIVE PARTY. A party in British politics which evolved from the old Tory party of the 19th century. It is on the right wing of politics, but unlike some similar parties in other European countries, has some liberal views on social and welfare

82

matters. The party has always been an opponent of Socialist ideas, and tends to aim at alleviating taxes, rather than using them to implement dogmatic notions.

CORPORATE STATE. A system of government in which the ruling body consists of representatives from the various factions within the country, such as farmers, workers, employers, professional people, etc. No state has yet been successfully run on a system such as this.

DICTATORSHIP. The rule of one or more persons with absolute power over the rest of the people. There have been dictatorships of both the left wing and of the right.

FASCISM. This word dates from the 1920s, and is given to the political movement headed by Benito MUSSOLINI in Italy. Although beginning his career as a Socialist, Mussolini's ideas went rapidly towards a right-wing, militaristic, anti-Socialist movement. The Fascist regime in Italy took power under Mussolini in 1922, and continued for 21 years. All other parties were banned, and Mussolini became virtual dictator of the country, notwithstanding the fact that the nomimal head of Italy was the king.

Although an assembly existed, supposedly on the lines of a CORPORATE STATE, the members did little more than rubber-stamp the decrees commanded by the leader, Mussolini, known as *Il Duce*.

Secret police were installed, and all opposition was crushed, although leading businessmen and the Roman Catholic church were allowed some measure of independence.

One aspect of Fascism was the belief in the superiority of the nation. Italy was encouraged to glory in the past, linking its history with that of Rome. Italian Fascism influenced movements in other countries, particularly the National Socialists, or Nazis, in Germany, the Falangist party in Spain, and the Peronista movement in Argentina.

LABOUR PARTY. In Britain, the Labour party started in 1900 as the Labour Representation Committee.

Previously, there had been an Independent Labour Party which had been formed in 1893 under James Keir HARDIE, who had always wanted such a body to be represented in Parliament. At the time, most working men were strongly Liberal in outlook, and the first Labour MPs were elected with Liberal support.

In 1906, the body became the Labour party, largely supported by the trades unions, but still with a strong Liberal connection. During World War I, Socialist thought entered the party's programme. Unlike Socialist parties elsewhere in Europe, the doctrines of the Labour party were largely based on the theories of such people as Robert Owen, Sidney Webb, and on the intellectual Socialism of the Fabian Society.

The first Labour government, from 1923 to 1924, was a minority one, in which the Liberals and the Labour party outnumbered the Conservative party. Needing Liberal support, the Labour government lasted only a year, and it was not until 1929 that Labour held office again. This time, Labour held an overall majority. After World War II, the Labour party was returned in 1945 with a very large majority. A moderate number of Socialist reforms have been made by the party, which remains one committed to parliamentary democracy and progressive non-Marxist Socialism.

LEAGUE OF NATIONS. Set up after World War I, largely owing to the efforts of President Woodrow WILSON of the United States, this international organization was intended as an instrument to preserve peace. The USA never became a member, and the Soviet Union only joined in 1934. It was replaced after World War II by the United Nations organization, although some of the old League's bodies were taken over.

LIBERAL PARTY. Descended from the Whig party of the 18th and 19th century, the Liberal party at the beginning of the century was one of the two major political parties in Britain. After the rise of the Labour party, the Liberals grew less in number, and now stood as a rather poor third party. In 1988 the Liberals merged with the Social Democratic Party to become the Social and Liberal Democrats. Liberal parties in other Commonwealth countries have been more successful, the Australian Liberals being almost equivalent to the British Conservatives, while the Liberal party of Canada, more traditional in its politics, has been in government frequently.

NATIONAL SOCIALISM. A form of Fascism adopted in Germany by Adolf HITLER, who was leader of a party called the National Socialist German Workers' Party (in German, *Nationalsozialistische Deutsche Arbeiterpartei*, also abbreviated to NSDAP, but more often called the Nazi Party).

The most important and disagreeable character of National Socialism was its avowed belief in the superiority of the Germanic or Nordic people, who were referred to as 'Aryans'. According to its doctrines, all races could be classified in a descending scale, with the 'Aryans' at the top, and Jews and Negroes at the bottom. Such beliefs were of course, false and totally without foundation, but when the Nazis came to power, their ideas of a Master Race consisting of Germans, finally led to the outbreak of World War II.

Adolf Hitler became *Führer* (or leader) of the country, and cruel, inhuman measures were very soon taken against Jews, gypsies, and others. In Nazi opinion, Jews were the cause of all the ills which had beset Germany after the end of World War I. They would be overthrown, and the Third Reich, as the new regime termed itself, would last for a thousand years. As a result of these doctrines, over 6,000,000 innocent Jews were massacred in vile concentration camps.

Hitler had, in fact, explained his ideas and ambitions in a book, *Mein Kampf* (My Struggle) which was published in two volumes in 1925 and 1927. To further his aims, Hitler set up a private army, the brownshirted SA (initials of *Stormabteilung*, or storm troops), with a special bodyguard force, the black-uniformed SS (*Schutzstaffel*, or protective echelon).

Adolf Hitler came to power in 1933, and in the following year, all parties except the Nazi movement were illegal. The regime fell after Germany was conquered in 1945, when Hitler killed himself.

Benito Mussolini, dictator of Italy since the 1920s, led Italy into World War II on the side of the Germans, was deposed in 1943 and assassinated in 1945.

SOCIALISM. A system of government in which the means of production and distribution is publicly owned. Revolutionary Socialism was advocated by Karl Marx and others, while a more moderate, evolutionary course was propounded by such thinkers as Count Henri de St Simon (1760-1825), Charles Fourier (1772-1837) and Robert Owen (1771-1858). Only Owen's was truly Socialist in its ideas, but it was the Fabian Society, founded in 1884 by Beatrice and Sidney Webb, Graham Wallas and George Bernard Shaw, that was the source of British evolutionary Socialism.

WARS OF THE TWENTIETH CENTURY

The Algerian War (1954-62). France had ruled Algeria since the early 19th century, and the area was regarded as part of France. Many French people had settled there, and when Algerian nationalists went to war to seek independence, a large army of French soldiers was required to hold them. When it seemed that Algeria might be handed over to the local nationalists, there came a military revolt supported by French settlers. General DE GAULLE was brought back from retirement and the *colons* or settlers believed he would help them to keep Algeria as part of France. This did not happen. Instead, De Gaulle brought the Algerian war to an end by giving independence to the country in 1962.

The Balkan Wars (1912-1913). The first Balkan War in 1912 came when Montenegro, Bulgaria, Greece and Serbia joined together to fight Turkey, when most of the Turkish areas in Europe were gained by the four allies. In the second, Serbia, Greece, Romania and Turkey united against Bulgaria, after Serbia had made claims to Macedonia.

The Boer War (1899-1902). Although it began in the 19th century, the Boer War lasted for over two years, and was fought between Great Britain and two Boer republics: the Transvaal, or South African Republic, and the Orange Free State. Trouble had flared after gold was discovered in 1886 in the Transvaal. Prospectors poured in, and the local Boer government viewed the presence of these *Uitlanders* (foreigners) with some alarm. Most were British, and the refusal of the Boers to grant them citizenship and equal rights produced strong British objections.

In 1895, Dr (later Sir) Leander Starr Jameson, with 660 men, made a raid into Transvaal territory from Mafeking, hoping to reach Johannesburg, 140 miles (225 km) distant. He hoped to be joined there by local *uitlanders*, but was forced to surrender by the Boers.

By 1899, the situation in Johannesburg had become worse. Since the Treaty of Paris in 1814, Britain had regarded South Africa as coming within its jurisdiction. After Paul Kruger, the Transvaal president refused once again to grant citizenship to the *uitlanders*, troops were sent out from Britain. When Britain refused to withdraw them, the Transvaal, joined by the Orange Free State, declared war.

Great Britain had only 25,000 men in the area, while the Boers greatly outnumbered them, as well as having superior weapons. The war continued until the Orange Free State was overrun, and Transvaal fell. The first became the Orange River Colony, and the second the Transvaal colony, the Boers accepting British sovereignty under the Treaty of Vereeniging in 1902.

Falklands War (1982). The background to this conflict goes back some two hundred years during which the Argentine (and the previous Spanish government of the area) claimed the islands. Formal British possession dates from 1765.

In March, 1982, reports were received that 60 Argentinians were on South Georgia Island (one of the dependencies of the Falkland Islands), collecting scrap metal from a disused whaling station. They left, leaving a few men behind, and the Argentinian flag flying. On 1 April, news came that an Argentinian naval force was steaming towards the Falklands. On the following day, the Argentinians invaded by sea and air, and the 81 Royal Marines garrisoned there were taken prisoner. 5,000 Argentinian troops were landed, and their flag was raised over Government House in Stanley, the capital.

On 5 April, the British task force set sail from Portsmouth, led by the aircraft carriers *Invincible* and *Hermes*. The liner *Canberra* was also put under naval control. On 7 April, Britain declared a war zone of 200 miles radius around the Falkland Islands. On 9 April, *Canberra* sailed, carrying 2000 troops. On 25 April, Marines recaptured South Georgia. On 1 May Vulcan bombers flying from Ascension Island attacked Port Stanley airfield. On 2 May the British submarine *Conqueror* torpedoed the Argentine cruiser *General Belgrano*. British ships were attacked from the air; HMS *Sheffield* was hit by an Exocet missile and abandoned. The frigates *Ardent* and *Antelope* were also lost.

Reinforcements arrived on the liner *QE2* and other ships, and British troops captured Port Darwin and the Goose Green airstrip towards the end of May. A surprise overland attack took Port Stanley, the Argentine forces surrendering on 14 June. Argentina's defeat lead to the fall of its military junta.

The Iran-Iraq War (1980-1988). Fighting between Iran and Iraq began when Iraq's President Sadam Husain accused Iran's religious leader, the ayatollah Khomeini, of plotting his overthrow. Iraq invaded its larger neighbour, but the war settled into a slugging conflict of attrition, with large-scale tank and artillery battles. Iraq's forces, smaller but on the whole better-armed, resorted to the use of chemical weapons and there were bombing raids and missile exchanges.

All efforts at international mediation failing, US and other Western naval forces entered the Persian Gulf to safeguard shipping. There were several skirmishes between US ships and Iranian forces.

The war ended, with a cease-fire agreement in 1988. Both countries had suffered crippling human and financial losses. There were no victors.

Israeli-Arab Wars. When British troops withdrew from Palestine in 1948, the Jews created a provisional government, setting up the state of Israel. The Arab Legion immediately entered Jerusalem, with Egypt also intervening on the Arab side. After General NASSER nationalized the Suez Canal in 1956, Israeli forces invaded Egypt, and Anglo-French forces occupied the Canal Zone. Then came the Six-Day war of 1967, when Israel invaded Egypt and Jordan, capturing Jerusalem and the Sinai peninsula. The fourth war came in 1973, when Egypt and Syria attacked Israel.

The Korean War (1950-1953). In 1945, Korea, which had been under Japanese rule for 36 years, was declared independent. The USSR moved in and occupied the northern part, while the USA occupied the south, since free elections were planned. These elections did not take place. Instead, two separate and rival governments were set up, the North being Communist in complexion, the South being one friendly to the West.

In June, 1950, war broke out when North Korea, led by Kim Il-Sung, and with support from the Chinese, invaded the South, in an attempt to unite the country. The USA urged the United Nations to intervene, and the Security Council called for a cease-fire.

A United Nations force, largely consisting of American troops, and led by General Douglas MACARTHUR, drove the North Koreans back. The Chinese who were supporting the North, and the Americans, who supported the South, came very near to open War between themselves, but armistice talks were started in 1951, and agreed in 1953. The two parts of Korea are now effectively separate states, and divided roughly at the line of the 38th parallel.

The Russian-Japanese War (1904-5). Both Russia and Japan had become rivals in their ambitions to annex Manchuria and Korea.

After new moves by Russia into Korea, Japan attempted to come to agreement. Russia refused, and diplomatic relations were broken off. Within days, without declaring war, Japan attacked Port Arthur on mainland China. It had been leased to Russia by China, and the Japanese were able to trap the Russian fleet there.

To the surprise of the world, Japan secured a number of victories against the Russians, destroying their fleet. After the peace treaty in 1905, Korea fell under the influence of Japan, who annexed the country totally in 1910.

The reverses had a disastrous effect on Russia, one result being the general strike by workers in October 1905. The Tsar was forced to agree to the 'October Manifesto', giving wider powers to the Duma (parliament), electoral and civil liberties.

Poster warfare: American World War I recruiting poster (above left). The US entry into the war in 1917 gave the allies the strength needed to make a final push to victory. The Soviet poster (above) proclaims: 'We will defend Mother Volga'. They did: the Germans never crossed the river. Left: German poster advertising a local SS rally.

The Sino-Japanese War (1931-45). Having successfully fought China between 1894-95 for the capture of Korea, the Japanese went to war once again with the object of conquering the whole of China. In 1931-32, the Japanese occupied Manchuria, which was declared 'independent'. A Japanese protectorate was established, and the name was changed to 'Manchukuo'. Full-scale war broke out in 1937, in which the Japanese heavily bombed Chinese cities, an action condemned by the League of Nations. After appalling atrocities, Nanking fell, and at the end of December, 1937, the Japanese took Hangchow and later Tsingtao. A Japanese government was set up at Nanking.

The Spanish Civil War (1936-39). Spain had become a republic after the overthrow of the monarchy in 1931. The war began with a revolt in 1936 by leading army officers in Spanish Morocco, which spread to many towns in Spain itself. With the support of most of the army and the air force, as well as a large number of Moorish troops, the forces were headed by General FRANCO, who also had the support of right-wing factions.

The republican government at first was able to hold on to power, but soon, foreign governments took a hand. Right-wing countries, like Germany under HITLER and Italy under MUSSOLINI intervened on the side of Franco, sending so-called 'volunteers', while the Soviet Union aided the government, sending supplies and equipment. Idealists of all kinds from many countries genuinely did volunteer to serve in Spain.

The insurgents, under Franco made a number of successes, and Franco was appointed Chief of the Spanish State. By 1939, Franco had conquered most of the country.

The Vietnam Wars (1946-54 and 1964-75). After the collapse of Japan in 1945, HO CHI-MINH, a Communist leader, set up a republic in the northern part of Vietnam. France, who still regarded the country as part of her Empire in Indo-China, set out to reassert her rights, and war broke out between French troops and Ho Chi-Minh's forces. After some fierce fighting, the French occupied the fortress at Dien Bien Phu in 1953. In the following year, Ho Chi-Minh's forces, called the Viet-Minh, attacked the French and took Dien Bien Phu. A conference of 14 nations took place, and it was agreed that Vietnam was to be partitioned into two states; the North, a Communist one under Ho Chi-Minh, and supported by China, and the South, supported by Great Britain and the United States. The other two states of Indo-China, Laos and Cambodia, were to be independent.

However, the Communists had set up guerrilla groups in the South, called the Vietcong, whose aim was to defeat the government of the South, run by the Catholic nationalist, Ngo Dinh Diem. He received military aid from the United States, while the Vietcong were aided by North Vietnam.

In 1964, two American warships were attacked off the North Vietnamese coast, and the USA then bombed North Vietnam military targets. From then on, the United States was virtually at war with North Vietnam. Although peace talks took place in 1969, nothing was agreed.

The North Vietnamese started an offensive in 1972, and advanced into the South, and eventually a cease-fire was agreed in 1973. Later that year, all American troops were withdrawn, and the North secured a victory over the South in 1975. The war ended with the whole country being united under the Communist government.

Throughout the period, the neighbouring countries of Laos and Cambodia (now called Kampuchea) were invaded, and thus drawn into the Vietnam war.

World War I, (1914-18). Rivalry between

Above: Two Soviet soldiers fire from behind a ruined wall in Stalingrad during the Second World War. Above right: Ghostly stumps of shell-blasted trees, water and mud—all part of a First World War battle scene. Below: In the war in Indo-China in 1953 French paratroopers counter-attack.

the great powers in 19th and early part of the 20th century were the main causes of World War I, but the actual outbreak was due to the assassination in June, 1914, of the Archduke Francis Ferdinand in Sarajevo, Serbia. The Archduke was heir to the throne of the Austro-Hungarian Empire, and was on a state visit to the adjoining country, Serbia. The assassin, Gavrilo Princip, was a Serbian nationalist, and the Austrians believed that the Serbian government was involved in the assassination.

Some weeks later, an ultimatum was issued by Austria to Serbia, who agreed with most, but not all, the demands. Russia, Serbia's ally, promised help if trouble occurred. On 28 July, Austria declared war on Serbia, and Russia mobilized its troops. Germany, allied to Austria-Hungary, felt threatened, and declared war on Russia on 1 August. On 3 August, Germany, believing that France would go to Russia's aid, declared war on France. Germany had already entered Luxembourg, and asked Belgium for permission to cross that country in return for a guarantee to uphold Belgian integrity. Belgium refused, and was immediately invaded.

Belgium's neutrality had been guaranteed by Britain, so on 4 August, 1914, Britain declared war on Germany. From them on, other countries entered the war, choosing sides according to their political viewpoint. Germany and Austria-Hungary became known as the Central Powers, and those opposing them were called the Allies.

Fighting took place in many parts of the world, although most of the battles took place in France and Belgium (Western Front); Russian borders (Eastern Front); Northern Italy; In Serbia, Turkey and Romania (Balkan Front); in Egypt, Palestine and Mesopotamia (Turkish Front), in Africa and China.

During World War I, a number of new weapons were used: in 1914, aircraft were used in battle and in bombing, in 1915, tear gas was used against the Russians by Germany; poison gas was used by the Germans on the Western Front; the tank was employed, machine-guns were widely used, and submarine warfare developed. Sea battles took place off Heligoland, Coronel (Chile); the Falkland Islands; the Dogger Bank; in the Atlantic Ocean, the Dardanelles, and Jutland.

Nearly ten million people were killed .

During World War I, the British Empire mobilized 8,904,467 men, of whom 908,371 died, and the USA mobilized 4,355,000 men, of whom 126,000 died.

Russia, because of the Bolshevik Revolution, left the war in March, 1918. Other nations surrendered in that year: Bulgaria on 29 September, Turkey on 31 October, and Austria-Hungary on 3 November. Germany's forces were overcome, and an armistice produced an end to the fighting on 11 November, 1918.

World War II (1939-45). This began with the invasion of Poland on 1st September 1939 by German armed forces. After HITLER, the German chancellor had sent his troops into Czechoslovakia the year before, Neville CHAMBERLAIN, the British prime minister, had given in to Hitler's demands. A pact of peace had been signed, but after the Polish invasion, Britain had to assert itself, and, together with France, declared war on Germany.

Within weeks, Germany had concluded a treaty with the USSR to divide up Poland between them. The Soviet Union invaded Finland, who surrendered four months later. Germany annexed the free city of Danzig, and almost half of Poland, the USSR claiming the other half. In April, 1940, German troops occupied Denmark, and invaded Norway by sea and air. They met strong resistance from the Norwegians,

War artists: The painting above is of a 'dogfight' between fighter planes in the Battle of Britain during the Second World War. The painting below shows the destruction of a German U-boat.

losing four troopships and four cruisers. British naval units attacked the Germans at Narvik, sinking all the enemy ships. Other British and French forces had landed in southern Norway, but by June, all resistance ceased, and the Allies withdrew.

In May, suddenly, without warning, and using armoured columns in the 'blitzkrieg' (lightning war) method, German armed forces swept through Belgium, the Netherlands and Luxembourg. Belgium and the Netherlands had no choice but to surrender. German troops turned north towards the Channel, thus cutting off British and French troops in Belgium (Flanders).

In May, Neville Chamberlain resigned as Prime Minister, and was replaced by Winston CHURCHILL. The Germans took Brussels and Namur, driving the Allied troops to the sea. On 28 May, the British forces were on the beaches at Dunkirk, and due to heroic efforts by the Royal Navy and civilian seamen, 215,000 British, and 120,000 French troops were rescued.

As the Germans swept across France, Italy came into the War on the side of Germany, with Italian troops invading southern France. Meanwhile, on 13 June, the Germans occupied Paris, and a week later, France concluded an armistice with Germany. The aged Marshal PÉTAIN became head of the French government, with Germany occupying a large area of the country.

After the fall of France, Britain had lost a huge amount of arms and equipment, and Churchill appealed to the United States for arms and supplies. These were sent within three weeks, for although the United States had not entered the war, there was little doubt as to where its sympathies lay.

Germany occupied the Channel Islands, and soon came heavy bombing of British cities, lines of communication and factories. Thousands of German aircraft flew over Britain, with widespread bombing.

Germany, using its submarine fleet, had tried to starve out Britain, and indeed, food supplies were very short. British credit in the United States had now been used up, so buying of supplies had to cease.

In March, 1941, Congress passed the Lend-Lease Act, which allowed the President to send much-needed shipments of food to Britain. The Battle of Britain was almost won, for by late June, 1941, raids by the Luftwaffe had become noticeably fewer. By this time, Italy had invaded Greece, and Germany had occupied Yugoslavia.

Although Hitler's aerial onslaught had failed, Britain had still expected invasion at any time. Then, on 22 June, 1941, the German army invaded the USSR instead.

Quite suddenly, Japan entered the war, by making a surprise attack on the American bases at Hawaii, the Philippines and other Pacific islands, as well as on British bases in Hong Kong and Malaya.

On 7 December 1941, at Pearl Harbor, Hawaii, the USA lost a great part of its fleet. The United States immediately declared war on Japan, and with Germany and Italy declaring war on the United States, the war had become a global one. Germany and Italy had, in 1936, made a pact known as the Rome-Berlin Axis, and from that time on, the partners were known as the 'Axis' powers.

Germany made great advances into the USSR, for by winter of 1941, German troops had reached the outskirts of Moscow, with Leningrad also under siege. The weather was hard, and Soviet counter-attacks drove the Germans back some way.

Meantime, the Japanese had scored successes in the Pacific, capturing the Philippines, Indonesia, Malaya and Singapore, and with the coming of spring in Europe, the Germans once more drove the the Soviet troops back. In North Africa, the Germans were successful too, as Rommel's armies approached Cairo and Suez.

At last, the tide began to turn. Rommel was driven back by the British 8th Army under General MONTGOMERY, and Soviet troops scored a great victory at Stalingrad, destroying the German attackers.

In 1943, the Allied leaders, Churchill, ROOSEVELT and STALIN met to discuss future strategy. The first landing by the Allies was in Italy, when British and Americans moved up northwards. Then the USSR was completely occupied with the Germans in the East, and it was not until June, 1944, that the greatest of all landings were made.

Enormous numbers of Allied soldiers were landed in Normandy, France on 6 June, and by less than a year later, were advancing through northern Germany.

The act which finally brought the war to an end was the dropping of atomic bombs on Hiroshima and Nagasaki in Japan. After this terrible event, the Japanese surrendered, bringing World War II to an end on 2 September, 1945.

Suffragettes are led away by the police after demonstrating for women's rights.

WOMEN'S SUFFRAGE

In 1903, a militant women's suffrage movement was started in Britain under the leadership of Mrs Emmeline PANKHURST and her daughter Christabel. Called the Women's Social and Political Union, the organization was devoted to the advance of women's rights, and particularly the right to vote. At that time, no women in the country were allowed to vote at elections. They were denied *suffrage* - the right or privilege of voting.

The suffragettes launched a terrorist campaign by setting houses, railway stations and pillar boxes on fire. Women chained themselves to railings in prominent places, and there was a continuous programme of heckling political speakers. In one case, a suffragette, Emily Davidson, threw herself on to the race-course at the 1913 Derby in front of the king's horse, and was killed.

Offenders were sent to prison, where they frequently went on hunger-strike. However, at the outbreak of World War I in 1914, the Union threw its strength into the war effort, giving up militant activities. In 1918, women over the age of 30 were given the right to vote and ten years later, women between the ages of 21 and 30 ('the flappers' vote') also were able to vote.

Similar activities had also taken place in the United States under the leadership of Lucy Stone. Some states had already given women the vote, but in 1920, all American women were able to do so. In the Commonwealth, New Zealand had granted the right in 1893, Australia in 1902, and Canada in 1917.

On the continent, women did not receive voting rights in France until 1945, and in Belgium, in 1948. Dates in other countries were as follows: Denmark 1915, Germany 1919, Italy 1946, Norway 1907, South Africa (white women only) 1930.

DISASTERS OF THE CENTURY 1900 to 1988

1902 13 to 18 Feb: In Russia, an earthquake in Transcaucasia kills and injures 2000 people.
18 April: In Guatemala, Central America, an earthquake destroys eight towns and kills 900 people.
8 May: In Martinique in the Caribbean, the town of St Pierre is destroyed by the eruption of the volcano Mount Pelée, with the loss of 30,000 lives.
May: In St Vincent in the Caribbean, the volcano of Soufrière is active and 2000 people are killed.
16 Dec: In Turkestan, an earthquake kills 10,000 people.

1903 29 April: In Armenia, an earthquake destroys villages and kills 785 people.

1905 April: A severe earthquake in Northern India destroys many villages and kills over 19,000 people in Amritsar, Dharmsala, Kangra and other places.
8 Sept: In Italy, 2000 killed in an earthquake in Calabria, followed by another earthquake at Monterosso on 14 Sept. with the loss of 3000 lives.

1906 4 Jan: In Nicaragua, an earthquake and volcanic eruption destroys the town of Masaya, with thousands killed.
14 Feb: In Colombia, an earthquake and tidal wave destroys Boca Grande, with thousands killed.
17 March: In Formosa (Taiwan), an earthquake at Kagi kills 1228 people.
18 April: San Francisco is destroyed by an earthquake followed by fires. Over 1000 lives are lost.
17 Aug: In Chile, 2500 lives are lost in an earthquake at Valparaiso.

1907 14 Jan: In Jamaica, an earthquake at Kingston kills 1000 people.

1908 28 Dec: In Italy, a disastrous earthquake hits South Calabria and Sicily, with widespread destruction and over 150,000 lives lost.

1912 15 April: The White Star liner *Titanic* hits an iceberg and sinks on her maiden voyage, with the loss of 1513 lives.

1915 7 May: The Cunard liner *Lusitania* is sunk by a German U-Boat. 1198 lives are lost, including 124 Americans.

1917 12 Dec: In a derailment at Modane, France, 543 passengers are killed.

1923 1 Sept: An earthquake in Japan virtually destroys the city of Yokohama, and Tokyo is in ruins. Over 140,000 people lose their lives.

1926 31 Aug: The island of Fayal in the Azores is badly hit by an earthquake. The city of Horta is almost destroyed, but there is very little loss of life.

1928 23 to 29 April: In Greece, Corinth is destroyed in an earthquake. 15,000 are homeless, but few people are killed.

1931 3 Feb: In New Zealand, the cities of Napier and Hastings are almost destroyed in an earthquake. 212 people are killed, 950 injured, and 10,000 are homeless.

1933 19 Sept: In China, the autumn floods cause wide devastation, destroying over 2000 villages.

1934 15 Jan: In India, a violent earthquake strikes Northern Bihar and Nepal. This is one of the greatest earthquakes in history, affecting 120,000 square miles (300,000 sq.km.). 10,000 people are killed and 500,000 are homeless.

1935 31 May: In Quetta, India (now Pakistan), a huge earthquake strikes, killing over 20,000 people.

1939 26 Jan: An earthquake in Southern Chile devastates 80,000 sq.km. (50,000 sq.m.), and 30,000 people

The scene of devastation at Lice in eastern Turkey after it had been struck by an earthquake in 1975. Nearly 3,000 people were killed. In the following year nearly 4,000 people perished in another massive earthquake in Turkey.

are killed, mostly in Concepción and Chillon.

26 to 29 Dec: In an earthquake in Anatolia, Turkey, over 45,000 lose their lives; the town of Erzincan is almost destroyed.

1945 6 Aug: An atomic bomb is dropped on Hiroshima, Japan, killing over 91,000 people.

9 Aug: An atomic bomb is dropped on Nagasaki, Japan, killing over 36,000 people.

Nov: In India (now Pakistan), a tidal wave results in the loss of over 4000 lives near Karachi.

1948 June: In Japan, 4000 people lose their lives in an earthquake in Fukui.

1949 5 Aug: In Ecuador, a violent earthquake kills 7000 in the centre of the country.

1954 9 to 12 Sept: In Algeria, 1600 in Orleansville lose their lives in an earthquake.

1956 8 Aug: In a Belgian colliery, 250 men are trapped by fire.

1957 July. In Northern Iran, an earthquake kills over 2000 people.

13 Dec: In Iran, a violent earthquake kills over 2000 people.

21 Dec: In Ceylon, people 250 die in landslides and floods, with many thousands homeless.

1958 28 Sept: In Japan, a typhoon in Tokyo kills 1300 people, with many injured.

1959 10 Feb: In the USA, a tornado strikes St Louis, with 19 people killed and 265 injured.

18 Sept: In Scotland, after an outbreak of fire, 47 miners die at Auchengeich colliery.

1960 29 Feb: In Morocco, a violent earthquake strikes Agadir, with the loss of 12,500 lives in the town and surrounding villages.

10 Oct: In the Ganges delta of Pakistan, 3000 people die after a cyclone strikes.

19 Dec: In the USA, the aircraft-carrier *Constellation* catches fire in Brooklyn Navy Yard, with the loss of 42 lives.

1962 10 Jan: In Peru, after snow, ice and rock break away from Mount Huascaran, a huge avalanche sweeps down into a valley, destroying the village of Ranrahirca, and killing over 3000 people.

1 Sept: In Iran, an earthquake centred north of Hamadan (the ancient Ecbatana) destroys 300 villages and 12,000 people are killed.

1963 26th July: In Yugoslavia, an earthquake at Skopje, capital of Macedonia, kills 1000 people, and renders 135,000 homeless.

1964 30 May: In Peru, after a riot at a football stadium in Lima, 300 people die.

1965 28 March: An earthquake in Chile results in the deaths of over 400 people.

27 Dec: The BP oil rig *Sea Gem* capsizes, and sinks in the North Sea with the loss of 13 lives.

1966 19 Aug: Over 2000 people are killed in an earthquake in Turkey.

21 Oct: A coaltip at Aberfan, in Wales, collapses, engulfing a school, a row of cottages and a farm, and killing 124 people, including 116 children.

8 Dec: The Greek ferry *Heraklion*, sailing from Crete to Piraeus, the seaport of Athens, sinks in a storm with the loss of 200 lives.

1967 18 March: 700,000 barrels of oil are spilt when the tanker *Torrey Canyon* is grounded off the Cornish coast of England.

22 May: Over 300 are killed in a fire at a Brussels department store.

1968 10 April: The New Zealand ferry *Wahine* sinks at Wellington, with the loss of 104 lives.

31 Aug: An earthquake in Iran results in the loss of over 20,000 lives.

3 Nov: Severe storms and floods in Northern Italy result in more than 100 deaths.

18 Nov: After a fire at a warehouse in Glasgow, 22 people die.

1969 2 June: The US destroyer *Frank E. Evans* is cut in two after colliding with the Australian aircraft carrier *Melbourne* in the South China sea. Over 70 US sailors are missing.

15 June: In Spain, a newly built restaurant collapses at Los Angeles de San Rafael, killing 53 people and injuring 200.

1970 10 Feb: In the Swiss Alps, an avalanche at Val d'Isère kills 39 people.

4 March: The French submarine *Eurydice* sinks after an explosion, with the loss of 57 lives.

9 April: In a gale outside Genoa harbour, the British cargo ship *London Valour* sinks with the loss of 21 lives.

16 April: In the French Alps, an avalanche engulfs a sanatorium, killing 72 people, most of them children.

31 May: In an earthquake in Peru,

Rescue workers at Aberfan in Wales where a coaltip collapsed in October 1966 engulfing a school and killing 116 children.

an estimated 70,000 people lose their lives.

15 Oct: In Australia, a bridge over the Yarra river, Melbourne, collapses while being constructed, with the loss of 34 lives.

1 Nov: In France, at St Laurent du Pont, near Grenoble, fire breaks out in a dance hall, with the loss of 144 lives.

13 Nov: In East Pakistan, a cyclone and tidal waves cause the death of more than 500,000 people.

1971 2 Jan: At a football match at Ibrox Park, Glasgow, Scotland, 66 spectators were killed and 145 injured when crush barriers collapse.

9 Feb: In Southern California, an earthquake results in the loss of at least 61 lives.

23 May: In Turkey, an earthquake results in the death of nearly 1000 people.

1972 30 May: At Battersea fun fair, London, a Big Dipper crashes, killing four children and injuring 16 others.

6 June: In Wankie, Rhodesia (now Zimbabwe), 400 miners are killed in an explosion.

10 June: In the USA, torrential rain causes floods in the Black Hills of South Dakota, with the loss of 200 lives.

24 June: Floods in the Eastern USA follow a severe hurricane, with the loss of more than 120 lives.

5 July: After a fire at a hospital in Sherborne, Dorset, England, 30 mentally handicapped patients die.

23 Dec: In Managua, Nicaragua, more than 10,000 people die in an earthquake.

1974 26 Jan: In Australia, torrential rain causes floods in Queensland. Brisbane is cut off, five people die and over 8000 are homeless.

4 April: In the USA, tornadoes sweeping across the country result in more than 330 deaths.

1 June: An explosion at a chemical plant at Flixborough, Lincolnshire, kills 29 people.

4 Aug: A bomb explodes on a Rome-Munich express train, killing 12 people and injuring 40.

11 Aug: In Bangladesh, monsoon floods result in the deaths of over 2000 people.

31 Aug: At Zagreb, Yugoslavia, an express train is derailed, with the loss of more than 120 lives.

21 Sept: In Honduras, floods caused by hurricanes result in the deaths of more than 8000 people.

21 Nov: In Britain, bomb explosions in two Birmingham public houses cause the death of 21 people, and 182 others are injured.

1975 28 Feb: In London, an underground train crashes into the end of a blind tunnel at Moorgate, with the loss of 43 lives and 68 people injured.

6 Sept: In Turkey, a massive earthquake centred on Lice results in nearly 3000 deaths.

27 Dec: In Bihar, India, an explosion after a flood in a coalfield results in 372 deaths.

1976 4 Feb: In Guatemala, an earthquake devastates the country, and over 22,000 people are dead.

6 May: In Italy, an earthquake strikes the north east, and the town of Gemona is almost destroyed, with the loss of over 900 lives.

17 Aug: In the Philippines, a severe earthquake followed by tidal waves results in the loss of more than 3000 lives.

1 Oct: In Lower California, Mexico, a hurricane devastates La Paz and other areas nearby, with the loss of more than 600 lives.

24 Nov: In Turkey, the province of Van is devastated by a severe earthquake and 3700 people lose their lives.

1977 18th Jan. In Australia, a commuter train from Mount Victoria to Sydney, leaves the rails and crashes into bridge supports, with the loss of 80 lives.

4 March: Romania is struck by a massive earthquake, with the loss of 1570 lives.

28 May: In the USA, a nightclub at Southgate, Kentucky is engulfed by fire, with the loss of 158 lives.

1978 29 Jan: In the worst blizzard for 30 years, four motorists are found dead in their cars in the north of Scotland, and 70 passengers are rescued from a snowbound train.

27 April: In the USA, scaffolding on a cooling tower in West Virginia collapses, with the loss of 51 lives.

11 July: In Spain, a tanker truck carrying liquid gas explodes in a camp site on the east coast. 170 people die and 100 more are injured.

5 Sept: In India, the Jumna river bursts its banks, and 10,000 lives are estimated to have been lost in the floods.

16 Sept: In Iran, a violent earthquake in the east devastates the town of Tabas and surrounding villages, with the loss of more than 5000 lives.

1979 8 Jan: A French tanker, the *Betelgeuse*, explodes while discharging its cargo at Bantry Bay, Ireland, with the loss of 50 lives.

15 April: Earthquakes strike towns and villages in the Bay of Kotor area of Yugoslavia, with more than 200 lives lost.

30 Aug: A hurricane in the Caribbean devastates the island of Dominica, and sweeps on to the Dominican Republic, causing 1000 deaths.

13 Sept: A hurricane with 200 kph (130 mph) winds strikes the Gulf of Mexico, causing severe damage in Mobile, Alabama, and Pascagoula in Mississippi.

1980 1 Jan: In Northern Quebec, after a prank when a young man sets fire to party decorations, a fire kills 45 people.

27 March: In the North Sea's worst

oil rig disaster, the *Alexander Kielland* platform capsizes and 137 lives are lost.

18 May: In Washington State, USA, the Mount St Helens volcano, dormant for over 100 years, erupts. 85 people die.

10 Oct: In Algeria, the city of El Asnam is devastated by a severe earthquake, with the loss of more than 2000 lives.

23 Oct: In Spain, an explosion at a primary school in Ortuella kills 48 children and three adults.

21 Nov: In Las Vegas, USA, a 26 storey hotel is destroyed by fire, with the loss of 84 lives.

23 Nov: In Southern Italy, a violent earthquake devastates large areas, with the loss of more than 4000 lives.

1981 10 Feb: In a fire at the Hilton Hotel at Las Vegas, USA, eight people die and more than 200 are injured.

14 Feb: In Ireland, in the Dublin suburb of Artane, 48 young people die at a St Valentine's dance after a fire at a club.

7 Sept: In China, floods in the northern Shansi province kill 764 people, injure 5000 others, and leave 200,000 homeless.

19 Sept: In Brazil, 300 people are drowned after a river boat overturns in the Amazon.

22 Sept: In Turkey, 35 soldiers die during a NATO exercise after a jet crashes into infantry.

16 Oct: In Japan, 94 miners are killed by methane gas in a coal mine.

4 Dec: In India, 46 people are crushed to death after a stampede on a staircase in an old tower in New Delhi.

19 Dec: Eight crew members of the Penlee lifeboat at Mousehole, Cornwall, England, lose their lives attempting to rescue eight people (all of whom also die) from the coaster *Union Star.*

1982 6 Jan: In the USA, at least 21 people die after mudslides in a storm bury homes at Ben Lomond, near San Francisco.

27 Jan: A gas explosion at Cardowan colliery, near Glasgow, Scotland, injures 41 miners.

7 Feb: In Tokyo, a fire in a 10 storey hotel results in the deaths of 32 people.

15 Feb: The world's largest oil rig capsizes in a storm off the coast of Newfoundland, with the loss of 84 lives.

28 May: In Nicaragua and Honduras, at least 200 die and 70,000 are homeless after devastation by floods.

9 June: In Zimbabwe, 55 people are killed and 35 injured when a bus falls from a bridge into a river near Salisbury (Harare).

31 July: In France, 53 people are killed in a multiple crash on a motorway near Beaune.

16 Sept: In India, monsoon floods cause the deaths of hundreds of people, and render millions homeless.

20 Oct: In the USSR, over 110 people die after a crush at a soccer match at Lenin stadium, Moscow.

13 Dec: In North Yemen, an earthquake results in the deaths of at least 2,800 people, while 200,000 are homeless.

1983 13 Feb: In Italy, a cinema in Turin is destroyed by fire with the loss of 64 lives.

13 Feb: In Italy, three cable cars at a ski resort in the Val d'Aosta crash to the ground, with the loss of 10 lives.

16 Feb: In Australia, bush fires destroy a wide area in the south, with the loss of 68 lives and 800 people injured. 350,000 farm animals are also killed.

4 May: In Bangladesh, many people die, and 60,000 are homeless after

widespread floods.

23 Oct: 241 US Marines and 58 French paratroopers are killed after trucks loaded with explosives are driven into the peacekeeping force building in Beirut, Lebanon.

17 Dec: Six people die after a IRA car bomb explodes outside Harrods store in London.

1984 October: The continuing famine in Ethiopia and surrounding countries is probably the greatest disaster in history.

11 Oct: An IRA bomb at the Grand Hotel in Brighton, England kills four and injures 31 people, including government ministers.

3 Dec: In Bhopal, India, 500 people are killed after toxic gas leaks from the Union Carbide pesticide plant, and thousands of others are given hospital treatment.

1985 3 March: In Chile, more than 170 die and many thousands are left homeless by an earthquake.

11 May: 56 die in fire at Bradford City football ground, Yorkshire, England.

29 May: In Belgium, 39 die in Heysel stadium, Brussels, as football violence erupts during European Cup Final between Liverpool and Juventus.

31 May: In the USA tornadoes sweep across country, killing 88 and doing great damage particularly in Pennsylvania.

25 June: In Bangladesh as many as 40,000 are thought to have died in floods following a cyclone.

19 Sept: Earthquakes devastate Mexico City. More than 20,000 people are killed.

13 Nov: In Columbia a volcanic eruption causes mudslides and floods killing 25,000 people.

1986 26 April: In the USSR, the Chernobyl nuclear power station catches fire and explodes, sending toxic waste over a wide area. Radiation exposure claims 29 lives in the following year.

25 May: In Bangladesh, hundreds die when a double-decker river ferry capsizes in the River Meghna.

21 Aug: In Cameroon, more than 1500 people are killed by poisonous gas from a volcanic lake.

16 Sept: The worst mining disaster in South Africa's history when fire kills 177 miners in the Kinross gold mine east of Johannesburg.

1987 6 March: 137 die when the British ferry *Herald of Free Enterprise* capsizes off Zeebrugge, Belgium. The design of roll-on, roll-off car ferries is criticized in the wake of the tragedy.

28 May: A Korean Airlines Boeing 707 with 115 on board and a South African Airways Boeing 747 with 159 passengers and crew are blown up in separate terrorist-initiated incidents over Burma and the Indian ocean respectively.

16 Nov: After Britain's worst storm in three centuries, 15 million trees are blown down in south-east England. The hurricane produces Britains largest-ever insurance bill for damage.

18 Nov: 31 people die when fire breaks out beneath an escalator at Kings Cross underground station, London.

21 Dec: In the Philippines, after colliding with a tanker, the ferry *Dona Paz* sinks with the loss of more than 3000 people – the worst peacetime disaster at sea.

Dec: Throughout the year drought and famine, aggravated by civil war, devastate much of Sudan and Ethiopia despite emergency relief measures.

1988 6 July: 167 oil workers are killed when explosions and fire destroy the Piper Alpha platform in the North Sea.

Sept: One of the largest locust swarms ever recorded sweeps through central Africa. Some locusts are blown as far as the West Indies and Cornwall, England.

25 Oct: More than 450 people are killed when the Philippines ferry *Dona Marilyn* (sister ship of the *Dona Paz* lost in 1987) is capsized by a cyclone.

PEOPLE: POLITICAL AND MILITARY

ABDULLAH IBN HUSSEIN, [1882-1951]; first king of Jordan, and founder of that country during World War I during the Arab revolt against the Ottoman Empire.
ACHESON, Dean Gooderham [1893-1971]; American lawyer and Secretary of State 1949-53. A founder of NATO.
ADENAUER, Konrad [1876-1967]; German statesman and first Chancellor of the Federal Republic of Germany [1949-63]. Former mayor of Cologne.
ALEXANDER, Harold Rupert Leofric George (1st Earl) [1891-1969]; British general who commanded forces at Dunkirk, supervising evacuation; commander of Allied forces in Italy 1943-45, Gov.-Gen. of Canada.
ALLENBY, Edmund Henry Hynman (1st Viscount) [1861-1936]; British field marshal, who in 1917 captured Gaza and Jerusalem from Turkish forces.
ALLENDE (Gossens), Salvador [1908-73]; Chilean politician and physician. Founded the Socialist party in Chile, and president of Chile 1970-73.
AMIN DADA, Idi [1925-]; Infamous president of Uganda 1971-1979; expelled most of Asians from country, and caused deaths of about 90,000 people.
ASQUITH, Herbert Henry (1st Earl of Oxford and Asquith) [1852-1928]; British statesman and Liberal prime minister [1908-16]; responsible for Act limiting the power of the House of Lords, 1911.
ASTOR, Nancy Witcher (Viscountess Astor) [1879-1964]; American-born as Nancy Langhorne, became the first woman to take her seat as a British MP (Conservative) in 1919; a campaigner for women's rights and help for the poor.
ATATÜRK, Kemal (formerly Mustafa Kemal) [1881-1938]; Turkish statesman and reformer. Founder and first president of the Turkish republic; introduced the Latin alphabet for the Turkish language.
ATTLEE, Clement Richard (1st Earl) [1883-1967]; British statesman and Labour prime minister (1945-1952). Introduced and developed the Welfare state.

AYUB KHAN, Mohammad [1907-74]; Pakistani politician and military leader. President 1958-69.
BALDWIN, Stanley (1st Earl) [1867-1947]; British statesman and Conservative prime minister (1923-24, 1924-29, 1935-37). Handled the crisis when King EDWARD VIII abdicated in 1936.
BALFOUR, Arthur James (1st Earl) [1848-1930]; British statesman and Conservative prime minister 1902-05. As foreign secretary made the famous Balfour Declaration, approving of Zionism in 1917.
BEN-GURION, David (David Gruen) [1886-1973]; Israeli statesman and first prime minister of Israel (1948-1953, 1961-1963). Born in Poland.
BENES, Eduard [1884-1948]; Czechoslovak statesman and a founder of the country in 1918. After Nazi take-over, fled as President to London in 1938, returning in 1945.
BERIA, Lavrenty Pavlovich [1899-1953]; Soviet politician and secret police chief. After a power struggle following STALIN's death in 1953, was arrested, tried and executed.
BERNADOTTE, Count Folke [1895-1948]; nephew of King Gustavus V of Sweden; a Red Cross mediator, who was assassinated in Palestine.
BEVAN, Aneurin [1897-1960]; British statesman and a great orator. A leader in the Labour party.

Ben Gurion (left), first prime minister of Israel and Willy Brandt, Chancellor of West Germany (1969–74).

101

Left: Continuing constitutional monarchy—the Prince and Princess of Wales with Prince William.

BEVERIDGE, William Henry (1st Baron) [1879-1963]; British economist and reformer. Author of the famous Beveridge Plan which outlined the future Welfare state.

BEVIN, Ernest [1881-1951]; British statesman and trade union leader. A leader in the Labour party, was in wartime cabinet, organized labour and national service; helped found NATO.

BHUTTO, Zulfikar Ali [1928-79]; Pakistani politician, and president 1971-77; also prime minister 1973-77. Ousted from office, and eventually executed.

BIRKENHEAD, Frederick Edwin Smith (1st Earl) [1872-1930]; British lawyer and statesman. A Conservative, was Lord Chancellor 1919-22. As attorney-general engaged in the trial of Sir Roger Casement, Irish rebel.

BLUM, Léon [1872-1950]; French statesman and Socialist. Imprisoned by the Vichy regime, bravely defended himself.

BONDFIELD, Margaret Grace [1873-1953]; first British woman cabinet minister, and trade union leader. A member of the Labour party.

BOURGUIBA, Habib [1906-]; Tunisian politician and independence leader. The first prime minister, and later president of Tunisia.

BRANDT, Willy [Karl Herbert Frahn) [1913]; German statesman; chancellor of the Federal Republic 1969-74. Nobel peace prize 1971.

BREZHNEV, Leonid Ilyich [1906-82]; Soviet leader; Chairman of Supreme Soviet 1964-1982.

BUSH, George Herbert Walker [1924-]; 41st President (Republican) of the United States (from 1989). Vice-President (1981-1989); former ambassador to UN and director of the C.I.A.

BULGANIN, Nikolai Aleksandrovich [1895-1975]; Soviet leader, and prime minister of the USSR 1955-58.

BUNCHE, Ralph Johnson [1904-71]; American diplomat and educator. Negotiated Arab-Israeli armistice, 1949.

BUTLER, Richard Austen (Baron) [1902-82]; British statesman; a skilled (Conservative) politician and social reformer. Held many offices, (chancellor of the exchequer, home secretary).

CALLAGHAN, (Leonard) James [1912-]; British statesman, and former Labour prime minister. Leader of the Opposition 1979-80.

CARSON, Edward Henry (Baron Carson) [1854-1935]; British statesman, and member of the Unionist (Conservative) party. A bitter opponent of the separation of Ireland from Britain. Organizer of the Ulster Orange movement, leading to partition of North and South.

CARTER, Jimmy (James Earle Carter) [1924-]; 39th President (Democrat) of the United States

Left: Martin Luther King and J.F. Kennedy, civil rights leader and reforming US president—both assassinated. Above: Charles De Gaulle, French general and president with Haile Selassie, 'lion of

Judah' and emperor of Ethiopia. Above right: Moshe Dayan, the Israeli soldier and politician who commanded the Six-day war in 1967.

(1977-1981). First 'deep South' candidate elected since before the American Civil War.

CASTRO, Fidel [1926-]; Cuban political leader, who overthrew the corrupt Batista regime, and set up Cuba as the first Communist state in the Western Hemisphere.

CAVELL, Edith [1865-1915]; British nurse, who when in Brussels during World War I, was shot by the Germans for helping Allied soldiers to escape.

CEAUSESCU, Nicholae [1918-]; Romanian political leader, and first president of the Romanian Socialist republic from 1974. Although Communist, has shown an independent spirit in relations with Soviet Union.

CHAMBERLAIN; (Arthur) Neville [1869-1940]; British statesman and Conservative prime minister. Signed the Munich pact with HITLER as part of policy of appeasement, which finally resulted in the take-over of Czechoslovakia by Germany. Son of Joseph CHAMBERLAIN.

CHAMBERLAIN, Joseph [1836-1914]; British statesman and Liberal politician. Colonial secretary.

CHAMBERLAIN, Sir (Joseph) Austen [1863-1937]; British statesman, elder son of Joseph and half-brother of Neville CHAMBERLAIN. (Conservative) Foreign Secretary 1924-29. Awarded Nobel peace prize.

CHARLES, Prince of Wales (Charles Philip Arthur George) [1948-]; eldest son, and heir to HM Queen ELIZABETH II. Duke of Cornwall, and Prince of Wales from 1969. Married 1981, Lady Diana Spencer. They have two sons: Prince William (Arthur Philip Louis), b.1982, and Prince Henry ('Harry' Charles Albert David), b.1984.

CHIANG KAI-SHEK [1887-1975]; Chinese statesman and general, who succeeded SUN YAT-SEN as leader of the Nationalist party in 1928. President from 1943, defeated by Communists, he retired to Taiwan to continue government there in 1949.

CHOU EN-LAI [1898-1970]; Chinese Communist statesman, was prime minister from 1949.

CHURCHILL, Sir Winston Spencer Leonard [1874-1965] British soldier, statesman and author. Served in the Boer War, entered parliament as a Conservative and held offices as President of Board of Trade, Home Secretary and First Lord of the Admiralty (1911-15). Prime Minister during crucial years of World War II, he unified the people and led them to victory. Awarded Nobel prize for literature, 1953.

CLEMENCEAU, Georges [1841-1929]; French statesman and prime minister. A defender of DREYFUS, and a staunch democrat, he streng-

103

thened the alliance with Britain. A leader at the peace conference at Versailles.

CURZON, George Nathaniel (1st Marquess) [1859-1925]; British statesman, and viceroy of India 1898-1905. A Conservative, was lord privy seal and foreign secretary.

DARLAN, Jean François [1881-1942]; French admiral and politician. Strongly anti-British, was a member of the Vichy government. Changed sides in World War II, joined Allies, but assassinated in 1942.

DAYAN, Moshe [1915-81]; Israeli soldier and politician, who planned and commanded the Six-Day war in 1967. Foreign minister 1977-79.

DE GASPERI, Alcide [1881-1954]; Italian statesman, and leader of the Christian Democrat party. Prime minister 1945-53].

DE GAULLE, Charles André Joseph Marie [1890-1970]; French general and statesman. Formed and led the Free French movement after France fell in 1940. He was president between 1945 and 1946. Retired, but recalled as president of the Fifth Republic from 1959 to 1969.

DENG XIAOPING [1904-]; Chinese political leader, who ousted the 'Gang of Four' after the death of MAO TSE-TUNG. Inaugurated policy of economic reform and increased many contacts with the West.

DE VALERA, Eamon [1882-1974]; Irish statesman, and leader of Irish independence movement from 1916. Was prime minister 1937-48, 1951-54, and 1957-59. President, 1959-73.

DOENITZ, Karl [1891-1980]; German admiral and commander-in-chief of the Navy 1943-45. Chancellor after death of HITLER in 1945, surrendered to Allies.

DOWDING, Hugh Caswall Tremenheere (1st Baron) [1882-1970]; British air chief marshal and head of Fighter Command 1936-42. Defeated the Luftwaffe in the Battle of Britain, 1940.

DREYFUS, Alfred [1859-1935]; French army officer of Jewish origin. Victim of an antisemitic campaign, was falsely accused of spying and jailed for life, 1894. A wide campaign was launched by the writer Emile Zola, when evidence was shown to be false and Dreyfus acquitted, following a government scandal, 1906.

DUBCEK, Alexander [1921-]; Czech Communist party leader. His reforms were suppressed after invasion by the Soviet Union in 1968.

DULLES, John Foster [1888-1959]; American diplomat and statesman. As Secretary of State [1953-59] showed an inflexible policy against the Soviet Union.

DUVALIER, François ('Papa Doc') [1907-71]; Haitian politician and as president, was dictator of his country, maintaining a reign of terror.

EDEN, (Robert) Anthony [1st Earl of Avon] [1897-1977]; British statesman who resigned in 1938 as foreign secretary in protest at Neville Chamberlain's appeasement policy towards HIT-LER. Prime minister 1955, resigned after the Suez Crisis in 1956.

EDWARD VII (Albert Edward) [1841-1910]; popular, though pleasure-seeking monarch. His efforts did much to strengthen the British monarchy's position and British-international relations.

EDWARD VIII (Edward Albert Christian George Andrew Patrick David) [1894-1972]; succeeded his father, George V, as king. Never crowned, he abdicated in 1936 to marry the American divorcee Mrs Wallis Simpson. He was made Duke of Windsor.

EISENHOWER, Dwight David [1890-1969]; American general and statesman. Supreme commander of allied forces in Europe in World War II, led the invasion which brought the surrender of Germany, 1945. Was 34th President (Republican) of the USA, 1953-61.

Bidding for peace: British prime minister Neville Chamberlain on his way to meet the German Fuhrer, Hitler.

ELIZABETH II (Elizabeth Alexandra Mary) [1926-]; ; succeeded her father, GEORGE VI, becoming Queen and Head of the Commonwealth, 1952. Married Lieut. Philip Mountbatten (Prince Philip) in 1947. Children: Prince Charles; Princess Anne (Elizabeth Louise) b. 1950, Prince Andrew (Albert Christian Edward) b. 1960, and Prince Edward (Antony Richard Louis) b.1964.

FAISAL I (IBN HUSSEIN), [1885-1933]; Arab statesman, leader of the Arab revolt from Ottoman (Turkish) rule, 1916. King of Iraq from 1921.

FAROUK, [1920-65]; King of Egypt; reigned from 1936, but deposed by the military revolution in 1952 led by General NASSER. From that time, he lived in exile.

FISHER, John Arbuthnot (1st Baron) [1841-1920]; British admiral. Great naval administrator, was First Sea Lord at the outbreak of World War I.

FOCH, Ferdinand [1851-1929]; French soldier, who as supreme commander of all allied armies in 1918, became marshal of France.

FORD, Gerald Rudolph [1913-]; American statesman who replaced Spiro Agnew as vice-president in 1973. Became 38th President of the USA (Republican) after NIXON resigned.

FRANCO, Francisco [1892-1975]; Spanish dictator, who took power after his Nationalist forces overthrew the Spanish republic in 1936. Rightwing leader (El Caudillo) 1939-1975.

GAITSKELL, Hugh Todd Naylor [1906-63]; British statesman and leader of the Labour Party 195563. A widely acclaimed leader of the Opposition, he was never prime minister. Chancellor of the Exchequer, 1950-51.

GANDHI, Indira [1917-1984]; Indian stateswoman and prime minister. Daughter of Jawaharlal NEHRU, she married, 1942, Feroze Gandhi (not related to M.K. Gandhi), but later separated. Assassinated by her Sikh bodyguard, 1st November, 1984.

GANDHI, Mohandas Kamamchand (Mahatma) [1869-1948]; Indian political and spiritual leader and lawyer. Led non-violent campaign for political freedom. Assassinated by a Hindu fanatic.

GEORGE V (George Frederick Ernest Albert) [1865-1936]; The second son of King EDWARD VII he succeeded his father as king, since his elder brother, the Duke of Clarence (Albert Victor) had died in the 1892. Became Duke of York, 1892, and married, 1893, Princess Victoria Mary of Teck.

GEORGE VI (Albert Frederick Arthur George) [1895-1952]; The second son of GEORGE V, became king, succeeding his brother, EDWARD VIII

War leaders: Eisenhower, American general and supreme commander of allied forces in Europe with General Montgomery.

'Big Three' summit at Yalta in 1945—Churchill, Roosevelt and Stalin.

in 1936 after his abdication. Married, 1923, Elizabeth Angela Marguerite Bowes-Lyon, who is now the Queen Mother.

GISCARD D'ESTAING, Valéry [1926-]; French statesman and political leader. President of the Republic, 1974-1981.

GOEBBELS, (Paul) Joseph [1897-1945]; German Nazi leader, and notorious controller of press, radio, films, theatre, books, etc. Committed suicide in Berlin bunker.

GOERING, Hermann Wilhelm [1893-1946]; German Nazi leader, a former World War I flying ace. Built the Luftwaffe, founded the Gestapo. Committed suicide in jail, 1946.

GORBACHEV, Mikhail Sergeyevich [1931-]; Soviet statesman who succeeded Chernenko in 1985 as leader of the USSR; president from 1988. Introduced concepts of *glasnost* ('openness') and *perestroika* ('reconstruction').

GROMYKO, Andrei Andreyevich [1908-]; Soviet diplomat and statesman. Foreign minister since 1957 and first deputy prime minister 1983. Retired 1988.

GUDERIAN, Heinz Wilhelm [1888-1954]; German general who largely devised the 'blitzkrieg' style of warfare. Led forces into Poland in 1939 and into France in 1940.

GUEVARA, Che (Ernesto Guevara de la Serna) [1928-67]; Argentine-born guerrilla, joined CASTRO and served in his government in Cuba. Left for South America, disappearing in 1967.

HAIG, Douglas (1st Earl) [1861-1928]; British field marshal and commander-in-chief in France in World War I. His old-fashioned strategy resulted in much loss of life.

HAILE SELASSIE 'The Lion of Judah' (Tafari Makonnen) [1892-1975]; King of Abyssinia (later called Ethiopia) and emperor from 1930. Overthrown in a military coup, 1974.

HAMMARSKJÖLD, Dag [1905-61]; Swedish statesman and economist. Secretary-general of the United Nations, was killed in an air crash while acting as a mediator in Africa.

HARDIE, James Keir [1856-1915]; Scottish labour leader, a founder of the Labour party. The first Socialist to be elected to parliament.

HARDING, Warren Gamaliel [1865-1923]; 29th president (Republican) of the USA (1921-23). Scandal and corruption was rife during his term of office.

HARRIMAN, William Averell [1891-1986]; American diplomat and statesman. Ambassador to the Soviet Union (1943-46) and to Great Britain (1946). Ambassador-at-large 1963-65.

HEATH, Edward Richard George [1916-]; British statesman, and first elected leader of the Conservative party 1965-75. Prime minister 1970-74, he took Britain into the Common Market.

HENDERSON, Arthur [1863-1935]; British statesman, and active worker for disarmament. Labour home secretary (1924) and foreign secretary (1929-31).

HESS, Walther Richard Rudolf [1894-1987]; German Nazi leader who flew to Scotland in 1941 to negotiate peace. Jailed for life, 1946; died in Spandau prison.

HIMMLER, Heinrich [1900-1945]; German Nazi leader; chief of the Gestapo from 1936. Organized mass killings, captured in 1945, he committed suicide.

HINDENBURG, Paul von [1847-1934]; German field-marshal during World War I, and statesman. Second president of the Weimar republic, he made Adolf HITLER chancellor in 1933.

HITLER, Adolf [1889-1945]; German politician, and dictator from 1933. Born in Austria, went to Munich in 1913, becoming leader of the Nazi party in 1920. Chancellor from 1933, became Führer (leader) in 1934. Annexed Austria and Czechoslovakia 1938-39. Invaded Poland 1939, starting World War II. Married Eva Braun, 1945, committed suicide in Berlin.

HO CHI MINH (Nguyen That Thanh) [1890-1969]; Vietnamese revolutionary leader. As communist, fought Japanese during World War II, then conducted campaign against France. Head of state of North Vietnam.

HOOVER, Herbert Clark [1874-1964]; 31st president (Republican) of the USA (1929-33), leading the country through early years of the Great Depression.

HOOVER, John Edgar [1895-1972]; American lawyer and government official. Director of the Federal Bureau of Investigation (1924-72). Strongly anti-criminal and anti-Communist, he was criticized for his autocratic outlook.

HORTHY, Miklos von Nagybanya [1869-1957]; Hungarian admiral and politician. Commanded the Austro-Hungarian fleet in World War I, became regent of Hungary 1920-1944.

HOXHA, Enver [1908-1985]; Albanian Communist leader, who was head of state 1946-82.

HULL, Cordell [1871-1955]; US statesman and diplomat, who was secretary of state 1933-44, and a founder of the United Nations.

HUSSEIN IBN TALAL, King of Jordan [1935-]; liberal king of a constitutional monarchy, has been a pro-western leader, yet showing strong sympathy for Palestinians in their struggle with Israel.

JAURÈS, (Auguste Marie Joseph) Jean [1859-1914]; French politician, philosopher and socialist. He founded the newspaper *L'Humanité*. Made sincere efforts to avert World War I. Assassinated by Raoul Villain.

JINNAH, Mohammed Ali [1876-1948]; Pakistani statesman, who helped found that country in 1947. He became the first governor-general.

JOFFRE, Joseph Jacques Césaire [1852-1931]; French soldier, who became a marshal of France. He commanded the French armies on the Western Front, and later the Allied armies, in World War I.

JOHNSON, Lyndon Baines [1908-1973]; 36th President (Democrat) of the United States. He was a former Texas schoolteacher. Vice-president to John KENNEDY, he succeeded as president in 1963, being re-elected in 1964, retiring in 1969.

JUAN CARLOS I, [1938-]; King of Spain since 1975. Grandson of King Alfonso XIII (1886-

Adolf Hitler, dictator of Nazi Germany from 1933 to 1945 at a mass rally of the Nazi party.

1941), was nominated by General FRANCO to succeed him as head of state.

KENNEDY, John Fitzgerald [1917-1963]; 35th President (Democrat) of the United States [1961-1963], being the youngest and the first Roman Catholic to be elected. Took a strong line with Cuba and Soviet Union. Assassinated in Dallas, Texas.

KENNEDY, Robert Francis [1925-1968]; American politician and brother of John KENNEDY. While campaigning for 1968 Democratic nomination was assassinated in Los Angeles.

KENYATTA, Jomo (Kamau) [1889?-1978]; African political leader, and first prime minister of Kenya, later president [1964-78]. Was imprisoned after being convicted of leading Mau Mau organization.

KERENSKY, Alexander [1881-1970]; Russian revolutionary leader, a moderate socialist. Headed the provisional government in 1917, but was overthrown by Bolsheviks.

KESSELRING, Albert [1885-1960]; German air force general, who commanded air forces in Poland, France and Battle of Britain. Commander-in-chief on the Western Front in 1945.

KHOMEINI, Ruhollah (Ruhollah Hendi) [1901-]; Iranian religious and political leader (ayatollah), whose followers overthrew the Shah in 1979.

KHRUSHCHEV, Nikita Sergeyevich [1894-1971]; Soviet leader. First secretary of the Communist Party (1953) and prime minister (1958-64), he relaxed the harsh methods used by Stalin, improved relations with the West, although those with China deteriorated badly. Deposed in 1964.

KING, Martin Luther [1929-1968]; American Negro religious leader, foremost in the civil rights movement. Strong supporter of non-violence and racial amity; assassinated in Memphis, Tennessee.

KING, William Lyon Mackenzie [1874-1950]; Canadian statesman and Liberal leader. Prime Minister 1921-25, 1926-30, 1935-38.

KISSINGER, Henry [1923-]; American statesman and scholar. Adviser to President NIXON, and Secretary of State 1973-77. Shared Nobel peace prize, 1973.

KITCHENER, Horatio Herbert (1st Earl) [1850-1916]; British field marshal, and Secretary for War in 1914-16. Lost at sea on H.M.S.

Makarios, archbishop and first president of the Cyprus republic in 1960 (left). Jomo Kenyatta, first prime minister of Kenya.

Hampshire while on way to conference with the Russian Tsar.

KOSYGIN, Alexei Nikolayevich [1904-1980]; Soviet leader who succeeded KHRUSHCHEV as chairman of the Council of Ministers.

LaGUARDIA, Fiorello Henry [1882-1947]; American politician, who was mayor of New York 1933-45. Known for being straightforward and honest.

LANSBURY, George [1859-1940]; British politician and Labour MP. A non-smoker, teetotaller, churchman and socialist of spiritual conviction. Founder and first editor of the *Daily Herald*.

LAVAL, Pierre [1883-1945]; French politician, who miscalculated by collaborating with the Germans in the time of the Vichy government in World War II. Tried and executed in 1945.

LAW, Andrew Bonar [1858-1923]; British statesman, and leader of the Conservative party. Prime Minister 1922-23.

LENIN, (Vladimir Ilyich Ulanov) [1870-1924]; Soviet Communist leader and founder of Bolshevism. Exiled, he returned to Russia in 1917, overthrew the provisional government, and set up the Soviet Russian state of which he became the first leader.

LIDDELL HART, Basil Henry [1895-1970]; military historian and strategist. His new approach, or 'expanding torrent' method, and ideas about mechanized warfare, published in 1929, foresaw the German 'blitzkrieg' used in World War II.

LIE, Trygve [1896-1968]; Norwegian statesman who became first secretary-general of the United Nations 1946-52.

LLOYD GEORGE, David (1st Earl) [1863-1945]; British statesman and .Liberal leader. As chancellor of the exchequer, introduced social insurance 1908-11. Prime Minister 1916-1922.

LUCE, Clare Boothe [1903-]; American politician, journalist and diplomat. Editor of Vanity Fair 1930-34, ambassador to Italy 1953-57.

LUDENDORFF, Erich Friedrich Wilhelm [1865-1937]; German general, who, with Field Marshal von HINDENBURG, directed the German forces in World War I. He supported HITLER in 1923.

MacARTHUR, Douglas [1880-1964]; American general and commander-in-chief of Allied Forces, South-East Pacific in World War II. Led military government of Japan 1945-51; commanded UN forces in Korea, 1950-51. Dismissed by President TRUMAN after making statements critical of the president.

MacDONALD, James Ramsay [1866-1937]; British statesman and Labour party leader. Prime Minister 1924, 1929-31. Coalition Prime Minister 1931-35.

MACMILLAN, (Maurice) Harold (Earl of Stockton) [1894-1986]; British statesman and publisher. Chancellor of the Exchequer 1955-57, and Conservative Prime Minister. He was unable to gain entry for Britain into the Common Market. His speech in 1960 referred to the 'wind of change' in Africa.

MAKARIOS III (Mikhail Khristodolou Mouskos) [1913-1977]; an archbishop of the Orthodox Church of Cyprus, he led the ENOSIS (union with Greece) movement in the 1950s. Became first president of the Cyprus republic in 1960.

MALCOLM X (Malcolm Little) [1925-65]; American black nationalist leader, who was assassinated.

MANDELA, Nelson Rolihlahla [1918-]; South African black political leader, sentenced to life imprisonment in 1964.

MAO TSE-TUNG (Mao Zedong) [1893-1976]; Chinese Communist leader who split with CHIANG KAI-SHEK, fighting both Japanese and Nationalists in World War II. Winning control of China, was its head until his death.

MARSHALL, George Catlett [1880-1959]; American general, and Chief of Staff 1939-45. Secretary of State 1947-49, of Defence 1950-51. Pioneered the Marshall Plan for aid and reconstruction of Europe.

MASARYK, Jan Garrigue [1886-1948]; Czech statesman and Minister in London 1925-38. Son of Tomas MASARYK, was in exiled government in London. Returned to his country, and allegedly committed suicide (or perhaps was murdered) after the Communist take-over in 1948.

MASARYK, Tomas Garrigue [1850-1937]; Czech statesman and first president of Czechoslovakia 1918-35.

MATA HARI (Margaretha Geertruida Macleod [b. Zelle]) [1876-1917]; Dutch dancer and spy in the German service. Became friendly with Allied officers, whom she betrayed after learning official secrets. Arrested, convicted and executed by the French in 1917.

MEIR, Golda (Golda Mabovitch) [1898-1978]; Israeli stateswoman and prime minister 1970-74. Born in Kiev, Russia, brought up in the USA.

MALENKOV, Georgi Maksimilianovich [1902-]; Soviet politician, who succeeded STALIN in 1953 as head of state. Resigned 1955.

MENDES-FRANCE, Pierre [1907-]; French statesman, and prime minister 1954-55; opposed the return to power of General DE GAULLE.

MENZIES, Sir Robert Gordon [1894-1978]; Australian statesman and prime minister 1939-41, 1949-66.

METAXAS, Joannes [1871-1941]; Greek statesman and general. Dictator of Greece 1936-1941, he directed resistance against Italy and Germany.

MITTERAND, François Maurice Marie [1916-]; French statesman and socialist. Fourth president of the Fifth republic from 1981.

MOLOTOV, Vyachelsav Mikhailovitch [1890-1986]; Soviet Communist leader and diplomat. Editor and part-founder of *Pravda*. Originally named Scriabin, he is a relative of Alexander SCRIABIN, the composer and pianist. Expelled from the Communist Party in 1964, he was reinstated in 1984.

MOLTKE, Helmuth Johannes Ludwig, Graf von [1848-1916]; German general and chief of staff 1906-14.

MONNET, Jean Omer Marie Gabriel [1888-1979]; French economist and government official: 'father of the Common Market'. He advocated the European Coal and Steel community which developed into the Common Market.

MONTGOMERY, Bernard Law (1st Viscount) [1887-1976]; British field marshal, commander of the 8th Army in World War II, defeated German General ROMMEL; commander-in-chief, Allied Forces in Northern France 1944. Received German surrender.

MOSLEY, Sir Oswald Ernald [1896-1984]; British politician, leader of British Union of Fascists (1932-1940), and its successor the Union Movement from 1948. Interned during World War II, 1940-43.

MOUNTBATTEN, Louis Francis Albert Victor Nicholas, (1st Earl) [1900-1979]; British admiral and statesman. A cousin of the Queen, and son of the former Prince Louis of Battenberg. Supreme Allied Commander, South East Asia, 1943-46; last Viceroy of India, 1947, and governor-general 1947-48. Assassinated by an IRA terrorist.

MUSSOLINI, Benito [1883-1945]; Italian politician and leader of the Fascist Party, which he founded in 1919. Took over government 1922. Conquered Ethiopia, 1935. Entered World War II as an ally of Adolf HITLER, 1940. Dismissed by king, 1943; killed by partisans.

NAGY, Imre [1895-1958]; Hungarian politician, a Communist since World War I. As prime minister after the revolution in 1956, he promised free elections, but was overthrown when Soviet troops entered Hungary, and was executed.

NASSER, Gamal Abdel [1918-1970]; Egyptian statesman and first president of Egypt 1956, and of the United Arab Republic 1958. Helped depose King FAROUK, 1952. Nationalized Suez Canal, 1956.

NEHRU, Jawaharlal [1889-1970]; Indian statesman, the first prime minister of India 1947-64. Father of Indira GANDHI.

NIMITZ, Chester William [1885-1966]; American admiral and commander of US naval forces in the Pacific in World War II. Chief of naval operations 1945-47.

NIXON, Richard Milhous [1913-]; American lawyer and 37th President (Republican) of the United States, previously vice-president 1953-61.

Re-opened relations with China after 21 years lapse. Involved in Watergate scandal, and was forced to resign (the first US president to do so).

NKRUMAH, Kwame [1909-1972]; Ghanaian political leader who became prime minister and then first president of the Ghana republic (1960-66). He was overthrown, and fled.

NYERE, Julius Kambarage [1921-]; Tanzanian political leader, first prime minister of Tanganyika and then first president, 1962-1985. Responsible for the union with Zanzibar in 1964.

PADEREWSKI, Ignace Jan [1860-1941]; Polish pianist, composer and statesman, who became prime minister of Poland in 1919.

PANKHURST, Emmeline (Emmeline Goulden) [1882-1928]; British suffragette leader, who fought to obtain the vote for women.

PARETO, Vilfredo [1848-1923]; Italian economist and sociologist, who argued for the superiority of the elite, and whose work was the basis of Fascist ideology.

PATTON, George Smith [1885-1945]; American general and armoured-unit commander. Renowned for his outspoken and reckless remarks.

PAULUS, Friedrich [1890-1957]; German soldier, with the rank of field-marshal, who was forced to surrender to the Soviet Union forces at Stalingrad in 1943.

PEARSON, Lester Bowles [1897-1972]; Canadian statesman and diplomat. Led the Canadian delegation to the UN, and later [1952-53], president of the UN General Assembly. Nobel peace prize 1957, and Order of Merit 1971.

PERÓN, Eva Duarte de [1919-1952]; known as 'Evita', and wife of Juan PERÓN. Former radio and film star, was effectively Perón's partner as leader.

PERÓN, Juan Domingo [1895-1974]; Argentine politician and leader of the quasi-fascist Peronista movement. President 1946-55 and 1973-74. Succeeded by his second wife, Isabel.

PERSHING, John Joseph [1860-1948]; American general and commander-in-chief of the American Expeditionary Force in World War I.

PÉTAIN, Henri Philippe Omer [1856-1951]; French general and statesman. A military hero of World War I, became premier on the fall of France in 1940, heading the pro-German Vichy government until 1944. Jailed for life for treason.

PHILIP, Prince, Duke of Edinburgh [1921-];

Consort of the Queen; the son of Prince Andrew of Greece. In navy 1939-50, married the then Princess Elizabeth 1947, renouncing his Greek titles. Created Duke of Edinburgh.

POINCARÉ, Raymond Nicolas Landry [1860-1934]; French statesman; prime minister three times, and president 1913-20.

POMPIDOU, Georges-Jean-Raymond [1911-1974]; French statesman, who was president of the republic 1969-74, following lead set by DE GAULLE, but reversing the policy of opposing Britain's entry into the Common Market.

PRIMO DE RIVERA, Miguel, Marqués de Estella [1870-1930]; Spanish general who in 1923 established himself as dictator of Spain until 1929.

QUISLING, Vidkun Abraham Lauritz [1887-1945]; Norwegian politician and leader of fascist party. He collaborated with the German invaders of Norway, 1940-45, but was tried for treason in 1945 and executed.

RASPUTIN, Grigori Yefimovich [1871-1916]; Russian monk who greatly influenced the Tsarina Alexandra and the court of Nicholas II of Russia. After a debauched life, was murdered by nobles.

REAGAN, Ronald Wilson [1911-]; 40th President (Republican) of the United States 1981-89, a former film and TV actor and sports announcer. Governor of California 1967-74. Oldest person to be elected to the office of president.

RHODES, Cecil John [1853-1902]; British statesman, who prospered in the diamond mines in South Africa, becoming premier of the Cape Colony, 1890. Responsible for colonizing Rhodesia (now Zimbabwe) 1890-95. Withdraw from politics after the failure of the Jameson raid into Transvaal, 1896.

RIBBENTROP, Joachim von [1893-1946]; German diplomat and Nazi leader. Ambassador to Britain 1936-38; German foreign minister 1939-45. Executed as a war criminal.

RICKOVER, Hyman George [1900-1986]; American admiral and 'father of the atomic submarine', which he helped to develop, 1947-1954.

ROMMEL, Erwin Johannes Eugin [1891-1944]; German field marshal and commander of the German Afrika Korps in World War II (1941-43). Commanded the army in Normandy 1944; ordered to commit suicide for opposing HITLER.

ROOSEVELT, (Anna) Eleanor [1884-1962];

American political and social worker and writer. Wife of President F.D. ROOSEVELT. Chairman of the U.N. Human Rights Commission 1947-51.

ROOSEVELT, Franklin Delano [1882-1945]; 32nd president (Democrat) of USA, 1933-45. His 'New Deal' reforms were aimed to take the country out of the depression of the thirties. Stricken with polio in 1921, he continued energetically, leading the USA through World War II, and helping to draft the Atlantic Charter in 1941.

ROOSEVELT, Theodore [1858-1919]; 26th President (Republican) of the USA, who had led his volunteer regiment called 'Rough Riders' in Cuba during the Spanish-American war, 1898. Nobel peace prize, 1906.

SADAT, (Mohamed) Anwar El- [1918-1981]; Egyptian statesman and president of Egypt, 1970-81. Made a courageous move to make peace with Israel, despite Arab opposition. Assassinated.

SALAZAR, Antonio de Oliveira [1889-1970]; Portuguese politician; a quasi-fascist who became virtual dictator of the country from 1933.

SCHUMAN, Robert [1886-1963]; French statesman and founder of the European Coal and Steel Community which led to the Common Market.

SLIM, William Joseph (1st Viscount) [1891-1970]; British field marshal, commander of the 14th Army in Burma 1943-1945. Commander of Land Forces, South-East Asia, 1945-1946. Chief of the Imperial General Staff, 1948; governor-general, Australia, 1953-60.

SMITH, Ian Douglas [1919-]; Rhodesian politician, who founded the Rhodesian Front in 1961. As prime minister, declared independence unilaterally in 1965.

SMUTS, Jan Christian [1870-1950]; South African statesman and field marshal. Fought on the Boer side during the BOER WAR, but fought for Britain in World War I. Premier of South Africa 1919-24, 1939-48.

SOEKARNO, (orig. Kusnasosro), Achmad [1902-1970]; Indonesian political leader who led the movement against Dutch rule. Became President (1949-67) until coup by General Suharto.

SPAAK, Paul Henri [1899-1972]; Belgian statesman, first president of the General Assembly of the UN. Secretary-general of NATO 1957-61.

STALIN, Joseph (Iosif Vissarionovich Dzhugashvili) [1879-1953]; Soviet leader; a revolution-

ary who succeeded LENIN as leader of Soviet Russia in 1924. As dictator, using harsh and ruthless methods, he made the Soviet Union a major industrial country. He purged political opponents, and was leader during World War II.

STEVENSON, Adlai Ewing [1900-1965]; American statesman, lawyer and diplomat. Ambassador to the United Nations 1961-65, he was unsuccessful as the Democratic candidate against EISENHOWER in the presidential elections of 1952 and 1956.

SUN YAT-SEN [1867-1925]; Chinese statesman and revolutionary. In 1911, he overthrew the Manchus, and formed the Nationalist party, becoming president (1912, 1921-25).

TEDDER, Arthur William (1st Baron) [1890-1967]; British air marshal who, under General EISENHOWER in World War II became deputy supreme commander in Europe.

THATCHER, Margaret Hilda [1925-]; British stateswoman; the first woman Prime Minister in Britain (from 1979). Succeeded Edward HEATH in 1975 as leader of the Conservative party. Won three elections (1979, 1983, 1987).

Field Marshall Smuts, premier of South Africa.

TIRPITZ, Alfred von [1849-1930]; German admiral who created a strong high seas fleet when secretary to the German navy 1897-1916.

TITO, (Josip Broz) [1892-1980]; Yugoslav statesman who took power after leading Communist resistance during World War II. Prime minister 1945-53, president from 1953. The first Communist leader to take an independent line.

TOGLIATTI, Palmiro [1893-1964]; Italian political leader and head of the Communist party from 1924.

TOGO, Count Heihachiro [1847-1934]; Japanese admiral who defeated the Russians at Port Arthur in 1905.

TOJO, Hideki [1884-1948]; Japanese military leader and prime minister 1941-44. Executed by the Allies as a war criminal.

TROTSKY, Leo (Lev Davidovich Bronstein) [1879-1940]; Soviet Communist leader and revolutionary. He served under STALIN, but opposed him and went into exile 1929. Assassinated in Mexico.

TRUDEAU, Pierre Elliott [1919-]; Canadian statesman and prime minister 1968-79 and 198084. French and English became dual official languages while he was in office.

TRUMAN, Harry S. [1884-1972]; 33rd President (Democrat) of the USA, 1945-53. In 1945, made the decision to drop the atom bomb on Japan; and in 1950, decided to send US troops to Korea.

TUBMAN, William Vacanarat Shadrach [1895-1971]; Liberian political leader; a lawyer who became president 1944-71.

VENIZELOS, Eleutherios [1864-1936]; Greek statesman and diplomat. Leading political figure of modern Greece, born in Crete. From there he led a revolt against Turkey. Was Prime Minister of Greece eight times, opposed pro-German king Constantine and brought Greece into World War I on the Allied side.

VERWOERD, Hendrik Frensch [1901-1966]; South African political leader, exponent of the *apartheid* doctrine. As prime minister, broke with the Commonwealth and formed a republic in 1962. He was assassinated in 1966.

VOROSHILOV, Kliment Yefremovich [1881-1969]; Soviet general and statesman. Commanded defences of Leningrad in 1941, and USSR president 1953-60.

VORSTER, Balthazar Johannes [1915-]; South African political leader who became president 1978-79. He resigned after charges of irregularities were made.

WAINWRIGHT, Jonathan Mayhew [1883-1953]; American general who defended Bataan, but was taken prisoner in 1942. Rescued in 1945, became commander of Fourth Army until 1947.

WALDHEIM, Kurt [1918-]; Austrian diplomat and secretary-general of the United Nations 1972-81. Elected president of Austria in 1986.

WALLACE, George Corley [1919-]; American politician, and opponent of racial integration. Shot and paralyzed from the waist down, 1972.

WAVELL, Archibald Percival (1st Earl) [1883-1950]; British field marshal and commander-in-chief of the Middle East, 1939-41,defeating Italian forces. Commander-in-chief, South East Asia, 1941-43. Was Viceroy of India, 1943-47.

WILHELM II, (Friedrich Wilhelm Victor Albrecht) [1859-1941] king of Prussia and last Kaiser (emperor) of Germany. Grandson of Queen Victoria. Intelligent, but arrogant and impetuous, his support of Austria led to Germany's part in World War I. Abdicated 1918.

WILHELMINA, [1880-1962]; Became Queen of the Netherlands in 1890. Married Henry, Duke of Mecklenburg-Schwerin in 1901. Abdicated in favour of her only child, Juliana, in 1948.

WILSON, (James) Harold (Baron Wilson of Rievaulx) [1916-]; British statesman and leader of the Labour party 1963-76. Prime minister 1964-70 and 1974-76.

WILSON, Thomas Woodrow [1856-1924]; American statesman and 28th President (Democrat) of the USA, 1913-21. Brought the United States into World War I, and a prime mover in establishing the League of Nations, although the USA never became a member.

WINGATE, Orde Charles [1903-1944]; British general who led the Chindits or 'Wingate's Raiders' in World War II against the Japanese in Burma.

YAMAMOTO, Isoroku [1884-1943]; Japanese admiral, responsible for the attack on Pearl Harbor, 1941.

ZHUKOV, Georgi Konstantinovich [1896-1974]; Soviet general who directed the defence of Moscow in 1941 and Stalingrad 1942. He captured Berlin and accepted the German surrender.

BRITISH KINGS AND QUEENS WHO REIGNED DURING THE TWENTIETH CENTURY

House of Saxe-Coburg and Gotha

Edward VII (Albert Edward): Eldest son of Queen Victoria. Born at Buckingham Palace, 9 November, 1841. Married Alexandra (1844- 1925), eldest daughter of King Christian IX of Denmark. Succeeded his mother 22 January, 1901. Died 6 May, 1910.

House of Windsor

George V (George Frederick Ernest Albert): Second son of Edward VII. Born at Marlborough House, London. Married Mary, formerly Princess Victoria Mary Augusta Louise Olga Pauline Claudine Agnes of Teck (1867-1953). Succeeded his father 6 May, 1910. Died 20 January, 1936.

Edward VIII (Edward Albert Christian George Andrew Patrick David): eldest son of George V. Born at White Lodge, Richmond, Surrey, on 23 June, 1894. Succeeded his father 20 January, 1936, but abdicated on 11 December 1936 as a result of disapproval of his proposed marriage to Mrs Ernest Simpson, a divorcee (born Bessie Wallis Warfield (1896-). He was granted the title of Duke of Windsor, and married Mrs Simpson (who became the Duchess of Windsor), on 3 June, 1937. He died 18 May, 1972.

George VI (Albert Frederick Arthur George): second son of George V. Born at Sandringham, Norfolk, on 14 December, 1895. Married Lady Elizabeth Angela Marguerite Bowes-Lyon (1900-) on 26 April 1923. After the abdication of his brother, he succeeded to the throne on 12 December, 1936. Died 6 February, 1952.

Elizabeth II (Elizabeth Alexandra Mary): elder daughter of George VI. Born London, 21 April, 1926. Married Philip Mountbatten on 20 November, 1947. (As son of Prince and Princess Andrew of Greece, he had renounced all his Greek titles, and was created Duke of Edinburgh on 19 November, 1947, becoming known as Prince Philip in 1957). Succeeded her father on 6 February, 1952. Her eldest son, **Prince Charles Philip Arthur George**, Duke of Cornwall, born 14 November, 1948, is heir-apparent, and was given the title of Prince of Wales in 1958.

Below: Edward VII (left) and George V.
Bottom: Elizabeth II on a 'walkabout'.

PRESIDENTS OF THE UNITED STATES
DURING THE TWENTIETH CENTURY

No.	Name	Lived	Party	In Office
25	William McKINLEY*	1843-1901	Rep.	1897-1901
26	Theodore ROOSEVELT+	1858-1919	Rep.	1901-1905
				1905-1909
27	William Howard TAFT	1857-1930	Rep.	1909-1913
28	Woodrow WILSON	1856-1924	Dem.	1913-1917
				1917-1921
29	Warren Gamaliel HARDING	1865-1923	Rep.	1921-1923
30	Calvin COOLIDGE+	1872-1933	Rep.	1923-1925
				1925-1929
31	Herbert Clark HOOVER	1874-1964	Rep.	1929-1933
32	Franklin Delano ROOSEVELT	1882-1945	Dem.	1933-1937
				1937-1941
				1941-1945
				Jan-April 1945
33	Harry S. TRUMAN+	1884-1972	Dem.	1945-1949
				1949-1953
34	Dwight David EISENHOWER	1890-1969	Rep.	1953-1957
				1957-1961
35	John Fitzgerald KENNEDY*	1917-1963	Dem.	1961-1963
36	Lyndon Baines JOHNSON	1908-1973	Dem.	1963-1965
				1965-1969
37	Richard Milhous NIXON[1]	1913-	Rep.	1969-1973
				1973-1974
38	Gerald Rudolph FORD+	1913-	Rep.	1974-1977
39	Jimmy (James Earle) CARTER	1924-	Dem.	1977-1981
40	Ronald Wilson REAGAN	1911-	Rep.	1981-1984
				1984-1989
41	George Herbert BUSH	1924-	Rep.	1989-

*+Vice-presidents who first took office by succession
and not by election.   *Assassinated.*
[1]Resigned.*

US presidents: Hoover, F.D. Roosevelt, Truman, Eisenhower, Johnson.

EUROPEAN KINGS, QUEENS AND RULING PRINCES IN THE TWENTIETH CENTURY

ALBANIA

	Lived	Reigned
Zogu I	1895-1961	1928-1939
Victor Emmanuel III of Italy		1939-1944
Zogu I*		1944-1946

*Deposed

AUSTRO-HUNGARIAN EMPIRE

	Lived	Reigned
Franz Josef I	1830-1916	1848-1916
Karl I*	1887-1922	1916-1918

*Abdicated

BAVARIA (Absorbed into Germany, 1918)

	Lived	Reigned
Otto I+	1848-1916	1886-1913
Luitpold (regent)	1821-1912	1886-1912
Ludwig (regent)	1845-1921	1912-1913
Ludwig III*	1845-1921	1913-1918

+Incurably insane   *Deposed and exiled

BELGIUM

	Lived	Reigned
Leopold II	1835-1909	1865-1909
Albert I	1875-1934	1909-1934
Leopold III*	1901-1983	1934-1951
Baudouin I	1930-	1951-

*Abdicated.

BULGARIA

	Lived	Reigned
Ferdinand I*	1861-1948	1887-1918
Boris III	1894-1943	1918-1943
Simeon II+	1937-	1943-1946

*Abdicated.   +Deposed.

DENMARK

	Lived	Reigned
Christian IX	1818-1906	1863-1906
Frederick VIII	1843-1912	1906-1912
Christian X	1870-1947	1912-1947
Frederick IX	1899-1972	1947-1972
Margrethe II	1940-	1972-

GERMAN EMPIRE

	Lived	Reigned
Wilhelm II	1859-1941	1888-1918

GREECE

	Lived	Reigned
George I	1845-1913	1863-1913
Constantine I+	1868-1923	1913-1917
Alexander I	1893-1920	1917-1920
Constantine I*	1868-1923	1920-1922
George II	1890-1947	1922-1923

Republic 1923-1929

George II	1890-1947	1935-1941

German occupation 1941-1944
Regency under Bishop Damaskinos 1944-1946

George II	1890-1947	1946-1947
Paul I	1901-1981	1947-1964
Constantine II+	1940-	1964-1973

+Exiled   *Abdicated

Royal heads of state.

ITALY

	Lived	Reigned
Victor Emmanuel III*	1869-47	1900-1946
Umberto II	1904-83	1946

*Abdicated; Umberto reigned
for only a month.

LIECHTENSTEIN

	Lived	Reigned
Johann II	1840-1929	1858-1929
Franz I	1853-1938	1929-1938
Franz Josef II*	1906-	1938-

*Crown Prince Hans Adam took over
official duties in 1984, but Franz
Josef remains head of state.

LUXEMBOURG

	Lived	Reigned
Adolf of Nassau	1817-1905	1890-1905
William IV	1852-1912	1905-1912
Marie-Adelaide*	1894-1924	1912-1919
Charlotte*	1896-	1919-1964
Jean	1921-	1964-

*Abdicated

MONACO

	Lived	Reigned
Albert I	1848-1922	1889-1922
Louis II	1870-1949	1922-1949
Rainier III	1923-	1949-

MONTENEGRO (now part of Yugoslavia)

	Lived	Reigned
Nicholas I	1841-1921	
(as prince)		1860-1910
(as king)*		1910-1918

*Deposed

THE NETHERLANDS

	Lived	Reigned
Wilhelmina*	1880-62	1890-1948
Juliana*	1909-	1948-1980
Beatrix	1938-	1980-

*Abdicated

NORWAY

	Lived	Reigned
Haakon VII*	1872-1957	1905-1957
Olav V	1903-	1957-

*Previously Prince Carl of Denmark

PORTUGAL

	Lived	Reigned
Carlos I	1863-1908	1889-1908
Manuel II*	1889-1932	1908-1910

*Deposed

ROMANIA

	Lived	Reigned
Carol I	1839-1914	1881-1914
Ferdinand I	1865-1927	1914-1927
Michael I	1921-	1927-1930
Carol II	1893-1953	1930-1940
Michael I	1921-	1940-1947

RUSSIAN EMPIRE

	Lived	Reigned
Nicholas II*	1868-1918	1894-1918

*Abdicated; shot later.

SERBIA (now part of Yugoslavia)

	Lived	Reigned
Peter I	1844-1921	1903-1921

SPAIN

	Lived	Reigned
Alfonso XIII*	1886-1941	1902-1931
Juan Carlos I	1938-	1975-

*Deposed

SWEDEN

	Lived	Reigned
Oscar II*	1829-1907	1872-1907
Gustav V	1858-1950	1907-1950
Gustav VI Adolf	1882-1973	1950-1973
Carl XVI Gustav	1946-	1973-

*Until 1905, also king of Norway

TURKEY (OTTOMAN EMPIRE)

	Lived	Reigned
Abdul Hamid II*	1842-1918	1976-1909
Mehmed V	1844-1918	1909-1920
Mehmed VI*	1861-1926	1920-1922
Abdul Mejid II*	1868-1944	1922-1924

*Title of rulers was **Sultan** but the last-named was called **Caliph.***
Abdicated

YUGOSLAVIA

	Lived	Reigned
Alexander+	1888-1934	1922-1934
Peter II*	1923-1970	1934-1945

+*King of Serbs, Croats and Slovenes until 1929, then name changed to Yugoslavia.*
**Republic declared.*

BRITISH PRIME MINISTERS

Name	Party	In Office
Arthur James BALFOUR	Con.	1902-05
Sir Henry CAMPBELL-BANNERMAN	Lib.	1905-08
Herbert Henry ASQUITH	Lib.	1908-15
„ „ „	Co.*	1915-16
David LLOYD-GEORGE	Co.*	1916-22
Arthur Bonar LAW	Con.	1922-23
Stanley BALDWIN	Con.	1923-24
James Ramsay MacDONALD	Lab.	1924
Stanley BALDWIN	Con.	1924-29
James Ramsay MacDONALD	Lab.	1929-31
„ „ „	Co.*	1931-35
Stanley BALDWIN	Co.*	1935-37
(Arthur) Neville CHAMBERLAIN	Co.*	1937-40
Winston Leonard Spencer CHURCHILL	Co.*	1940-45
„ „ „ „	Con.	1945
Clement Richard ATTLEE	Lab.	1945-51
Winston CHURCHILL	Con.	1951-55
Sir (Robert) Anthony EDEN	Con.	1955-57
(Maurice) Harold MACMILLAN	Con.	1957-63
Sir Alexander Frederick DOUGLAS-HOME	Con.	1963-64
(James) Harold WILSON	Lab.	1964-70
Edward Richard George HEATH	Con.	1970-74
(James) Harold WILSON	Lab.	1974-76
(Leonard) James CALLAGHAN	Lab.	1976-79
Margaret Hilda THATCHER	Con.	1979-83
„ „ „	Con.	1983-87
„ „ „	Con.	1987-

**Coalition.*

Lloyd George (Liberal)
Attlee (Labour)

Thatcher (Conservative)

ASSASSINATIONS AND POLITICAL MURDERS

1900 29 July: King Humbert I of Italy, at Monza by an anarchist, Gaetano Bresci.
1901 14 Sept: President McKinley of the USA, by Leon Czolgosz. He is succeeded as president by Theodore Roosevelt.
1902 8 April: The Russian minister of the interior, Sipyagin.
1903 10 June: King Alexander I and Queen Draga, the royal family of Serbia, by Serbian officers.
1908 1 Feb: King Carlos I of Portugal and the Crown Prince Louis, duke of Braganza, in Lisbon, by Buica and Da Costa. Manuel II becomes King.
1909 26 Oct: Prince Ito of Japan, at Harbin, by a Korean.
1911 14 Sept: Piotr Stolypin, prime minister of Russia, in a theatre in Kiev, by a Jewish revolutionary, Mordka Bogrov.
1913 23 Jan: Nazim Pasha, prime minister of Turkey.
23 Feb: Francisco Indalecio Madero, president of Mexico.
18 March: King George I of Greece, in Salonika, by a Greek named Schinas.
1914 16 March: Gaston Calmette, editor of *Figaro*, in Paris, by Mme Caillaux.
28 June: The Archduke Franz Ferdinand and his wife, (Sophie Chotek, Duchess of Hohenburg) at Sarajevo, by a Bosnian nationalist, Gavrilo Princip.
30 July: Jean JAURÈS, a leading Socialist politician, in Paris.
1918 16 July: Tsar Nicholas and all Russian Royal Family, by revolutionaries, at Ekaterinburg (Sverdlovsk).
31 Oct: Count Stephen Tisza, prime minister of Hungary, in Budapest, by soldiers.
1922 22 June: Field-Marshal Sir Henry H.

Wilson, MP for North Down, Northern Ireland, in London.
24 June: Dr Walter Rathenau, German foreign minister, by young ex-naval officers, members of an anti-Semitic group.
22 Aug: Michael Collins, Sinn Fein leader, at Bandon, Co. Cork, by rebels.
16 Dec: Gabriel Narutowicz, first president of the Polish republic, by Capt. Niewadowski.
1923 10 May: Vaslav Vorovsky, Russian delegate at the Lausanne Conference.
29 June: General J.C. Gomez, first Vice-President of Venezuela.
20 July: General Francisco 'Pancho' Villa, at Parral, Mexico.
1924 10 June: Giacomo Matteotti, Italian Socialist deputy, by Fascist hirelings.
1927 10 July: Kevin O'Higgins, vice-president of the Irish Free State.
1928 17 July: General Alvaro Obregon, president of Mexico.
1932 1 May: Paul Doumer, president of France, by Paul Gargalov, a Russian emigré.
1933 30 April: Luis Sanchez Cerro, president of Peru, by Abelardo Hurtado de Mendoza.
8 Nov: King Nadir Shah, of Afghanistan, by a student, Abdul Khallig.
1934 30 June: The Nazis stage a blood purge in their own party. Von Schleicher, Roehm and others are executed in the 'Night of the Long Knives'.
25 July. Engelbert DOLLFUSS, chancellor of Austria, by Austrian Nazis, in a bid for power.
9 Oct: King Alexander of Yugoslavia and Louis Barthou, French foreign minister, at Marseilles by Georgief, a Croatian terrorist.
1 Dec: Sergei Kirov, an associate of Josef STALIN. Afterwards, the Communist party in Russia is purged.

Below: Mahatma Gandhi (1869–1948) led a non-violent campaign to free India from British rule.

Tsar Nicholas II of Russia with his family aboard the royal yacht before the First World War. During the Revolution of 1917 the family were captured and imprisoned at Ekaterinburg. It is thought that they were assassinated.

1935 8 Sept: Senator Huey Long, of Louisiana, at Baton Rouge, by Dr Carl A. Weiss.

1939 26 Jan: Professor Cristescu, Iron Guard leader, and Armand Calinescu, prime minister of Romania, by the Iron Guard.

1940 19 July: Samuel H. Chang, director of American newspaper firm, in Shanghai.

21 Aug: Leon TROTSKY, exiled Russian leader, at Coycacan, Mexico, by Jacques Mornard, alias Frank Jacson, a Belgian born in Iran.

1941 26 July: Marx Dormoy, French Socialist leader, at Montelimar, France, by a time bomb.

1942 5th Jan: Yves Paringaux, French chief of staff in the Vichy interior ministry, at Melun, France.

31 May: Reinhard Heydrich, German 'protector' of Bohemia and Moravia (Czechoslovakia), by Czech patriots.

24 Dec: Admiral Jean DARLAN, French naval officer and politician, in Algiers, by a French monarchist.

1943 11 Jan: Carlo Tresca, antifascist leader and editor of an Italian language newspaper in New York, in New York.

1945 24 Feb: Ahmed Maher Pasha, prime minister of Egypt, in the parliament building, Cairo.

28 April: Benito MUSSOLINI, by Italian partisans.

1948 20 Jan: Mohandas GANDHI, Indian religious and political leader, at New Delhi, by Natheram Jodre, a Hindu fanatic.

119

17 Sept: Count Folke BERNADOTTE, UN mediator, in Jerusalem, by Jewish terrorists.

28 Dec: Nokrashy Pasha, prime minister of Egypt.

1951 20 July: King ABDULLAH of Jordan, in Jerusalem.

6 Oct: Henry Gurney, British high commissioner for Malaya.

16 Oct: Liaquat Ali Khan, prime minister of Pakistan, by Said Akbar.

1958 14 July: King Faisal II and the prime minister of Iraq, Nuri-es-Said, at Baghdad.

1959 25 Sept: S.W.R.D. Bandaranaike, prime minister of Ceylon (Sri Lanka), by a Buddhist monk.

1960 29 Aug: Hazza el-Majali, prime minister of Jordan.

1963 8 Feb: Abdul Karim Kassem, prime minister of Iraq, at Baghdad.

1 Nov: Ngo Dinh Diem, prime minister of South Vietnam, during an army coup.

22 Nov: US President John F. KENNEDY, in Dallas, Texas, by Lee Harvey Oswald. Lyndon B. JOHNSON becomes president.

1965 21 Feb: Malcolm X, Black Muslim leader, in Manhattan, New York.

1966 6 Sept: Dr Verwoerd, South African prime minister, in the House of Assembly, Cape Town.

1967 25 Aug: George Rockwell, American Nazi leader.

1968 4 April: Martin Luther KING, US civil rights leader, in Memphis, Tennessee.

5 June: Robert KENNEDY, US senator, in Los Angeles, by Sirhan Bishara Sirhan, a Jordanian Arab. (Dies 25 hours later).

1969 5 July: Tom Mboya, minister of economic planning, in Nairobi, Kenya.

1971 28 Nov: Wasfi Tal, prime minister of Jordan, in Cairo.

12 Dec: Jack Barnhill, a Northern Ireland senator, at his home near the Irish Republic border.

1973 2 March: Cleo Noel, US ambassador to the Sudan, George Curtis Moore, chargé d'affaires, Guy Eid, Belgian chargé d'affaires, in the Saudi Arabian embassy at Khartoum. Terrorists demanded the release of Sirhan Sirhan, who killed Senator Robert KENNEDY.

10 March: In Bermuda, the Governor, Sir Richard Sharples, and his aide, Captain Hugh Sayers, at Government House.

20 Dec: Luis Carrero Blanco, prime minister of Spain, in Madrid.

1974 12 March: A Protestant member of the Dublin parliament, Senator Billy Fox, in Co. Monaghan, Irish Republic, by the 'Ulster Freedom Fighters'.

30 June: Mrs Albert King, mother of the late Martin Luther King, while playing the organ at a church at Atlanta, Georgia.

1975 25 March: In Saudi Arabia, King Faisal, by his 'mentally deranged' nephew. Crown Prince Khalid ibn Abdul Aziz succeeds to the throne.

15 Aug: In Bangladesh, Sheikh Mujibur Rahman in a military coup. Khandakar Mushtaque Ahmed is sworn in as president.

24 Oct: In Paris, the Turkish Ambassador, Ismail Erez, in his car.

27 Nov: Ross McWhirter, writer, publisher and co-editor of the *Guinness Book of Records*, at his home in Enfield, near London.

23 Dec: In Athens, Richard Welch, US diplomat and head of CIA activities in Greece.

1976 13 Feb: The Nigerian head of state, General Murtala Mohammed, during an attempted coup.

16 June: In the Lebanon, the US ambassador Francis Meloy, his economic counsellor, Robert Waring, and their Lebanese chauffeur, after being kidnapped in Beirut.

21 July: Christopher Ewart-Biggs, British ambassador to Ireland, and

his secretary, by a bomb placed under their car a few miles from Dublin.

1978 16 March: Aldo Moro, five times prime minister of Italy, after being kidnapped in Rome by terrorists. His five bodyguards are shot dead.

10 April: The body of Baron Charles Bracht, a Belgian millionaire kidnapped on 7 March, is found in Antwerp.

1979 14 Feb: The US ambassador to Afghanistan, Adolph Dubs, after Afghan soldiers storm the hotel where he is being held hostage.

22 March: In the Netherlands, the British ambassador, Sir Richard Sykes and his footman.

30 March. Airey Neave, British Conservative MP, after a bomb explodes in his car as he leaves the House of Commons.

27 Aug: Admiral of the Fleet Earl MOUNTBATTEN, his 14-year-old grandson, Nicholas, and 15-year-old boatman Paul Maxwell, after an IRA bomb explodes in their boat in Sligo Bay, Ireland. Three others are seriously injured, while 82-year-old Lady Brabourne dies the next day.

7 Dec: In Paris, Prince Chahryar Shafik, a nephew of the Shah of Iran.

1980 24 March: The archbishop of San Salvador, Monsignor Oscar Romero, as he celebrates Mass.

12 April. President William Tolbert of Liberia in a military coup by army Master Sergeant Samuel Doe.

17 Sept: General Anastasio Somoza, former president of Nicaragua, in Asunción, capital of Paraguay.

1981 30 May: President Ziaur Rahman of Bangladesh, at Chittagong, by rebel army officers.

30 Aug: In Iran, the president and the prime minister, Mohammad Ali Rajai and Mohammad Javad Bahonar, by a bomb explosion.

6 Oct: President Anwar SADAT of Egypt, in Cairo. Three other people are also killed, and 27 injured.

14 Sept: The president-elect of Lebanon, Bashir Gemayel, in a bomb explosion in East Beirut.

1982 21 Aug: In the Philippines, Benigno Aquino, opposition leader, as he arrives at Manila airport after spending three years in exile in the USA.

1983 9 Oct: In Rangoon, Burma, four South Korean cabinet ministers, after a bomb explosion.

19 Oct: In Grenada, Maurice Bishop, the prime minister, and three other ministers, shot dead by troops during a state of disorder.

1984 3 Feb: In Birmingham, England, Ravindara Mhatre, Indian diplomat, after being kidnapped two days before.

28 Mar: Kenneth Whitty, first secretary at the British Embassy in Athens, Greece, shot dead while driving home for lunch.

31 Oct: In India, Mrs Indira GANDHI, the prime minister, shot dead by her own Sikh bodyguards.

1985 20 Aug: in the Punjab, India, Sant Harchand Singh Longowal, moderate Sikh leader, shot by fellow Sikhs.

7 Nov: in Columbia 12 judges are among many killed when government troops storm the Palace of Justice in Bogota, held by left-wing guerrillas.

1986 28 Feb: Sweden's prime minister Olof Palme, shot in a Stockholm street by unknown assailants.

1987 1 June: Lebanese premier Rashid Karami, killed by a bomb in his helicopter.

20 March: Italian air force general Licio Giorgeri shot in Rome by Red Brigade terrorists.

1988 28 June: US military attaché Capt William E. Nordeen, killed in Athens by a booby trapped car bomb.

17 Aug: Pakistan's President Zia ul-Haq dies in a plane crash reportedly caused by sabotage.

Science and Medicine

AEROSOL A container pressurized by an inert gas, used for packaging paints, chemicals, insecticides and other liquids.

AIR CONDITIONING A system, developed by W.H. CARRIER, for cleaning and purifying air, and controlling its temperature and humidity in rooms, buildings and manufacturing.

AIRCRAFT, POWERED A fixed-wing heavier-than-air flying machine, usually divided into seaplanes, landplanes and amphibians. The first successful aircraft was flown in 1903 by the WRIGHT brothers.

AIRSHIP A power-driven lighter-than-air flying machine, which can be rigid (with an internal frame), semi-rigid (with a structured keel), or non-rigid, built without a main structure, and relying on internal gas pressure for its shape and size.

APPLETON LAYER Also known as the F-layer, this is most distance of the three regions of the IONOSPHERE. It is the upper ionized layer resulting from ultraviolet radiation from the sun, and can reflect radio waves back to earth.

AQUALUNG An apparatus used in underwater exploration, consisting of a close-fitting face-mask, a breathing-tube and a compressed-air container. It was invented in 1942 by J. COUSTEAU and E. Gagnan.

ATOMIC NUMBER The number of ELECTRONS orbiting around the NUCLEUS of the atoms of an element, or the number of PROTONS in the nucleus.

AUTOGIRO A rotating-wing aircraft which relies mainly on the action of the air upon its freely-revolving rotors for its support in the air. Invented in 1923 by J.L. de la CIERVA.

BAKELITE The first plastic or synthetic resin, invented in 1908 by L.H. BAEKELAND.

BALL-POINT PEN A writing instrument whose point consists of a very small ball-bearing, which receives semi-liquid ink from a reservoir above. Invented in 1919 by L. BIRO.

BATHYSCAPHE A vessel used for undersea exploration containing a spherical cabin, and with ballast and buoyancy compartments. Invented in 1948 by A. PICCARD.

BATHYSPHERE A spherical diving apparatus used for deep-sea observation and exploration; large enough to contain two men and their instruments, and capable descending to great depths. Invented in 1930 by W. BEEBE.

BATTERY, SOLAR A photo-electric cell or battery which converts light-energy from the Sun's radiation into electrical energy. Frequently used in artificial satellites. Invented in 1954 by D. PEARSON, C. FULLER and G. PEARSON.

BETATRON A machine which accelerates ELECTRONS in a circular magnetic field to produce a continuous stream of high-energy particles. Invented in 1939 by D. KERST.

BIG BANG THEORY The theory that a giant explosion marked the beginning of the universe as we know it. It is considered to have occurred about 20,000 million years ago, and that the universe has been expanding ever since.

CARBON-14 DATING A system of dating very early remains. Living organisms absorb radio-active carbon-14 from carbon-dioxide in the atmosphere, and this decays after death at a measurable rate. It is, therefore,

*A micro-computer as a mathematical aid.
Right: A bathyscaphe—a vessel used for
undersea exploration.*

possible to compute the period from death.
Discovered in 1947 by W.F. WILLARD.

CAROTENOIDS A group of orange-red or
yellow plant pigments, also found in certain
animal structures, such as feathers.

CELLOPHANE (Trade name) A glossy
transparent cellulose wrapping material, invented in 1908 by J. BRANDENBERGER.

CHLOROPHYLL The characteristic green
colouring matter found in plants, actually
consisting of two green and two yellow
pigments.

CLOUD-CHAMBER A term used in nuclear engineering for a chamber in which
saturated gas or air can be cooled by
expansion. This makes the tracks of ionizing
particles visible as a row of droplets. Invented in 1911 by C.T.R. WILSON.

COMPRESSION IGNITION ENGINE
See DIESEL ENGINE.

COMPUTER, ANALOGUE A computer
which operates with varying numerical am-
plitudes, based on electric current, voltage
and resistance.

COMPUTER, DIGITAL A computer
which operates by the use of digits related to
impulses, suitably coded.

CONTINENTAL DRIFT The theory propounded by A.L. WEGENER which supposes
the slow movement of continents from one
single land-mass to their present positions.

CORDITE An explosive made from nitro-
glycerine, cellulose nitrate and petroleum
jelly, pressed into ropes, rods or *cords*.
Invented in 1889 by DEWAR and ABEL.

COSMIC RAYS Extremely penetrating rays
coming from outer space.

CRYSTALLOGRAPHY The study and
classification of the structure of crystals.

CYBERNETICS The theory of control
mechanism and communication in machines
and living creatures.

123

CYCLOTRON An accelerator for imparting energy to charged particles of atomic magnitudes, which passes them repeatedly through an electromagnetic field. Invented by E. Lawrence in 1931.

DACRON See TERYLENE.

DDT An insecticide, full name DichloroDiphenylTrichloroethane, discovered in 1931 by P. MÜLLER.

DIELS-ALDER REACTION The formation of a cyclic compound by reaction between an aldehyde, acid or ester and a conjugated diene. Produced in 1928 by Otto DIELS and Kurt ALDER.

DIESEL ENGINE A compression-ignition engine in which a fuel pump injects fuel into a cylinder where it is highly compressed, so producing ignition. Invented in 1892 by Rudolf DIESEL.

DIODE A thermionic valve or tube with two electrodes: a cathode and an anode. Invented in 1904 by Sir J.A. FLEMING.

DNA Abbreviation for deoxyribonucleic acid, the 'brains' behind the living cell. It takes the form of long, thread-like molecules in chromosomes and viruses. The nucleic acids (see also RNA) play a large part in hereditary characteristics.

ELECTRIC LIGHT BULB A glass bulb containing a wire or filament, usually made of tungsten; the bulb being filled with an inert gas. The filament glows when an electric current is passed through it. Invented in 1879 by T.A. EDISON.

ELECTRON A small, negatively charged sub-atomic particle. Every electrically-charged neutral atom has as many orbiting electrons as PROTONS in nucleus.

ELINVAR A variety of nickel-steel alloy with variable proportions of manganese and tungsten. It is used for the hair-springs of watches since its elasticity is almost unaffected by temperature changes. See also INVAR. Invented in 1896 by C.E. GUILLAUME.

FILM, SOUND The first successful showing of a sound-on-film process was in 1923, using the Phonofilm process invented by L. DE FOREST.

FREON A compound of ethane or methane used as a refrigerant in fire-extinguishers or in AEROSOLS. Discovered in 1930 by T. MIDGLEY.

FUEL CELL A cell in which the oxidation of a fuel is used to produce electricity. It is somewhat like an accumulator, but uses fuel (such as oxygen and hydrogen) to operate, instead of being recharged with electricity. Invented in 1959 by F. BACON.

GAS TURBINE An engine which converts the chemical energy of a liquid fuel into mechanical energy by internal combustion.

GEIGER COUNTER An instrument for detecting and measuring radio-activity, invented in 1913 by J.H.W. GEIGER.

GEODESIC STRUCTURES Buildings or structures which are put together by means of a trellis-work of steel struts. These are either triangular or polygon shaped, so that the weight is evenly distributed throughout.

GEOMAGNETISM The natural magnetism of the earth itself.

GRAMOPHONE A machine for recording sound, which uses a revolving disc which contains a continuous spiral groove. A stylus is placed in contact with this, through which the sound is reproduced. In the USA, it is generally known as the phonograph.

GRAMOPHONE RECORD, LONG-PLAYING The modern disc record will play at $33\frac{1}{3}$ revolutions per minute (first produced in 1948), or at 45 rpm. The disc gramophone was invented in 1888 by Emile Berliner, following the cylinder phonograph of T.A. EDISON (1878). Stereo discs appeared in 1958, compact discs in the 1980s.

GYROSCOPIC MONORAIL A type of monorail which ran on one single rail, being kept upright by a gyroscopic system. Invented by Louis BRENNAN.

HAEMOGLOBIN The red colouring matter present in the red blood cells, which carries the oxygen around the body.

HELICOPTER A flying machine with rotors instead of wings. These are power-driven, and fixed vertically, so that the machine can take off or land vertically.

HELIUM, LIQUID Helium is an inert gas, and liquid helium has many unusual properties, including superfluidity.

HOLOGRAPHY A system of reproducing three-dimensional images without cameras or lenses; instead a laser is used. Invented in 1947 by D. GABOR.

HOVERCRAFT A vehicle or craft which hovers, or moves across water or land, being held away from the surface by a cushion of air pushing downwards. Invented in 1955 by Sir C. COCKERELL.

HYDROFOIL A fast ship whose hull is fitted with struts on which winglike constructions, or foils, are set. The craft is propelled by jets, or by a propeller, either in the water or in the air. At speed, the hull may be lifted entirely clear of the water.

HYDROGEN BOMB An atomic bomb whose atoms are condensed to form helium, during which process, enormous energy is released. Its explosive power is one thousand times more powerful than an atomic bomb such as was used over Japan at the end of World War II.

ICONOSCOPE A camera tube which forms the basis of the television camera, converting optical images into electronic impulses.

INSULIN A hormone secreted in the pancreas of vertebrate animals, which controls the sugar metabolism. Its use lowers the blood sugar content, and is therefore important for treatment of diabetes. Discovered in 1921 by BANTING and BEST.

INTERNAL COMBUSTION ENGINE An engine, such as a petrol or diesel engine, in which the energy produced by burning fuel is transformed into mechanical energy by controlling the combustion in an enclosed cylinder behind a piston.

INVAR An alloy of iron, nickel and carbon which expands only very minutely.

IONOSPHERE Those layers of the upper atmosphere which reflect radio signals, and thus make it possible to make radio transmissions across the globe.

IRON LUNG An apparatus to contain the human body, in which artificial respiration is performed mechanically by pumps. Invented in 1927 by P. Drinker.

ISOTOPE One of two or more forms of an element with the same atomic number (i.e., number of protons in the nucleus), but different atomic masses (due to different numbers of neutrons in the nucleus).

JET ENGINE A gas turbine producing a stream of hot gas, which allows an aircraft to be propelled through the atmosphere by reaction propulsion. Invented in 1930 by Sir Frank WHITTLE.

KINESCOPE A cathode-ray tube used in television for the electronic reproduction of transmitted images.

LASER A word coined from the initials: Light Amplification by Stimulated Emission of Radiation; a device invented in 1954 by C.H. TOWNES. It produces an intense, directional beam of light, which, when highly concentrated and focused, produces an intense point of heat. See also MASER.

LITHIUM A silvery-white metal, the lightest solid known. It resembles sodium, but is less active; is used in alloys, and is the basis for a lubricant grease.

MAGNETRON A thermionic valve which produces high power oscillations in the microwave region, and largely used in RADAR.

MASER A microwave amplifier that uses energy changes within atoms or molecules; abbreviation for Microwave Amplification by Stimulated Emission of Radiation. See LASER.

MESON One of a group of unstable sub-atomic particles with masses between those of the ELECTRON and the PROTON.

MICROSCOPE, ELECTRON Similar to the light microscope, but with much greater resolving power. The object is subjected to a parallel beam of electrons fired from an electron gun, giving magnifications of 1500 times. Invented in 1933 by Knoll and Rushka.

MOTION PICTURE CAMERA A camera with intermittent motion, arranged so that the opening of the shutter is mechanically synchronized with the movement of the film through the camera. Normal speeds are between 16 and 24 frames per second.

NEOPRENE A synthetic rubber, which is stronger than natural rubber, and has better resistance to heat.

NEPTUNIUM An element made during the temporary stage in the formation of plutonium from uranium.

NEUTRINO A stable elementary particle emitted during the decay of NEUTRONS and MESONS. They have zero mass and are electrically neutral.

NEUTRON An uncharged sub-atomic particle found in the nuclei of all atoms except hydrogen.

NUCLEAR REACTOR An atomic pile, a large-scale assembly in which nuclear reactions in fissile material are controlled by introducing moderators (non-fissile material).

NUCLEIC ACID These are large molecules consisting of chains of nucleotides, and are present in all living matter, since they are the means by which all the genetic codes are stored and transferred. See DNA and RNA.

NYLON A plastic material, any of a group of long-chain synthetic polymeric amines, which are used to make a fabric of great tensile strength.

PHONOGRAPH See GRAMOPHONE.

PHOTON A quantum of electro-magnetic radiation, such as light.

POLYESTER A polymer formed from a polyhydric alcohol and a polybasic acid. Polyesters are used in the manufacture of synthetic resins, fibres and plastics.

POLYETHYLENE A waxy plastic material, also known as polythene or Alkathene. It is flexible, and chemically resistant, and is used as an insulating material.

POLYMER A high-molecular weight chemical compound obtained by polymerization. Most plastics are polymers.

POSITRON A positive electron; an elementary particle with the same mass as the ELECTRON and with an equal electrical charge, but opposite sign.

QUANTUM THEORY The theory that light and other forms of energy are given off as discrete packets (quanta) of energy.

RADAR This is an abbreviation of RAdio Detection And Ranging, and describes any system employing microwaves for locating, indentifying, and navigating ships, aircraft, missiles, satellites or similar moving objects.

RADIO The transmission of information or sounds by means of electro-magnetic waves.

RADIO TELESCOPE Instead of collecting light, as does an optical telescope, the radio telescope uses a directional aerial to pick up radio energy from the sky.

RADIO-ACTIVITY The emission of radiation, such as alpha-rays, beta-rays and gamma-rays from unstable elements by spontaneous splitting of their atomic nuclei.

RADIOMETER An instrument which measures the conversion of radiant energy into mechanical energy.

RELATIVITY, THEORY OF Einstein's theory that it is impossible to measure motion absolutely, but only within a given frame of reference, which also always involves time, such as space-time.

RNA Abbreviation for ribonucleic acid. Similar to DNA, except that the thymine is replaced by uracil.

SILICON CHIP A wafer of silicon bearing a miniaturized circuit. In complex electronic devices, a great many silicon chips are used.

SPECTROGRAPH An instrument for producing and photographing spectra. See SPECTRUM.

SPECTROHELIOGRAPH An instrument used for photographing the Sun, with the light of a particular wavelength.

SPECTRUM Any series of bands and lines observed through a SPECTROGRAPH, when light or other radiation is diffracted.

STEADY-STATE THEORY This was put forward in 1948 by F. HOYLE, H. BONDI, and T. Gold, that the expansion of the universe is compensated by a continuous creation of matter throughout space.

TELEVISION The transmission of visible moving images by electronic means. Significant experimentation was done by J.L. BAIRD and W. ZWORYKIN.

TERYLENE Also known as Dacron, this is the trade name for a synthetic fibre, made from a straight-chain polyester, similar to Nylon.

TETRA-ETHYL LEAD A colourless oily liquid, used as an anti-knock additive in petrol.

THALLIUM A soft metal whose physical properties closely resemble those of lead. Its compounds are very poisonous.

THYROXINE An amino-acid containing iodine, produced by the thyroid gland.

TRANSISTOR A semi-conductor device that can amplify electric current.

TRANSURANIC ELEMENTS Elements in the periodic table beyond uranium; which are elements of atomic number greater than 92. All are radioactive.

TRIODE A thermionic valve containing three electrodes; an anode, a cathode and a control grid. Invented in 1906 by L. DE FOREST.

UNCERTAINTY PRINCIPLE The indeterminacy principle. It is impossible to measure the position and momentum of a particle simultaneously with more than limited precision. The more accurately the position is known, the less accurately is it possible to determine the momentum.

X-RAYS Very short wavelength electromagnetic waves produced when a stream of high-energy electrons bombards matter.

XEROGRAPHY A type of photographic copying in which an electrostatic image is formed on a surface coated with selenium when it is exposed to an optical image. The system was invented in 1948 by C.F. CARLSON.

ZEEMAN EFFECT The splitting up of the individual components of the line spectrum of a substance when placed in a strong magnetic field. Discovered in 1896 by P. ZEEMAN.

Automation at work in a car factory.

127

INVENTIONS OF THE TWENTIETH CENTURY

Invention	Inventor(s)	Country	Year
Aeroplane	Wilbur & Orville Wright	USA	1903
Aerosol	L.D. Goodhue & W.N. Sullivan	USA	1941
Aqualung	Jacques Cousteau & Emile Gagnan	France	1942
Autogiro	Juan de la Cierva	Spain	1923
Bakelite	Leo Baekeland	Belgium/USA	1908
Ball-point pen	Laszlo Biro	Hungary	1938
Bathyscaphe	Auguste Piccard	Belgium	1948
Battery, solar	D.Pearson, C.Fuller, G.Pearson	USA	1954
Betatron	Donald Kerst	USA	1939
Brakes, disc	Dr F. Lanchester	England	1902
Camera, Polaroid	Edwin Land	USA	1947
Cellophane	Jacques Brandenberger	Switzerland	1908
Combine harvester	Benjamin Holt	USA	1911
Computer, analogue	Vannevar Bush	USA	1925
Computer, automatic digital	Howard Aiken	USA	1944
Computer, electronic	J.G. Brainerd, J.P.Eckert & John W.Mauchly	USA	1946
Cyclotron	Ernest Lawrence	USA	1931
Electric blanket	Simmons Co.	USA	1946
Film, sound	Dr Lee De Forest	USA	1923
Food,frozen process	Clarence Birdseye	USA	1925
Fork-lift truck	Coventry-Climax Co.	England	1947
Fuel cell	Francis Bacon	England	1959
Gas turbine engine	R. Armengaud & C.Lemale	France	1903
Geiger counter	Hans Geiger	England	1913
Glass, laminated safety	John Wood	England	1905
Helicopter	Paul Cornu	France	1907
Holography (3-D photography)	Dennis Gabor	England	1965
Hovercraft	Sir Christopher Cockerell	England	1955
Hydrofoil	Enrico Forlamini	Italy	1903
Iron lung	Philip Drinker	USA	1927
Jet engine	Sir Frank Whittle	England	1930
Jukebox	John C. Dunton	USA	1905
Lamp, neon	Georges Claude	France	1910
Lamp, tungsten filament	Irving Langmuir	USA	1915
Laser	Theodore Maiman	USA	1960
Launderette	J.F. Cantrell	USA	1934
Lie detector	John A. Larson	USA	1921
Loudspeaker	Horace Short	England	1900
Magnetron	Sir John Randall and Dr H.A.H. Boot	England	1939
Maser	Charles H. Townes	USA	1954

Meson	Carl Anderson	USA	1935
Microscope, electron	M. Knoll & E. Ruska	Germany	1933
Neon lamp	Georges Claude	France	1910
Nylon	Wallace Carothers	USA	1935
Parking meter	Carlton Magee	USA	1935
Photo-copier			
(Rectigraph)	George C. Beidler	USA	1907
Photographic			
colour film	Leopold Godowsky	USA	1935
Photon	Arthur H. Compton	USA	1923
Radar	Dr Albert H. Young and		
	Leo C. Young	USA	1922
Radar	Sir Robert Watson-Watt	Scotland	1935
Radio (frequency			
modulation)	Edwin H. Armstrong	USA	1933
Radio telegraphy,			
transatlantic	G. Marconi	Italy	1901
Radio telephone	Reginald Fessenden	USA	1902
Razor, safety	King Camp Gillette	USA	1901
Razor, electric	Jacob Schick	USA	1928
Record,			
long-playing	Peter Goldmark	USA	1948
Rifle, automatic	John Browning	USA	1918
Road studs, catseye	Percy Shaw	England	1934
Rocket, liquid fuel	Robert H. Goddard	USA	1926
Rubber, latex foam	Dunlop Rubber Co.	England	1928
Scanner, EMI	Godfrey Hounsfield	England	1971
Self-starter	Charles E. Kettering	USA	1911
Talking picture,			
sound-on-film	Emile Lauste	France	1913
Steel, stainless	Harry Brearley	England	1913
Tank, Military	Sir Ernest Swinton	England	1914
Tape Recorder			
(Blattnerphone)	Louis Blattner	England	1929
(Plastic tape			
Magnetophone)	AEG Company	Germany	1935
Cassette recorder	Philips Company	England	1963
Television	John Logie Baird	Scotland	1925
Television,			
electronic	Vladimir Zworykin	USA	1923
Television, videotape			
recording	A. Poniatoff	USA	1951
Terylene	J.R. Whinfield & J.T. Dickson	England	1946
Transistor	John Bardeen, Walter Brattain		
	and William Shockley	USA	1948
Triode	Dr Lee De Forest	USA	1906
Vacuum cleaner	Cecil Booth	England	1910
Washing machine,			
electric	Hurley Machine Co.	USA	1911
Xerography	Chester Carlson	USA	1948

LEADING NAMES IN SCIENCE, TECHNOLOGY AND INVENTION

AIKEN, Howard Hathaway [1900-73]; American mathematician, who invented the first modern digital computer in 1944. It weighed 35 tons (35 tonnes).

ALDER, Kurt [1902-58]; German chemist, who, with Otto DIELS, produced the Diels-Alder reaction in 1928. It is the basis of many modern synthetic products.

APPLETON, Sir Edward Victor [1892-1965]; British physicist, who in 1926, discovered the Appleton or F layer of the ionosphere, making long-distance radio communication possible.

ARRHENIUS, Svante August [1859-1927]; Swedish chemist, who, about 1884, founded the basis for modern physical chemistry.

ASTON, Francis William [1877-1945]; British chemist, who in 1920, developed the mass spectrograph, aiding discovery of various isotopes.

BAADE, Walter [1893-1960]; German astronomer, later at the Mount Wilson observatory, Pasadena, California, and Mount Palomar. His discoveries increased by twenty-fold our estimates of the size of the universe.

BAEKELAND, Leo Hendrik [1863-1944]; American chemists, born in Belgium, who in

Washing machine, 1920

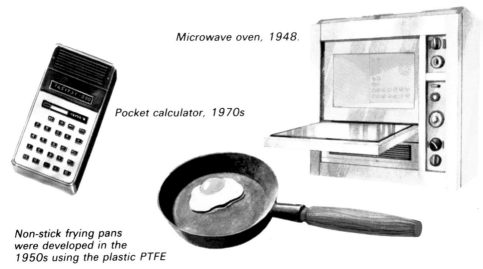

Microwave oven, 1948.

Pocket calculator, 1970s

Non-stick frying pans were developed in the 1950s using the plastic PTFE

1909, invented Bakelite, one of the first plastics.

BAIRD, John Logie [1888-1946]; British engineer, who in 1924 gave the first demonstration of a television image, and first demonstrated objects in motion on television in 1926. He used a mechanical scanning system.

BELL, Alexander Graham [1847-1922]; American inventor of Scottish birth, who invented the articulating telephone in 1876, the photophone in 1880, and the graphophone in 1887.

BENZ, Karl Friedrich [1844-1929]; German engineer, who in 1885, designed and built the first practical internal combustion automobile.

BERNAL, John Desmond [1901-71]; British physicist, born in Ireland. He was responsible for development of crystallography.

BETHE, Hans Albrecht [1906-]; American physicist born in Alsace (then Germany). His outstanding work has been concerned with atomic nuclei and nuclear interaction.

BIRÓ, László [1900-]; Argentinian inventor, born in Hungary, where in 1938, he produced the first ball-point pen.

BLACKETT, Patrick Maynard Stuart (1st Baron) [1897-1974]; British physicist, who was able to photograph subatomic particle reaction, and who worked with cosmic rays.

BOHR, Niels Hendrik David [1885-1962]; Danish physicist, who worked in nuclear physics and the on the atomic bomb, but who organized the Atoms for Peace conference in 1955.

BONDI, Hermann [1919-]; British mathematician and cosmologist, born in Austria, who, with Fred HOYLE and Thomas Gold, propounded the 'steady-state' theory of the universe.

BOSCH, Carl [1874-1940]; German chemist, who developed the use of synthetic nitrogen (discovered by Fritz HABER) as a fertilizer.

BRAGG, Sir (William) Lawrence [1890-1971]; British physicist, born in Australia, who, with his father, Sir William Henry BRAGG, was a pioneer in X-ray crystallography.

BRAGG, Sir William Henry [1862-1942]; British physicist, whose work with his son, Sir Lawrence BRAGG led to the analysis of substances such as DNA.

BRAUN, Wernher Magnus Maximilian von [1912-77]; American engineer, German-born in what is now Poland. A pioneer in rocketry, who led in the development of the V-2 missiles in Germany, and of the American rockets used to explore space.

BRENNAN, Louis [1852-1932]; British inventor, born in Ireland. He invented the Brennan torpedo and the gyroscopic monorail.

BRODE, Wallace Reed [1900-]; American physicist, who developed the use of the spectroscope in investigating the nature of chemical substances.

BUSH, Vannevar [1890-1974]; American electrical engineer, who in 1925, built the first analogue computer, and who headed research into uranium for use in the atomic bomb.

CALVIN, Melvin [1911-]; American biochemist, who investigated the photosynthesis process by which plants use light, carbon dioxide and water to form starch and oxygen.

CARLSON, Chester Floyd [1906-68]; American inventor, who in 1938, produced the first xerographic image, leading to the widespread use of Xerography in copying documents.

CAROTHERS, Wallace Hume [1896-1937]; American chemist, who in 1931, invented the first type of nylon, and the first successful synthetic rubber, called neoprene.

CARRIER, Willis Havilland [1876-1950]; American engineer and inventor, who developed air-conditioning, and who invented a system used for high-rise buildings.

CARVER, George Washington [1864-1943]; American botanist, son of slave parents, who developed agricultural research, and was able to produce 300 by-products of peanuts, and over 100 from sweet potatoes.

CHADWICK, Sir James [1891-1974]; British physicist, who in 1932, discovered the neutron, which aided the development of nuclear fission.

CHAPMAN, Sydney [1888-1970]; British mathematician and geophysicist; whose special work was in geomagnetism, and who worked on the subject of lunar and solar tides. His name is given to a layer in the ionosphere.

CIERVA, Juan de la (Cierva Cordoniu) [1895-1936]; Spanish aeronautical engineer, who in 1928, invented the autogiro. He died in an aircraft accident at Croydon, England.

COCKCROFT, Sir John Douglas [1897-1967]; British physicist, who, with E.T.S. WALTON, developed the high-voltage generator as a particle

131

accelerator, used in splitting atoms.

COCKERELL, Christopher Sydney [1910-]; British radio engineer and inventor of the hovercraft.

COMPTON, Arthur Holly [1892-1962]; American physicist, a leading authority on nuclear energy, and X-rays, and who in 1923, discovered the photon.

CROOKES, Sir William [1832-1919]; British physicist, who discovered thallium in 1861, and invented the radiometer in 1875. He was a pioneer in the development of the vacuum electronic tube.

CURIE, Marie (b. Manya Sklodowska) [18671934]; French physicist of Polish birth, married in 1895, Pierre Curie, physicist. Together they investigated radio-activity, a word they invented.
                                                    •
DE BROGLIE, Prince Louis-Victor-Pierre-Raymond (7th Duke) [1892-1960]; French physicist, who in 1929, discovered the wave nature of electrons. His elder brother, Maurice [1875-1960] was also a distinguished physicist.

DE FOREST, Lee [1873-1961]; American inventor, who after researching into radio waves, invented the triode valve in 1906, and the first sound-on-film system in 1923.

DEWAR, Sir James [1842-1923]; British physicist, who in 1898, was first to liquefy hydrogen, and first in 1899, to solidify it. He was also the inventor of the vacuum flask [also known as the Dewar or Thermos flask] . (1892), and cordite, with Sir Frederick Abel, (1889).

DIELS, Otto Paul Hermann [1876-1964]; German chemist, who with Kurt ALDER, discovered Diels-Alder reaction.

DIESEL, Rudolf [1858-1913]; German inventor, born in Paris, who in 1892, invented the compression-ignition Diesel engine.

DIRAC, Paul Adrien Maurice [1902-84]; British physicist, a pioneer of wave mechanics. In 1928 he predicted the existence of the positron, confirmed in 1932 by Carl David Anderson.

DORNBERGER, Walter Robert [1895-1980]; German engineer, who after experimentation with rockets, developed the German V-2 rocket, and moved to the USA in 1947 for work with the Bell Aircraft Corporation.

EASTMAN, George [1854-1932]; American inventor, who in 1884, produced the first photographic roll-film, using a paper roll; using a celluloid

roll in 1889, and using a cellulose acetate film in 1924.

EDISON, Thomas Alva [1847-1931]; American inventor, responsible for a large number of innovations. Inventions include: the telegraphic stock ticker (1869), the phonograph (1877), and the electric light bulb (1879). He held 1300 patents.

EIFFEL, Alexandre-Gustave [1832-1923]; French engineer, who built many bridges, and the framework for the Statue of Liberty. He is best known for the Eiffel tower in Paris, built 1887-89.

EINSTEIN, Albert [1879-1955]; American physicist, born in Germany, but naturalized Swiss at the age of 15. In 1905, he propounded his theory of relativity ($E = mc^2$).

FERMI, Enrico [1901-54]; American physicist, born in Italy. He was a pioneer in the study of neutrons and neutron bombardment, and directed the first controlled nuclear chain reaction in 1942. He also worked on the atomic bomb at Los Alamos, New Mexico.

FISCHER, Hans [1881-1945]; German organic chemist, who worked on the composition of the colouring matter in leaves and in blood.

FLEMING, Sir (John) Ambrose [1849-1945]; British electrical engineer, who in 1904, invented the two-electrode radio rectifier valve (diode).

FRANCK, James [1882-1964]; American physicist, who, with Gustav Hertz, bombarded gases with electrons to produce light emissions, showing that the gas atoms were excited by the electrons.

FRIESE-GREENE, William [1855-1921]; British pioneer in cinematography, who in 1889, produced the first practical motion-picture camera. He also experimented with stereoscopic and colour film.

FULLER, (Richard) Buckmaster [1895-1983]; American engineer, philosopher and author, who worked out architectural themes on engineering principles, including the three-dimensional 'geodesic dome', and mass-produced houses on engineering lines.

GABOR, Dennis [1900-79]; British physicist, born in Hungary, who in 1947, invented holography, a system of three-dimensional photography.

GEIGER, (Johannes) Hans Wilhelm (1882-1945]; German physicist, who in 1913, introduced the Geiger counter, a device for measuring radioactivity.

GODDARD, Robert Hutchings [1882-1945]; American physicist, and pioneer in the development of rockets. He made the first liquid-fuelled rocket in 1926, and one which exceeded the speed of sound in 1935.

GOLDMARK, Peter Carl [1906-77]; American inventor, born in Hungary, who in 1940 demonstrated the first practical colour TV system, and in 1948, developed the long-playing 33⅓ rpm gramophone record.

GUILLAUME, Charles Edouard [1861-1938]; Swiss physicist, who in 1896, invented the nickel-steel alloys invar and elinvar, whose character-

Right: Marie and Pierre Curie. Below: Max Planck (left); Lord Rutherford (centre) and Albert Einstein. Bottom: Marconi and Fermi (right).

istics are that they vary little, no matter what the temperature. The metals are used for measures and precision instruments.

HABER, Fritz [1868-1934]; German chemist who produced ammonia synthetically. During World War I, he helped to develop poison gas, but in 1933, resigned his post at the Kaiser Wilhelm Institute in Berlin in protest at the dismissal of Jewish scientists.

HAHN, Otto [1879-1968]; German chemist, who in 1938, discovered uranium fission. Worked on nuclear fission during World War II, but stressed the dangers of nuclear war after the dropping of the bomb over Hiroshima in 1945.

HALE, George Ellery [1868-1935]; American astronomer, who founded the Yerkes Observatory in 1897, the Mount Wilson Observatory in 1908, and the Mount Palomar Observatory in 1948. He was the inventor of the spectroheliograph.

HAWORTH, Sir (Walter) Norman [1883-1950]; British chemist who worked on carbohydrates and Vitamin C. In 1933, he was the first to synthesize a vitamin.

HEISENBERG, Werner Karl [1901-76]; German physicist who discovered the 'uncertainty principle' or indeterminacy. During World War II, he directed the unsuccessful atomic bomb project.

HESS, Victor Franz [1883-1964]; American physicist, born in Austria, a pioneer in the investigation of cosmic rays.

HILLIER, James [1915-]; American physicist, born in Canada, who in 1937, made the Model B electron microscope, a great improvement on anything previously produced.

HINSHELWOOD, Sir Cyril Norman [1897-1967]; British physicist and chemist, who worked on the reaction of gases, and the growth of bacteria. He spoke six languages, including Latin and Russian.

HINTON, Lord (Christopher Hinton) [1901-83]; British nuclear engineer, who was responsible for the building of the nuclear power station at Calder Hall, Cumberland, England.

HODGKIN, Dorothy Crowfoot [1910-]; British biochemist, who has worked on the structure of pencillin, vitamin B12 (to combat pernicious anaemia) and zinc insulin. 'She was the second woman (after Florence Nightingale) to be awarded the Order of Merit (1965).

HOLLAND, John Philip [1841-1914]; American inventor, born in Ireland, who built the first successful submarines. His *Holland*, launched in 1898, was purchased by the US Navy.

HOYLE, Sir Fred [1915-]; British astronomer, mathematician and science-fiction writer. Proponent of the 'steady-state' theory of the universe. *Nature of the Universe* (1952), *Frontiers of Astronomy* (1955), *The Black Cloud* (science fiction, 1957), *Of Men and Galaxies* (1966), *Life Cloud* (1979).

HUBBLE, Edwin Powell [1889-1953]; American astronomer, who in 1924 discovered that other galaxies were far from the galaxy of the Sun, and propounded the idea of an expanding universe.

HUTCHISON, Sir (William) Kenneth [1903-]; British engineer, who has been responsible for gas production in the United Kingdom. This included work during the war (hydrogen for balloons in the barrage, oxygen for high flying aircraft), and development of North Sea gas.

INGOLD, Sir Christopher Kelk [1893-1970]; British chemist, who did important work in the field of aromatic compounds.

JANSKY, Karl Guthe [1905-50]; American radio engineer, and a pioneer of radio astronomy. In 1932 he was the first to discover the source of radio waves from outside the solar system.

JUNKERS, Hugo [1859-1935]; German aeronautical designer, who in 1915, built the J.1, the first all-metal aircraft.

KAMERLINGH ONNES, Heike [1853-1926]; Dutch physicist, who in 1908, was the first to liquefy helium, and discovered superconductivity.

KARRER, Paul [1889-1971]; Swiss chemist, who in 1931, discovered the constitution of Vitamin A.

KENDALL, Edward Calvin [1886-1972]; American biochemist, who in 1916, isolated thyroxine, the substance of the thyroid hormone, and by the 1930s had isolated most other hormones.

KUHN, Richard [1900-67]; Austrian chemist, who researched into carotenoids. In 1938, he was instructed by the Nazi government to decline the Nobel Prize for chemistry.

LAND, Edwin Herbert [1909-]; American inventor, who in 1932 invented the Polaroid lens, and in 1947, invented the instant camera.

LANDAU, Lev Davidovitch [1908-68]; Russian physicist, who worked on low-temperature physics, especially liquid helium.

The radio telescope at Jodrell Bank, near Manchester, England. It was set up under the direction of Sir Bernard Lovell.

LANGEVIN, Paul [1872-1946]; French physicist who is best known for his work on the theory of magnetic materials. During World War I, he developed an ultrasonic device for detecting U-boats.

LANGMUIR, Irving [1889-1957]; American chemist; who improved light bulbs, invented a hydrogen blowtorch, and studied mononuclear films.

LAUE, Max Theodor Felix von [1879-1960]; German physicist, who determined the diffraction of X-rays by crystals. He opposed Nazi interference with science.

LIBBY, Willard Frank [1908-1980]; American chemist, who in 1947, discovered the carbon-14 dating technique.

LOVELL, Sir (Alfred Charles) Bernard [1913-]; British astronomer, and a leader in radio astronomy. Under his direction, the radio telescope at Jodrell Bank, near Manchester, England, was completed in 1957.

MARCONI, Guglielmo (Marchese) [1874-1937]; Italian physicist, who invented radio (1895-1901), and transmitted signals across the Atlantic in 1901.

MAXIM, Sir Hiram Stevens [1840-1916]; British inventor, born in the United States, who in 1883 invented the fully-automatic machine gun.

MEITNER, Lise [1878-1968]; Swedish physicist, born in Austria. who worked on the physics of radio-activity, spending much of her working life with Otto HAHN.

MIDGLEY, Thomas [1889-1944]; American chemist, who in 1921 discovered the anti-knock property of tetra-ethyl lead in petrol, and in 1930, discovered the refrigerant Freon.

MILLIKAN, Robert Andrews [1868-1953]; American physicist, who proved in 1910 that electricity consists of particles, and who invented the term 'cosmic rays'.

MITCHELL, Reginald Joseph [1895-1937]; British aircraft designer, who designed the Sea Lion seaplane in 1921, and in 1935, the prototype of the Spitfire.

MOSELEY, Henry Gwyn Jeffreys [1887-1915]; British physicist, born in Turkey. He showed that the chemical properties of an element are determined by its atomic number. He died in action at Gallipoli, his birthplace.

MUELLER, Erwin Wilhelm [1911-77]; American physicist, born in Germany, who in 1956 invented the field ion microscope, with which he was able to produce images of single atoms.

MÜLLER, Paul [1899-1965]; Swiss chemist, who discovered the insecticide DDT in 1939.

McMILLAN, Edwin Mattison [1907-]; American physicist, who in 1940, discovered the element neptunium, and worked out improvements to the CYCLOTRON.

NATTA, Giulio [1903-1979]; Italian chemist, whose work on polymers has led to important developments in plastics and industrial chemicals.

OBERTH, Hermann [1894-]; German physicist and engineer, born in Transylvania, now Romania. He foresaw modern use of rockets in space, and in 1927 founded a German Society for Space Travel. *Die Rakete zu den Planeträumen* (The Rocket into Interplanetary Space), 1923.

OPPENHEIMER, (Julius) Robert [1904-67]; American physicist, whose work led to the discovery of the positron. He worked on the first A-bombs, but was disinclined to continue with the development of the H-bomb.

OSTWALD, Friedrich Wilhelm [1853-1932]; German chemist, born in Latvia. He was a founder of modern physical chemistry, building up a school at Leipzig University.

PANETH, Friedrich Adolf [1887-1958]; Austrian chemist, who spent much time in studying radiations, using radio-active tracers. Was able to date rocks by their helium content.

PAULI, Wolfgang [1900-58]; American physicist, born in Austria. He postulated the existence of neutrinos.

PAULING, Linus Carl [1901-]; American chemist, who described the structure of molecules and the nature of chemical bonds. He has advocated the taking of large doses of vitamin C to counter the common cold.

PLANCK, Max Karl Ernst Ludwig [1858-1947]; German physicist, who in 1900 developed the QUANTUM THEORY.

POULSEN, Valdemar [1869-1942]; Danish electric engineer, who invented the telegraphone, an early type of 'tape' recorder, which magnetized steel wire, ribbon or disc.

POWELL, Cecil Frank [1903-69]; British physicist, who photographed nuclear processes, and proved the existence of the pion in 1947.

RAMAN, Sir Chandrasekhara Venkata [1888-1970]; Indian physicist, who in 1928, proved that light changed wavelengths when scattered.

REBER, Grote [1911-]; American radio astronomer, who in 1937 built the first radio telescope.

ROBINSON, Sir Robert [1886-1975]; British chemist, who investigated the structure of natural compounds, including akaloids, and their synthesis.

RUTHERFORD, Ernest (1st Baron) [1871-1937]; British physicist, born in New Zealand, who discovered alpha, beta and gamma radiation, and who referred to the 'half-life' of radioactivity. He was the first to achieve nuclear reaction in 1917, yet he never believed that there could be any practical use for atomic energy.

RYLE, Sir Martin [1918-84]; British astronomer, a supporter of the 'big bang' theory of the origin of the universe. He was director of the Mullard Astronomy observatory at Cambridge, and Astronomer Royal 1972-82.

SANGER, Frederick [1918-]; British biochemist, who in the 1950s was first to establish a protein-amino-acid sequence, based on insulin. He is the only person to receive two Nobel prizes in the same category; in this case, chemistry.

SCHRADER, Gerhard [1903-]; German chemist, who has worked in insecticides, especially of the organo-phosphorus type, which are important in crop protection.

SCHRÖDINGER, Erwin [1887-1961]; Austrian physicist, who worked on wave mechanics and the QUANTUM THEORY. He was exiled to Ireland during World War II.

SEABORG, Glen Theodore [1912-]; American physicist, who helped to discover five of the transuranic elements. He was chairman of the US Atomic Energy Commission 1961-71.

SEMENOV, Nikolai Nikolayevitch [1896-1986]; Russian chemist, who worked on chemical chain reactions and thermal explosions.

SHOENBERG, Sir Isaac [1880-1963]; British electrical engineer, born in Russia, who installed the first radio stations in Russia. Principal inventor of hi-fi television system.

SIKORSKY, Igor Ivan [1889-1972]; American aeronautical engineer, born in Russia. Designed and built his own helicopter, 1909; the world's first multi-engined aircraft, 1913; the *American Clipper* amphibian, 1931.

SODDY, Frederick [1877-1956]; British chemist, who with Lord RUTHERFORD developed the theory of atomic disintegration of radio-active elements.

STAUDINGER, Hermann [1881-1965]; German chemist, who studied polymers and developed the long-chain-molecule theory of chemistry.

SUNDBACK, Gideon [1880-1954]; American engineer, born in Sweden, who in 1914, perfected the zip fastener.

SZILARD, Leo [1898-1964]; American physicist, who in 1934, developed the first method of separating isotopes of radio-active elements, and who, with Enrico FERMI, built the first nuclear reactor in 1942.

TELLER, Edward [1908-]; American physicist, born in Hungary. During World War II, he worked on the hydrogen bomb, and is referred to as 'father of the H-bomb'.

THOMSON, Sir Joseph John [1856-1940]; British physicist who in 1897, discovered the electron, and who was responsible for the study of sub-atomic physics.

TIZARD, Sir Henry Thomas [1885-1959]; British chemist, who, as chairman of the Committee for Scientific Survey of Air Defence, was largely responsible for the development of radar in Britain's defence.

TODD, Sir Alexander Robertus (Baron) [1907-]; British biochemist, whose research in the 1940s into synthesizing nucleic acid prepared the way for the study of DNA.

TOWNES, Charles Hurd [1915-]; American physicist, who, in 1953, invented the MASER, and who helped to develop the LASER.

TSIOLKOVSKY, Konstantin Eduardovich [1857-1935]; Russian physicist, and a pioneer in rocket and space research. He worked out the theory of rockets for space flight as early as 1883.

WALLIS, Sir Barnes Neville [1887-1979]; British engineer and inventor, who designed the R100 airship in 1928, and who devised the 'bouncing bombs' which demolished the Möhne and Eder dams during World War II.

WALTON, Ernest Thomas Sinton [1903-]; Irish physicist, who, with Sir John COCKCROFT, in 1932, disintegrated lithium by proton bombardment.

WATSON-WATT, Sir Robert Alexander [1892-1973]; British physicist, who in 1935, invented the first practical radar.

WEAVER, Warren [1894-1978]; American mathematician, who developed the science of CYBERNETICS, which deals with the study of communication and control, especially needed in modern automation.

WEGENER, Alfred Lothar [1880-1930]; German meteorologist, geophysicist and Arctic explorer, who put forward the hypothesis of CONTINENTAL DRIFT.

WHINFIELD, John Rex [1901-66]; British chemist, who in 1941, invented the first polyester fibre and film, and eventually developed Terylene.

WHITTLE, Sir Frank [1907-]; British aeronautical engineer, who in 1941, successfully developed the jet engine for aircraft. A jet engine had been designed in Germany by Dr Hans von Ohain in 1939. Whittle's first patent, on the other hand, had been taken out in 1930, and was bench-tested in 1937, and German developments were based on this.

WIENER, Norbert [1894-1964]; American mathematician, who founded the science of CYBERNETICS, the study of communications and control.

Sir Frank Whittle who successfully developed the jet engine for aircraft.

WILLSTÄTTER, Richard Martin [1872-1942]; Swiss chemist, born in Germany. He studied the constitution of plant materials and alkaloids; and also worked on chlorophyll and haemoglobin.

WILSON, Charles Thomson Rees [1869-1959]; British physicist, who in 1911 invented the cloud-chamber, used in the development of atomic physics.

WRIGHT, Wilbur [1867-1912] and **Orville** [1871-1948]; American inventors, who in 1903 made the first powered aircraft flight in a machine of their own design.

ZEEMAN, Pieter [1865-1943]; Dutch physicist, who in 1896 discovered the ZEEMAN EFFECT.

ZEPPELIN, Ferdinand Adolf August Heinrich, Graf von [1838-1917]; German soldier and inventor, in 1900, of the first rigid airship.

ZIEGLER, Karl Waldemar [1898-1973]; German chemist, who researched into long-chain polymers, and particularly in the development of polyethylene.

ZWORYKIN, Vladimir Kosma [1889-1982]; American engineer and inventor, born in Russia, who invented the ICONOSCOPE in 1923, and KINESCOPE in 1929. These led to the first electronic TV system. His work also made the electron microscope possible.

137

LEADING NAMES IN NATURE, MEDICINE, ANTHROPOLOGY AND BIOLOGY

ADRIAN, Edgar Douglas (1st Baron) [1889-1977]; British physiologist, who worked on sensation and muscular control by nerve impulses, and later on electrical activity of the brain.

ATTENBOROUGH, David Frederick [1926-]; Broadcaster and writer on natural history and related matters. Has taken part in many zoological expeditions, filmed and presented by the BBC.

BANTING, Sir Frederick Grant [1891-1941]; Canadian physiologist, who first prepared (with Charles H. Best) insulin to treat diabetes.

BARNARD, Christiaan [1922-]; South African surgeon, who performed the first heart transplant in 1967.

BARR, Murray [1908-]; Canadian anatomist, who, with a colleague named Bertram, discovered a method of sex determination of a child before birth.

BATESON, Gregory [1904-1980]; American (British-born) anthropologist, whose studies in social psychology amongst primitive peoples have developed into theories concerning schizophrenia.

BAWDEN, Sir Frederick [1908-]; British plant pathologist, who has worked with virus structures and the mechanism of protein formation.

BEADLE, George Wells [1903-]; American biochemist, who discovered that genes regulate chemical events.

BEHRING, Emil Adolf von [1854-1917]; German bacteriologist, who discovered an anti-diphtheria serum, and an anti-toxin for tetanus.

BIFFEN, Sir Rowland Harry [1874-1949]; British geneticist, plant breeder and botanist, who introduced scientific methods into plant breeding.

BINET, Alfred [1854-1911]; French psychologist who devised the Binet tests for measuring intelligence.

BOVET, Daniel [1907-]; Swiss-Italian pharmacologist, who developed antihistamines and other drugs for treating asthma and hay fever, and who researched into tranquilizers and anaesthetics.

BURNET, Sir (Frank) Macfarlane [1899-1985]; Australian physiologist, and an authority on virus diseases.

CALMETTE, Leon Charles Albert [1863-1933]; French bacteriologist, who with Alphonse Guérin, developed the BCG vaccine against tuberculosis.

CANNON, Walter Bradford [1871-1945]; American physiologist, who researched into the digestion and nervous systems of the human body.

CARRELL, Alexis [1873-1944]; French-born American surgeon and biologist, who worked on artificial heart machines, and whose techniques for transplanting arteries, etc., helping to avoid amputations during World War I.

CHAIN, Ernst Boris [1906-1979]; British biochemist, born in Germany, who, with H.W. FLOREY, was able to isolate penicillin.

CRICK, Francis Harry Compton [1916-]; British biophysicist, who helped to discover the structure of DNA (deoxyribonucleic acid, the 'brains' behind the living cell), advancing the understanding of genetics.

DALE, Sir Henry Hallett [1875-1968]; British physiologist, who worked on the chemical transmission of nerve impulses.

DART, Raymond Arthur [1893-]; Australian, later South African anthropologist, who discovered the remains of australopithecines; upright-walking, man-like apes.

DE VRIES, Hugo Marie [1845-1935]; Dutch botanist and plant geneticist, who independently discovered the Mendelian laws of heredity.

DICK-READ, Grantly [1890-1959]; British obstetrician, and author of *Childbirth Without Fear*.

DOBZHANSKY, Theodosius [1900-75]; American geneticist, born in the Ukraine, whose work has been largely in the field of human populations.

DOMAGK, Gerhard [1895-1964]; German biochemist, who discovered the therapeutic use of sulpha drugs, pioneering the way for further research.

DURKHEIM, Emile [1858-1917]; French sociologist, whose work included an important study of suicide and its causes.

ECCLES, Sir John [1903-]; Australian physiologist who discovered the chemical means by which signals are communicated by nerve cells.

EHRLICH, Paul [1854-1915]; German bacteriologist, who worked with Robert KOCH. He discovered chemicals that act on disease-producing organisms without harming normal cells.

EIJKMAN, Christiaan [1858-1930]; Dutch physician and pathologist, who discovered the vita-

Above: Sigmund Freud developed psychoanalysis; Heyerdahl (below) sailed the Atlantic in a papyrus reed boat.

mins which when lacking, cause beriberi.

EINTHOVEN, Willem [1860-1927]; Dutch physiologist who invented a string galvanometer, a precursor of the electro-cardiograph.

ENDERS, John Franklin [1897-1985]; American microbiologist, who discovered a method to culture viruses, which led to the production of anti-polio vaccine.

FABRE, Jean-Henri Casimir [1823-1915]; French entomologist who closely studied the habits of insects and spiders.

FLEMING, Sir Alexander [1881-1955]; British bacteriologist, who in 1928, discovered the curative qualities of penicillin.

FLOREY, Howard Walter [Baron] [1898-1968]; British pathologist, who with Ernst CHAIN, produced purified penicillin for medical use.

FLYNN, John [1880-1951]; Australian Presbyterian minister, who in 1928 launched the Flying Doctor Services in Australia, which served remote areas with flying ambulances, called up by radio

transmitters operated by foot-pedal power.

FRANKLIN, Rosalind [1920-1958]; British X-ray crystallographer who helped uncover the secrets of DNA. Associated with F.H. CRICK, J.D. WATSON and M.H.F. WILKINS.

FREUD, Sigmund [1856-1939]; Austrian neurologist who developed psychoanalysis, teaching that doctors should listen, understand, and interpret. Associated with Carl JUNG.

GALTON, Sir Francis [1822-1911]; British scientist, who constructed weather charts, applied statistics in human heredity, and devised a method of comparing fingerprints.

GEMZELL, Carl [1910-]; Swedish gynaecologist, whose researches helped a large number of infertile women to bear children.

GRAY, Sir James [1891-1975]; British zoologist, whose studies of animal movement greatly changed zoological ideas. He was editor of the *Journal of Experimental Biology*.

HAMMOND, John Hugo [1889-1964]; American electrical and radio engineer, inventor of remote control devices and the variable ship's propeller.

HAUSER, Gayelord [1895-1978]; American nutritionist, born in Austria. Writer on diets and nutrition, and leader of the natural food movement.

HEYERDAHL, Thor [1914-]; Norwegian anthropologist, whose 'Kon-Tiki' expedition in 1947 established the possibility that Polynesians could have originated in South America.

HODGKIN, Sir Alan Lloyd [1914-]; British physiologist, who, with A.F. Huxley, discovered the chemical processes of communication along nerves.

HOPKINS, Sir Frederick Gowland [1861-1947]; British biochemist, who in 1912 discovered the existence of vitamins.

HOUNSFIELD, Godfrey Newbold [1919-]; British engineer, who led in the design of Britain's first computer, and worked on the application of computer techniques to X-rays.

HUGGINS, Charles Brenton [1900-]; American scientist, born in Canada, who in 1966 discovered hormonal treatment for cancer.

HUXLEY, Sir Julian Sorell [1887-1975]; British biologist, and author on biological and zoological subjects. Director-general of UNESCO, 1946 to 1948.

ISAACS, Alick [1921-1967]; British medical scientist of Lithuanian origin, who worked on influenza viruses, and was discoverer of the antivirus Interferon.

JACOB, François [1920-]; French biologist, who studied genetic elements of viruses, and the control of bacterial enzyme production.

JUNG, Carl Gustav [1875-1961]; Swiss psychiatrist, who differentiated people according to types, extraverted and introverted. Associated with Sigmund FREUD.

KELLER, Helen Adams [1880-1968]; American writer and scholar, who became blind and deaf at the age of 19 months. Her struggle against handicap became an inspiration for others.

KENDREW, Sir John Cowdrey [1917-]; British biochemist who determined the structure of proteins, and who worked on myoglobin.

KOCH, Robert [1843-1910]; German bacteriologist, who discovered the cause of anthrax, tuberculosis and cholera.

KÖHLER, Wolfgang [1887-1967]; German psychologist, born in Estonia, an authority on *Gestalt* psychology, which involves the appreciation of patterns rather than of single objects.

KOLFF, Willem [1911-]; American physician, born in the Netherlands, who in 1944 developed the artificial kidney.

KREBS, Sir Hans Adolf [1900-1981]; British biochemist, born in Germany, who discovered the Krebs cycle, which involves the manner in which animals absorb food.

LANDSTEINER, Karl [1868-1943]; Austrian pathologist, who in 1901 discovered the four main human blood groups.

LEAKEY, Louis Seymour Bazett [1903-72]; British anthropologist, who in East Africa, discovered the remains of early types of man, particularly *Zinjanthropus*, 1,750,000 years old.

LEDERBERG, Joshua [1925-]; American geneticist, who, with Edward TATUM, discovered sexual reproduction in bacteria.

LEVI-STRAUSS, Claude [1908-]; French anthropologist, born in Belgium. The founder of structual anthropology.

LISTER, Lord Joseph [1827-1912]; British surgeon, who introduced the useF of carbolic acid spray to kill germs during operations, and thus saved many lives.

LORENZ, Konrad Zacharias [1903-]; Austrian

psychologist and esearcher into animal behaviour; particularly showing that young animals will identify with the species with which it spends is younger years.

MALINOWSKI, Bronislaw [1884-1942]; British anthropologist, born in Poland, who introduced a method of comparison between different racial activities.

MEAD, Margaret [1901-1978]; American anthropologist, whose work includes the idea that the modern world can learn much from other societies.

MEDAWAR, Sir Peter Brian [1915-1987]; British biologist and medical scientist, born in Brazil, who discoverd that immunity is acquired in the embryo stage, or in early infancy.

MINOT, George Richards [1885-1950]; American physician, who specialized in research into the use of the liver.

MONIZ, Antonio Caetano de Abreu Freire Egas [1874-1955]; Portuguese surgeon and statesman; foreign minister of Portugal, 1918 to 1919. He invented prefrontal lobotomy for certain mental patients.

MONOD, Jacques-Lucien [1910-76]; French biochemist, who proposed the mechanism of genetics by means of 'messenger' RNA (ribonucleic acid) synthesis.

MORGAN, Thomas Hunt [1866-1945]; American biologist, the propounder of the theories of genes, and a founder of modern genetics.

MULLER, Hermann Joseph [1890-1967]; American geneticist who worked on artificial transmutation of genes by X-rays.

NORTHROP, John Howard [1891-]; American biochemist, who in 1930 proved that enzymes are proteins.

PAPANICOLAOU, George Nicholas [1883-1962]; American physiologist of Greek birth, who devised the simple Pap smear test for cervical cancer.

PAVLOV, Ivan Petrovich [1849-1936]; Russian physiologist, who discovered how the autonomic nerves control the digestive process.

PERUTZ, Max Ferdinand [1914-]; British biochemist born in Austria, who worked out the structure of the blood protein haemoglobin.

PETERSEN, William Earl [1892-]; American dairy scientist, who experimented on milk secretion and milk fever. Today, milking of cows is

conducted on lines based on his findings.

PIRIE, Norman Wingate [1907-]; British biochemist, who, with Sir Frederick BAWDEN, produced a virus in crystalline form, which led the way to more detailed genetic study.

RICHET, Charles-Robert [1850-1935]; French physiologist, who worked on the reaction of muscles (anaphylaxis), and who also studied psychical phenomena.

RORSCHACH, Hermann [1884-1822]; Swiss psychiatrist, who developed the ink blot test known by his name, and which is used in psychopathological diagnosis.

SABIN, Albert Bruce [1906-]; American microbiologist, born in Russia, who developed the oral vaccine for polio, using live attenuated viruses.

SCHOLL, William [1882-1968]; American physician, who commercially developed the arch support for the foot. A chain of shops was set up in 1904, and in 1910 opened in Britain.

SCHWEITZER, Albert [1875-1965]; French medical missionary (born in Alsace, then Germany), theologian and musician. He established a mission hospital at Lambaréné, in French Equatorial Africa (Gabon).

SHEA, John [1924-]; American surgeon, and a pioneer in the surgery of deafness. Using a plastic replacement for a diseased bone in the middle ear, he restored hearing to sufferers.

SHERRINGTON, Sir Charles [1857-1952]; British physiologist who worked on the nervous system and the effects of reflex actions.

SPOCK, Benjamin McLane [1903-]; American physician, and author of many books on the care of babies. *A Baby's First Year* (1950).

STANLEY, Wendell [1904-1971]; American biochemist who worked on the purification and crystallization of viruses, and who developed a preventive vaccine for influenza.

SUMNER, James Batcheller [1887-1955]; American biochemist, who was the first to crystallize an enzyme.

SZENT-GYORGI, Albert von [1893-1986]; Hungarian-born American biochemist. He worked on the adrenal glands, and studied the biochemistry of muscular contractions.

TATUM, Edward Lawrie [1909-1975]; American biochemist who with G.W. BEADLE researched into molecular genetics, showing how mutations affect genetic chemical reactions.

TEILHARD DE CHARDIN, Pierre [1881-1955]; French palaeontologist, philosopher and R.C. priest, who showed a way of reconciling Christianity and evolutionary theories. In China, was involved in the discovery of the fossil skull of Peking Man (*Homo erectus*).

TEMPLEMAN, William [1911-1970]; British agricultural scientist, who developed selective weed-killers, which kill weeds but leave the main crop unharmed.

THOMPSON, Sir D'Arcy Wentworth [1860-1948]; British zoologist and classicist, famed for his book *On Growth and Form* (1917).

THORNDIKE, Edward Lee [1874-1949]; American psychologist, who devised intelligence tests, and who was a pioneer in the study of animal intelligence.

TINBERGEN, Nikolas [1907-]; Dutch experimental zoologist, and a pioneer in the work of studying animal behaviour.

TISELIUS, Arne Wilhelm Kaurin [1902-1971]; Swedish chemist, who applied electrophoresis to the analysis of proteins, especially serum proteins.

TJIO, Joe Hin [1919-]; American geneticist, of Indonesian birth. He has done important work in the field of chromosomes, discovering that Man has 46, not 48, as was formerly thought.

TSWETT, Mikhail Semenovich [1872-1919]; Russian chemist and botanist, and inventor of the technique of chromatography.

TURING, Alan Mathison [1912-1954]; British mathematician who pioneered early computer programming techniques.

WAKSMAN, Selman Abraham [1888-1973]; American microbiologist, born in Russia, who isolated two antibiotics: antimycin and streptomycin.

WALLACE, Alfred Russel [1823-1913]; British naturalist, who independently from Charles Darwin developed the theory of natural selection. *Contributions to the Theory of Natural Selection* (1870).

WATSON, James Dewey [1928-]; American biologist, who with F.H.C. CRICK, established the structure and function of DNA;.

WEISMANN, August Friedrich Leopold [1834-1914]; German geneticist, remembered for his chromosome theory of heredity.

WILKINS, Maurice Hugh Frederick [1916-]; British biophysicist, who suggested that the molecules of DNA had a helical structure.

ZUCKERKANDL, Emile [1906-]; French biochemist, of Austrian birth. His study of the chemical differences of animals added a new dimension to investigations into evolution.

ZUCKERMAN, Sir Solly (Baron) [1904-]; British zoologist and educationalist. Researched extensively on vertebrates, and was also scientific advisor to the British Defence Ministry.

Louis Blériot became the first person to fly the English Channel in a heavier-than-air craft on 25 July 1909.

A famous fighter of World War II – the British Supermarine Spitfire.

Transport and Exploration

AIR EVENTS AND MAJOR DISASTERS OF THE TWENTIETH CENTURY

1903 17 December: The WRIGHT brothers make their first controlled aeroplane flight.

1906 3 March: The Vuia I aircraft, built by the Romanian aviator Trajan Vuia, is fitted with pneumatic tyres and tested at Montesson, France. November: In France, the firm of Voisin Frères sets up in Billancourt for the manufacture of aircraft.
22 August: The Brazilian, Alberto Santos-Dumont, makes the first aircraft flight in Europe.

1907 August: In France, at Issyles-Moulineaux, the first aerodrome, complete with hangars, is built.
13 November: French cycle-dealer Paul Cornu flies a twin rotor helicopter in a test near Lisieux, France.

1908 10 June: In the USA, the first flying-club, the Aeronautical Society of New York, starts.
17 September: In the USA, Lieut. Thomas Selfridge is killed after a crash in an aircraft with Orville Wright at Fort Meyer, Virginia.
30 October: In France, Henry Farman, in a 50hp Voisin, flies 20 miles across country from Mourmelon to Rheims.

1909 28 June to 18 July: In France, the air display Concours d'Aviation takes place at Douai.
25 July: Louis BLÉRIOT, French aviator, makes the first flight across the English Channel in 37 minutes.
29 August: The world's first air race is held in Rheims, France. The Gordon Bennett Cup is won by Glenn Curtiss, of the USA.
7 September: Eugéne Lefebvre, a pilot testing a Wright A aircraft at Juvisy, France, is killed.

Experiments with gliders led the Wright brothers to make the first controlled, powered flight in a heavier-than-air craft on 17 December 1903.

1910 28 March: The world's first sea-plane, designed by Henri Fabre, takes off from the water at Marti-gues, near Marseilles.
28 April. Claude Grahame-White makes the first flight by night from Roade, Northants, to Lichfield, Staffs, in England.
10 May: The first air display is held at Hendon, near London.
2 June: C.S. ROLLS flies the English Channel both directions in a Short-Wright biplane.
12 July: C.S. Rolls, piloting a Wright Flyer near Bournemouth, England, crashes and is killed.
27 September: The first twin-en-gined aircraft is test-flown in France.
2 October: In Milan, Italy, two aircraft collide: Captain Dickson's Farman, and M. Thomas's Antoin-ette.
23 October: The Infante Don Al-fonso, cousin of King Alfonso of Spain, becomes a qualified pilot.
October: The first fighter aircraft is shown at the Paris Aero Show. It is a Voisin biplane fitted with a machine-gun.
14 November: In the USA, the pilot Eugéne Ely takes off in a Curtiss biplane from the flight-deck of the light cruiser Birmingham.
1911 12 April: Pierre Prier flies non-stop from London to Paris in a 50hp BLÉRIOT in 3 hours 56 minutes.
11 July: J. Beaumont flies a com-plete circuit of the British Isles.
August: In the USA, Hugh Robinson lands a seaplane on Lake Michigan to rescue a pilot who had crashed.
9 September: The British Post Office starts the first air mail service in the world. Mail is flown from Hendon, near London, to Windsor, Berks.
17 September: At Hendon, near London, Lieut. R.A. Cammell of the Air Battalion, Royal Engineers, is killed after his Valkyrie monoplane crashes.

18 September: The Short S.39, Britain's first twin-engined aircraft, is test flown at Eastchurch.
18 November: At Barrow-in-Fur-ness, Britain's first seaplane flies, piloted by Comdr. Oliver Schwann of the Royal Navy. The machine is an adapted Avro D biplane.
1912 10 January: The world's first flying-boat, designed by Glenn Curtiss, makes its maiden flight at Ham-mondsport, New York State.
12 June: In Tripoli, North Africa, the 2nd Aerial Company of the Italian Aviation Corps makes a night air raid on Turkish lines.
9 September: J. Vedrines becomes the first man to fly at over 100 mph, reaching a speed of 107 mph (172 kph).
1913 13 May: Igor SIKORSKY, Russian en-gineer, builds and flies the first four-engined aircraft.
20 August. In France, Adolphe Pég-oud is the first pilot to parachute from an aircraft.
August: In the USA, at Hammonds-port, N.Y., an automatic pilot is fitted to a Curtiss flying boat.
6 September: Adolphe Pégoud is the first pilot to loop the loop.
1914 1 January: In the USA, the world's first airline starts operating. It is the St PetersburgTampa Airboat line, of St Petersburg, Florida.
February: The first aerial torpedo is released from a Farman biplane by General A. Guidoni, of the Italian army.
6 June: The first flight taking an aircraft out of sight of land is made, on a journey from Scotland to Nor-way.
1915 19 February: Two RFC B.E.2C air-craft make a raid on Cambrai aero-drome by night.
31 May: An LZ 38 Zeppelin makes an air raid on London, hitting a house at Stoke Newington, North London.

12 December: The first all-metal aircraft, a Junkers J.1, is test-flown at Dessau, Germany.

1916 15 to 19 April: 19,000 pounds (8600kg.) of supplies are air-lifted to a besieged garrison at Kut al-Imara, Iraq, by the 30th Squadron, RAF, which makes 140 flights in all.

November: The first heavy British bomber to become operational, the Handley Page O/100, is delivered to the Royal Naval Air Service at Dunkirk.

1919 6 February: In Germany, the first continuing airline, Deutsche Luft-Reederei, is established, flying between Berlin and Weimar. Passengers were carried from 28 February.

16 to 25 May: Lieut.-Comdr. A.C. Read and five crew members of the US Navy fly a Curtis NC-4 flying boat from Newfoundland to Lisbon in 52 hours 31 minutes.

May: The Duke of York (later King GEORGE VI) becomes a pilot.

14 to 15 June: Capt. John ALCOCK and Lieut. Arthur Whitten BROWN fly a Vickers Vimy aircraft non-stop from Newfoundland to Galway, Ireland in 16 hours 27 minutes.

July: The British airship R34 makes the first two-way transatlantic flight, from Scotland to New York and back. 32 people are on board.

25 August: The first regular international airline service begins between London and Paris, operated by Aircraft Transport and Travel Ltd., using converted biplane bombers.

7 October: British Aerial Transport start a London-Amsterdam airline service.

12 November to 13 December: Ross and Keith Smith in a Vickers Vimy, fly from London to Australia in 135 hours.

1920 4 February to 20 March: The first flight from Britain to South Africa is made, by two South Africans, Lieut.-Col. Pierre van Ryneveld and Flt.-

Lieut. C.J. Quinton Brand.

3 July: The Royal Air Force hold an Air Display at Hendon, North London.

14 December: A Handley Page airliner en route from Cricklewood to Paris, crashes at Golders Green, with the loss of four lives.

1921 21 - 24 February: In the USA, Lieut. William Coney flies across the country from San Diego, California to Jacksonville, Florida.

3 August: The first aerial crop-dusting operation takes place at Troy, Ohio, when Lieut. John B. Macready flies a Curtiss JN6 over a patch of ground infested with caterpillars.

1922 7 April: In France, a Farman Goliath aircraft of Grands Express collides with a Daimler Airways DH18 over Poix.

1923 9 January: Juan de la Cierva makes his first flight in Madrid in his autogiro.

1924 1 April: In Britain, the airline Imperial Airways is formed.

7 April to 28 April: The first round the world flight is made by US aviators Lieut. L.H. Smith in a Douglas *Chicago* and Lieut. Erik Nelson in a Douglas *New Orleans*, flying from, and returning to, Seattle, and making 57 stops.

1926 March: Alan COBHAM flies from Croydon, near London, to Cape Town and back.

8 to 9 May: Lieut.-Comdr. Richard BYRD of the US Navy, and Floyd Bennet make the first successful flight over the North Pole, using a Fokker monoplane.

28 December: Imperial Airways begins its passenger and mail service to India.

1927 1 May: Cooked meals are served for the first time on a British airliner, on Imperial Airways' London to Paris service.

20 to 21 May. Charles A. LINDBERGH

flies from New York to Paris in $33\frac{1}{2}$ hours, in the first solo non-stop transatlantic flight, in his Ryan monoplane, *Spirit of St Louis.*

1928 7 to 22 February: Bert Hinkler makes the first solo flight from England to Australia.

31 May to 9 June: The Australian aviator, Charles Kingsford SMITH and three others in *Southern Cross,* a Fokker F.VIIb-3m aircraft, fly from Oakland, San Francisco to Brisbane, in the first aerial crossing of the Pacific.

1929 24 to 26 April: The first non-stop flight is made from England (Cranwell, Lincs) to India (Karachi).

8 to 29 August: The German airship *Graf Zeppelin* makes a round the world flight.

1930 5 to 24 May: Amy JOHNSON becomes the first woman to fly solo from England to Australia. The flight takes $19\frac{1}{2}$ days.

7 October: The British airship R101 crashes near Beauvais, France. Only six people survive of the 54 aboard.

Frank WHITTLE, British engineer, patents a design for a jet engine.

1932 27 April: Imperial Airways starts its Britain-South Africa airmail service.

20 to 21 May: Amelia EARHART becomes the first woman to fly solo across the Atlantic. She flies from Newfoundland to Ireland in 15 hours 18 minutes.

18 to 19 August: J.A. MOLLISON makes the first solo transatlantic flight from east to west.

1933 6 to 8 February: O.R. Gayford and G.R. Nicholetts set up a world record for non-stop distance flying of 5341 miles (8531km) (from Cranwell, England, to Walvis Bay, S.W. Africa).

13 April: Lord Clydesdale flies over the summit of Mount Everest.

15 to 22 May: Wiley POST, flying the Lockheed Vega *Winnie Mae,* makes the first round the world solo flight

in 7 days, 18 hours and 49 minutes.

9 December: Imperial Airways and Indian Trans-Continental Airways start the London - Singapore airline service.

1934 30 January: The Russian balloon *Osoaviakhim* ascends 13 miles (21km) into the stratosphere. During the descent, the car tears loose and crashes, killing the three occupants.

24 September: Imperial Airways starts its England-Australia airmail service.

22 October to 4 November: Charles Kingsford SMITH and A. Taylor make the first Australia-USA flight over the Pacific.

1935 13 April: Imperial Airways and Qantas start a London - Australia airline service, which allows $12\frac{1}{2}$ days to Brisbane.

Pan American Airways begin a trans-Pacific service from California, U.S.A.

1936 August to October: 8899 Moorish troops with guns and equipment are carried from Spanish Morocco to Spain in 20 Junkers 52/3 aircraft to support General Franco's invasion during the Spanish Civil War.

29 September: F.R.D. Swain sets up a world altitude record of 49,967 feet (15,230 metres).

5 to 16 October: Jean BATTEN makes the first direct flight from England to New Zealand.

1939 27 to 28 June: Pan American Airways start the first transatlantic passenger flights, using the Boeing 314 flying-boat *Yankee Clipper* between Botwood, Newfoundland and Southampton, England.

24 August: The first turbojet aircraft flies; a Heinkel He 178 designed by Dr Hans von Ohain and flown by Flug Kapitän Erich Warsitz at Rostock-Marienhe, Germany.

2 December: Imperial Airways and British Airways merge to form the

British Overseas Airways Corporation.

1941 15 May: The first British turbojet aircraft, the Gloster-Whittle E28/39, flies; designed by Frank Whittle and flown by Flt.Lieut. P.E.G. Sayer at Cranwell.

1942 24 December: The German V1 guided missile is first launched at Peenemünde.

1944 2 January: Helicopters are used in warfare for the first time, when three Sikorsky R.4s perform patrol duty with an Atlantic convoy.
25 July: The Messerschmitt 262 is the first jet fighter to be used in combat.
27 July: The Gloster Meteor is the first British jet fighter to be used in combat.

1945 17 November: H.J. Wilson sets up a new world speed record of 606 mph (975 kph) in an RAF Meteor jet.

1947 14 October: Capt. Charles Yeager of the USAF flies at 670 mph (1078 kph) supersonic speed in a Bell XS-1 rocket plane, in California.

1948 23 March: John Cunningham sets up a world altitude record of 59,492 feet (18,133 metres).
12 July: Six RAF de Havilland Vampires are the first jet aircraft to fly the Atlantic.
16 July: The first British turboprop airliner flies: the Vickers Viscount V.630.

1953 18 May: In the USA, Jacqueline Cochrane, piloting a North American F-86 Sabre, becomes the first woman to fly faster than sound.

1954 3 August: The first VTOL (vertical take-off and landing) aircraft, the 'Flying Bedstead', or Rolls-Royce TMR is flown.

1955 23 August: A Canberra PR7 flies from Croydon, near London, to New York and back in 14 hours 45.4 seconds.
28 December: The Comet 3 aircraft completes its round-the-world flight.

Amy Johnson, the first woman to fly solo from England to Australia.

finishing the Montreal-London sector in 6 hours 18 minutes.

1956 10 March: A Fairey Delta 2 research aircraft flown by Peter Twiss sets up a new world speed record of 1132 mph (1823 kph).
30 June: Two US airliners collide in a thunderstorm in Arizona, with the loss of 128 lives.

1957 January: Three USAAF Stratofortresses fly round the world non-stop, covering 23,452 miles (40,960km) in 45 hours.
29 June: A Bristol Britannia completes the first non-stop flight by a civil aircraft from London to the US Pacific Coast; 5100 miles (8207km) in 14 hours 40 minutes.
16 July: A US Navy Crusader flies non-stop across America; 2460 miles (3958km) in 3 hours 23.5 minutes.
20 August: A USAAF balloon sets up a world altitude record of 102,000 feet (310,896 metres)

6 November: The world's first vertical take-off airliner flies near Maidenhead, England.

1958 1 January: A BOAC Britannia sets up a world record airline flight of 7 hours 57 minutes for London-New York.

6 February: Seven members of the British football team Manchester United are among 21 people killed in an air crash at Munich, West Germany.

7 May: Major H. Johnson, of the USAAF, in a Lockheed Starfighter, sets up an altitude record of 91,248 feet (27,812 metres) [17.28 miles; 27.8km].

16 May: Capt. W. Irwin, of the USAAF, in a Lockheed Starfighter, sets up a world speed record of 1404.18 mph (2259.7km).

4 October: A Comet 4 airliner leaves London on the first passenger jet service over the Atlantic.

1959 17 February: An aircraft taking the Turkish Prime Minister, Mr Menderes, to Britain, crashes at Gatwick Airport with the loss of 15 lives. Mr Menderes is unhurt.

1960 4 August: A USAAF rocket-propelled research aircraft sets up a speed record for manned aircraft of 2150 mph (3460 kph).

12 August: A USAAF rocket aircraft sets up an altitude record of 131,000 feet (119,786 metres) [24.8 miles; 39.9km].

19 November: The Hawker Siddeley P.1127 (Kestrel) VTOL aircraft is flown.

16 December: In the US, two airliners collide in a snowstorm over New York, with the loss of 137 lives.

1961 26 May: A USAAF bomber flies the Atlantic in little more than three hours at a average speed of 1000 mph (1600kph). The aircraft crashes a few days later.

1967 9 July: Sheila SCOTT lands at Cape Town, breaking the women's solo flight record set up by Amy Johnson in 1936.

11 December: The prototype of the supersonic airliner Concorde is shown for the first time in Toulouse, France.

1968 31 December: The Russian TU-144 is the first supersonic airliner to fly.

1969 9 February: The Boeing 747, world's largest airliner, makes its maiden flight.

2 March: Concorde makes a 27-minute flight from Toulouse. This Anglo-French aircraft is the first supersonic airliner to fly in France or Britain.

9 April: Concorde makes a 22-minute maiden flight near Bristol, England.

1970 4 January: The London to Sydney air race is won by two Britons, Capt. William Bright and Capt. Frank Buxton.

12 January: The first jumbo jet, a Pan American Boeing 747, lands at London Heathrow.

25 March: British Concorde 002 makes its first supersonic flight, reaching a speed of 700 mph (1127 kph).

21 October: Caledonian Airways takes over British United Airways.

1971 14 April: A BOAC jumbo jet makes its first flight between London and New York.

30 July: A Japanese Boeing 727 collides in mid-air with a jet fighter, with the loss of 162 lives.

1972 8 March: The 192ft (59 metre) airship Europa flies in Britain; the first one to do so for 20 years.

28 August: While taking part in an air race, Prince William of Gloucester and his co-pilot are killed when their plane crashes soon after take-off near Wolverhampton, England.

1973 3 June: At the Paris Air Show, a Russian Tupolev-144 supersonic airliner explodes and crashes on the town of Goussainville, with the loss of 14 lives.

26 September: Concorde flies from Washington to Paris in three hours 33 minutes.

1974 3 March: In the world's worst air disaster to date, a Turkish DC10 crashes after take-off from Orly airport in Paris, with the loss of 346 lives.

1975 4 April: A US aircraft carrying Vietnamese orphans to the USA crashes after take-off from Saigon, with the loss of 206 lives.

29 November: British racing driver Graham HILL, piloting a light plane, dies with five others after a crash in thick fog at Elstree, England.

26 December: The Russian Tupolev TU-144 starts its scheduled flights by carrying mail and freight from Moscow to Alma Ata, a distance of 2000 miles (3200km).

1976 21 January: Concorde scheduled passenger flights are started by British Airways and Air France.

24 May: Concordes of Air France and British Airways fly to Washington, inaugurating the first commercial supersonic flights to North America.

10 September: A British Airways Trident en route from London to Istanbul, and a Yugoslav DC-9 en route to Cologne from Split, collide at 33,000 ft (10,000 metres) over Yugoslavia, with the loss of 176 lives.

13 December: A Pan Am Boeing 747 makes the longest non-stop passenger flight from Sydney to San Francisco in 13 hours 14 minutes.

1977 27 March: In the world's worst air disaster, a Pan Am jumbo jet collides with a KLM jumbo jet at Tenerife, with the loss of 576 lives.

29 April: Hawker Siddeley, British Aircraft Corporation and Scottish Aviation combine to form the British Aerospace Corporation.

22 November: Concordes of British Airways and Air France start regular scheduled flights from London and Paris to New York.

1978 20 April: A South Korean Boeing 707, 1000 miles (1600km) off course, is fired at by a Russian fighter aircraft and forced to land at Murmansk. Two passengers are killed and 13 others injured.

17 August: The first balloon crossing of the Atlantic, from Presque Isle, Maine, USA, to Evreux, Normandy, France, is completed by three Americans in 137 hours, six minutes.

1979 12 June: Bryan Allen, an American, makes the first man-powered flight across the English Channel, pedalling his *Gossamer Albatross* from Folkestone to Cap Gris Nez in 2 hours 50m minutes.

28 November: A New Zealand DC-10 aircraft crashes on to the slopes of an Antarctic volcano, with the loss of 257 lives.

1980 19 August: A Saudi Arabian TriStar aircraft bursts into flames as it crash-lands at Riyadh, with the loss of 301 lives.

4 December: The Prime Minister of Portugal, Dr Francisco da Carneiro, is killed after a light aircraft crashes at Lisbon, with the loss of six other lives.

1981 27 May: Off the Florida coast, an electronic warfare aircraft crashes on to the flight deck of the US aircraft carrier *Nimitz* with the loss of 14 lives.

7 July: The first flight across the English Channel by a solar-powered machine is made by the American-built *Solar Challenger*.

22 August: Julian Knott makes the first crossing of the English Channel by solar-powered balloon in one and a quarter hours.

1982 5 February: The British airline Laker Airways collapses with debts of

£270,000,000 ($351,000,000).

1983 14 April: A Spitfire fighter plane from World War II is sold for £260,000 ($338,000).

1984 19 July: Lynn Rippelmeyer is the first woman to captain a Boeing 747 across the Atlantic.

25 July: Patrick Lindsay flies a replica of Louis Blériot's aircraft from Calais to Dover to mark the 75th anniversary of Blériot's flight. This is a sponsored event to raise money for charity.

1985 12 Aug: A Japan Airlines Boeing 747 crashes into Mt Osutaka; only four of the 525 people on board survive the worst-ever air disaster involving one aircraft.

1986 2 April: A terrorist bomb explodes on board a TWA jet flying from Rome to Athens: four passengers die.

23 Dec: Dick Rutan and Jeana Yeager in *Voyager* complete a nine-day non-stop flight around the world, covering 40,269 km at an average speed of 186 km/hr.

1987 28 May: Mathias Rust, a West German teenager, lands a Cessna light plane in Moscow's Red Square, hav-

Concorde, the supersonic airliner, can cruise at a speed of 2000Km/hr (1200 mph) for almost three hours. The nose can be moved down to give the pilot a better view of the runway at take-off and landing. Concorde *carries up to 140 passengers.*

ing flown through Soviet air defences. Rust is jailed; Soviet generals are reportedly sacked.

2-3 July: *Virgin Atlantic Flyer* is the first hot-air balloon to fly the Atlantic (west-east). Crew are Richard Branson and Per Lindstrand.

1988 9 March: US B1-B bomber is cleared for low-level operations after suspension following a fatal crash in Colorado in October 1987.

4 Sept: Italian airforce jets collide during display at a West German air show. More than 50 people die.

21 Oct: British Airways (which now includes British Caledonian) announces it will add more Boeings to its fleet, in preference to the European Airbus A320.

THE EXPLORATION OF SPACE

1957 4 Oct: In USSR, the world's first artificial satellite, Sputnik 1, is launched from Baikonur.
3 Nov: The USSR launches Sputnik 2, which carries the dog, Laika.

1958 31 Jan: The first American artificial satellite, Explorer 1, is launched from Cape Canaveral, by Juno I ballistic missile.
1 Oct: In the USA, the National Aeronautics and Space Administration (NASA) is inaugurated.
12 Dec: A Jupiter missile is launched in the USA, with a nose-cone containing a monkey, but this is lost at sea.
18 Dec: The USA initiates 'Project Score', and launches an Atlas missile which sends back a tape-recorded message of President Eisenhower's Christmas message.

1959 2 Jan: The USSR launches Luna 1 in an attempt to reach the Moon, but the projectile misses, and goes into orbit around the Sun.
28 May: A nose-cone containing two monkeys is launched from Cape Canaveral, and this is later recovered. One monkey dies.
12 Sept: The USSR launches Luna 2, which reaches the Moon.
4 Oct: Luna 3 is launched, which reaches the Moon, and circles it, photographing the far side.

1960 11 Aug: Discoverer 13 is launched by the US Air Force, and the capsule parachutes back into the sea.
12 Aug: In the USA, NASA launches Echo 1, the first communications satellite.
18 Aug: Discoverer 14 is launched by the US Air Force, and the capsule is recovered in the air by the aircraft C-119.
19 to 20 Aug: The USSR launches Sputnik 5, containing the two dogs, Strelka and Belka, which are recovered alive after making 17 orbits of the Earth.
1 Dec: The USSR launches Sputnik 6, containing two more dogs, Pchelka and Mushka. The satellite orbits Earth for 24 hours, but on re-entry, it burns up, destroying its passengers.

1961 31 Jan: A chimpanzee named Ham is recovered from a Mercury capsule after a sub-orbital flight.
25 March: The USSR makes a trial launching of a Vostok spacecraft, which contains two dogs, Zvesdochka and Chernushka.
12 April: The USSR launches a man into space. He is Lieut. Yuri Gagarin, in Vostok 1, who makes a complete circuit of the Earth in 108 minutes.
5 May: In the USA, NASA launches the Mercury 3 spacecraft *Freedom 7*, carrying Comdr. Alan B. Shepard on a suborbital flight.

The space rocket Apollo 2 at take-off.

151

21 July: NASA launches the Mercury 4 spacecraft *Liberty Bell 7*, carrying Lieut.-Col. Virgil I. Grissom on a suborbital flight. The spacecraft splashes down and sinks, but Grissom is recovered.

6 to 7 Aug: The USSR launches Vostok 2, with cosmonaut Major Gherman Titov aboard. The spacecraft completes 17 Earth revolutions in 25 hours 18 minutes.

29 Nov: NASA launches Mercury 5 capsule with the chimpanzee Enos aboard. The animal is recovered later after the capsule makes two orbits.

1962 20 Feb: Lieut.-Col. John Glenn becomes the first American to orbit the Earth in space, after Mercury 6 capsule *Friendship 7* is launched. It makes three Earth revolutions in a flight lasting 4 hours 55 minutes. The capsule is recovered safely in the Atlantic.

24 May: Lieut.-Comdr. M. Scott Carpenter is launched in Mercury 7 spacecraft *Aurora 7* and makes three Earth revolutions in 4 hours 56 minutes. The capsule is recovered in the Atlantic.

10 July: *Telstar 1* is launched, the first private communications satellite, which allows live TV to be transmitted between Europe and America.

11 to 15 Aug: In the USSR, Major Andrian Nikolayev in Vostok 3, makes 64 Earth revolutions in 94 hours 22 minutes. Televised pictures are transmitted.

12 to 15 Aug: In Vostok 4, Lieut.-Col. Pavel Popovich makes 48 Earth revolutions in 70 hours 57 minutes. The spacecraft passes within four miles of Vostok 3.

27 Aug: NASA launches Mariner 2 spacecraft to explore Venus.

3 Oct: NASA launches Mercury 8 spacecraft *Sigma 7*, with astronaut Comdr. Walter M. Schirra aboard. He completes six revolutions of the Earth in 9 hours 13 minutes, 11 seconds. The capsule is safely recovered in the Pacific.

14 Dec: Mariner 2 flies close to Venus, and discovers that the planet has a heavy atmosphere consisting mostly of carbon dioxide.

1963 7 May: *Telstar 2* is launched.

16 to 19 June: Soviet cosmonaut Jr.-Lieut. Valentina Tereshkova becomes the first woman in space. She is aboard Vostok 6, which makes 48 Earth revolutions in 70 hours 50 minutes, and which passes within 3 miles of Vostok 5.

1964 28 July: NASA launches Ranger 7 to reach the Moon and take photographs.

19 Aug: NASA launches Syncom 3 communications satellite which relays the opening ceremony of the Olympic Games from Tokyo.

12 to 13 Oct: Three Soviet cosmonauts, Col. Vladimir Komarov, Dr Konstantin Feoktistov and Dr Boris Yegorov in Voskhod 1 make 16 Earth revolutions in 24 hours 17 minutes 3 seconds. This is the first three-man crew in space.

28 Nov: NASA launches Mariner 4 to explore Mars.

1965 18 to 19 March: Soviet cosmonauts Col. Pavel Belyayev and Lieut.-Col. Alexei Leonov in Voskhod 2 make 17 Earth revolutions in 26 hours 2 minutes 17 seconds. Col. Leonov makes the first space walk, lasting 10 minutes.

23 March: US astronauts Lieut.-Col. Virgil I. Grissom and Lieut.-Comdr. John W. Young in Gemini 3 make three revolutions of the Earth in 4 hours 53 minutes. This is the first US two-man space crew. The spacecraft is pilot-manoeuvred during orbit.

6 April: The commercial communications satellite *Early Bird* (Intelsat 1) is launched from Cape Canaveral. It is first used for TV on 2nd May.

3 to 7 June: NASA launches Gemini 4, with astronauts Capt. James A. McDivitt and Capt. Edward H. White aboard. It completes 62 Earth revolutions in 97 hours 56 minutes 31 seconds. Captain White makes a space-walk lasting 21 minutes, manoeuvring in space by using a gas gun.

14 July: Mariner 4 reaches Mars and takes 21 close-up pictures, showing surface craters, but no artificial 'canals'. The atmosphere is mostly carbon dioxide.

4 to 18 Dec: NASA launches Gemini 7, with astronauts Major Frank Borman and Lieut.-Comdr. James A. Lovell aboard. It makes 206 Earth revolutions in 330 hours 35 minutes 17 seconds, and meets Gemini 6 in orbit.

15 to 16 Dec: NASA successfully launches Gemini 6, with astronauts Comdr. Walter M. Schirra and Capt.

Thomas P. Stafford aboard. It completes 16 Earth revolutions in 25 hours 51 minutes 43 seconds, meeting Gemini 7 in orbit.

1966 31 Jan: The USSR launches Luna 9 to reach the Moon.

3 Feb: Luna 9 reaches the Moon, landing in the Ocean of Storms. TV pictures are sent back to Earth.

18 March: Astronauts Neil A. Armstrong and Capt. David R. Scott aboard Gemini 8 are launched by NASA. They complete $6\frac{1}{2}$ Earth revolutions in 10 hours 41 minutes 26 seconds. During the flight, the spacecraft docks with Gemini Agena target vehicle. A thruster malfunctions, but the astronauts return safely.

31 March: The USSR launches Luna 10 to reach the Moon.

3 April: Luna 10 reaches the Moon and becomes its first artificial satellite.

10 May: NASA launches Surveyor 1 to reach the Moon.

1 June: Surveyor 1 makes a soft landing on the Moon in the Ocean of Storms, after a flight lasting 63 hours 36 minutes, and sends back TV pictures.

3 to 6 June: NASA launches Gemini 9, with astronauts Capt. Thomas P. Stafford and Lieut. Eugene A. Cernan aboard. It makes 45 Earth orbits in 72 hours 20 minutes 50 seconds. An attempt is made to dock in space with a Target Docking Adaptor, but the Target's nose shroud fails to jettison. Lieut. Cernan makes a 2 hour 8 minute spacewalk.

11 to 15 Nov: NASA launches Gemini 12, with Lieut.-Comdr. James A. Lovell and Major Edwin E. Aldrin aboard. It makes 59 orbits in 94 hours 34 minutes 31 seconds, and docks with an Agena target vehicle, with Major Aldrin working outside the spacecraft for over five hours. The first photograph is made in space of a solar eclipse.

21 Dec: The USSR launches Luna 13 to reach the Moon.

24 Dec: Luna 13 reaches the Moon, landing in the Ocean of Storms, and making close-up pictures of objects.

1967 27 Jan: Lieut.-Col. Virgil I. Grissom, Lieut.-Col. Edward H. White, and Lieut.-Comdr. Roger Chaffee die after their command module catches fire during a launch rehearsal.

23 to 24 April: In the USSR, Col. Vladimir Komarov, cosmonaut, is killed in spacecraft Soyuz 1, when the parachute lines of the re-entry module become entangled after returning from orbit. The module crashes to Earth from a height of four miles (6.5 km).

12 June: The USSR launches Venera 4 to reach Venus.

14 June: NASA launches Mariner 5 to reach Venus.

18 Oct: Venera 4 reaches Venus, releasing a 1-metre spherical package at 28,000 miles (45,000 km) which parachutes on to the planet. The atmosphere is almost entirely carbon dioxide, and there is no magnetic field.

1968 27 March: Col. Yuri Gagarin and Col. Vladimir Seryogin die in an aircraft accident.

14 Sept: The USSR launches Zond 5 to reach and orbit the Moon. It carries tortoises, wine flies, mealworms, bacteria, plants and seeds. It returns successfully, to splash down in the Indian Ocean.

11 to 22 Oct: Capt. Walter M. Schirra, Major Donn F. Eisele and R. Walter Cunningham in Apollo 7 are launched by NASA and make 163 orbits in 260 hours 9 minutes and 3 seconds. They make live TV broadcasts from space.

21 to 27 Dec: NASA launches Apollo 8 to orbit the Moon. Aboard are Col. Frank Borman, Capt. James A. Lovell, Lieut.-Col. William Anders. The Moon is orbited 10 times in 20 hours 6 minutes, reaching to within 70 miles of the Moon's surface, and sending TV pictures back to Earth.

1969 14 to 17 Jan: The USSR launches Soyuz 4, with cosmonaut Col. Vladimir Shatalov aboard. It completes 48 orbits in 71 hours 14 minutes, and docks in space with Soyuz 5.

15 to 18 Jan: The USSR launches Soyuz 5, with cosmonauts Col. Boris Volynov, Alexei Yeliseyev and Col. Yevgeny Khrunov aboard. It docks with Soyuz 4, when Yeliseyev and Khrunov space-walk to that spacecraft and return to Earth on board. Col. Khrunov returns alone in Soyuz 5.

24 Feb: NASA launches Mariner 6 to approach Mars. 3 to 13 March: NASA launches Apollo 9 into orbit around the

Earth. Aboard are Col. James A. McDivitt, Col. David R. Scott, and Russell L. Schweickart. It completes 151 orbits in 241 hours 54 seconds. Two astronauts transfer from the command module to the lunar landing vehicle for about seven hours, and Schweickart makes a spacewalk of 37½ minutes.

27 March: NASA launches Mariner 7 to approach Mars.

18 to 26 May: NASA launches Apollo 10 in a full rehearsal for the Moon landings. Aboard are Col. Thomas P. Stafford, Comdr. John W. Young, and Comdr. Eugene A. Cernan. The spacecraft orbits the Moon, and two astronauts in the lunar module *Snoopy* are separated from the command module *Charlie Brown* to fly within 9½ miles of the Moon's surface. The command module makes 31 orbits of the Moon, in 61 hours 34 minutes.

13 July: The USSR launches the automatic Luna 15 which crashes into the Sea of Crises. This coincides with the Apollo 11 mission, but does not interfere with it.

16 to 24 July: NASA launches Apollo 11, with Neil A. Armstrong, Lieut.-Col. Michael Collins, and Col. Edwin E. Aldrin aboard. While in orbit around the Moon, the lunar module *Eagle* separates from the command module *Columbia*, carrying Armstrong and Aldrin to the Moon's surface. *Eagle* lands in the Sea of Tranquility, and on 20 July, Armstrong sets foot on the Moon, followed 15 minutes later by Aldrin. They stay on the Moon 21 hours 36 minutes 21 seconds, collecting samples, blasting off in the *Eagle* lunar module, and linking up with the command module *Columbia*. They splash down safely in the Pacific.

31 July: Mariner 6 flies by Mars, taking photographs, and approaching to within 2000 miles (3200 km) of the planet.

5 Aug: Mariner 7 flies by Mars, taking photographs, and showing surface character of the planet.

7 to 14 Aug: The USSR launches Zond 7 on a flight to orbit the Moon. This is a computer-controlled operation, and the spacecraft approaches to within 1243 miles (2000 km) of the Moon's surface. The craft lands back in the USSR.

11 to 16 Oct: The USSR launches Soyuz 6, with Col. Georgi Shonin and Valery Kubasov aboard. It makes 75 orbits in 118 hours 42 minutes. The spacecraft makes a group flight with Soyuz 7 and Soyuz 8, during which Kubasov performs welding and smelting experiments in space.

12 to 17 Oct: The USSR launches Soyuz 7, with Col. Viktor Gorbatko aboard. It makes 75 orbits in 118 hours 41 minutes, and takes part in group flight with Soyuz 6 and Soyuz 8.

13 to 18 Oct: The USSR launches Soyuz 8, with Col. Vladimir Shatalov and Alexei Yeliseyev aboard. It makes 75 orbits in 118 hours 41 minutes, and takes part in a group flight with Soyuz 6 and Soyuz 7.

14 to 24 Nov: NASA launches Apollo 12 on a mission to the Moon. Aboard are Comdr. Charles Conrad, Comdr. Richard F. Gordon, and Comdr. Alan L. Bean. Lunar module *Intrepid* separates from the command module *Yankee Clipper*, and lands in the Ocean of Storms, carrying Conrad and Bean, who spend a total of nearly eight hours on the surface on two days. They blast off and link up with the command module, after spending 31 hours, 31 minutes on the Moon. The command module makes 45 orbits of the Moon in 88 hours 56 minutes. The total flight time in all is 244 hours 36 minutes 25 seconds.

1970   11 Feb: Japan launches an artificial satellite, *Ohsumi*, from Kagoshima Space Centre.

10 Nov: The USSR launches Luna 17 on mission to the Moon. Aboard is the first remote-controlled Moon vehicle, *Lunokhod 1*. It lands on the Sea of Rains, and the vehicle is steered on the surface, sending back many pictures.

12 Dec: An Italian crew launch the satellite Explorer 42 from the Kenya coast.

15 Dec: The Soviet spacecraft Venera 7 reaches Venus, and makes first landing on the planet after a parachute descent.

1971   31 Jan. to 9 Feb: NASA launches Apollo 14 on a Moon mission. Aboard are Alan B. Shepard, Major Stuart A. Roosa, and Lieut.-Comdr. Edgar D. Mitchell. Lunar module *Antares* separates from the command module *Kitty Hawk*, and lands Shepard and Mitchell near the Fra Mauro crater. Using a small handcart, they make two Moon walks totalling 9 hours 33 minutes, and collect samples. Total time on the Moon is 33 hours 31 minutes, while the command module makes 34 Moon orbits in 66 hours 39 minutes. Whole flight takes 216 hours 1 minute 57 seconds.

19 April: The USSR launches Salyut 1 space station.

23 to 25 April: The USSR launches Soyuz 10, with Col. Vladimir Shatalov, Alexei Yeliseyev and Nikolai Rukavishnikov aboard. It completes 32 Earth orbits in 47 hours 46 minutes. The spacecraft docks with Salyut 1 for 5½ hours.

19 May: The USSR launches Mars 2 on a mission to Mars.

28 May: The USSR launches Mars 3 spacecraft.

6 to 29 June: The USSR launches Soyuz 11 with Lieut.-Col. Georgi Dobrovolsky, Vladislav Volkov and Viktor Patsayev aboard. It docks with Salyut 1 for 22 days for trials and experiments. On return, a pressure valve malfunctions, and the crew are dead on arrival.

26 July to 7 Aug: NASA launches Apollo 15 on a mission to the Moon. Aboard are Col. David R. Scott, Lieut.-Col. James B. Irwin, and Major Alfred M. Worden. Lunar module *Falcon* separates from the command module *Endeavour*, carrying Scott and Worden to the Moon's surface, landing near the Apennine Mountains. They make three Moon walks totalling 18 hours 36 minutes, and collect rock and soil samples. A Lunar Roving Vehicle is used, which travels over 17 miles (27 km). Time on the Moon totals 66 hours 55 minutes, and the command module makes 74 orbits. The total flight time is 295 hours 11 minutes 53 seconds.

28 Oct: At Woomera, Australia, Britain launches the *Prospero* technology satellite into orbit. It weighs 145lb (65kg).

27 Nov: The Soviet spacecraft Mars 2 reaches Mars, ejecting a capsule which crashlands on the planet. Mars 2 goes into orbit and sends back TV pictures and information.

1972 3 March: NASA launches Pioneer 10 on a mission to fly close to Jupiter.

16 to 27 April: NASA launches Apollo 16 on a mission to the Moon. Aboard are Capt. John W. Young, Comdr. Thomas K. Mattingly, and Col. Charles M. Duke. The lunar module *Orion* separates from the command module *Casper*, and lands in the Descartes region, carrying Young and Duke. They make three Moon walks totalling 20 hours 14 minutes. The roving vehicle travels nearly 17 miles (27 km), and the astronauts collect samples and set up an astronomical observatory. They stay on the Moon for a total of 71 hours 2 minutes, while the command module makes 64 orbits around the Moon. The total flight time is 265 hours 51 minutes 5 seconds.

7 to 19 Dec: NASA launches Apollo 17 on a mission to the Moon. Aboard are Capt. Eugene A. Cernan, Lieut.-Comdr. Ronald E.Evans, and Dr Harrison H. Schmitt. The lunar module *Challenger*

American astronaut Edwin Aldrin, the second man on the Moon, descending the Apollo 2 lunar module's ladder.

separates from the command module *America*, carrying Cernan and Schmitt to the Moon's surface in the Taurus-Littrow area. They make three Moon walks totalling 22 hours 5 minutes. They stay a total of 74 hours 50 minutes 38 seconds on the Moon.

1973 16 Jan: The USSR launches Luna 21, which lands by the Le Monnier crater on the Sea of Serenity. The remote-controlled Moon vehicle *Lunokhod 2* is used.

6 April: NASA launches Pioneer 11 on a mission to fly near Jupiter and Saturn.

14 May: NASA launches Skylab 1 into Earth orbit, but this is damaged by air pressure, and teams of astronauts in Skylabs 2, 3 and 4 later carry out repairs.

25 May to 22 June: NASA launches Skylab 2 ferry, with Capt. Charles Conrad, Dr Joseph Kirwin, and Capt. Paul J. Weitz aboard. They dock with Skylab 1 and effect repairs.

21 July: The USSR launches Mars 4 on a mission to reach Mars.

25 July: The USSR launches Mars 5 on a mission to reach Mars.

28 July to 25 Sept: NASA launches Skylab 3 ferry, with Capt. Alan L. Bean, Major Jack R. Lousma, and Dr Owen K. Garriott aboard.

5 Aug: The USSR launches Mars 6 on a mission to reach Mars.

9 Aug: The USSR launches Mars 7 on a mission to Mars.

27 to 29 Sept: The USSR launches Soyuz 12.

3 Nov: NASA launches Mariner 10 on a mission to Venus and Mercury.

16 Nov. to 8 February 1974: NASA launches Skylab 4 ferry.

18 to 26 Dec: The USSR launches Soyuz 13, with Major Pyotr Klimuk and Valentin Lebedev aboard. The crew carry out biological experiments.

1974 5 Feb: Mariner 10 reaches Venus.

10 Feb: The Soviet Mars 4 spacecraft passes Mars at a distance of 1367 miles (2200 km). It fails to go into orbit.

12 Feb: The Soviet Mars 5 spacecraft goes into orbit around Mars.

9 March: The Soviet Mars 7 spacecraft reaches Mars and ejects a capsule, but this misses the planet by 808 miles (1200 km).

12 March: The Soviet Mars 6 spacecraft reaches Mars and ejects a capsule which parachutes on to the surface, but which stops transmitting just before it lands.

29 March: Mariner 10 reaches Mercury, obtaining pictures of the planet's surface. It also detects a magnetic field.

30 May: NASA launches Applications Technology Satellite ATS6, which provides educational programmes to 5000 villages in India.

25 June: The USSR launches Salyut 3 space laboratory into orbit.

3 to 19 July: The USSR launches Soyuz 14.

26 to 28 Aug: The USSR launches Soyuz 15.

2 to 8 Dec: The USSR launches Soyuz 16.

26 Dec: The USSR launches Salyut 4 space laboratory into orbit.

1975 11 Jan. to 9 Feb: The USSR launches Soyuz 17, with Lieut.-Col. Alexei Gubarev and Georgi Grechko aboard. It docks with Salyut 4 for experiments.

24 May to 26 July: The USSR launches Soyuz 18B, with Lieut.-Col. Pyotr Klimuk and Vitaly Sevastyanov aboard. It docks with Salyut 4 for experiments.

8 June: The USSR launches Venera 9 on a mission to orbit Venus.

14 June: The USSR launches Venera 10 on a mission to orbit Venus.

15 to 21 July: The USSR launches Soyuz 19.

15 to 24 July: NASA launches Apollo 18, with Brig-Gen. Thomas P. Stafford, Vance D. Brand, and Donald K. Slayton aboard. They take part in a link-up with the Soviet Soyuz 19, docking with that spacecraft on 17 July, remaining together for two days.

26 July: China launches China 3 military satellite into orbit.

20 Aug: NASA launches Viking 1 on a mission to reach Mars.

9 Sept: NASA launches Viking 2 on a mission to reach Mars.

17 Nov. to 6 Feb: The USSR launches an unmanned spacecraft, Soyuz 20, which docks automatically with Salyut 4.

26 Nov: China launches China 4, which returns the military satellite to Earth.

1976 10 Feb: Pioneer 10, on its way out of the Solar System, crosses the orbit of Saturn.

19 June: The Viking 1 spacecraft reaches Mars and goes into orbit.
22 June: The USSR launches Salyut 5 space laboratory into orbit.
6 July to 24 Aug: The USSR launches Soyuz 21, with Col. Boris Volynov and Lieut.-Col. Vitaly Zholobov aboard. It docks with Salyut 5, and cosmonauts make series of experiments.
20 July: Viking 1 releases a landing device, *Chryse Planitia*. This transmits pictures from the Martian surface and examines the soil.
7 Aug: The Viking 2 spacecraft reaches Mars and goes into orbit.
18 Aug: The Soviet Luna 24 spacecraft goes into orbit around the Moon, and soft-lands in the Sea of Crises. It returns to Earth with soil samples.
3 Sept: Viking 2 releases a landing device, *Utopia Planitia*, which transmits pictures from the surface and examines soil in its automatic laboratory.
15 to 23 Sept: The USSR launches Soyuz 22.

14 to 16 Oct: The USSR launches Soyuz 23.
22 Oct: The Soviet spacecraft Venera 9 reaches Venus and goes into orbit around it. A capsule is released which reaches the surface and for 53 minutes transmits TV pictures of conditions. Surface temperature on Venus is recorded at 485°C.
25 Oct: The Soviet spacecraft Venera 10 reaches Venus and goes into orbit. It releases a capsule which reaches the surface and transmits for 65 minutes, sending TV pictures.
1977 7 to 25 Feb: The USSR launches Soyuz 24, with Col. Viktor Gorbatko and Lieut.-Col. Yuri Glazkov aboard. It docks with Salyut 5, where cosmonauts work on experiments.

Left: First woman in orbit—Valentina Tereshkova who was launched into space on 16 June 1963 in the Soviet spacecraft Vostok 6. Below: First Man on the Moon—Neil Armstrong.

20 Aug: NASA launches Voyager 2 spacecraft on a mission to fly near Jupiter, Saturn, Uranus and Neptune.
5 Sept: NASA launches Voyager 1 on a mission to fly near Jupiter and Saturn.
29 Sept: The USSR launches Salyut 6 space laboratory into orbit.
10 Dec. to 16 March 1978: The USSR launches Soyuz 26, with Lieut.-Col. Yuri Romanenko and Georgi Grechko aboard. It docks with Salyut 6.

1978 10 to 16 Jan: The USSR launches Soyuz 27, with Lieut.Col. Vladimir Dzhanibekov and Oleg Makarov aboard. This craft docks at a second port on Salyut 6, which is already docking Soyuz 26. The two crews switch ships, returning in each other's spacecraft.
2 to 10 March: The USSR launches Soyuz 28, with Col. Alexei Gubarev and the Czechoslovak Capt. Vladimir Remek aboard. They dock with Salyut 6, joining Romanenko and Grechko who are already there with Soyuz 27. They conduct experiments and return to Earth.
20 May: NASA launches Pioneer Venus 1 on a mission to Venus. 15 June to 2 Nov: The USSR launches Soyuz 29, with Col. Vladimir Kovalenok and Alexander Ivanchenkov aboard. It docks with Salyut 6, where the cosmonauts remain to conduct experiments.
27 June to 5 July: The USSR launches Soyuz 30, with Col. Pyotr Klimuk and the Polish Major Miroslaw Hermanszewski aboard. They dock with Salyut 6, meeting the crew of Soyuz 29 already there.
8 Aug: NASA launches Pioneer Venus 2 to reach Venus.
26 Aug. to 3 Sept: The USSR launches Soyuz 31, with Col. Valery Bykovsky and the East German Lieut.-Col. Sigmund Jähn aboard. It docks with Salyut 6 and Soyuz 29. They conduct experiments, and Bykovsky and Jähn return in Soyuz 29.
4 Dec: Pioneer Venus 1 reaches Venus, and goes into orbit, conducting a survey of the planet.
9 Dec: Pioneer Venus 2 reaches Venus, separating into five probes which measure atmosphere as they descend to the surface.
27 Dec: The Soviet spacecraft Venera 11 and 12 reach Venus, and release cap-sules on to the surface, which relay scientific data.

1979 25 February to 19 Aug: The USSR launches Soyuz 32, with Lieut.-Col. Vladimir Lyakhov and Valery Ryumin aboard. It docks with Salyut 6. Cosmonauts remain to conduct experiments.
5 March: Voyager 1 flies to within 177,720 miles (285,950 km) of the clouds of Jupiter, and relays information. Jupiter's atmosphere is composed of hydrogen and helium. The Great Red Spot is an atmospheric storm. Jupiter's moon, Io, has at least nine active volcanos. The thin ring around the planet is between 18 and 20 miles (29 and 32 km) thick.
10 to 12 April: The USSR launches Soyuz 33, with Nikolai Rukavishnikov and the Bulgarian Major Georgi Ivanov aboard. It fails to dock with Salyut 6. Cosmonauts are recalled.
13 May to 9 June: The USSR launches the unmanned Progress 6 spacecraft to reach Salyut 6 with supplies.
9 July: Voyager 2 flies to within 399,560 (642,890 km) miles of the clouds of Jupiter. Three new satellites of the planet are discovered, and the moons Io, Europa, Callisto, Ganymede and Amalthea are examined.
1 Sept: Pioneer 11 flies within 12,560 miles (20,210 km) of the clouds of Saturn. Photographing and measuring lasts 10 days. Two new outer rings are discovered, and also an 11th moon. Saturn has a magnetic field.
24 Sept. to 13 Oct: The USSR launches Cosmos 1129 satellite, carrying white rats, quail eggs, carrot seeds and carrot slices inoculated with plant bacteria. Experiments on breeding are to be carried out.
24 Dec: The European Space Agency launches the Ariane heavy satellite vehicle from the French space centre at Kourou, Guiana, and places a CAT satellite in orbit.

1980 27 March to 26 April: The USSR launches the unmanned cargo spacecraft Progress 8, which docks with Salyut 6.
9 April to 11 Oct: The USSR launches Soyuz 35, with Lieut.-Col. Leonid Popov and Valery Ryumin aboard. It docks with Salyut 6
26 May to 3 June: The USSR launches

Soyuz 36, with Valery Kubasov and the Hungarian Capt. Bertalan Farkas aboard. It docks with Salyut 6 and Soyuz 35, and the resident crew join with those of Soyuz 36 in experiments. Popov and Ryumin return to Earth in Soyuz 35.

5 to 9 June: The USSR launches Soyuz T-2, with Lieut.-Col. Yuri Malyshev and Vladimir Aksyonov aboard. It docks with Salyut 6 and Soyuz 36, and the two cosmonauts eventually return to Earth.

29 June to 19 July: The USSR launches the unmanned cargo craft Progress 10, which automatically docks with Salyut 6, carrying supplies.

18 July: India launches an artificial test satellite weighing 78lb (35.4 kg) from Sriharikota island, 62 (100 km) miles from Madras.

18 to 26 Sept: The USSR launches Soyuz 38, with Lieut.Col. Yuri Romanenko and the Cuban Lieut.-Col. Arnaldo Tamayo Mendez aboard. It docks with Salyut 6 and Soyuz 37.

12 Nov: Voyager 1 flies to within 77,000 miles (124,000 km) of the clouds of Saturn, where the rings are examined in detail. The largest Moon of Saturn is Titan, 3,175 miles (5108 km) across, which has an atmosphere mostly of nitrogen.

27 Nov: The USSR launches Soyuz T-3, with Lieut.-Col. Leonid Kizim, Oleg Makarov and Gennady Strekalov aboard. It docks with Salyut 6 and Progress 11.

6 Dec: The first of a new series of nine Intelsat 5 satellites is launched from Cape Canaveral. It is the largest communications satellite to date, capable of relaying 12,000 telephone calls and two colour TV programmes.

1981 12 March: The USSR launches Soyuz T-4, with Col. Vladimir Kovalyonok and Viktor Savinykh aboard. It docks with Salyut 6.

22 March: The USSR launches Soyuz 39, with Vladimir Dzhanibekov and the Mongolian Jugderdemidiyn Gurragcha aboard. It docks with Salyut 6, joining the crew of Soyuz T-4.

12 April: NASA launches the shuttle spacecraft Columbia, with Comdr. John Young and Capt. Robert Crippen aboard. After 54 hours in space and 36 orbits of the Earth, Columbia, the first re-usable spacecraft, returns to Edwards Air Force base in California.

26 Aug: Voyager 2 reaches Saturn, and relays pictures of the its rings and moons.

1982 14 May: The USSR launches a new space station, Salyut 7, with Anatoly Beregovoi and Valentin Lebedev aboard.

25 June: The USSR launches Soyuz T-6, with two Soviet, and one French cosmonaut aboard. It docks with Salyut 7

19 Aug: The USSR launches Soyuz T-7, with Svetlana Savitskaya (the second woman in space) and two other cosmonauts aboard. It docks with Salyut 7.

11 Nov: NASA launches the space shuttle Columbia from Cape Canaveral. Aboard is a four-man crew, and two commercial satellites are also carried. It returns on 16 Nov.

10 Dec: Two Soviet cosmonauts, Anatoly Beregovoi and Valentin Lebedev return to Earth after a record 211 days in the space station Salyut 7.

1983 4 April: NASA launches a second space shuttle, Challenger, from Cape Cavaveral. Aboard is a crew of four astronauts. It returns safely on 9 May.

20 April: The USSR launches Soyuz T-8, with three cosmonauts aboard, but it fails to dock with Salyut 7, and returns to Earth.

18 June: NASA launches the space shuttle Challenger on a six-day mission from Cape Canaveral. The crew of five

Lunakhod—'Moon-Walker'—the robot vehicle used by the Russians to explore the Moon by remote control.

159

includes a woman astronaut, Dr Sally Ride. The shuttle returns safely on 24 June.

27 June: The USSR launches Soyuz T-9, with two cosmonauts aboard. It docks with the space station Salyut 7.

30 Aug: NASA launches the space shuttle *Challenger* on a night-time launch, with five astronauts aboard. It returns safely, also at night, on 5 Sept.

23 Nov: After spending five months in space, Vladimir Lyakhov and Alexander Alexandrov, two Soviet cosmonauts return to Earth.

28 Nov: Six astronauts, including a West German, are launched in the space shuttle, returning 10 days later.

1984 3 Feb: US space shuttle *Challenger* is launched (returning 11 February).

6 Feb: *Challenger* launches a satellite, but it is a failure.

7 Feb: Capt Bruce McCandless is the first astronaut to go freely into space without a lifeline as he leaves US space shuttle *Challenger*.

8 Feb: Soviet spacecraft Soyuz T-10 is launched, with three cosmonauts aboard, to link up with orbital station Salyut 7.

5 March: The European Space Agency rocket Ariane is launched into space.

4 April: Soviet spacecraft T11 with three cosmonauts aboard (including the first Indian), docks with orbital space station Salyut 7. They return on 11 April.

6 April: Five US astronauts are launched in space shuttle Challenger. During flight they repair a faulty satellite, and return on 13 April.

25 July: Soviet cosmonaut Svetlana Savitskaya is the first woman to walk in space as she leaves Soyuz T-12 for three hours outside the station. The craft returns on 29 July.

1985 29 Nov: During shuttle *Atlantis* mission, US astronauts Jerry Ross and Sherwood Spring practice construction techniques in space.

17 June: Soviet Vega 2 probe ceased transmitting data from a balloon in the atmosphere of Venus.

27 June: The Soviet Salyut 7 orbiting space station was further enlarged by the addition of a new module.

1986 23 Jan: US Voyager probe flies by the planet Uranus, its camera revealing a featureless surface. Ten new satellites of

Uranus are spotted (making 15 in all).

28 Jan: The US shuttle *Challenger* explodes 73 seconds after lift-off from Cape Canaveral. All seven astronauts on board are killed. The fault is later traced to defective seals in the rocket boosters.

19 Feb: The USSR launches its new Mir ('Peace') space station.

14 March: European Space Agency's Giotto spacecraft passes within 600 km of Halley's comet, the closest of several probes sent to investigate the world's best-known comet.

5 May: Soviet cosmonauts Solovyov and Kizim transfer from Mir to Salyut 7 in a Soyuz T15 spacecraft – the first ever crew transfer between orbital space stations.

28 May: Solovyov and Kizim deploy a 15-metre long metal tower in orbit to test building techniques.

5 Sept: US carries out rocket interception tests as part of its research into Strategic Defence Initiative ('Star Wars') defence systems.

1987 15 May: USSR launches its new Energia rocket, the world's most powerful at three million kilograms thrust.

25 July: Cosmos 1870 is the largest-ever Earth-observation satellite, weighing 15 tonnes.

23 July: Soviet TM3 craft carries Russian cosmonauts Aleksandrov and Viktorenko and Syria's first spaceman, Muhammad Faris.

15 Sept: The redesigned third stage works well on Europe's Ariane rocket. Launch no. V19 puts two communications satellites into orbit.

29 Dec: Yuri Romanenko of the USSR lands after 326 days in space aboard the Mir space station – a duration record.

1988 29 Sept: The USA returns to manned spaceflight with the successful launch and return of the space shuttle *Discovery*.

20 Oct: Soviet cosmonauts Titov and Manorov complete the most difficult space repair job hitherto attempted – the repair of an Anglo-Dutch telescope launched in 1987.

23 Oct: Soviet TV shows first pictures of Russia's space shuttle. The first unmanned launch of the craft is postponed because of a technical hitch but takes place on 15 November.

16 Nov: Soviet shuttle Buran (unmanned) makes successful flight.

HISTORY AND EXPLORATION: SOME WELL-KNOWN PEOPLE

ALDRIN, Edwin Eugene [1930-]; American astronaut; in 1969, the second man to set foot on the Moon.

ALCOCK, Sir John William [1892-1919]; British aviator, who on 14 June, 1919, with Sir Arthur Whitten BROWN, was first to fly the Atlantic. Died of injuries in an aircraft crash.

AMUNDSEN, Roald [1872-1928]; Norwegian polar explorer, who, in 1911, was the first man to reach the South Pole, in advance of Robert Falcon SCOTT.

ARMSTRONG, Neil Alden [1930-]; American astronaut, in 1969, the first man to set foot on the Moon.

BADEN-POWELL, Robert Stephenson Smyth (1st Baron) [1857-1941]; British soldier, renowned for his defence of Mafeking during the BOER WAR. Founded the Boy Scouts, 1907; and with his sister, Agnes, founded the Girl Guides.

BATTEN, Jean Gardner [1909-]; British aviator, who in 1934 set up a women's record in flying solo to Australia, and who in 1935 was the first woman to complete the return flight. Other world records, 1935-1937.

BLÉRIOT, Louis [1872-1936]; French aviator and inventor, who in 1909 made the first flight across the English Channel.

BROWN, Sir Arthur Whitten [1886-1948]; British aviator, born in Glasgow of American parents. With Sir John ALCOCK, made the first transatlantic flight, 1919.

BRYANT, Sir Arthur [1899-1984]; British author, historian and lawyer. Former lecturer in history at Oxford. *The American Ideal*, 1936, *The Years of Endurance*, 1942, *The Story of England* 1953- .

BYRD, Richard Evelyn [1888-1957]; American admiral, aviator and explorer. Made first flight over the North Pole, 1926, and South Pole, 1928.

CHILDE, (Vere) Gordon [1892-1957]; Australian archaeologist, who synthesized European prehistory, and originated concepts, such as 'culture'. *The Dawn of European Civilization* (1929).

COBHAM, Sir Alan John [1894-1973]; British aviator and aviation consultant, who made many long-distance flights, pioneering the London-Cape Town route. He invented a system for refuelling aircraft while in the air.

CODY, William Frederick; 'Buffalo Bill' [1846-1917]; American army scout, Indian fighter and showman, whose exploits were told in fiction form in American magazines. Organized his own Wild West Show which toured the world.

COUSTEAU, Jacques-Yves [1910-]; French undersea explorer, film-maker and author. Inventor of the aqualung, and designed underwater dwellings for underwater exploration.

EARHART, Amelia (Putnam) [1898-1937]; American aviator, the first woman to fly solo over the Atlantic. She disappeared while making a round-the-world flight in 1937.

Above: Hillary and Tensing, first to climb Everest, in 1953. Right: Amelia Earhart, the first woman to cross the Atlantic by air. Far right: Robert Peary reached the North Pole in 1909.

GAGARIN, Yuri Alekseyevich [1934-1968]; Soviet cosmonaut, and the first man to travel in space in 1961. Killed in an aircraft accident.

GLENN, John Herschel [1921-]; American astronaut, and the first man to orbit the Earth in 1962. Later became a US senator.

HILLARY, Sir Edmund Percival [1919-]; New Zealand mountaineer, who, with Sherpa Tenzing, was the first to reach the summit of Everest in 1953.

JOHNSON, Amy [1903-1941]; British aviator, who flew solo from England to Australia in 1930, and who made new records in flying to Japan in 1931 and to Cape Town in 1932. During World War II, while in the Air Transport Auxiliary, she baled out over the Thames Estuary and was drowned.

LINDBERGH, Charles Augustus [1902-74]; American aviator, who made the first solo nonstop flight across the Atlantic in 1927. In 1932, his infant son was kidnapped and murdered.

MOLLISON, James Allan [1905-59]; British aviator, who made a record-breaking flight to Australia in 1931 (8 days 19 hours 28 minutes). Married Amy JOHNSON in 1932; marriage dissolved 1938.

NAMIER, Sir Louis Bernstein [1888-1960]; British historian of Russian origin, whose methods involved microscopic analysis of the subject matter. *Structure of Politics at the Accession of George III*, 1929.

NEVINS, Allan [1890-1971]; American historian, especially noted for political biography. *Ordeal of the Union*, 1947-1971.

POST, Wiley [1899-1935]; American aviator, who in 1933 made the first round-the-world solo flight. Killed in a aircraft crash with the humorist, Will Rogers.

PETRIE, Sir (William Matthew) Flinders [1853-1942]; British archaeologist, particularly associated with ancient Egypt, were he was a founder of scientific methods of excavation.

PICCARD, Auguste [1884-1962]; Swiss physicist and explorer of the ocean depths and the stratosphere. *In Balloon and Bathyscaphe*, 1956.

SCOTT, Robert Falcon [1868-1912]; British Antarctic explorer, who died with his companions after reaching the South Pole in 1912, one month after Roald AMUNDSEN.

SCOTT, Sheila Christine [1927-1988]; British aviator, a former actress, who in 1967 set up a new solo record in flying to Cape Town. She achieved other records and won many air races.

SHACKLETON, Sir Ernest Henry [1874-1922]; British Antarctic explorer, first with Robert Falcon SCOTT, and later in his ship, *Endurance*.

SMITH, Sir Charles Edward Kingsford [1897-1935]; Australian aviator, who made a record flight around Australia, 1927; from California to Brisbane, 1928; and from Australia to England, 1929. Lost while en route to Singapore on flight from Australia to England.

TAWNEY, Richard Henry [1880-1962]; British economic historian, best known for 16th and 17th century studies.

TAYLOR, Alan John Percivale [1906-]; British historian, especially of the inter-war years of the 20th century. *The Origins of the Second World War*, 1961.

TERESHKOVA, Valentina Vladimirovna [1937-]; Soviet cosmonaut; the first woman to travel into space, in 1963.

TOYNBEE, Arnold [1899-1975]; British historian, best known for his study of the development and decline of civilization, *A Study of History* in 12 volumes, 1934-61.

TREVELYAN, George Macauley [1876-1962]; British historian and biographer. *Giuseppe Garibaldi*, 3 vols., 1907-11; *British History in the Nineteenth Century, 1782-1901*, 1922.

VENTRIS, Michael George Francis [1922-1956]; British architect and scholar, who deciphered the ancient Mycenaean script, Linear B, and recognizing it as early Greek.

WEDGWOOD, Dame (Cicely) Veronica [1910-]; British author and historian of the English Civil War period. *The King's Peace*, 1955; and *The King's War*, 1958.

WHEELER, Sir (Robert Eric) Mortimer [1890-1976]; British archaeologist of flamboyant style, who did much to delineate the Indus valley civilization and by excavations at Mohenjodaro, Pakistan.

WILKINS, Sir George Hubert [1888-1958]; Australian polar explorer, who spent many years in the Arctic. *Flying the Arctic*, 1928, *Undiscovered Australia*, 1928, *Under the North Pole*, 1931.

Arts of the Century

ABBEY THEATRE This Dublin theatre was, from 1904 until the late 1920s, the home of the forward-looking Irish drama, and in particular, the Irish National Theatre Society, which flourished under the leadership of W.B. YEATS and Lady Gregory. Dramatists involved included W.B. Yeats, J.M. SYNGE and Sean O'CASEY.

ABSTRACT An art form that represents ideas (by means of geometric and other designs instead of natural forms. Pioneered by KANDINSKY and taken up by MIRÓ and de Kooning.

ABSTRACT EXPRESSIONISM A combination of abstract art and EXPRESSIONISM consisting mainly of dripping and smearing paint at random. Pioneered by Jackson POLLOCK.

ACTION PAINTING A type of ABSTRACT EXPRESSIONISM

ACTIVISM The theory that playwrights should look for a realistic solution to social problems.

ART NOUVEAU A movement based on the use of linear flowing forms, which started in Europe and the USA in the late 1890s. Probably inspired by the introduction of Japanese art into the West. In Germany, known as *Jugendstil*, and in Italy as *Stile Liberty*. Typified by A. Mucha, William Morris, Aubrey Beardsley and the architect Charles Mackintosh.

BAUHAUS A school of art, design and architecture founded in Germany in 1919, and based on the ideas of the WERKBUND. It was run by Walter GROPIUS, but was closed down by the Nazis in the early 1930s.

BEBOP (or BOP) An intellectual type of jazz which started in the 1940s in an attempt to break the monotonous rhythm of earlier jazz.

BLAUE REITER (blue rider) A group of Munich artists (1911) who highlighted various modern art forms; started by KANDINSKY and Marc, joined later by KLEE.

BLUES A form of jazz using 12-bar melodic section. Essentially vocal, the music is often slow and sad.

BOOGIE WOOGIE A jazz barrelhouse style of piano playing, with repetitive bass in the left hand and stylized melodic variations in the right.

BROADWAY A general term for American professional theatre; from the New York street where many theatres are located. Compare WEST END.

BRUTALISM A movement in modern architecture starting in the 1950s, aimed at the straight-forward, often rough, use of materials, based on the uncompromising ruthlessness of the architects LE CORBUSIER and MIES VAN DER ROHE.

BURLESQUE A play that mocks or parodies another. In the USA, a vulgar kind of variety performance for male audiences.

CABARET An intimate entertainment performed while the audience wines and dines.

CALYPSO Folk music of the West Indies, usually sung, in 4/4 time.

CATWALK A narrow platform above the stage from which stage-hands adjust scenery, etc.

COLLAGE A picture built up from pieces of fabric or paper stuck on to a ground, and possibly embellished with paint.

COUNTRY AND WESTERN Topical and traditional rural music, mainly vocal and American, evolved from folk, blues and hillbilly music; now known simply as 'country'.

CUBISM An important movement in modern French painting started by PICASSO and BRAQUE in 1907. Cubists aimed to reduce objects to basic shapes of cubes, spheres, cylinders and cones.

CYCLORAMA A curved wall at the back of a stage, on which light patterns or pictures can be projected.

DADAISM An outrageous and nihilistic movement started in Zurich (1916) as a protest against all artistic and civilized standards. Duchamp was a leading exponent. From the French word *dada*, a hobby-horse.

DIRECTOR A person who stages a play and instructs. In Britain, the word PRO-DUCER was until recently, always used in this sense.

DIXIELAND JAZZ Originally, early Negro jazz; later applied to the music of white imitators.

DOWNSTAGE The part of the stage nearest the audience.

ETHNIC ART A term used increasingly, particularly in the USA, when describing art produced by distinct groups, such as Puerto Ricans and negroes, and reflecting the increased importance given to the rights of minority groups.

ENTR'ACTE A diversion between acts, usually musical.

EPILOGUE A speech delivered at the end of a play, usually in verse, and by a member of the cast.

EXPRESSIONISM In the theatre, this was a German movement of the 1920s, which concentrated on psychology rather than events. In art, a movement that aims at expressing the artist's inner feelings and experiences, rejecting reality and idealism even to the point of distortion. It began in the late 1800s. Van Gogh, Gauguin, MATISSE, PICASSO and Rouault were adherents at various times. It was also an architectural movement.

FARCE An extravagant comedy based on toruous manipulation of the situation rather than wit.

FAUVES (Wild beasts) A group of Parisian painters of the early 1900s (DUFY, MATISSE, Rouault, Vlaminck, etc.) who shocked the critics by their brilliant use of colour.

FLATS A flat piece of scenery used to build up a three-dimensional set.

FLIES The space above the PROSCENIUM, from which scenes are controlled.

FOOTLIGHTS Stage lights arranged across the front of the stage at stage level.

FOURTH WALL The theory of drama that the audience is viewing the action through a

A scene from Endgame *by Samuel Beckett, the Irish playwright of the absurd. He writes mainly in French.*

wall which has been removed without the actors knowing it.

FUNCTIONALISM In architecture, the modern principle that the form of a building should follow from its proposed function and that of its parts.

FUTURISM An Italian artistic movement (1905-15) which emphasized violence, machinery and politics, and which was anti-cultural and anti-romantic. Painters used CUBIST forms and strong colours.

GALLERY The uppermost tier of seats in a theatre, traditionally the cheapest; also called the Gods, from their nearness to heaven.

GOUACHE A non-transparent water-colour paint that provides an easy way of obtaining oil-painting effects.

GRAND GUIGNOL A play built round a sensational situation, with an element of horror.

IMAGISM A school of poetry of the early 1900s, concerned with precise language, direct treatment, and freedom of form.

IMPRESSIONISM An important movement that developed among French painters in the mid-19th century. Impressionists were particularly concerned with light and its effects. They put down on canvas their immediate impressions of nature. MONET, RENOIR, Pissarro, Sisley, Cézanne and Degas were leading impressionists.

INGÉNUE A stock character of an innocent young girl.

INTERNATIONAL STYLE A term given to a modern style of architecture that evolved in western Europe in the 1920s, and became popular in the United States. Its basic concepts are generally cubic shapes, often asymmetrical, and a great deal of window space; principles employed in buildings ranging from houses to skyscrapers.

INTIMISME A kind of IMPRESSIONIST technique applied to intimate and familiar interiors instead of landscape; adopted by a small group of French painters, led by Bonnard and Vuillard.

JAZZ Music which arose in the United States from the negroes' African music in the environment of the American south. It became centred on New Orleans, and took the form of improvisation by the performers on a harmonic sequence against the background of a defined rhythm.

JITTERBUGGING An improvised, all-in, athletic form of dancing, originating in the late 1930s with the development of BOOGIE WOOGIE.

JIVE A later, slightly more sober and respectable form of JITTERBUGGING.

KITCHEN-SINK In the theatre, a term for realistic working-class drama, originating in the 1950s. In painting, applied to a group depicting REALISM in the 1950s; pioneered by David Bomberg and John Bratby.

LEGITIMATE THEATRE Straight drama, without music.

LONDON GROUP A group of painters, founded in 1913, by the union of the Camden Town group and the Vorticists. Members included Gilman and SICKERT. It still exhibits, including many avant-garde works.

MAINSTREAM JAZZ Middle-of-the-road jazz that avoids extremes of TRAD or progressive jazz.

MANAGER In the United Kingdom, a person responsible for the business side of a production, as against the dramatic side. In the USA, he is called the PRODUCER.

MATINEE A daytime performance in a theatre, especially when held in the afternoon.

MELDRUM SCHOOL An Australian group of painters inspired by Max Meldrum, founded in 1913.

METHOD, THE Acting based on living the part, in which the actor loses himself or herself completely in the role.

MIME Acting without speech, by exaggerated action and gesture; particularly popular in France.

MONTAGE Sticking one layer on top of another; it may be combined with painting to make a picture.

MUSICAL COMEDY Lighthearted entertainment with songs and dances held together by a loose plot.

MUSIC HALL Entertainment popular in Britain (mid-1800s to early 1900s, latterly revived as old-time music hall) which includes a variety of turns; singers, comic acts, acrobats, etc.

MUSIQUE CONCRÈTE Music based on pre-recorded sound patterns rearranged electronically.

NATURALISM A style that portrays objects with photographic detail. Compared with REALISM it is often stilted and monotonous.

NEO-IMPRESSIONISM A type of painting that developed in France in the late 19th century. It relied largely on formal composition and application of pure blobs of colour. Pioneered by Seurat and Signac. Also called Pointillism.

NEO-ROMANTICISM The Romantic realism of the 1900s in England, inspired by the words of Blake and the works of Palmer and Calvert. Typified by the paintings of Sutherland, Nash and Piper.

NEW WAVE A term applied to a movement in literature and the cinema, originating in France (*la Nouvelle vague*) in the late 1950s that attempted to eschew fixed values, revealing a character by the way he experienced objects and events, which were often meticulously described. It was also applied to a movement in pop music beginning in the 1970s, which included PUNK ROCK and offbeat arrangements, and also heavy ROCK.

OP ART (Optical art) A modern technique with which the painter creates optical illusions by means of dazzling patterns.

ORPHISM A French ABSTRACT movement founded in 1912. Followers described it as 'art of painting new structures out of elements that have .... been created entirely by the artist himself.' Delaunay was one of the founders. It was later called Simultaneism.

PANTOMIME In the USA, this is mime, or acting without words. In the UK, it is an extravagant Christmas entertainment, loosely based on a fairy tale.

PIT In the theatre, the ground floor of the auditorium.

POP The term for currently popular music or song, generally launched and performed with maximum publicity and with an eye to record sales.

POP ART A movement born independently in Great Britain and the USA in the 1950s and 1960s. It uses photographs, strip cartoons, advertisements, etc. as sources, often enlarged and painted surrealistically in garish colours. Paolozzi, JOHNS and Rauschenberg were among the pioneers.

POST-IMPRESSIONISM The work of French painters that followed IMPRESSIONISM between 1885 and 1905. Artists experimented freely with expression, form and design, instead of representing nature realistically. Typified by Cézanne, Gauguin, Van Gogh, RENOIR and Degas.

PRODUCER In the UK, the person who directs the action (the US DIRECTOR); in the USA, the MANAGER.

PROMPTER The person who holds a copy of the play and reminds actors if they forget their lines.

PROMPT SIDE The side of the stage where the prompter sits: to the actors' left in the UK, to the right in the USA. OP means 'opposite prompt', the other side of the stage.

PROPERTIES Articles required on stage apart from costume, furniture and scenery.

PUNK ROCK Rock music with outrage-

Punk—an outrageous movement soon to become outmoded.

ous, often obscene words, accompanied by equally outrageous behaviour by its performers.

RAGTIME Essentially Negro piano music based on a rigidly syncopated pattern. It had some influence on JAZZ.

REALISM A movement begun in the late 19th century towards a natural style of acting, away from histrionics and contrived drama. Also applied to art, an approach to painting that began wth Courbet in France in the 1800s. Its adherents tried to portray an impression of everyday life.

REGGAE A West Indian type of rock jazz with a simple 2-beat rhythm.

REPERTORY THEATRE A theatre with a repertoire of plays and a permanent company of actors.

REPRESENTATIONAL ART A type of painting that shows objects as nearly as possible as they actually are. The opposite of ABSTRACT ART.

REVUE An entertainment comprising a number of short items (sketches, songs, etc.) often topical or satirical.

ROCK AND ROLL (also ROCK) Rhythmic development of the blues and skiffle, with undisguised emphasis on the beat and body movements of the dancers.

SCIENCE FICTION Literature based on scientific fact or fantasy, often set in the

Left: Marcel Marceau, perhaps the greatest exponent of mime. Above: A scene from a No play, Japanese theatre which has not changed for over 300 years.

distant future. Early pioneers in the form were Jules VERNE and H.G. WELLS.

SKIFFLE Makeshift jazz music (in vogue during the mid-1950s) that included guitars, banjos, mandolins and a number of home-made instruments such as washboard, tea-chest bass, and paper-and-comb. The reper-toire was largely folk music with a beat.

SON ET LUMIÈRE An open-air entertain-ment (held in a castle, cathedral, etc.) relating to the history of the place, using special lighting and sound effects.

SOUBRETTE A coquettish maidservant in comedy; a female member of the company specializing in such roles.

SOUL MUSIC Popular, often religious music written and performed by Negroes and used for dancing.

STEEL BANDS West Indian percussion bands, originating in Trinidad, that use as instruments the tops of oil drums, tuned to various pitches.

STOCK COMPANY In the USA, the equivalent of the British REPERTORY com-pany, sometimes a travelling one.

SURREALISM A 20th century art move-ment that aimed at escaping control of reason and tried to express the subconscious mind pictorially. ERNST, ARP and DALI have been leading exponents.

SWING Commercialized jazz featured by the big bands; The period 1935-46 is known as the swing era.

SYNCOPATION In music, the shifting of the accent on to a beat not normally accented.

TABS The front curtain; sometimes used for curtains on stage.

THEATRE OF THE ABSURD Drama based on fantastic, unreal situations, aban-doning all logical thought and processes. Pioneered by Samuel BECKETT, Ionesco, PINTER, etc.

TIN PAN ALLEY Originally 28th Street in New York City, where most of the commer-cial song hits were published. Today, the term describes any well-known area of the pop publishing business. London's equiva-lent is Denmark Street.

TORMENTORS In the theatre, the sides of the PROSCENIUM arch.

TRAD (or Traditional jazz) Jazz that ad-

167

heres to the old traditional New Orleans highly improvised, contrapuntal sounds.

UPSTAGE The back of the stage away from the audience; to upstage an actor means to manoeuvre him into a less favourable position.

VAUDEVILLE The US equivalent of the British music hall, popular from the late 1890s to the advent of talking pictures.

VORTICISM An English avant-garde art movement started in 1912 by Wyndham Lewis. Adherents painted in an ABSTRACT style.

WERKBUND A group founded in Germany in 1907 by the architect Hermann

Papa Celestin's Original Tuxedo Orchestra, New Orleans 1928. New Orleans was the home of jazz.

Muthesius, who had been influenced by William Morris. It attempted to harness the artist to machine production, and to achieve quality through durable work and genuine materials.

WEST END In London, the area where most theatres are located. By analogy, the professional theatre. Compare BROADWAY.

WINGS The side scenery in the theatre; the sides of the stage.

THE ARTS, LITERATURE, ARCHITECTURE, MUSIC

AALTO, (Hugo) Alvar (Henrick) [1898-1976]; Finnish architect and town planner; a leader in Scandinavian design.

ABERCROMBIE, Sir (Leslie) Patrick [1879-1957]; British architect and town planner.

ACHEBE, Chinua [1930-]; Nigerian writer, and leading literary celebrity of Africa. *Things Fall Apart* (1958), *Arrow of God* (1964).

ALBEE, Edward Franklin [1928-]; American playwright, author of *Who's Afraid of Virginia Woolf?* (1962).

ANOUILH, Jean [1910-]; French playwright and screenwriter with pessimistic themes. *Antigone* (1952), *The Waltz of the Toreadors* (1952).

APOLLINAIRE, Guillaume (Wilhelm Apollinaris Kostrowitzki) [1880-1918]; Poet and friend of artists, born in Italy of Polish parentage, but of adopted French nationality. *L'Hérésiarch & Cie* (1910).

ARP, (Hans) Jean [1886-1966]; French abstract painter, sculptor and poet, born in Strasbourg (then Germany). A founder of the DADA movement.

AUDEN, Wystan Hugh [1907-73]; British-born American poet and essayist. Attracted by Communism, which he later rejected. *The Dance of Death* (1933).

AYCKBOURN, Alan [1939-]; British playwright, actor and director (Scarborough theatre). A modern successful dramatist: *Absurd Person Singular* (1975), *The Norman Conquests* (1975).

BABEL, Isaak Emmanvilovich [1894-1941]; Russian short-story writer who is believed to have died in prison. *Red Cavalry* (1926).

BACON, Francis [1909-]; British painter (Irish-born) of expressionistic style. *Studies After Velazquez' Portrait of Pope Innocent X* (1951-53).

BAKST, Leon (Lev Nikolayevich) [1866-1924]; Russian scenic artist and painter. Designed sets for the Russian ballet.

BARBIROLLI, Sir John (Giovanni Battista Barbirolli) [1899-1970]; British conductor and musical director of British National Opera.

BARRIE, Sir James Matthew [1860-1937]; British playwright and novelist, the author of *Peter Pan* (1904). *The Admirable Crichton* (1902).

BARTÓK, Béla [1881-1945]; Hungarian composer and pianist, who wrote operas: *Bluebeard's Castle* (1911) and ballets.

BECKETT, Samuel [1906-]; Irish-born British playwright and novelist of the absurd, who writes mainly in French: *Waiting for Godot* (1952).

BEECHAM, Sir Thomas [1879-1961]; British conductor; founder of British National Opera the London Philharmonic and the Royal Philharmonic Orchestras.

BEHRENS, Peter [1868-1940]; German architect and designer, originally in the ART NOUVEAU style. Designed domestic appliances, such as cookers.

BELLOC, (Joseph) Hilaire (Pierre René) [18701953]; French-born British author and poet. A Liberal MP for four years. Famed for his *Cautionary Tales* (1907). *The Path to Rome* (1902).

BELLOW, Saul [1915-]; Canadian-born American novelist. Nobel prize for literature 1976: *Humboldt's Gift* (1975).

BENNETT, (Enoch) Arnold [1867-1931]; British novelist and playwright, who wrote about the pottery towns. *Clayhanger* (1910), *Riceyman Steps* (1923).

BERG, Alban [1885-1935]; Austrian composer, and well-known for his opera *Wozzeck* (1925).

BERGSON, Henri Louis [1859-1941]; French philosopher, awarded Nobel prize for literature, 1927. *Creative Evolution* (1911).

BERNSTEIN, Leonard [1918-]; American composer and conductor (New York Philharmonic). Wrote music for *West Side Story* (1957).

BETJEMAN, Sir John [1906-84]; British poet whose works have been very popular in recent years Poet Laureate 1972-84. *Collected Poems.*

BLOK, Aleksander Aleksandrovich [1880-1921]; Russian poet, leader in the symbolist style. *The Scythians* (1920).

BLYTON, Enid Mary [1897-1968]; writer for children; number of titles exceeded 400. Her characters, the Famous Five, and Noddy, appeared in many books.

BOCCIONI, Umberto [1882-1916]; Italian painter and sculptor in the FUTURIST style.

BOMBERG, David Garshen [1890-1957]; British painter, mainly of still-lifes, landscapes and the human head.

BONNARD, Pierre [1867-1947]; French painter and printmaker, a POST-IMPRESSIONIST.

BORGES, Jorge Luis [1899-1986]; Argentine poet and short-story writer.

BOULEZ, Pierre [1925-]; French conductor and composer. Musical director of the New York Philharmonic 1971-77.

BOULT, Sir Adrian Cedric [1889-1983]; British conductor, founded the BBC Symphony Orchestra, 1930.

BRANCUSI, Constantin [1876-1957]; French (Romanian-born) sculptor; *The Kiss,* (1908).

BRAQUE, Georges [1882-1963]; French painter, sculptor and designer. Founder of modern art, and developed CUBISM with PICASSO.

BRECHT, Bertolt [1898-1956]; German playwright and poet. In America during war years, wrote *The Threepenny Opera* (1928).

BRETON, André [1896-1966]; French poet, essayist and novelist, founder of the SURREALIST movement.

Below: Picasso's Cat and Bird, *1939. Right:* Madonna and Child *by Henry Moore (Tate Gallery).*

BREUER, Marcel Lajos [1902-1981]; Hungarian-born American `architect; designed UNESCO building in Paris (1953-58).

BRITTEN, (Edward) Benjamin [1913-76]; British composer famed for operas *Peter Grimes* (1945), *Billy Budd* (1951), *Gloriana* (1953).

BROMFIELD, Louis [1896-1956]; American novelist, author of *The Green Bay Tree* (1924), *The Rains Came* (1937).

BROOKE, Rupert Chawner [1887-1915]; British poet, known for his poems of World War I; died of blood poisoning while in Royal Navy. His poem beginning 'If I should die' (*The Soldier*, 1915) showed great promise.

BUCHAN, John (1st Baron Tweedsmuir) [18751940]; popular British author of adventure books: *Prester John* (1910), *The Thirty-Nine Steps* (1915). Governor-General of Canada, 1935-40.

BUSONI, Ferruccio Benvenuto [1866-1924]; Italian pianist and composer. *Turandot* (1917).

CAGE, John Milton [1912-]; American composer who uses 'new sounds' in music, and was first to compose music on magnetic tape: *Imaginary Landscape No. 5* (1952).

CALLAS, Maria (Cecilia Sophia Anna Maria Kalogeropoulos) [1923-1977]; American prima donna soprano of Greek parentage. She had a superb, and highly individual voice.

CAMUS, Albert [1913-60]; French novelist, playwright and journalist, born in Algiers. Like Jean-Paul SARTRE, an EXISTENTIALIST. Works include *The Plague* (1948), *The Rebel* (1951).

CAPEK, Karel [1890-1938]; Czech novelist and playwright. The word 'robot' became international, from his play *R.U.R.* (1920).

CARO, Anthony [1924-]; British sculptor who uses industrial steel and aluminium in his work.

CARTIER-BRESSON, Henri [1908-]; French photographer of international fame, with a subtle and understanding technique.

CARUSO, Enrico [1873-1921]; Outstanding Italian operatic tenor, one of the very first to be recorded for the gramophone.

CASALS, Pablo [1876-1973]; Spanish cellist and conductor. Foremost of great cellists in his time.

CASSON, Sir Hugh Maxwell [1910-]; British architect and president of the Royal Academy from 1976.

CHAGALL, Marc [1887-1985]; French painter (Russian-born), of colourful scenes of Russian and Jewish life.

CHALIAPIN, Fyodor Ivanovich [1873-1938];

Russian operatic bass with a very powerful voice.

CHANDLER, Raymond [1888-1959]; American writer of short stories and novels of the tough crime type. Created the private detective 'Philip Marlowe'.

CHESTERTON, Gilbert Keith [1874-1936]; British novelist, essayist and poet. Also wrote detective stories featuring his hero 'Father Brown'. *All Things Considered* (1908), *Collected Poems* (1933).

CHOMSKY, Noam [1928-]; American educationist and linguist. He has stated that there is a universal grammar underlying all languages.

CHRISTIE, Agatha Mary Clarissa [1891-1976]; British novelist and playwright, especially of detective stories featuring her sleuth 'Hercule Poirot'. Her play, *The Mousetrap*, has been running in London since 1952.

COCTEAU, Jean [1889-1963]; French poet, novelist, playwright and film-maker. Books include *Les Enfants Terribles* (1929) and the film *La Belle et le Bête* (1946).

COLETTE (Sidonie-Gabrielle Colette) [1873-1954]; French novelist, known for her stories of 'Claudine': *Chéri* (1920), *La Fin de Chéri* (1926).

CONRAD, Joseph (Jozef Teodor Konrad Nalecz Korzeniowski) [1857-1924], British (Polish-born) novelist and short-story writer. In adult life, learned English, and wrote novels in that language: *Typhoon* (1902), *The Secret Agent* (1907).

CORBUSIER, Le (Charles-Edouard Jeanneret) [1887-1965]; Swiss architect, among whose works is the Palais des Nations, Geneva.

DALI, Salvador (Felipe Jacinto, Marquis of Pubol); [1904-]; Spanish surrealist painter. Also stage and film designer.

D'ANNUNZIO, Gabriele [1863-1938]; Italian novelist, playwright and poet. Also, was leader of 12,000 men who captured Fiume in 1919. Later supported Mussolini. *Il Fuoco* (1900).

DAY LEWIS, Cecil [1904-72]; Irish-born British poet, novelist, and detective-story writer (as 'Nicholas Blake'). Poet Laureate 1958-72. *Overtures to Death* (1938).

DE LA MARE, Walter John [1873-1956]; British poet, and outstanding as a writer for children. *Songs of Childhood* (1902).

DE MONTHERLANT, Henri-Marie-Joseph Millon [1896-1972]; French novelist, athlete and bullfighter. His novels glorify force and virility. *The Bullfighters* (1927).

DEBUSSY, Claude Achille [1862-1918]; French composer of romantic music. *Claire de Lune* (1890-1905).

DELIUS, Frederick [1862-1934]; British composer of German parentage. Composed operas, concertos and tone poems. *Over the Hills and Far Away* (1895).

DOUGLAS, Norman [1868-1952]; British writer, a former diplomat. *Late Harvest* (1946).

DREISER, Theodore Herman Albert [1871-1945]; American novelist. *Sister Carrie* (1900), *An American Tragedy* (1925).

DUFY, Raoul [1877-1953]; French painter and designer. Bright colours characterize his work, such as *Bois de Boulogne* (1929).

DURRELL, Lawrence (George) [1912-]; British novelist, poet and playwright (born in India). *The Alexandria Quartet* (1957), *Clea* (1960).

EAMES, Charles [1907-1978]; American designer, especially well known for his moulded plywood furniture of the 1940s.

EHRENBURG, Ilya [1891-1967]; Russian novelist and journalist. Novels include *The Storm* (1941), *The Thaw* (1954).

ELGAR, Sir Edward William [1857-1934]; British composer, especially of orchestral and choral works. *Enigma Variations* (1896), *Dream of Gerontius* (1900).

ELIOT, Thomas Stearns [1888-1965]; American-born British poet and playwright. *The Waste Land* (1922), *Murder in the Cathedral* (1935).

ERNST, Max [1891-1976]; German painter and sculptor; associated with the SURREALIST and DADA movements.

EVANS, Bergen [1904-78]; American writer, critic and grammarian. A man concerned with words; who wrote and made radio and TV appearances in this field. *Dictionary of Contemporary American Usage* 1968.

FALLA, Manuel de [1876-1946]; Spanish composer, especially of Spanish folk themes. *The Three-Cornered Hat* (ballet, 1919).

FAULKNER, William Harrison [1897-1962]; American novelist, particularly dealing with the American South. *The Sound and the Fury* (1929), *The Reivers* (1962).

FITZGERALD, (Francis) Scott (Key) [1896-

1940]; American novelist and short-story writer. His stories of the 1920s were immediately successful. *The Great Gatsby* (1925), *Tender is the Night* (1934).

FLAGSTAD, Kirsten [1895-1962]; Norwegian operatic soprano, best-known in Wagner's operas.

FLESCH, Carl [1873-1944]; Hungarian violinist and teacher of some of the best-known violinists of the present day.

FORSTER, Edward Morgan [1879-1970]; British novelist, well-known for his *A Passage to India* (1924), as well as *Howards End* (1910), and *Maurice* (1971).

FRANCE, Anatole (Jacques Anatole François Thibault) [1844-1924]; French novelist, poet and critic. Nobel prize for literature, 1921. *The Crime of Sylvester Bonnard* (1881), *Penguin Island* (1909).

FROST, Robert Lee [1874-1963]; American poet, who usually wrote about New England. *Collected Poems* (1931).

FRY, Christopher (Christopher Harris) [1907-]; British playwright of verse plays: *The Lady's Not for Burning* (1949), *Venus Observed* (1950).

FURTWÄNGLER, Wilhelm [1886-1954]; German conductor, pianist and composer. Conductor of the Berlin Philharmonic, he remained in Germany, despite his opposition to the Nazis.

GALSWORTHY, John [1867-1933]; British novelist and playwright. Famed for *The Forsyte Saga* (1922). Nobel prize for literature, 1932.

GENET, Jean [1910-1986]; French playwright and essayist. An EXISTENTIALIST, after spending his youth in prisons and reformatories. *The Maids* (1948), *The Blacks* (1959).

GIACOMETTI, Alberto [1901-66]; Swiss sculptor and painter, mainly of solitary figures.

GIDE, André Paul Guillaume [1869-1951]; French novelist and essayist. *The Immoralist* (1902), *Strait is the Gate* (1909).

GILL, (Arthur) Eric (Rowton) [1882-1940]; British typographer, stone-carver, engraver and author. Designed the 'Perpetua' and Gill Sans typefaces.

GOLDING, William (Gerald) [1911-]; British novelist, best known for *Lord of the Flies* (1954). *Pincher Martin* (1956). Nobel prize for literature, 1983.

GORKY, Maxim (Aleksei Maximovich Pyesh-

kov) [1868-1936]; Russian novelist,¦ playwright and short-story writer. A critic of Lenin, his death is something of a mystery. *The Lower Depths* (1902), *Mother* (1907).

GRASS, Günter [1927-]; German novelist and playwright. *The Tin Dum* (1959), *Dog Years* (1965).

GRAVES, Robert Ranke [1895-1985]; British poet, novelist and critic. *Goodbye to All That* (1929), *Claudius the God* (1934).

GREENE, Graham [1904-]; British novelist and playwright. *The Power and the Glory* (1940), *The Third Man* (1949), *The Quiet American* (1955).

GREY, Zane [1875-1939]; American novelist of Western tales. Among the 54 titles are *The Last of the Plainsmen* (1908) and *Riders of the Purple Sage* (1912).

GROPIUS, Walter Adolph [1883-1969]; German architect; founder and director of the BAUHAUS at Weimar 1919-28.

HARDY, Thomas [1840-1928]; British novelist and poet. Began as an architect, writing his first novel *Desperate Remedies* in 1871. Others were *Far From the Madding Crowd* (1874), and *Jude the Obscure* (1896). His *Collected Poems* appeared in 1931.

HEARTFIELD, John (Helmut Herzfeld) [1891-1968]; German born artist, strongly anti-Nazi. Changed his name to an English version in 1913 as a protest against German militarism.

HEIFETZ, Jascha [1901-]; American (Russian-born) violinist; a virtuoso and child prodigy who was able to play a Mendelssohn concerto at the age of 7.

HEMINGWAY, Ernest Miller [1899-1961]; American novelist and short-story writer. *A Farewell to Arms* (1929), *For Whom the Bell olls* (1940). Nobel prize for literature, 1954.

HEPWORTH, Dame Barbara [1903-75]; British sculptor with a semi-abstract style. *Reclining Figure* (1932), *Four Square* (1966).

HINDEMITH, Paul [1895-1963]; American composer (German-born) and viola player. Operas *Wir Bauen Eine Stadt* (for children, 1931), *Mathis der Maler* (1934, banned by the Nazis).

HOCKNEY, David [1937-]; British painter and designer, noted for his Californian 'swimming pool' paintings and for photomontage collection *Cameraworks*.

HOLST, Gustav (Gustavus Theodor von Holst)

Composer Benjamin Britten (far left); Poet T.S. Eliot (left) and actress Sarah Bernhardt (see page 189).

[1874-1934]; British composer of Swedish descent. His best-known work is *The Planets*.

HOWARD, Sir Ebenezer [1850-1928]; British town planner and originator of the Garden City movement; founder of Letchworth and Welwyn Garden cities. Began as a shorthand writer.

HUGHES, Richard Arthur Warren [1900-76] British novelist, playwright and poet. *A High Wind in Jamaica* (1929), *The Fox in the Attic* (1961).

HUXLEY, Aldous Leonard [1894-1963]; English novelist and essayist. *Brave New World* (1932), *Eyeless in Gaza* (1936).

JOHN, Augustus Edwin [1878-1961]; British painter, mainly in portraits (of LLOYD GEORGE, Bernard SHAW and T.E. LAWRENCE) and landscapes.

JOHNSON, Philip Cortelyou [1906-]; American architect, particularly associated with steel and glass constructions.

JOYCE, James Augustine [1882-1941]; Irish novelist, poet and playwright, one of the foremost of the century. *A Portrait of the Artist as a Young Man* (1914), *Ulysses* (1922), *Finnegan's Wake* (1939).

KAFKA, Franz [1883-1924]; Austrian-Jewish novelist and short-story writer. *The Trial* (1925), *America* (1927).

KAHN, Louis Isadore [1901-1974]; American architect, more recently in the romantic classicist style, including government buildings in Bangladesh and the Palace of Congresses, Venice.

KANDINSKY, Wassily [1866-1944]; Russian painter in ABSTRACT style. With *The Blue Rider* group, 1911-14.

KARAJAN, Herbert von [1908-]; Austrian conductor; of the Vienna State Opera 1945-64; musical director of Berlin Philharmonic.

KHATCHATURIAN, Aram Ilyich [1903-1978]; Russian composer and folksong student, whose music became popular in the west. *Sabre Dance, Gayaneh, Masquerade, Sparticus*.

KIPLING, (Joseph) Rudyard [1865-1936]; British novelist, poet and short-story writer, born in India. Poems include *Mandalay, The White Man's Burden, If, Gunga Din*; books *The Jungle Book* (1894), *Stalky & Co* (1899), *Kim* (1901).

KLEE, Paul [1879-1940]; Swiss painter and etcher in SURREALIST style.

KODALY, Zoltán [1882-1967]; Hungarian composer and teacher. Closely associated with Béla BARTÓK.

KOKOSCHKA, Oscar [1886-1980]; Austrian painter of portraits and landscapes in EXPRESSIONISTIC style. *The Tempest* (1914).

KREISLER, Fritz [1875-1962]; American (Austrian-born) violin virtuoso since the age of 12.

LARKIN, Philip Arthur [1922-1985]; British poet, novelist and editor. His work is witty and cynical.

LAWRENCE, David Herbert [1885-1930]; British novelist and short-story writer, son of a coalminer. *The White Peacock* (1911), *Sons and Lovers*

(1913), *Lady Chatterley's Lover* (1928).

LEGER, Fernand [1881-1965]; French painter in the CUBIST style.

LEONCAVALLO, Ruggiero [1858-1919]; Italian operatic composer, best known for *I Pagliacci* (1892).

LEWIS, (Harry) Sinclair [1885-1951]; American novelist, first in the USA to be awarded Nobel prize for literature, 1930. *Main Street* (1920), *Babbitt* (1922), *Arrowsmith* (1925); *Elmer Gantry* (1927), *Dodsworth* (1929).

LONDON, Jack (John Griffith London) [1876-1916]; American novelist and short-story writer, previously a sailor, tramp, and factory worker. Author of 51 books, including *The Call of the Wild* (1903), *The People of the Abyss* (1903), *The Sea-Wolf* (1904), *Martin Eden* (1909).

LORCA, Federico Garcia [1899-1936]; Spanish poet and playwright, murdered by supporters of FRANCO. *Blood Wedding* (1933) *The Poet in New York* (1940).

LUTYENS, Sir Edwin Landseer [1869-1944]; British architect. Works include the Viceroy's House, New Delhi (1912-30), The Cenotaph, Whitehall (1919), British Embassy, Washington (1926-29).

MACKENZIE, Sir (Edward Montague) Compton [1883-1972]; British novelist. *Carnival* (1914), *Sinister Street* (1913-14), *Whisky Galore* (1947).

MacNEICE, (Frederick) Louis [1907-63]; Irish poet and playwright. Also an outstanding translator. *The Dark Tower* (BBC 1947).

MAETERLINCK, Maurice Polydore Marie Bernard [1862-1949]; Belgian playwright, poet and prose writer. Nobel prize for literature 1911. *Pelléas et Mélisande* (1892), *L'Oiseau Bleu* (1908).

MAGRITTE, René François-Ghislain [1898-1967]; Belgian SURREALIST painter. *The Rape* (1934), *Golconda* (1953).

MAHLER, Gustav [1860-1911]; Austrian composer and conductor. Director of the Vienna Imperial Opera, 1897-1907, and Metropolitan Opera, New York, 1907. Conductor of New York Philharmonic 1908-11.

MALAMUD, Bernard [1914-1986]; American novelist and short-story writer, especially on Jewish themes. *The Fixer* (1966), *The Tenants* (1971).

MALRAUX, André [1901-1976]; French novelist

and politician. Has taken part in revolutions and wars, and was a Resistance leader. *La Condition Humaine* (1933), *L'Espoir (1937)*.

MANN, Thomas [1875-1955]; German (later American) novelist, opposed to Nazis. Nobel prize for literature 1929. *Buddenbrooks* (1900), *The Magic Mountain* (1924).

MARTIN, Sir Leslie [1908-]; British architect in partnership with Sir Robert MATTHEW.

MASCAGNI, Pietro [1863-1945]; Italian composer, best known for his one-act opera *Cavalleria Rusticana* (1890).

MASEFIELD, John Edward [1878-1967]; British poet and novelist. Poet Laureate 1930-67. Well-known for sea poems and stories: *Salt Water Ballads* (1902), *Lost Endeavour* (1910).

MATISSE, Henri-Emile-Benoit [1869-1954]; French painter, leader of 'Les Fauves'; a group of artists renowned for their bright and violent colour. *Woman with the Hat* (1905), *The Red Studio* (1911).

MATTHEW, Sir Robert [1906-]; British architect, in partnership with Sir Leslie MARTIN. Responsible for The Royal Festival Hall, London (1949-51) and town centres.

MAUGHAM, William Somerset [1874-1965]; British novelist, playwright and masterful short-story writer. Plays include: *Lady Frederick* (1907), *The Constant Wife* (1927). Novels include: *Of Human Bondage* (1915), *The Moon and Sixpence* (1919), *Cakes and Ale* (1930).

MAURIAC, François [1885-1970]; French novelist and playwright. Nobel prize for literature, 1952. *Le Baiser au Lépreux* (1923), *Le Noeud de Vipères* (1932).

MAUROIS, André (Emile Salomon Wilhelm Herzog) [1885-1967] French novelist and biographer (of many leading people). *Lelia* (1952), *Olympio* (1954).

MAYAKOVSKY, Vladimir Vladimirovich [1893-1930]; Russian poet *A Cloud in Trousers* (1914), *The Backbone Flute* (1915).

MELBA, Dame Nellie (Helen Porter Mitchell) [1861-1931]; Australian operatic soprano, whose repertoire numbered 26 roles.

MENUHIN, Yehudi [1916-]; American-born violin virtuoso from the age of 7. Often performed with his sister Hephzibah (1920-1981).

MESSIAEN, Olivier [1908-]; French composer and organist. *Les Oiseaux Exotiques* (1956).

MIES VAN DER ROHE, Ludwig [1886-1969]; German-born American architect. Designed the Seagram Building, New York City.*

MILLER, Henry Valentine [1891-1980]; American novelist whose works were often banned. *Tropic of Cancer* (1934), *Tropic of Capricorn* (1939).

MILNE, Alan Alexander [1882-1956]; British author, best-known for his children's books: *When We Were Very Young* (1924), *Winnie-the-Pooh* (1926).

MIRÓ, Joan [1893-1983]; Spanish surrealist painter, similar in style to Paul KLEE.

MODIGLIANI, Amedeo [1884-1920]; Italian painter and sculptor, famed for his elongated heads. *Cellist* (1910).

MONDRIAN, Piet (Pieter Cornelis Mondiaan) [1872-1944]; Dutch ABSTRACT painter, leader of the De Stijl (the Style) movement, using rectangles of colour. *Broadway Boogie Woogie* (1943).

MONET, Claude [1840-1926]; French painter whose landscape painting *Impression: Sol Levant* (1874) gave rise to the term IMPRESSIONIST. *Rouen Cathedral* (1894).

MOORE, Henry [1898-1986]; British sculptor in a semi-abstract style. *North Wind* (1928).

MUSIL, Robert von [1880-1942]; Austrian novelist, who died leaving his many-volumed work *A Man Without Qualities* unfinished.

NABOKOV, Vladimir [1899-1977] Russian-born American novelist, best-known for his book *Lolita* (1955).

NAIPAUL, Vidiadhar Surajprasad [1932-]; West Indian (of Indian parentage) novelist. Stories deal with life in Trinidad: *The Mystic Masseur* (1957), *A House for Mr Biswas* (1961).

NERVI, Pier Luigi [1891-1979]; Italian architectural engineer and designer. Inventor of reinforced concrete. Designed the Turin Exhibition Hall (1948-9), and the Rome Sports Palace (1959).

NEWMAN, Barnett [1905-70]; American abstract EXPRESSIONIST painter.

NICHOLSON, Ben [1894-82] British abstract painter, son of Sir William Nicholson [1872-1949], also an artist.

O'CASEY, Sean (John Casey) [1880-1964]; Irish playwright who was associated with the Abbey Theatre in Dublin. *Juno and the Paycock*

Lady with Umbrella *by Claude Monet, the only impressionist artist fully recognized in his own time.*

(1924), *The Plough and the Stars* (1926).

OISTRAKH, David [1908-74]; Russian violinist and conductor. His son, Igor, is also a renowned violinist.

O'NEILL, Eugene Gladstone [1888-1953]; American playwright. Nobel prize for literature 1936. *Beyond the Horizon* (1920), *Anna Christie* (1922), *The Iceman Cometh* (1946).

ORWELL, George (Eric Arthur Blair) [1903-50]; British novelist (born in India), essayist and critic. *Animal Farm* (1945), *Nineteen Eighty-Four* (1949).

OSBORNE, John James [1929-]; British playwright. One of the 'angry young men' of the 1950s. *Look Back in Anger* (1956), *The Entertainer* (1957), *West of Suez* (1971).

PARKER, Dorothy (Dorothy Rothschild) [18931967]; American writer, poet and humorist. Her work often appeared in *The New Yorker* magazine. *Enough Rope* (1926).

PARTRIDGE, Eric Honeywood [1894-1979]; British etymologist and lexicographer, born in New Zealand. His life was devoted to the study of words, as revealed in such works as *A Dictionary of Slang and Unconventional English*, 1937; *Usage and Abusage*, 1942; and *A Dictionary of Catch Phrases*, 1977.

PASTERNAK, Boris Leonidovich [1890-1960]; Russian poet and novelist. Nobel prize for literature 1958. *Doctor Zhivago* (1957).

PEVSNER, Sir Nikolaus [1902-83]; German-born British art and architectural historian. His multi-volume 'Buildings of England' series set out to cover the whole of the country.

PICASSO, Pablo Ruiz [1881-1974]; Spanish painter and sculptor. Founded the CUBIST movement with Georges BRAQUE. Pictures include *Guernica* (1937) which depicted the horrors of the SPANISH CIVIL WAR.

PINTER, Harold [1930-]; British playwright. *The Caretaker* (1959), *The Birthday Party* (1960), *The Servant* (1962), *The Homecoming* (1965).

PIRANDELLO, Luigi [1867-1936]; Italian playwright and novelist. Nobel prize for literature 1934. *Six Characters in Search of an Author* (1921).

POLLOCK, (Paul) Jackson [1912-56]; American painter in the abstract EXPRESSIONIST style, and leader of the OP ART movement. *Autumn Rhythm* (1953).

POTTER, (Helen) Beatrix [1866-1943]; British writer and illustrator for children. *The Tale of Peter Rabbit* (1902), *The Tale of Squirrel Nutkin* (1903).

POULENC, Francis [1899-1963]; French composer, whose style was witty yet serious in purpose. Opera: *Dialogues of the Carmelites* (1953-56).

POUND, Ezra Weston Loomis [1885-1972]; American poet and critic. Greatly influenced other poets, he had occasional bouts of insanity, and during World War II broadcast fascist propaganda from Italy. *Cantos* (192560).

PRIESTLEY, John Boynton [1894-1984]; British novelist and playwright. *The Good Companions* (1929), *Time and the Conways* (play, 1937).

PROKOFIEV, Sergei Sergeyevich [1891-1953]; Russian composer. Music for film *Alexander Nevsky* (1938), ballets *Romeo and Juliet* (1935-36), Peter and the Wolf (1936).

Cathedral of Christ the King, Liverpool, by Sir Frederick Gibberd (above) and a country house by Lutyens (opposite).

PROUST, Marcel [1871-1922]; French novelist, best known for his eight-volume work *Remembrance of Things Past* (1913-27).

PUCCINI, Giacomo [1858-1924]; Italian composer of operas. *La Boheme* (1896), *Tosca* (1900), *Madame Butterfly* (1904).

RACHMANINOV, Sergei Vasilievich [1873-1943]; American (Russian-born) composer and piano virtuoso. *Rhapsody on a Theme by Paganini* (1934).

RAVEL, Maurice Joseph [1875-1937]; French composer. *Pavanne for a Dead Infanta* (1899), *Bolero* (1928).

RENOIR, Pierre Auguste [1841-1919]; French IMPRESSIONIST painter, a leader of that movement. *Le Moulin de la Galette* (1876), *Les Parapluies* (1883).

RICHARDS, Frank (Charles Harold St.John Hamilton) [1875-1961]; British author, the main contributor to the boys' papers *Magnet* and *Gem*, principally between the two World Wars. His famous creation was the character 'Billy Bunter'.

RILKE, Rainer Maria [1875-1926]; Austrian poet (b. Prague). *Stories of God* (1904), *Poems from the Book of Hours* (1905).

ROBBE-GRILLET, Alain [1922-]; French novelist and film director. *The Erasers* (1953), *Towards a New Novel* (1963).

RODIN, Auguste (François-Auguste-René) [18401917]; French sculptor. *The Thinker* (1880), *The Kiss* (1886).

ROTHKO, Mark (Marcus Rothkovitch) [1903-70]; American (Russian-born) abstract expressionist painter.

RUBINSTEIN, Artur [1886-1982]; Polish-born American violinist, particularly known for his performances of Chopin.

SAARINEN, Eero [1910-1961]; Finnish-born American architect. Designed the American Embassy, London.

SAINT-SAËNS, (Charles) Camille [1835-1921]; French composer and pianist. *Samson & Delilah* (1877), *Carnival of the Animals* (1886).

SALINGER, Jerome David [1919-]; American novelist and short-story writer. *The Catcher in the Rye* (1951).

SANTAYANA, George [1863-1952]; Spanish-born American philosopher and poet. *The Last Puritan* (1935).

SARGENT, Sir (Harold) Malcolm [1895-1967]; British conductor and organist. Chief conductor of the BBC Symphony Orchestra and of the Henry Wood Promenade Concerts.

SARTRE, Jean-Paul [1905-81]; French philosopher and novelist, leader of the EXISTENTIALIST movement.

SCHOENBERG, Arnold Franz Walter [1874-1951]; Austrian-born American composer who devised a new method of composition using a 12-tone series.

SCRIABIN, Aleksander Nikolayevich [1872-1915]; Russian composer and pianist. *Prometheus* (tone poem, 1911).

SEGOVIA, Andrés [1894-1987]; Spanish guitar virtuoso, who re-established the instrument in modern times.

SENGHOR, Leopold Sedar [1906-]; Sengalese poet, and first president of that country from 1960.

SHAW, George Bernard [1856-1950]; Irish playwright whose works are both witty and of political import. Nobel prize for literature, 1925. *Arms and the Man* (1894), *Man and Superman* (1905), *Pygmalion* (1913), *Saint Joan* (1923).

SHOLOKHOV, Mikhail Aleksandrovich [1905-84]; Russian novelist, particularly known for the 4-volume *And Quiet Flows the Don* (1928-40)

SHOSTAKOVICH, Dmitri [1906-75]; Russian composer, criticized by officialdom in the USSR for his operas *The Nose* (1930) and *A Lady Macbeth of Mtsensk* (1934).

SIBELIUS, Jean (Johan Julius Christian) [1865-1957]; Finnish composer, especially of Finnish national music. *Finlandia* (1900).

SICKERT, Walter Richard [1860-1942]; Germanborn British painter, influenced by Degas. *Ennui* (1914), *Pulteney Bridge* (1918).

SIMENON, Georges Joseph Christian [1903-]; Belgian novelist, a very large number of his books being concerned with the detective 'Inspector Maigret'. A long semi-autobiographical work *Pedigree*, appeared in 1948.

SINCLAIR, Upton Beall [1878-1968]; American novelist. *The Jungle* (1906), *Oil!* (1927), *Dragon's Teeth* (1942).

SITWELL, Dame Edith [1887-1964]; British poet, novelist and critic, renowned for her strong personality. *The Mother* (1915), *Façade* (1923), *I Live Under a Black Sun* (1937).

SITWELL, Sir Francis Osbert (5th Baronet) [1892-1969]; British poet, playwright and novelist; brother of Dame Edith SITWELL, *Mrs Kimber* (1937), *The Man Who Lost Himself* (1929), *Noble Essences* (1950).

SNOW, Baron (Charles Percy Snow) [1905-80]; British novelist and scientist. *The Two Cultures of the Scientific Revolution* (1959), *Strangers and Brothers* (series, 1940-70).

SOLZHENITSYN, Alexander Isaievich [1918-]; Russian novelist, historian and playwright. After receiving Nobel prize for literature in 1970, was accused of treason, and forced to leave Russia. *One Day in the Life of Ivan Denisovich* (1962), *The Gulag Archipelago* (1974).

SPENCE, Sir Basil Urwin [1907-76]; British architect. In 1951 he produced the winning design for the modern Coventry Cathedral.

SPENCER, Sir Stanley [1891-1959]; British artist. *Resurrection, Cookham* (1923-7), *Resurrection, Port Glasgow* (1947-50).

STEIN, Gertrude [1874-1946]; American writer. *The Autobiography of Alice B. Toklas* (1933).

STEINBECK, John Ernst [1902-68]; American novelist. Nobel prize for literature 1962. *Of Mice and Men* (1937), *The Grapes of Wrath* (1940), *East of Eden* (1952).

STEPHEN, Sir Leslie [1832-1904]; British critic and biographer, and editor, with Sir Sidney Lee, of the *Dictionary of National Biography* from 1890.

STEVENS, Wallace [1879-1955]; American poet. *Collected Poems* (1954).

STOCKHAUSEN, Karlheinz [1928-]; German composer, and creator of electronic music. *Kontakte* (1960), *Momente* (1962).

STRAUSS, Richard Georg [1864-1949]; German composer and director of Vienna State Opera. *Der Rosenkavalier* (1911), *Ariadne auf Naxos* (1912).

STRAVINSKY, Igor Fyodorovich [1882-1971]; Russian-born American composer, well-known for his ballets. *The Firebird* (1910), *Petrouchka* (1911), *The Rite of Spring* (1913).

SUTHERLAND, Graham Vivian [1903-80]; British painter, often of war-torn cities, landscapes, and portraits. His tapestry *Christ in Glory* (1962) is in Coventry Cathedral.

SUTHERLAND, Dame Joan [1926-]; Australian coloratura soprano, who gained overnight fame with her 'Lucia' in *Lucia di Lammermoor*.

SYNGE, John Millington [1871-1909]; Irish playwright and poet. A director of the Abbey theatre. *Riders to the Sea* (1905), *The Playboy of the Western World* (1907).

TAGORE, Sir Rabindranath [1861-1941]; Indian (Bengali) poet, novelist and playwright and painter. Nobel prize for literature 1913. *The Golden Boat* (1893).

TETRAZZINI, Luisa [1871-1940]; Italian operatic coloratura soprano.

THOMAS, Dylan Marlais [1914-53]; British (Welsh) poet. *Deaths and Entrances* (1946), *Under Milk Wood* (1954).

THURBER, James Grover [1894-1961]; American humorist and cartoonist. *The Owl in the Attic* (1931), *My Life and Hard Times* (1934).

TIPPETT, Sir Michael Kemp [1905-]; British composer. *The Midsummer Marriage* (1955), *A Child of Our Time* (1944).

TOLKIEN, John Ronald Reuel [1892-1973]; British author, scholar and philologist. Creator of the adult fairy stories in *The Hobbit* (1938), *The Lord of the Rings* (1954), *Silmarillion* (1977).

TOSCANINI, Arturo [1867-1957]; Italian conductor, and musical director of La Scala, Milan from 1898. Conductor of New York Philharmonic 1928-36; director of NBC Symphony Orchestra 1937-54.

UNDSET, Sigrid [1882-1949]; Norwegian novelist. Nobel prize for literature, 1928. *Kristin Lavransdatter* (three vols, 1920-22).

VALERY, Paul Ambroise Toussaint Jules [1871-1945]; French poet and critic. *La Jeune Parque* (1917), *Variété* (5 vols, 1922-44).

VAUGHAN WILLIAMS, Ralph [1872-1958]; British composer who used folk songs in his themes. *A London Symphony* (1914), *A Pastoral Symphony* (1921), *Hugh the Drover* (1924).

VERNE, Jules [1828-1905]; French novelist; the father of science fiction. *Five Weeks in a Balloon* (1863), *A Journey to the Centre of the Earth* (1864), *20,000 Leagues Under the Sea* (1870), *Around the World in Eighty Days* (1873).

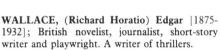
French novelist, Jules Verne (left) and Australian soprano Joan Sutherland.

WALLACE, (Richard Horatio) Edgar [1875-1932]; British novelist, journalist, short-story writer and playwright. A writer of thrillers.

WALTER, Bruno (Bruno Walter Schlesinger) [1867-1962]; German conductor, Vienna Opera, Metropolitan Opera, New York Philharmonic.

WALTON, Sir William Turner [1902-1983]; British composer. *Façade* (1926), *Belshazzar's Feast* (1931).

WARHOL, Andy [1930-1987]; American painter and film-maker, who helped start the POP ART movement, which featured paintings of soup tins.

WAUGH, Evelyn (Arthur St.John) [1903-66]; British novelist, often humorous and strongly satirical. *Decline and Fall* (1928), *Vile Bodies* (1930), *Brideshead Revisited* (1945).

WEBERN, Anton von [1883-1945]; Austrian composer, who used the 12-tone system of Arnold SCHOENBERG.

WEILL, Kurt [1900-50]; German composer of popular operas. *The Rise and Fall of the City of Mahagonny* (1927), *The Threepenny Opera* (1928).

WELLS, Herbert George [1866-1946]; British novelist and historian. Comedies include *Love and Mr Lewisham* (1900), *Kipps* (1905), *The History of Mr Polly* (1910). Science fiction titles include *The Time Machine* (1895), *The Invisible Man* (1897), *The Shape of Things to Come* (1933).

WEST, Dame Rebecca (Cicily Isabel Fairfield) [1892-1983]; British novelist, journalist and critic, and for a brief time, an actress. *The Return of the Soldier* (1918), *The Judge* (1922), *The Birds Fall Down* (1966).

WHITE, Patrick Victor Martindale [1912-]; Australian novelist, playwright and short-story writer. Nobel prize for literature 1973. *Happy Valley* (1939), *The Eye of the Storm* (1973).

WILLIAMS, Tennessee (Thomas Lanier Williams) [1911-83]; American playwright. *The Glass Menagerie* (1944), *A Streetcar Named Desire* (1947), *Cat on a Hot Tin Roof* (1955).

WILSON, Edmund [1895-1972]; American critic, playwright, poet and novelist. *Axel's Castle* (1931), *To the Finland Station* (1940).

WODEHOUSE, Pelham Grenville [1881-1975]; British novelist, short-story writer, playwright. Humorous novels deal with upper-class life, with famed characters such as Jeeves and Bertie Wooster. *Leave it to Psmith* (1923), *Carry on, Jeeves* (1925).

WOOD, Sir Henry Joseph [1869-1944]; British conductor, and in charge of promenade concerts at Queen's Hall, and later, the Royal Albert Hall.

WOOLF, (Adeline) Virginia (Virginia Stephen) [1882-1941]; British novelist and critic who married Leonard Sidney Woolf. *Orlando* (1928), *The Waves* (1931). Committed suicide.

WRIGHT, Frank Lloyd [1867-1959]; American architect, one of the most outstanding of the century. Designed the Guggenheim Museum, New York (1943).

YEATS, William Butler [1865-1939]; Irish poet and playwright, one of the leading poets of the century. Nobel prize for literature, 1923. *The Countess Cathleen* (play, 1892), *Last Poems* (1940).

SOME BOOKS PUBLISHED DURING THE TWENTIETH CENTURY

Where books by foreign authors are shown with English titles, the date given is for the English translation.

Abbreviations: Aus= Australian; Bel= Belgian; Braz= Brazilian; Can= Canadian; Cz= Czech; Fr= French; GB= Great Britain; Ger= German; Ire= Ireland; It= Italian; NG= Nigerian; Nor= Norwegian; Rus= Russia; SA= South Africa; Sw= Sweden; USA= United States; USSR= Soviet Union

1900

Lord Jim	Joseph Conrad (GB)
Love and Mr Lewisham	H.G. Wells (GB)
The Tale of Peter Rabbit	Beatrix Potter (GB)
The Web of Life	Robert Herrick (USA
Sister Carrie	Theodore Dreiser (USA)
The Wonderful World of Oz	Frank Baum (USA)

1901

Kim	Rudyard Kipling (GB)
Hawthorn and Lavender	W.E. Henley (GB)
The Octopus	Frank Norris (USA)

1902

Just So Stories	Rudyard Kipling (GB)
Typhoon	Joseph Conrad (GB)
Heart of Darkness	Joseph Conrad (GB)
The Hound of the Baskervilles	Sir Arthur Conan Doyle (GB)
The Path to Rome	Hilaire Belloc (GB)
Mrs Craddock	W. Somerset Maugham (GB)
Salt Water Ballads	John Masefield (GB)
The Golden Bowl	Henry James (USA)

1903

The Way of All Flesh	Samuel Butler (GB)
The Private Papers of Henry Ryecroft	George Gissing (GB)
The Call of the Wild	Jack London (USA)
The Story of My Life	Helen Keller (USA)

1904

Nostromo	Joseph Conrad (GB)
Traffics and Discoveries	Rudyard Kipling (GB)
The Island Pharisees	John Galsworthy (GB)
The Common Lot	Robert Herrick (USA)
The Sea Wolf	Jack London (USA)

1905

The Lake	George Moore (GB)
The Return of Sherlock Holmes	Sir Arthur Conan Doyle (GB)
Kipps	H.G. Wells (GB)
Where Angels Fear to Tread	E.M.Forster (GB)

1906

The Man of Property	John Galsworthy (GB)
The Railway Children	E. Nesbit (GB)
The Jungle	Upton Sinclair (USA)
The Devil's Dictionary	Ambrose Bierce (USA)

1907

The Secret Agent	Joseph Conrad (GB)
The Longest Journey	E.M. Forster (GB)
Cautionary Tales	Hilaire Belloc (GB)

1908

Anne of Green Gables	L.M. Montgomery (Can)
The Old Wives' Tale	Arnold Bennett (GB)
The Man Who Was Thursday	G.K. Chesterton (GB)
All Things Considered	G.K. Chesterton (GB)
A Room With a View	E.M. Forster (GB)
Autobiography of a Super-Tramp	W.H. Davies (GB)
The Wind in the Willows	Kenneth Grahame (GB)
A Lume Spento	Ezra Pound (USA)

1909

The Blue Bird	Maurice Maeterlinck (Bel)
Penguin Island	Anatole France (Fr)
Tono Bungay	H.G. Wells (GB)
The History of Mr Polly	H.G. Wells (GB)
Ann Veronica	H.G. Wells (GB)
Three Lives	Gertrude Stein (USA)

1910

Clayhanger	Arnold Bennett (GB)
The Ball and the Cross	G.K.Chesterton (GB)
Howards End	E.M. Forster (GB)
Psmith in the City	P.G. Wodehouse (GB)
Lost Endeavour	John Masefield (GB)
Prester John	John Buchan (GB)

1911

Under Western Eyes	Joseph Conrad (GB)
The Card	Arnold Bennett (GB)
Mr Perrin and Mr Traill	Hugh Walpole (GB)
The White Peacock	D.H. Lawrence (GB)
Zuleika Dobson	Max Beerbohm (GB)
The Secret Garden	Frances Hodgson Burnett (GB)

1912

The Unbearable Bassington	Saki (GB)
In Accordance with the Evidence	Oliver Onions (GB)
The Financier	Theodore Dreiser (USA)

1913
Chance	Joseph Conrad (GB)
Sinister Street	Compton Mackenzie (GB)
Sons and Lovers	D.H. Lawrence (GB)
A Boy's Will	Robert Frost (USA)
The Custom of the Country	Edith Wharton (USA)

1914
Vandover and the Brute	Frank Norris (USA)
North of Boston	Robert Frost (USA)
The Titan	Theodore Dreiser (USA)

1915
Green Mansions	W.H. Hudson (GB)
The Good Soldier	Ford Madox Ford (GB)
Of Human Bondage	W. Somerset Maugham (GB)
1914 and Other Poems	Rupert Brooke (GB)
The Thirty-Nine Steps	John Buchan (GB)

1916
Caprice	Ronald Firbank (GB)
A Portrait of the Artist as a Young Man	James Joyce (Ire)
The Man Against the Sky	Edward Arlington Robinson (USA)

1917
A Diversity of Creatures	Rudyard Kipling (GB)
South Wind	Norman Douglas (GB)
Nocturne	Frank Swinnerton (GB)
The Old Huntsman	Siegfried Sassoon (GB)

1918
The Magic Pudding	Norman Lindsay (Aus)
Piccadilly Jim	P.G. Wodehouse (GB)
The Return of the Soldier	Rebecca West (GB)
My Antonia	Willa Cather (USA)
The Magnificent Ambersons	Booth Tarkington (USA)

1919
The Moon and Sixpence	W. Somerset Maugham (GB)
Reynard the Fox	John Masefield (GB)
Valmouth	Ronald Firbank (GB)
The Gunroom	Charles Morgan (GB)
The Dark River	Sarah Gertrude Millin (SA)
Winesburg, Ohio	Sherwood Anderson (USA)

1920
Chéri	Colette (Fr)
In Chancery	John Galsworthy (GB)
Women in Love	D.H. Lawrence (GB)
The Story of Dr Doolittle	Hugh Lofting (GB)
Poor White	Sherwood Anderson (USA)
This Side of Paradise	F. Scott Fitzgerald (USA)
Main Street	Sinclair Lewis (USA)
The Age of Innocence	Edith Wharton (USA)

PENGUIN BOOKS

THE BODLEY HEAD · ARIEL ANDRÉ MAUROIS · THE BODLEY HEAD

COMPLETE · UNABRIDGED

1921
Héloise and Abelard	George Moore (GB)
To Let	John Galsworthy (GB)
Chrome Yellow	Aldous Huxley (GB)
Three Soldiers	John Dos Passos (USA)

1922
Remembrance of Things Past*	Marcel Proust (Fr)
Hassan	James Elroy Flecker (GB)
The Waste Land	T.S. Eliot (GB)
Futility	William Gerhardie (GB)
Lady into Fox	David Garnett (GB)
The Judge	Rebecca West (GB)
Ulysses	James Joyce (Ire)
The Enormous Room	E.E. Cummings (USA)
Babbitt	Sinclair Lewis (USA)
One of Ours	Willa Cather (USA)
Three Soldiers	John Dos Passos (USA)
	*Beginning (ends 1970)

1923
Black Bryony	T.F. Powys (GB)
Antic Hay	Aldous Huxley (GB)
Harmonium	Wallace Stevens (USA)

1924
Strait is the Gate	André Gide (Fr)
Lord Raingo	Arnold Bennett (GB)
Some Do Not...	Ford Madox Ford (GB)
A Passage to India	E.M. Forster (GB)
The Spanish Farm	R.H. Mottram (GB)
The Inimitable Jeeves	P.G. Wodehouse (GB)
Ukridge	P.G. Wodehouse (GB)
Sard Harker	John Masefield (GB)

Pastors and Masters	Ivy Compton-Burnett (GB)
The Green Bay Tree	Louis Bromfield (USA)
So Big	Edna Ferber (USA)

1925

The Desert of Love	François Mauriac (Fr)
No More Parades	Ford Madox Ford (GB)
Portrait of a Man	
With Red Hair	Hugh Walpole (GB)
Mrs Dalloway	Virginia Woolf (GB)
Those Barren Leaves	Aldous Huxley (GB)
The Sailor's Return	David Garnett (GB)
Turbott Wolfe	William Plomer (SA)
An American Tragedy	Theodore Dreiser (USA)
Manhattan Transfer	John Dos Passos (USA)
The Great Gatsby	F. Scott Fitzgerald (USA)
Arrowsmith	Sinclair Lewis (USA)

1926

The World of William Clissold	H.G. Wells (GB)
A Man Could Stand Up	Ford Madox Ford (GB)
Winnie-the-Pooh	A.A. Milne (GB)
Soldiers Pay	William Faulkner (USA)
Early Autumn	Louis Bromfield (USA)

1927

The Bullfighters	Henry de Montherlant (Fr)
Jeremy at Crale	Hugh Walpole (GB)
Meet Mr Mulliner	P.G. Wodehouse (GB)
To the Lighthouse	Virginia Woolf (GB)
Tarka the Otter	Henry Williamson (GB)
The Magic Mountain	Thomas Mann (Ger)
Death Comes for the Archbishop	Willa Cather (USA)
The Grandmothers	Glenway Westcott (USA)
Elmer Gantry	Sinclair Lewis (USA)
Oil!	Upton Sinclair (USA)
The Bridge of San Luis Rey	Thornton Wilder (USA)

1928

Mr Blatsworthy on Rampole Island	H.G. Wells (GB)
Last Post	Ford Madox Ford (GB)
Ashenden	W. Somerset Maugham (GB)
Point Counter Point	Aldous Huxley (GB)
Decline and Fall	Evelyn Waugh (GB)
Orlando	Virginia Woolf (GB)
John Brown's Body	Stephen Vincent Benét (USA)

1929

The Fortunes of	
Richard Mahony	Henry Handel Richardson (Aus)
Les Enfants Terribles	Jean Cocteau (Fr)
Living	Henry Green (GB)
The Testament of Beauty	Robert Bridges (GB)
Death of a Hero	Richard Aldington (GB)
Good-bye to All That	Robert Graves (GB)
Brothers and Sisters	Ivy Compton-Burnett (GB)

The Good Companions	J.B. Priestley (GB)
The Man Within	Graham Greene (GB)
A High Wind in Jamaica	Richard Hughes (GB)
The Near and the Far	L.H. Myers (GB)
A Farewell to Arms	Ernest Hemingway (USA)
The Sound and the Fury	William Faulkner (USA)
Sartoris	William Faulkner (USA)
Little Caesar	W.R. Burnett (USA)

1930

The Immoralist	André Gide (Fr)
A True Story	Stephen Hudson (GB)
Cakes and Ale	W. Somerset Maugham (GB)
The Apes of God	Percy Wyndham Lewis (GB)
Nothing to Pay	Caradoc Evans (GB)
Vile Bodies	Evelyn Waugh (GB)
Kristin Lavransdatter	Sigrid Undset (Nor)
As I Lay Dying	William Faulkner (USA)

1931

Buttercups and Daisies	Compton Mackenzie (GB)
Tobit Transplanted	Stella Benson (GB)
The Waves	Virginia Woolf (GB)
Swallows and Amazons	Arthur Ransome (GB)
Grand Hotel	Vicki Baum (USA)

1932

Brave New World	Aldous Huxley (GB)
Light in August	William Faulkner (USA)
Tobacco Road	Erskine Caldwell (USA)
The Good Earth	Pearl Buck (USA)

1933

The Bulpington of Blup	H.G. Wells (GB)
The Shape of Things to Come	H.G. Wells (GB)
The Dance of Death	W.H. Auden (GB)
A Glastonbury Romance	John Cowper Powys (GB)
Murder Must Advertise	Dorothy L. Sayers (GB)
Testament of Youth	Vera Brittain (GB)
Great Circle	Conrad Aiken (USA)
God's Little Acre	Erskine Caldwell (USA)
The Autobiography of	
Alice B. Toklas	Gertrude Stein (USA)
Miss Lonelyhearts	Nathanael West (USA)

1934

I, Claudius	Robert Graves (GB)
The Artificial Princess	Ronald Firbank (GB)
Resurrection	William Gerhardie (GB)
Voyage in the Dark	Jean Rhys (GB)
Tender is the Night	F. Scott Fitzgerald (USA)
Tropic of Cancer	Henry Miller (USA)
Appointment in Samarra	John O'Hara (USA)
Call it Sleep	Henry Roth (USA)
And Quiet Flows	
the Don	Mikhail Sholokhov (USSR)

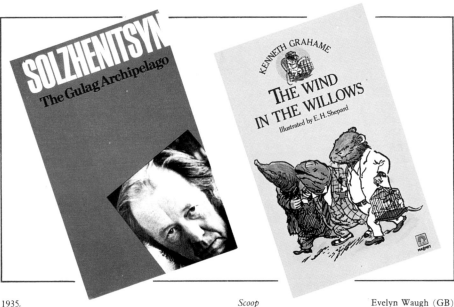

1935.

The Last Puritan	Sherwood Anderson (USA)
Journeyman	Erskine Caldwell (USA)
Tortilla Flat	John Steinbeck (USA)
Judgement Day	James T. Farrell (USA)
Of Time and the River	Thomas Wolfe (USA)
The Last Puritan	George Santayana (USA)

1936

Eyeless in Gaza	Aldous Huxley (GB)
Absalom, Absalom!	William Faulkner (USA)
Black Spring	Henry Miller (USA)
Men and Brethren	James Gould Cozzens (USA)
Gone With the Wind	Margaret Mitchell (USA)

1937

Days of Hope	André Malraux (Fr)
The Four Winds of Love	Compton Mackenzie (GB)
The Revenge for Love	Percy Wyndham Lewis (GB)
A Handful of Dust	Evelyn Waugh (GB)
To Have and Have Not	Ernest Hemingway (USA)
The Late George Apley	John P. Marquand (USA)
I Can Get It for You Wholesale	Jerome Weidman (USA)
Of Mice and Men	John Steinbeck (USA)
The Rains Came	Louis Bromfield (USA)

1938

House of All Nations	Christina Stead (Aus)
Count Belisarius	Robert Graves (GB)

Scoop	Evelyn Waugh (GB)
Brighton Rock	Graham Greene (GB)
In Hazard	Richard Hughes (GB)
Overtures to Death	Cecil Day Lewis (GB)
The Hobbit	J.R.R. Tolkien (GB)
America	Franz Kafka (Ger)
U.S.A.	John Dos Passos (USA)
The Fathers	Allen Tate (USA)
The Yearling	Marjorie Kinnan Rawlings (USA)
Night Rider	Robert Penn Warren (USA)

1939

Foveaux	Kylie Tennant (Aus)
Happy Valley	Patrick White (Aus)
My Friend Maigret	Georges Simenon (Bel)
Finnegan's Wake	James Joyce (Ire)
What's Become of Waring?	Anthony Powell (GB)
Goodbye to Berlin	Christopher Isherwood (GB)
The Grapes of Wrath	John Steinbeck (USA)
Night Rider	Robert Penn Warren (USA)
Tropic of Capricorn	Henry Miller (USA)
Wickford Point	John P. Marquand (USA)
The Day of the Locust	Nathanael West (USA)
The Nazarene	Sholem Asch (USA)
The Big Sleep	Raymond Chandler (USA)

1940

The Man Who Loved Children	Christina Stead (Aus)
The Power and the Glory	Graham Greene (GB)
Strangers and Brothers	C.P. Snow (GB)

Darkness at Noon	Arthur Koestler (GB)
World's End	Upton Sinclair (USA)
The Heart is a	
Lonely Hunter	Carson McCullers (USA)
Native Son	Richard Wright (USA)
Trouble in July	Erskine Caldwell (USA)
For Whom the Bell Tolls	Ernest Hemingway (USA)
Of Mice and Men	John Steinbeck (USA)
The Hamlet	William Faulkner (USA)
The Don Flows Home	
to the Sea	Mikhail Sholokhov (USSR)

1941
Between the Acts	Virginia Woolf (GB)
Parents and Children	Ivy Compton-Burnett (GB)
The Last Tycoon	F. Scott Fitzgerald (USA)
H.M. Pulham, Esq.	John P. Marquand (USA)
The Storm	Ilya Ehrenburg (USSR)

1942
Put Out More Flags	Evelyn Waugh (GB)
Dragon's Teeth	Upton Sinclair (USA)

1943
Georgia Boy	Erskine Caldwell (USA)
So Little Time	John P. Marquand (USA)
Western Star	Stephen Vincent Benét (USA)

1944
The Razor's Edge	W. Somerset Maugham (GB)
A Woman in Sunshine	Frank Swinnerton (GB)
The Burning of the Leaves	Laurence Binyon (GB)
The Horse's Mouth	Joyce Cary (GB)
The Shrimp and the Anemone	L.P. Hartley (GB)
Boston Adventure	Jean Stafford (USA)

1945
Bonjour Tristesse	Françoise Sagan (Fr)
Loving	Henry Green (GB)
The Story of Ragged Robyn	Oliver Onions (GB)
Brideshead Revisited	Evelyn Waugh (GB)
Animal Farm	George Orwell (GB)
The Unquiet Grave	Cyril Connolly (GB)
Black Boy	Richard Wright (USA)
A Bell for Adano	John Hersey (USA)

1946
The Outsider	Albert Camus (Fr)
Late Harvest	Norman Douglas (GB)
All the King's Men	Robert Penn Warren (USA)
The Member of	
the Wedding	Carson McCullers (USA)
Paterson	William Carlos Williams (USA)

1947
Thérèse: A Portrait	
in Four Parts	François Mauriac (Fr)

The Roads to Freedom	Jean-Paul Sartre (Fr)
An Avenue of Stone	Pamela Hansford Johnson (GB)
Under the Volcano	Malcolm Lowry (GB)
The Diary of Anne Frank	Anne Frank (Ger)
Mafeking Road	H.C. Bosman (SA)
The Mountain Lion	Mary McCarthy (USA)
The Victim	Saul Bellow (USA)
The Stoic	Theodore Dreiser (USA)
The Middle of the Journey	Lionel Trilling (USA)
Tales of the South Pacific	James A.Michener (USA)
Mother	Maxim Gorky (USSR)

1948
The Aunt's Story	Patrick White (Aus)
Man's Estate	André Malraux (Fr)
Poems	Gerard Manley Hopkins (GB)
Complete Poems	Richard Aldington (GB)
The Loved One	Evelyn Waugh (GB)
The Heart of the Matter	Graham Greene (GB)
A Summer to Decide	Pamela Hansford Johnson (GB)
Joseph and His Brethren	Thomas Mann (Ger)
Cry the Beloved Country	Alan Paton (SA)
Guard of Honour	James Gould Cozzens (USA)
The Home Place	Wright Morris (USA)
The Naked and the Dead	Norman Mailer (USA)
The Pisan Cantos	Ezra Pound (USA)

1949
The Third Man	Graham Greene (GB)
The Meaning of Treason	Rebecca West (GB)
Nineteen Eighty-Four	George Orwell (GB)
The Woman of Rome	Alberto Moravia (It)
Sexus	Henry Miller (USA)

1950
The Go-Between	L.P. Hartley (GB)
The Grass is Singing	Doris Lessing (GB)
Molloy	Samuel Beckett (Ire)
The Family Moskatt	Isaac Singer (USA)

1951
The Masters	C.P. Snow (GB)
A Question of Upbringing	Anthony Powell (GB)
The Daughter of Time	Josephine Tey (GB)
The Cruel Sea	Nicholas Monsarrat (GB)
Venture to the Interior	Laurens van der Post (SA)
Lie Down in Darkness	William Styron (USA)
The Grass Harp	Truman Capote (USA)
The Catcher in the Rye	J.D. Salinger (USA)
The Cain Mutiny	Herman Wouk (USA)
From Here to Eternity	James Jones (USA)

1952
Mr Nicholas	Thomas Hinde (GB)
A Step in Silence	P.H. Newby (GB)
Hemlock and After	Angus Wilson (GB)
The Borrowers	Mary Norton (GB)

Museum Pieces	William Plomer (SA)
The Invisible Man	Ralph Ellison (USA)
East of Eden	John Steinbeck (USA)
The Natural	Bernard Malamud (USA)
The Old Man and the Sea	Ernest Hemingway (USA)

1953

The Voices of Silence	André Malraux (Fr)
Hurry On Down	John Wain (GB)
The Castle	Franz Kafka (Ger)
Junkie	William Burroughs (USA)
Go Tell it on the Mountain	James Baldwin (USA)
The Adventures of Augie March	Saul Bellow (USA)

1954

Quite Early One Morning	Dylan Thomas (GB)
Lucky Jim	Kingsley Amis (GB)
Under the Net	Iris Murdoch (GB)
Self-Condemned	Percy Wyndham Lewis (GB)
Lucy in Her Pink Jacket	A.E. Coppard (GB)
Lord of the Flies	William Golding (GB)
The Lord of the Rings	J.R.R. Tolkien (GB)
The Huge Season	Wright Morris (USA)
In Love	Alfred Hayes (USA)
Pictures from an Institution	Randall Jarrell (USA)
The Thaw	Ilya Ehrenburg (USSR)

1955

Mother and Son	Ivy Compton-Burnett (GB)
The Quiet American	Graham Greene (GB)
The Picnic at Sakkara	P.H. Newby (GB)
The Less Deceived	Philip Larkin (GB)
Academic Year	D.J. Enright (GB)
The Day of the Monkey	David Karp (USA)
The Human Age	Percy Wyndham Lewis (GB)
The Confessions of Felix Krull	Thomas Mann (Ger)
The Trial	Franz Kafka (Ger)
A Charmed Life	Mary McCarthy (USA)
Lolita	Vladimir Nabokov (USA)

1956

Along the Arno	Brian Glanville (GB)
Collected Poems	W.B. Yeats (GB)
Anglo-Saxon Attitudes	Angus Wilson (GB)
The Towers of Trebizond	Rose Macaulay (GB)
The Fountain Overflows	Rebecca West (GB)
Pincher Martin	William Golding (GB)
*The Malayan Trilogy**	Anthony Burgess (GB)
A Dance in the Sun	Dan Jacobson (SA)
Six Feet in the Country	Nadine Gordimer (SA)
*Beginning (ends 1959)	

1957

Voss	Patrick White (Aus)
The Mandarins	Simone de Beauvoir (Fr)
Collected Poems	Edith Sitwell (GB)
Poems of Many Years	Edmund Blunden (GB)

The Ordeal of Gilbert Pinfold	Evelyn Waugh (GB)
Justine	Lawrence Durrell (GB)
Room at the Top	John Braine (GB)
Pnin	Vladimir Nabokov (USA)
The Assistant	Bernard Malamud (USA)
By Love Possessed	James Gould Cozzens (USA)

1958

Second Thoughts	Michel Butor (Fr)
The Bankrupts	Brian Glanville (GB)
Saturday Night and Sunday Morning	Alan Sillitoe (GB)
The Once and Future King	T.H. White (GB)
Mount Olive	Lawrence Durrell (GB)
Balthazar	Lawrence Durrell (GB)
The Unspeakable Skipton	Pamela Hansford Johnson (GB)
Things Fall Apart	Chinua Achebe (NG)
The Sibyl	Pär Lagerkvist (Sw)
Paterson	William Carlos Williams (USA)
Breakfast at Tiffany's	Truman Capote (USA)
Doctor Zhivago	Boris Pasternak (USSR)

1959

The Lost Domain	Alain-Fournier (Fr)
Jealousy	Alain Robbe-Grillet (Fr)
Mémoires d'Hadrien	Marguerite Yourcenar (Fr)
The Loneliness of the Long Distance Runner	Alan Sillitoe (GB)
Memento Mori	Muriel Spark (GB)
Cider With Rosie	Laurie Lee (GB)
The Naked Lunch	William Burroughs (USA)
Advertisements for Myself	Norman Mailer (USA)
Advise and Consent	Allen Drury (USA)
Goodbye Columbus	Philip Roth (USA)
The Vertebrate Story	Alfred S. Romer (USA)

1960

The Plague	Albert Camus (Fr)
Clea	Lawrence Durrell (GB)
Complete Poems	A.E. Housman (GB)
This Sporting Life	David Storey (GB)
The Violent Bear it Away	Flannery O'Connor (USA)
To Kill a Mockingbird	Harper Lee (USA)
The Magician of Lublin	Isaac Singer (USA)
Any Number Can Play	Clifton Fadiman (USA)

1961

Riders in the Chariot	Patrick White (Aus)
Scenes from Provincial Life	William Cooper (GB)
A Fox in the Attic	Richard Hughes (GB)
The Old Men at the Zoo	Angus Wilson (GB)
Lady Chatterley's Lover	D.H. Lawrence (GB)
A Severed Head	Iris Murdoch (GB)
The Prime of Miss Jean Brodie	Muriel Spark (GB)
The Tin Drum	Günter Grass (Ger)
The Heart of the Hunter	Laurens van der Post (SA)

Herzog	Saul Bellow (USA)
The Edge of Sadness	Edwin O'Connor (USA)
Catch 22	Joseph Heller (USA)
What Makes Sammy Run?	Budd Schulberg (USA)
Rabbit, Run	John Updike (USA)

1962

Gabriela, Clove and Cinnamon	Jorge Amado (Braz)
A Clockwork Orange	Anthony Burgess (GB)
The Golden Notebook	Doris Lessing (GB)
Lindmann	Frederic Raphael (GB)
As a Man Grows Older	Italo Svevo (It)
The Confessions of Zeno	Italo Svevo (It)
Ship of Fools	Katherine Anne Porter (USA)
Another Country	James Baldwin (USA)
Who's Afraid of Virginia Woolf?	Edward Albee (USA)
The Reivers	William Faulkner (USA)
The Sot-Weed Factor	John Barth (USA)
The End of the Road	John Barth (USA)
The Wall	John Hersey (USA)
The Slave	Isaac Singer (USA)
The Long March	William Styron (USA)

1963

The Watcher on the Cast-Iron Balcony	Hal Porter (Aus)
The Shoes of the Fisherman	Morris West (Aus)
Honey for the Bears	Anthony Burgess (GB)
Electra	Henry Treece (GB)
The Group	Mary McCarthy (USA)
Letting Go	Philip Roth (USA)
The Bell Jar	Sylvia Plath (USA)
One Day in the Life of Ivan Denisovich	Alexander Solzhenitsyn (USSR)

1964

The Little Girls	Elizabeth Bowen (GB)
The Snow Ball	Brigid Brophy (GB)
Nothing Like the Sun	Anthony Burgess (GB)
Corridors of Power	C.P. Snow (GB)
Arrow of God	Chinua Achebe (NG)
The Keepers of the House	Shirley Ann Grau (USA)
Julian	Gore Vidal (USA)

1965

Lost Empires	J.B. Priestley (GB)
Der Steppenwolf	Hermann Hesse (Ger)
An American Dream	Norman Mailer (USA)

1966

The Solid Mandala	Patrick White (Aus)
The Microcosm	Maureen Duffy (GB)
The Comedians	Graham Greene (GB)
The Birds Fall Down	Rebecca West (GB)
The Magus	John Fowles (GB)
The Late Bourgeois World	Nadine Gordimer (SA)

In Cold Blood	Truman Capote (USA)
The Wide Sargasso Sea	Jean Rhys (West Indies)

1967

The Pyramid	William Golding (GB)
The Mazemaker	Michael Ayrton (GB)
Miss Mamma Aimee	Erskine Caldwell (USA)
The Fixer	Bernard Malamud (USA)
Giles Goat-Boy	John Barth (USA)
When She Was Good	Philip Roth (USA)
The Chosen	Chaim Potok (USA)
The Confessions of Nat Turner	William Styron (USA)
Cancer Ward	Alexander Solzhenitsyn (USSR)

1968

The Painted Bird	Jerzy Kosinski (USA)
King, Queen, Knave	Vladimir Nabokov (USA)
Couples	John Updike (USA)

1969

Complete Poems	Walter De la Mare (GB)
Something to Answer For	P.H. Newby (GB)
The French Lieutenant's Woman	John Fowles (GB)
Portnoy's Complaint	Philip Roth (USA)
Mr Bridge	Evan S. Connell (USA)

1970

Last Things	C.P. Snow (GB)
Collected Poems	John Betjeman (GB)
The Millstone	Margaret Drabble (GB)
The Elected Member	Bernice Rubens (GB)
Mr Sammler's Planet	Saul Bellow (USA)
Bech	John Updike (USA)
Jonathan Livingston Seagull	Richard Bach (USA)
The Confederates	Thomas Keneally (AUS)

1971

Books Do Furnish a Room	Anthony Powell (GB)
Maurice	E.M. Forster (GB)
In a Free State	V.S. Naipaul (GB)
The Tenants	Bernard Malamud (USA)
Rabbit Redux	John Updike (USA)
The Winds of War	Herman Wouk (USA)
Fourth Street East	Jerome Weidman (USA)

1972

Ways of Seeing	John Berger (GB)
G	John Berger (GB)
Watership Down	Richard Adams (GB)
Enemies: A Love Story	Isaac Singer (USA)
The Optimist's Daughter	Eudora Welty (USA)

1973

The Eye of the Storm	Patrick White (Aus)
The Siege of Krishnapur	J.G. Farrell (GB)
Pentimento	Lillian Hellman (USA)
Fear of Flying	Erica Jong (USA)

Burr: A Novel	Gore Vidal (USA)	**1982**	
Slaughterhouse Five	Kurt Vonnegut (USA)	A Moving Target	William Golding (GB)
		Monsignor Quixote	Henry Graham Greene (GB)
1974		Constance, or	
The Good Soldier Schweik	Jaroslav Hasek (Cz)	Solitary Practices	Lawrence Durrell (GB)
The Rain Forest	Olivia Manning (GB)	Schindler's Ark	Thomas Keneally (Aus)
Falstaff	Robert Nye (GB)		
High Windows	Philip Larkin (GB)	**1983**	
Bring Forth the Body	Simon Raven (GB)	Waterland	Graham Swift (GB)
Holiday	Stanley Middleton (GB)	Stanley and the Women	Kingsley Amis (GB)
The Conservationist	Nadine Gordimer (SA)	Swallow	D.M. Thomas (GB)
Working	Studs Terkel (USA)	The Philosopher's Pupil	Iris Murdoch (GB)
The Gulag		The Life and Times of Michael K	J.M. Coetzee (SA)
Archipelago	Alexander Solzhenitsyn (USSR)	The Anatomy Lesson	Philip Roth (USA)
		Him With His Foot in His Mouth	Saul Bellow (USA)
1975			
Changing Places	David Lodge (GB)	**1984**	
Heat and Dust	Ruth Prawer Jhabvala (GB)	Mr Noon	D.H. Lawrence (GB)
Humboldt's Gift	Saul Bellow (USA)	The Fourth Protocol	Frederick Forsyth (GB)
Shogun	James Clavell (USA)	This Real Night	Rebecca West (GB)
Roll, Jordan, Roll	Eugene Genovese (USA)	Flaubert's Parrot	Julian Barnes (GB)
		Down from the Hill	Alan Sillitoe (GB)
1976		De Alfonce Tennis	J.P. Donleavy (USA)
California Time	Frederic Raphael (GB)	Parachutes and Kisses	Erica Jong (USA)
Saville	David Story (GB)	Tough Guys Don't Dance	Norman Mailer (USA)
Roots	Alex Haley (USA)	God Knows	Joseph Heller (USA)
1977		**1985**	
Silmarillion	J.R.R. Tolkien (GB)	Gentlemen in England	A.N. Wilson (GB)
Staying On	Paul Scott (GB)	Hawksmoor	Peter Ackroyd (GB)
Guest of Honour	Nadine Gordimer (SA)	Linden Hills	Gloria Naylor (USA)
The Uses of Enchantment	Bruno Bettelheim (USA)	Carpenter's Gothic	William Gaddis (USA)
Falconer	John Cheever (USA)		
		1986	
1978		The Old Devils	Kingsley Amis (GB)
The Sea, The Sea	Iris Murdoch (GB)	The Fisher King	Anthony Powell (GB)
Jake's Thing	Kingsley Amis (GB)	The Handmaid's Tale	Margaret Atwood (Can)
The Singapore Grip	J.G. Farrell (GB)	What's Bred in the Bone	Robertson Davies (Can)
		World's Fair	E.L. Doctorow (USA)
1979			
Darkness Visible	William Golding (GB)	**1987**	
Offshore	Penelope Fitzgerald (GB)	Moon Tiger	Penelope Lively (GB)
Life on Earth	David Attenborough (GB)	The Colour of Blood	Brian Moore (Ire)
Sophie's Choice	William Styron (USA)	The Book and the Brotherhood	Iris Murdock (GB)
Old Patagonian Express	Paul Theroux (USA)	Her Story	Dan Jacobson (SA)
		Rich in Love	Josephine Humphreys (USA)
1980		More Die of Heartbreak	Saul Bellow (USA)
Rites of Passage	William Golding (GB)	Beloved	Toni Morrison (USA)
A Brother's Tale	Stan Barstow (GB)		
Earthly Powers	Anthony Burgess (GB)	**1988**	
Nuns and Soldiers	Iris Murdoch (GB)	The Making of the Atomic Bomb	Richard Rhodes (USA)
The Middle Ground	Margaret Drabble (GB)	The Counterlife	Philip Roth (USA)
The Cut-Rate Kingdom	Thomas Keneally (Aus)	The Bonfire of the Vanities	Tom Wolfe (USA)
		A Brief History of Time	Stephen Hawking (GB)
1981		Nice Work	David Lodge (GB)
Midnight's Children	Salman Rushdie (GB)	The Satanic Verses	Salman Rushdie (Ind)
Weekend with Claude	Beryl Bainbridge (GB)	Oscar and Lucinda	Peter Carey (Aus)
The Sirian Experiments	Doris Lessing (GB)		
Loitering with Intent	Muriel Spark (GB)		

CINEMA, THEATRE, TV, RADIO, PERFORMERS AND ENTERTAINERS

ANTONIONI, Michelangelo [1912-]; Italian film director and scriptwriter. *Le Amiche* (1959), *Blow-up* (1967), *Zabriskie Point* (1969).
ARMSTRONG, Louis Daniel [1900-71]; 'Satchmo'. American black musician, a leading jazz trumpeter. Film: *Satchmo the Great* (1957).
ARTAUD, Antonin [1896-1948]; French drama critic and writer.
ASHCROFT, Dame Peggy (Edith Margaret Emily) [1907-]; British stage actress, particularly associated with Shakespearean roles. Also in films and TV. Awarded an Oscar in 1985.
ASHTON, Sir Frederic (William Mallandine) [1904-1988]; British ballet choreographer and director of the Royal Ballet 1952-70.
ASTAIRE, Fred (Frederick Austerlitz) [1899-1987]; American dancer and actor (stage and film). Often teamed with Ginger ROGERS. *Top Hat* (1935).
BACHARACH, Burt [1929-]; American pianist and composer. *Raindrops Keep Falling on My Head* (1970).
BALANCHINE, George (Georgi Melitonovich Balanchivadze) [1904-1983]; American (Russian-born) choreographer.
BARA, Theda (Theodosia Goodman) [1890-1955]; American silent-screen star, renowned for her 'vamp' roles. *A Fool There Was* (1916).
BARDOT, Brigitte [Camille Javal] [1934-]; French film star, known as the 'sex kitten'. *The Truth* (1961), *Love on a Pillow* (1962).
BARRAULT, Jean-Louis [1910-]; French stage and film actor. *Les Enfants du Paradis* (1944).
BASIE, Count (William Basie) [1904-84]; American jazz musician, band leader, composer and pianist.
BAYLIS, Lilian Mary [1874-1937]; British theatre manager, who changed the Old Vic from a music hall to the home of Shakespeare performances, and created Sadler's Wells as the centre of opera and ballet.
BEATLES, The (John Lennon [1940-80], Paul McCartney [1942-]; Ringo Starr [1940-]; George Harrison [1943-]); British pop group, who had a phenomenal and lasting success from their beginning in the 1960s.

BEIDERBECKE, Bix (Leon Bismarck Beiderbecke) [1903-31]; American jazz musician, cornet-player and composer.
BENNY, Jack (Benjamin Kubelsky) [1894-1974]; American comedian and film actor. In vaudeville from 1911, famed for his comic violin-playing. *Hollywood Revue of 1929*, *The Horn Blows at Midnight* (1945).
BERGMAN, (Ernst) Ingmar [1918-]; Swedish film director and screenwriter. *Prison* (1948), *Wild Strawberries* (1957), *Through a Glass Darkly* (1961).
BERGMAN, Ingrid [1915-82]; Swedish actress and film star. *Casablanca* (1943), *Anastasia* (1956).
BERKELEY, Busby (William Berkeley Enos) [1895-1976]; American stage and film director, renowned for his spectacular musicals. *Forty-Second Street* (1933), *Dames* (1934).
BERLIN, Irving (Israel Baline) [1888-]; American composer of over 1000 popular songs. *Alexander's Ragtime Band* (1911), *Easter Parade* (1948), *White Christmas* (1954).
BERNHARDT, Sarah (Henriette Rosine Bernard) [1844-1923]; French stage actress, famed for her tragic roles; briefly in silent films.
BOGART, Humphrey De Forest [1899-1957]; American film star, usually as the tough guy. *Dead End* (1937), *Casablanca* (1943), *The African Queen* (1952).
BOLDEN, Buddy (Charles Joseph) [1868-1931]; American cornet-player, who in 1895, formed the first jazz band in the U.S.
BOW, Clara [1905-65]; American film actress who, as the 'It' girl, depicted the young 'flapper' of the 1920s. *Mantrap* (1926), *It* (1927).
BOYER, Charles [1899-1978]; French film star. famous as the 'great lover'. *Caravan* (1934), *The Garden of Allah* (1936), *Algiers* (1938).
BRANDO, Marlon [1924-]; American stage and film star, a METHOD actor. *The Men* (1950), *A Streetcar Named Desire* (1951), *The Young Lions* (1958).
BROOK, Peter Stephen Paul [1925-]; British theatrical and film director: co-director of the Royal Shakespeare theatre. Film: *Lord of the Flies* (1969).
BUÑUEL, Luis [1900-1983]; Spanish film director and writer. *Robinson Crusoe* (1952), *Belle de Jour* (1966).

BURTON, Richard (Richard Jenkins) [1925-1984] ; British film and stage star. *Look Back in Anger* (1959), *Cleopatra* (1962), *Anne of a Thousand Days* (1970).

CAGNEY, James [1899-1986]; American film star, famed for his cocky personality. *The Public Enemy* (1931), *Angels With Dirty Faces* (1938), *Yankee Doodle Dandy* (1942).

CAMPBELL, Mrs Patrick (Beatrice Stella Tanner) [1865-1940]; British stage actress, a friend of George Bernard SHAW, who created the part of Eliza Doolittle for her.

CANTOR, Eddie (Edward Israel Iskowitz) [1892-1964]; American comedian and song and dance man, who appeared in Broadway musicals and films. *Kid Boots* (1926); *Roman Scandals* (1933). A film based on his life, *The Eddie Cantor Story* was made in 1953.

CAPRA, Frank [1897-]; American (Italian-born) film director. *It Happened One Night* (1934), *Mr Deeds Goes to Town* (1936), *Arsenic and Old Lace* (1944).

CARMICHAEL, Hoagy (Hoagland Howard Carmichael) [1899-1981]; American composer, pianist and singer. Songs: *Georgia on My Mind, Stardust, In the Cool, Cool, Cool of the Evening.*

CARNE, Marcel [1903-]; Leading French film director. *Le Jour Se Lève* (1939), *Les Enfants du Paradis* (1944).

CHAPLIN, Sir Charles Spencer (Charlie Chaplin) [1889-1977]; British film actor, director and producer. Famed for his role in silent films as the 'Little Tramp'. *The Gold Rush* (1924), *City Lights* (1931), *The Great Dictator* (1940). A film, *The Life Story of Charles Chaplin*, was made in Britain in 1926, but was never shown because of a threat of legal action.

CHEVALIER, Albert [1861-1923]; British comedian and songwriter, son of a French teacher. Famed for his cockney coster songs and sketches.

CHEVALIER, Maurice [1887-1972]; French singer, entertainer and film star. *The Love Parade* (1930), *Le Silence d'Or* (1947), *Gigi* (1958).

CLAIR, René (René Chomette) [1898-1981]; French film director of light comedy. *Sous Les Toits de Paris* (1929), *I Married a Witch* (1942), *Les Belles de Nuit* (1946).

COCHRAN, Sir Charles Blake [1872-1951]; British stage impresario, famed for his smart

The Beatles.

Ginger Rogers and Fred Astaire.

189

revues of the 1920s and 30s: *This Year of Grace* (1928), *Wake Up and Dream* (1929).

COLE, Nat 'King' (Nathaniel Adams Coles) [1919-65]; American singer and pianist, who popularized *Too Young*, *Unforgettable*, etc.

COOPER, Gary (Frank James Cooper) [1901-61]; American film star with a slow, deliberate manner. *A Farewell to Arms* (1932), *City Streets* (1932), *Mr Deeds Goes to Town* (1936), *For Whom the Bell Tolls* (1943).

COPEAU, Jacques [1878-1949]; French theatrical manager and director. His Paris 'home' was the Theatre du Vieux Colombier, where he used imaginative, simplified scenery.

CORNELL, Katharine [1898-1974]; American stage actress. After playing in stock companies, became one of Broadway's best-known leading ladies.

COWARD, Sir Noel Pierce [1899-1973]; British playwright, composer, actor and director. He wrote and appeared in his own plays, including *Hay Fever* (1925), *Private Lives* (1930), *Design for Living* (1932), *Blithe Spirit* (1941). He acted in, wrote and produced the film *In Which We Serve* (1941).

CRAWFORD, Joan (Lucille le Sueur) [1906-77]; American film star. *Grand Hotel* (1932), *Rain* (1932), *Mildred Pierce* (1945).

CROSBY, Harry Lillis (Bing) [1903-78]; American singer, a leading crooner of the 1930s and 40s, radio and film star. *Anything Goes* (1936), *Road to Singapore* (1940), *Going My Way* (1944).

CUNNINGHAM, Merce [1919-]; American dancer and choreographer of abstract dancing.

DAVIS, Bette (Ruth Elizabeth Davis) [1908-]; American film star, renowned for dramatic roles. *Of Humage Bondage* (1934), *Dangerous* (1935), *Jezebel* (1938), *The Little Foxes* (1941), *The Corn is Green* (1945).

DE HAVILLAND, Olivia [1916-]; British-born film star, sister of Joan Fontaine. *Gone With the Wind* (1939), *The Heiress* (1949).

DE MILLE, Cecil Blount [1881-1959]; American film director, a pioneer in Hollywood. *The Squaw Man* (1913), *The Ten Commandments* (1923, 1956), *The Sign of the Cross* (1932), *The Plainsman* (1936).

DE SICA, Vittorio [1902-76]; Italian film director and actor. *Bicycle Thieves* (1948), *Miracle in Milan* (1951), *Yesterday, Today and Tomorrow* (1964).

DE VALOIS, Dame Ninette [1898-]; Founder of the Royal Ballet, and director 1931-63. Former prima ballerina, and a leading choreographer.

DIAGHILEV, Serge Pavlovich [1872-1929]; Russian impresario of ballet, art and music. Formed the *Ballets Russes* 1911-29.

DIETRICH, Marlene (Maria Magdalena von Losch) [1901-]; German-born film star of glamorous legend. *The Blue Angel* (1930), *Shanghai Express* (1932), *Destry Rides Again* (1939), *Witness for the Prosecution* (1957).

DISNEY, Walter Elias (Walt) [1901-66]; American cartoon animator and film producer. Creator of Mickey Mouse, who first appeared in *Steamboat Willie* (1928). Other cartoon successes include *Snow White* (1937), *Pinocchio* (1939), *Fantasia* (1940).

DOUGLAS, Kirk (Issur Danielovitch Demsky) [1918-]; American film star. *The Strange Love of Martha Ivers* (1946), *Lust for Life* (1956), *Spartacus* (1960), *Cast a Giant Shadow* (1966).

DOVZHENKO, Alexander [1894-1956]; Russian film director and writer. *Arsenal* (1929), *Earth* (1930), *Aerograd* (1935).

DREYER, Carl [1889-1968]; Danish film director. *Leaves from Satan's Book* (1920), *Day of Wrath* (1943).

DUNCAN, Isadora [1878-1927]; American dancer who specialised in free form dancing.

DUSE, Eleonora [1858-1924]; Italian stage actress, especially known for her portrayal of *Hedda Gabler*. She was married to Gabrielle D'ANNUNZIO.

DYLAN, Bob (Robert Zimmerman) [1941-]; American singer and songwriter. *Blowin' in the Wind*.

EISENSTEIN, Sergei Mikhailovich [1898-1948]; Russian film director. *The Battleship Potemkin* (1925), *Alexander Nevsky* (1938), *Ivan the Terrible* (1944).

ELLINGTON, 'Duke' (Edward Kennedy Ellington) [1899-1974]; American jazz musician, bandleader, pianist and composer. *Mood Indigo*, *Don't Get Around Much Anymore*.

EVANS, Dame Edith Mary Booth [1888-1976]; British stage and film actress. Well-known in classic roles, and especially as Lady Bracknell in *The Importance of Being Earnest*.

FAIRBANKS, Douglas (Douglas Elton Thomson Ullman) [1883-1939]; American star of silent films in swashbuckling roles. *The Mark of Zorro* (1920), *Robin Hood* (1921). His son, Douglas Fairbanks Jnr (b. 1909) is also a film actor. He was made an honorary K.B.E. in 1949.

FIELDS, Gracie (Grace Stansfield) [1898-1979]; British singer, comedienne and film actress. *Sally in Our Alley* (1931), *Sing as We Go* (1934).

FIELDS, W.C. (William Claude Dukinfield) [1879-1946]; American comedian, film star and eccentric. *It's a Gift* (1934), *David Copperfield* (1934), *My Little Chickadee* (1940). A film, *W.C.Fields and Me* was made in 1976, with Rod Steiger in the part.

FITZGERALD, Ella [1918-]; American jazz singer and entertainer. Film: *St Louis Blues* (1955).

FLAHERTY, Robert Joseph [1884-1951]; American documentary film maker. *Nanook of the North* (1920), *Man of Aran* (1934), *Elephant Boy* (1937).

FLYNN, Errol [1909-59]; Tasmanian-born film star. *Captain Blood* (1935), *The Charge of the Light Brigade* (1936), *The Sea Hawk* (1940), *Gentleman Jim* (1942).

FOKINE, Mikhail Mikhailovich [1880-1942]; American (Russian-born) dancer and chief choreographer for the *Ballets Russes*.

FONDA, Henry Jaynes [1905-82]; American film and stage star. *Young Mr Lincoln* (1939), *The Grapes of Wrath* (1940), *Twelve Angry Men* (1957).

FONDA, Jane [1937-] ; American actress and social activist; daughter of Henry FONDA. *Cat Ballou* (1965), *Barbarella* (1968).

FONTANNE, Lynn [1887-1983]; American stage actress (British-born). With her husband, Alfred LUNT, became a famous theatrical couple.

FONTEYN, Dame Margot (Margot Fonteyn de Arias, born Margaret Hookham) [1919-]; British prima ballerina. President of the Royal Academy of Dancing since 1954.

FORD, John (Sean O'Feeney) [1895-1973]; American film director, especially of Western and adventure films. *The Informer* (1935), *Stagecoach* (1939), *The Grapes of Wrath*, (1940), *The Quiet Man* (1952).

GABLE, (William) Clark [1901-1960]; American film star of strongly masculine roles. *It*

Mickey Mouse with his creator, Walt Disney.

Margot Fonteyn and Rudolph Nureyev.

191

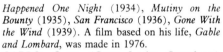

Happened One Night (1934), *Mutiny on the Bounty* (1935), *San Francisco* (1936), *Gone With the Wind* (1939). A film based on his life, *Gable and Lombard*, was made in 1976.

GARBO, Greta (Greta Lovisa Gustafsson) [1905-]; Swedish film star who became one of the Hollywood 'greats'. *Flesh and the Devil* (1927), *Anna Christie* (1930), *Queen Christina* (1933), *Ninotchka* (1939).

GARDNER, Ava (Lucy Johnson) [1922- ; American film star. *The Hucksters* (1947), *Show Boat* (1951), *The Barefoot Contessa* (1954).

GARLAND, Judy (Frances Gumm) [1922-69]; American film star and entertainer. *The Wizard of Oz* (1930), *Babes in Arms* (1939), *Meet Me in St Louis* (1944), *A Star is Born* (1954).

GERSHWIN, George [1898-1937]; American composer of Broadway musicals, concert music and popular songs. *Rhapsody in Blue* (1924), *Porgy and Bess* (1925), *Lady Be Good* (1924), *An American in Paris* (1928).

GERSHWIN, Ira (Israel) [1896-1983] American lyric-writer, who collaborated with his brother George GERSHWIN.

GIELGUD, Sir (Arthur) John [1904-]; British actor on stage and film. Famous as Shakespearean actor, notably as Hamlet in 192930.

GILLESPIE, Dizzy (John Birks Gillespie) [1917-]; American jazz trumpeter and composer. A modern jazz innovator, he formed his own orchestra in 1945.

GISH, Lilian (Lillian de Guiche) [1896-1984]; American silent film star; also more recently in modern films. *Birth of a Nation* (1914).

GODARD, Jean-Luc [1930-]; French film writer and director, semi-surrealist of the 'new wave'. *A Bout de Souffle* [Breathless] (1960).

GOLDWYN, Samuel (Samuel Goldfish) [1884-1974]; Polish-American film producer; *Wuthering Heights* (1939); *The Kid from Brooklyn* (1946) *The Secret Life of Walter Mitty* (1947).

GOODMAN, Benny (Benjamin David Goodman) [1909-]; American clarinettist and bandleader; *Hello, Beautiful* (1942).

GRAHAM, Martha [1893-]; American dancer and choreographer; a main influence on modern dance. She created, *c*.150 ballets developing body movement as emotional expression. *Appalachian Spring* (1944); *Clytemnestra* (1958).

GRANT, Cary (Archibald Leach) [1904-1986]; British-born debonair film actor; *I'm No Angel* (1933); *I Was a Male War Bride* (1949).

GRIERSON, John [1898-1972]; British documentary film maker. Founded GPO Film Unit and produced *Night Mail* (1936).

GRIFFITH, D.W. [David Wark Griffith] [1874-1948]; American film producer, the first major producer-director. He introduced many now familiar techniques with spectacular films: *The Birth of a Nation* [1915].

GROCK (Charles Adrien Wettach) [1880-1959]; Swiss musical clown and a master of mime.

Far left: Bob Hope in My Favourite Brunette, *1946. Centre left: Swedish star Greta Garbo. Left: D.W. Griffith, the first major film producer, on location in 1914.*

GUINNESS, Sir Alec [1914-]; British stage and film actor; impersonates a wide range of characters. *The Bridge on the River Kwai* (1957).

GUTHRIE, Sir Tyrone [1900-1971]; British theatre director. Working with the Old Vic and at Sadler's Wells, he had a fresh approach to traditional plays, especially Shakespeare.

HALEY, Bill (William John Clifton Haley) [1927-1981]; American musician, originator of 'rockabilly'. Best known with the band 'The Comets'.

HALL, Sir Peter Reginald Frederick [1930-]; British theatrical and film producer. Director of the National Theatre (1973-1988).

HAMMERSTEIN, Oscar II [1895-1960]; American lyricist. Working wth the composer Richard RODGERS he wrote *Oklahoma* (1943), *South Pacific* (1949) and *The Sound of Music* (1959).

HANDLEY, Thomas Reginald (Tommy) [1902-1949]; British radio comedian, famous for his long-running *ITMA* series during World War II.

HARDY, Oliver Nowell [1892-1957]; American film comedian, who in partnership with Stan LAUREL, made over 200 slapstick films. *Another Fine Mess.*

HARLOW, Jean (Harlean Carpenter) [1911-1937]; American blonde film star of the early '30s. *Hell's Angels* (1930); *Red Dust* (1932). Two films based on her life have been made: both called *Harlow*, and made in 1965.

HARRISON, Rex (Reginald Carey Harrison) [1908-]; British actor, appearing in many films, such as *Anna and the King of Siam* [1946], *The Ghost and Mrs Muir* (1947), and *My Fair Lady* (1964).

HART, Lorenz Milton [1895-1943]; American lyricist, writing with Richard RODGERS. *The Lady is a Tramp.*

HAWKS, Howard Winchester [1896-1977]; American film director of comedies and action dramas. *His Girl Friday* (1940); *The Big Sleep* (1946).

HAYES, Helen (Helen Brown) [1900-]; American stage and film actress. *Anastasia* (1956) *Airport* (1969).

HAYWORTH, Rita (Margarita Carmen Casino) [1918-1987]; American actress and dancer, often in fiery roles. *Gilda* (1946).

HELPMANN, Sir Robert [1909-1986]; Australian ballet dancer, choreographer and actor. *Miracle in the Gorbals* (1944).

HEPBURN, Katharine [1907-]; American stage and film actress. Many of her best films were made with Spencer TRACY. She has won three Academy Awards. Films: *Morning Glory* (1933); *Guess Who's Coming to Dinner* (1967); *The Lion in Winter* (1968).

HESTON, Charlton (John Charlton Carter) [1924-]; American film actor, particularly in Biblical and mediaeval epics. *Ben Hur* (1959); *El Cid* [1961].

HITCHCOCK, Alfred [1899-1984]; British film and TV director of suspense thrillers. *Blackmail* (1929); *The Thirty-Nine Steps* (1935) *Psycho* (1960) *The Birds* (1963).

HOFFMAN, Dustin [1937-]; American film actor. *The Graduate* (1967), *Kramer vs. Kramer* (1979).

HOLIDAY, Billie (Eleonora) [1915-59]; Black American singer of blues and jazz, who fought her drug addiction. *Lady Sings the Blues* (1956).

193

HOLLOWAY, Stanley [1890-1982]; British character actor, singer and comedian. In many films, including *My Fair Lady* (1964) as Dolittle.
HOPE, Leslie Townes (Bob) [1903-]; American comedian for forty years. Famous for troop shows and films with Bing CROSBY and Dorothy Lamour, especially 'The Road' series.
HOUDINI, Harry (Erik Weisz) [1874-1926]; American showman and escapologist.
HUGHES, Howard Robard [1905-76]; American businessman, aviator and film producer. *Hell's Angels* (1930); *Scarface* (1932). Later became an eccentric recluse.
JOHNSON, Celia [1908-82]; British actress on stage, film and TV, in 'well-bred' roles. *Brief Encounter* (1946).
JOLSON, Al (Asa Joelson) [1886-1950]; American singer and entertainer, who starred in the first talking picture *The Jazz Singer* (1927). Two films based on his life *The Jolson Story* (1946) and *Jolson Sings Again* (1949) have been made.
KAYE, Danny (David Daniel Kaminsky) [1913-1988]; American entertainer on stage, film and TV. *The Secret Life of Walter Mitty* (1947).
KAZAN, Elia (Elia Kazanjoglous) [1909-]; American director of films and stage. *A Streetcar Named Desire* (1951); *On the Waterfront* (1954).
KEATON, Buster (Joseph Francis Keaton) [1895-1966]; American film actor and comedian, mainly in silent comedies. Called 'Old Stoneface' for his unsmiling appearance. *The Navigator* (1924); *The General* (1926); *Steamboat Bill Junior* (1927). Two films have been made based on his life: *The Buster Keaton Story* (1957), and *The Comic* (1969).
KELLY, Gene Curran [1912-]; American dancer, singer and film actor. Best known for *Singin' in the Rain* (1952).
KELLY, Grace (Princess Grace of Monaco) [1929-82]; American film actress renowned for her 'cool' beauty. *High Society* (1956). Retired from acting on marriage to Prince Rainer of Monaco. Killed in a motor accident.
KERN, Jerome David [1885-1945]; American composer, especially of musical comedies. *Show Boat* - which contained the song *Ol' Man River* (1927); *Roberta* (1933). Other songs include *Smoke Gets In Your Eyes*, and *The Last Time I Saw Paris*.

KOMISARJEVSKY, Theodore [1882-1954]; British theatrical producer and designer, born in Italy of Russian parents. *Macbeth* (1933).
KORDA, Sir Alexander (Sandor Corda) [1893-1956]; British film producer and director, born in Hungary. He revived the British film industry with *The Private Life of Henry VIII* (1933), and *Rembrandt* (1936).
KUBRICK, Stanley [1928-]: American writer and film producer-director, mainly of psychological thrillers. *Dr Strangelove* (1963); *2001: A Space Odyssey* (1969): *A Clockwork Orange* (1971).
KUROSAWA, Akira [1910-]; Japanese film director, who adapted typical Japanese drama to the cinema. *Rashomon* (1951); *The Seven Samurai* (1954).
LA ROCCA, Nick [Dominick James La Rocca] [1889-1961]; American cornetist, who in 1916 formed the Original Dixieland Jazz Band.
LANCASTER, Burt [1913-]; American film actor; a former circus acrobat, which experience he often uses in films. *The Flame and the Arrow* (1950); *Birdman of Alcatraz* (1962).
LANG, Fritz [1890-1976]; American film director born in Vienna, best known for his silent films. *Dr Mabuse, der Spieler* (1922); *Metropolis* (1926).
LAUGHTON, Charles [1899-1962]; British-born, later American stage and film actor. Later in life, he was consumed by self-doubts, but he had been highly acclaimed earlier. *The Private Life of Henry VIII* (1933); *Rembrandt* (1936); *The Hunchback of Notre Dame* (1939).
LAUREL, Stan (Arthur Stanley Jefferson) [1890-1965]; British-born film comedian, famed for his partnership with Oliver HARDY. *Way Out West* (1936); *A Chump at Oxford* (1940).
LAWRENCE, Gertrude (Gertrud Alexandra Dagmar Lawrence-Klasen) [1898-1952]; British actress in musical comedy and revues, many by Noel COWARD. *Private Lives* (1930); *Tonight at Eight-Thirty* (1936); *The King and I* (1951).
LEIGH, Vivien (Vivien Hartley) [1913-1967]; British actress, for many years the wife of Laurence OLIVIER. Famed for her role as Scarlett O'Hara in *Gone With the Wind* (1939); *A Streetcar Named Desire* (1951).
LEMMON, Jack [1925-]; American actor, mainly in light comedy films. *Mister Roberts* (1955), *Some Like It Hot* (1959), *Save the Tiger* (1973).

'Ascot Opening Day' from the film musical My Fair Lady.

LERNER, Alan Jay [1918-1986]; American lyricist and writer. He wrote the film *An American in Paris* (1951); the score of *Gigi* (1958), and collaborated in *My Fair Lady* (1964).

LIFAR, Serge [1905-1986]; Russian dancer and choreographer. He was the spirit behind the Paris Opera *Creatures de Promethée* (1929).

LITTLEWOOD, Joan [1914-]; British stage director, who founded a repertory company known for advanced ideas.

LLOYD, Harold Clayton (1893-1971); American film comedian of the silent and early sound era, famous for his timid character but dangerous stunts. *Safety Last* (1923); *The Freshman* (1925); *The Kid Brother* (1927).

LLOYD, Marie (Matilda Wood) [1870-1922]; British music hall singer with ribald Cockney personality. Famous for songs such as *Oh, Mr Porter*, and *A Little of What You Fancy*.

LOCKWOOD, Margaret (Margaret Day) [1916-]; British leading film actress of the 30s and later TV actress. *The Wicked Lady* (1945); *Cast a Dark Shadow* (1957).

LOEWE, Frederick [1901-1988]; American composer, born in Berlin, famed for his collaboration with Alan Jay LERNER in musicals. *My Fair Lady* (1956); *Gigi* (1958); *Paint Your Wagon* (1969).

LONDON, Tom (Leonard Clapham) [1883-1963]; American character actor playing small roles, but who appeared in more films than any other actor. The total was over 2000.

LOREN, Sophia (Sophia Scicoloni) [1934-]; Italian film actress, later internationally known. *Two Women* (1961); *The Millionairess* (1961).

LORRE, Peter (Laszlo Loewenstein) [1904-64]; Hungarian-born actor of timid manner and rolling eyes. Many films as 'Mr Moto'. *M* (1930); *The Maltese Falcon* (1941); *The Mask of Dimitrios* (1944).

LUBITSCH, Ernst [1892-1947]; German film director and comic actor. The 'Lubitsch Touch' indicated light sexual innuendo. *Trouble in Paradise* (1932); *To Be or Not to Be* (1942).

LUNT, Alfred [1893-1977]; American stage actor and producer. Appeared in many productions with his wife, Lynn FONTANNE. *Pygmalion* (1926); *Idiot's Delight* (1936).

MacMURRAY, Fred (Frederick Martin MacMurray) [1908-]; American film actor, a leading man in the 30s and later famed in roles with Walt Disney comedies. *The Gilded Lily* (1935); *Sing You Sinners* (1938)]; *The Absent-Minded Professor* (1961).

McQUEEN, Steve [1930-83]; American film actor of tough roles. *The Magnificent Seven* (1960); *Papillon* (1973).

MAKAROVA, Natalia [1940-]; Russian ballerina, best known for her performances of Giselle.

MARCH, Fredric (Frederic McIntyre Bickel) [1897-1975]; American film and stage actor. *Dr Jekyll and Mr Hyde* (1932); *A Star is Born* (1937); *The Best Years of Our Lives* (1946).

195

MARKOVA, Dame Alicia (Lilian Alicia Marks) [1910-]; British ballerina, originally with the Diaghilev company, later with the London Festival Ballet. Her style is in the Russian classical tradition.

MARX BROTHERS [Chico (Leonard) 1891-1961, Groucho (Julius Henry) 1895-1977, Gummo (Milton) 1893-1977, Harpo (Adolph Arthur) 1893-1964, Zeppo (Herbert) 1901-79]; Family of Jewish-American comic actors of impossible manic humour. Most remembered are Harpo, the simple mute, and Groucho, of the painted moustache and cigar. *Duck Soup* (1933); *At the Circus* (1939); *A Night at the Opera* (1935).

MASON, James [1909-84]; British film and stage actor, playing wide-ranging roles. *The Seventh Veil* (1945); *A Star is Born* (1954); *Journey to the Centre of the Earth* (1959); *Lolita* (1962).

MASSINE, Leonide [1895-1979]; Russian ballet dancer and choreographer. Principal dancer and choreographer of Diaghilev's *Ballets Russes*. Main ballets: *La Boutique Fantasque* and *Le Sacré du Printemps*.

MAYER, Louis Burt [1885-1957]; American founder (with Sam GOLDWYN) of Metro-Goldwyn-Mayer, the Hollywood film-makers.

MELIES, Georges [1861-1938]; French film pioneer before World War I, especially of trick films. *Voyage to the Moon* (1902); *Twenty Thousand Leagues Under the Sea* (1907).

MILLER, Glenn [1904-44]; American trombonist, dance-band leader and composer. His smooth sound was popular during World War II. Songs: *Chatanooga Choo-Choo, Moonlight Serenade, In the Mood.*

MILLS, Sir John [1908-]; British character actor, originally in musical comedy. *Great Expectations* (1946); *In Which We Serve* (1942); *Ryan's Daughter* (1971).

MISTINGUETT [Jeanne-Marie Bourgeois] [1875-1956]; French star of the Paris music halls often in partnership with Maurice CHEVALIER.

MONROE, Marilyn (Norma Jean Baker or Mortenson) [1926-1962]; American sexy film star, formerly a model. *Niagara* (1952); *Gentlemen Prefer Blondes* (1953); *Some Like It Hot* (1959). Two films have been made based on her life: *Goodbye, Norma Jean* (1975), and *Marilyn.*

MONTGOMERY, Robert [1904-1981]; American actor, and later director of the smooth, smart

Laurence Olivier as Hamlet.

type of film. Later in politics. *Night Must Fall* (1937); *Here Comes Mr Jordan* (1941).

MORTON, 'Jelly Roll' [Ferdinand Joseph La Menthe Morton] [1885-1941]; American pianist and jazz musician. *Jelly Roll Blues.*

NEWMAN, Paul [1925-]; American film actor. *Cat on a Hot Tin Roof* (1958); *Butch Cassidy and the Sundance Kid* (1969); *The Sting* (1973).

NIJINSKY, Vaslav Fomich [1888-1950]; Russian ballet dancer, of Polish descent. Performed in DIAGHILEV's *Ballets Russes* with great grace and agility. Became insane from 1917.

NIVEN, James David [1909-83]; British actor with a light and debonair manner; latterly a writer. *Raffles* (1940); *Around the World in Eighty Days* (1956).

NUREYEV, Rudolf Hametovich [1938-]; Russian, later British, ballet dancer; a soloist with the Kirov Ballet. Defected to Paris, 1961. Later with the Royal Ballet.

OLIVIER, Lord (Laurence Olivier) [1907-]; British actor and director, famed for his Shakespearean roles as Hamlet and Othello, also in films. First director of the National Theatre. Films: *Wuthering Heights* (1939); *The Entertainer* (1960); *Marathon Man* (1976).

PARKER, Charlie (Charles Christopher Parker) [1920-55]; American jazz musician. A saxophonist, and a leading exponent of bebop.

The Marx Brothers in A Day at the Races.

Nijinsky dancing in Le Spectre de la Rose (1911).

PAVLOVA, Anna (Anna Pavlovna) [1881-1931]; Russian ballerina of classical style, famous for her solo performances.
PECK, Gregory [1916-]; American actor of upright character. *To Kill a Mockingbird* (1963); *The Boys from Brazil* (1978).
PIAF, Edith (Edith Giovanna Gassion) [1915-63]; French singer, of strong earthy character. Her style is typified in the song *Je Ne Regrette Rien*.
PICKFORD, Mary (Gladys Mary Smith) [1893-1979]; Canadian film actress in the age of silent films, known as 'the world's sweetheart'. *Pollyanna* (1919); *Little Lord Fauntleroy* (1921).
PISCATOR, Erwin [1893-1966]; German theatrical producer and director in expressionist form.
POITIER, Sidney [1927-]; Black American actor and director, whose film successes helped the breakdown of racial barriers. *Guess Who's Coming to Dinner* (1967); *In the Heat of the Night* (1967).
PORTER, Cole Albert [1893-1964]; American composer and lyricist, known for his witty lyrics. Musical productions: *Anything Goes* (1934); *Kiss Me Kate* (1949). Songs include: *Night and Day, You're the Top, I've Got You Under My Skin*.
POWELL, William [1892-1984]; American film actor, famed for his 'Thin Man' character 1934-47. *The Great Ziegfeld* (1936); *My Man Godfrey* (1936); *Mister Roberts* (1955).
PRESLEY, Elvis Aron [1935-1977]; American rock-and-roll singer and actor. Became an international cult figure, and was known as 'the Pelvis' because of his gyrating style. *Love Me Tender* (1956); *G.I. Blues* (1960).
PUDOVKIN, Vsevolod Illarionovich [1893-1953]; Russian film director and theorist. *Mother* (1926); *General Suvorov* (1941).
RAMBERT, Dame Marie (Cyvia Rambam, later Miriam Ramberg) [1888-1982]; British ballet teacher and director, born in Poland. Founded the Ballet Rambert in London, 1931.
RATTIGAN, Sir Terence Mervyn [1911-77]; British playwright whose subjects ranged from farce to historical drama. *French Without Tears* (1936); *The Winslow Boy* (1946); *Adventure Story* (1949); *Separate Tables* (1954).
REDFORD, Robert [1937-]; American film actor and director. *Butch Cassidy and the Sundance Kid* (1969); *The Candidate* (1972); *The Sting* (1973); *Out of Africa* (1985); Oscar for direction of *Ordinary People* (1980).

197

Above left: Singer Frank Sinatra, 1954. Above right: Elvis Presley. Right: Clark Gable and Vivien Leigh in Gone with the Wind, *1939.*

REDGRAVE, Sir Michael Scudamore [1908-85]; British stylish actor of stage and screen. *The Importance of Being Earnest* (1952); *The Dam Busters* (1955).

REDGRAVE, Vanessa [1937-]; British film actress and political activist. Daughter of Sir Michael REDGRAVE. *Isadora* (1968); *Julia* (1977).

REED, Sir Carol [1906-76]; British film director, at his best during the late 1940s. *The Fallen Idol* (1948); *The Third Man* (1949).

REINHARDT, Django (Jean-Baptiste) [1910-53]; Belgian-born French guitarist of gypsy parentage; an original European jazz musician.

REINHARDT, Max (Max Goldmann) [1873-1943]; Austrian-born theatrical producer. Director of the Deutsches Theater, Berlin, he specialized in spectacular productions.

RENOIR, Jean, [1894-1979]; French film director, son of the painter, Pierre Auguste RENOIR. *Nana* (1926); *Une Partie de Campagne* (1936); *La Grande Illusion* (1937); *French Cancan* (1956).

RESNAIS, Alain [1922-]; French film director. *Hiroshima Mon Amour* (1959); *Last Year at Marienbad* (1961).

RICHARDSON, Sir Ralph [1902-83]; British actor, mainly on the stage, but also in films and TV. In Shakespeare, but often in whimsical and eccentric roles. *The Fallen Idol* (1948); *Dr Zhivago* (1965).

ROBBINS, Jerome [1918-]; American dancer and choreographer, especially of such films as *West Side Story* (1961).

ROBINSON, Edward G. (Emanuel Goldenburg) [1893-1973]; American film star of Roman-

ian origin. Often played villains or policemen. *Little Caesar* (1930); *The Woman in the Window* (1944); *Double Indemnity* (1944); *Key Largo* (1948).

RODGERS, Richard [1902-79]; American composer, who collaborated with lyricists Lorenz HART and Oscar HAMMERSTEIN. Music for productions *Pal Joey* (1957); *South Pacific* (1958); *The Sound of Music* (1965). Songs include: *People Will Say We're in Love, Some Enchanted Evening, My Favourite Things.*

ROGERS, Ginger (Virginia Katharine McMath) [1911-]; American actress and dancer, especially with Fred ASTAIRE. *Top Hat* (1935); *Lady in the Dark* (1943).

ROSSELINI, Roberto [1906-1977]; Italian film director, married Ingrid BERGMAN. *Stromboli* (1949); *Vanina Vanini* (1960).

ROTHAPFEL, Samuel [1882-1936]; American showman, known as 'Roxy'. Father of the super-cinema, he opened the world's largest cinema in New York, the Radio City Music Hall, also the Roxy on 7th Avenue.

RUTHERFORD, Dame Margaret [1892-1972]; British actress and comedienne, famous for her rather eccentric elderly ladies. Was Madame Arcati in *Blithe Spirit* (1941); Miss Prism in *The Importance of Being Earnest* (1952); and Miss Marple in films of Agatha Christie novels.

SANDERS, George [1906-72]; British actor, born in St Petersburg, Russia. Of suave appearance and manner, played crooks, cads and swindlers with success. *Rebecca* (1940); *The Picture of Dorian Gray* (1945); *All About Eve* (1950).

SELZNICK, David Oliver [1902-65]; American film producer. *The Prisoner of Zenda* (1937); *Gone With the Wind* (1939); *Duel in the Sun* (1946).

SENNETT, Mack (Michael Sinnott) [1880-1960]; American producer of short slapstick films in the silent era. *Tillie's Punctured Romance* (1914).

SHARIF, Omar [Michel Shalhouz] [1932-]; Egyptian actor who plays strong romantic heroes. *Genghis Khan* (1965); *Dr Zhivago* (1965).

SHEARER, Norma [1904-1983]; Canadian-born American film actress of the 20s and 30s. *Smilin' Through* (1932); *The Barretts of Wimpole Street* (1934); *Idiot's Delight* (1939).

SINATRA, Frank (Francis Albert) [1915-]; American actor, singer and producer. *On the Town* (1949); *From Here to Eternity* (1953); *Pal Joey* (1957).

SMITH, Bessie [1894-1937]; American blues singer of earthy character. Called the 'Empress of the Blues', she recorded over 200 songs.

SOUSA, John Philip [1854-1932]; American bandmaster and composer, mainly of spirited marches, including *Stars and Stripes Forever, The Washington Post, El Capitan*.

STANISLAVSKY, Konstantin (Konstantin Sergeyevich Alexeyev) [1865-1938]; Russian actor and producer. Co-founder and director of the Moscow Art Theatre, devising the method whereby actors express themselves naturally.

STANWYCK, Barbara (Ruby Stevens) [1907-]; American leading lady in films and TV, usually in dramatic roles. *Stella Dallas* (1937); *Double Indemnity* (1944); *Sorry, Wrong Number (1948)*. TV series The Big Valley (1965-69).

STEWART, James Maitland [1908-]; American leading man in films, usually comedies. *You Can't Take it With You* (1938); *Destry Rides Again* (1939); *Philadelphia Story* (1940); *Harvey* (1950).

STRASBERG, Lee [1901-]; Austrian-born American drama teacher, who founded the Actors' Studio and co-founded the Group Theatre, where he used the STANISLAVSKY methods.

STREISAND, Barbra (Barbara Joan Streisand) [1942-]; American singer, actress and director. *Funny Girl* (1968); *Hello Dolly* (1969); *Yentl* (1984).

STROHEIM, Erich von (Hans Erich Maria Stroheim von Nordenwall) [1885-1957]; Aus-

trian born actor and director, usually playing Prussians or villains. *The Great Gabbo* (1930); *Sunset Boulevard* (1950). A film based on his life, *The Man You Love to Hate* was made in 1979.

STURGES, John [1911-]; American director of action films. *Bad Day at Black Rock* (1954); *Gunfight at the OK Corral* (1957); *The Magnificent Seven* (1960).

SWANSON, Gloria (Gloria May Josephine Swenson) [1897-1983]; American film star mainly of the silent era, but who appeared in *Sunset Boulevard* (1950), portraying an ageing former star. *Sadie Thompson* (1928); *Indiscreet* (1931).

TATI, Jacques (Jacques Tatischeff) [1908-1982]; French comic actor, pantomimist and director. *Jour de Fête* (1949); *Monsieur Hulot's Holiday* (1952);

TAYLOR, Elizabeth [1932-]; British-born leading actress, who was evacuated to Hollywood as a child. Married several times to Richard BURTON. *National Velvet* (1944); *Cleopatra* (1962); *Who's Afraid of Virginia Woolf?* (1966).

TEMPLE, Shirley (Shirley Temple Black) [1928-]; American child star of films in the 30s, now in politics. *Little Miss Marker* (1934); *Curly Top* (1935); *Wee Willie Winkie* (1937).

TERRY, Dame Ellen Alice [1847-1929]; Distinguished British stage actress. Appeared with Henry Irving in Shakespeare. Married for one year to the painter, G.F. Watts.

THORNDIKE, Dame Sybil [1882-1976]; British stage actress, renowned for classical Greek drama, and as Joan of Arc in G.B. SHAW's *St Joan*.

TILLEY, Vesta (Lady de Frece, born Matilda Alice Powles) [1864-1952]; British music hall performer, famed as a male impersonator. Known for her song *Burlington Bertie*.

TOLAND, Gregg [1904-1948]; American cameraman who worked mainly with Sam GOLDWYN. *Wuthering Heights* (1939).

TRACY, Spencer [1900-67]; American film actor, usually appearing as the tough, honest hero. Often played opposite Katherine HEPBURN. *Captains Courageous* (1937); *Boys' Town* (1938); *Adam's Rib* (1949); *Guess Who's Coming to Dinner.*

TREE, Sir Herbert Draper Beerbohm [1853-1917]; British actor-manager, and half-brother of the critic and caricaturist Sir Max Beerbohm. Renowned for lavish productions of Shakespeare.

Romantic idol of the silent screen—Rudolph Valentino as a sheikh.

WAYNE, John (Marion Michael Morrison) [1907-79]; One of the most successful of all American film actors, usually in action films, especially Westerns. *Stagecoach* (1939); *The Quiet Man* (1952); *True Grit* (1969). He appeared in 153 films in all, playing the lead in all but 11.

WELLES, Orson [1915-1985]; American actor and producer, large in all things. His 1938 radio version of H.G. WELL'S *War of the Worlds* panicked America. Films include: *Citizen Kane* (1941); *The Magnificent Ambersons* (1946); *Macbeth* (1947). He was founder of the Mercury Theatre in 1937.

WESKER, Arnold [1932-]; British playwright, of Russian-Jewish parentage; a background looming large in his plays: *Chicken Soup with Barley* (1959); *Roots* (1960); *Chips With Everything* (1962).

WEST Mae [1892-1980]; American entertainer and film actress; a sex symbol of the 1930s. Wrote and performed her own material. Films include: *I'm No Angel* (1933); *My Little Chickadee* (1939).

WHITEMAN, Paul Samuel [1891-1967]; American bandleader and musician, known as the 'King of Jazz'. Gave first performance of GERSHWIN'S *Rhapsody in Blue* in 1924.

WILDER, Billy (Samuel Wilder) [1906-]; Austrian-born American film director. *Ninotchka* (1939); *Double Indemnity* (1941); *Sunset Boulevard* (1950); *Some Like It Hot* (1959).

ZANUCK, Darryl Francis [1902-79]; American production chief in the film industry. Helped to found 20th Century Productions, which later merged with Fox, when he became chief executive.

ZEFFIRELLI, Franco [1923-]; Italian film, stage and opera director and designer. Films: *Romeo and Juliet* (1968), *Brother Sun and Sister Moon* (1973).

ZIEGFELD, Florenz [1867-1932]; American impresario of extravagant stage shows featuring glamorous girls. *The Ziegfeld Follies* (1907-30); *Show Boat* (1927); *Rio Rita* (1927); *Bitter Sweet* (1929).

ZUKOR, Adolph [1873-1976]; Hungarian-born film pioneer and executive, who founded companies which became Paramount Pictures in 1927.

TUCKER, Sophie (Sophia Abuza) [1884-1966]; Russian-born American vaudeville star and singer, active until the last, and known as the 'Last of the Red-Hot Mamas'. Her own signature song was *Some of These Days.*

USTINOV, Peter Alexander [1921-]; British playwright, author, actor and director, of White Russian parentage. His writing is witty and satirical. Plays include: *The Love of Four Colonels* (1951); *Romanoff and Juliet* (1956).

VALENTINO, Rudolph (Rodolpho Alfonso Raffaelo Pierre Filibert Guglielmo di Valentina d'Antonguolla) [1895-1926]; Italian-born American film actor, a romantic idol of the silent era. *The Four Horsemen of the Apocalypse* (1921); *The Sheik* (1921). Two films have been made, based on his life: both are called *Valentino* (1951) and (1977).

VIGO, Jean (Jean Almereyda) [1905-34]; French director of dream-like films. *Zero de Conduite* (1932).

WALLER, Fats (Thomas Wright Waller) [1904-43]; American jazz pianist and composer. Songs include: *Ain't Misbehavin', Honeysuckle Rose.*

WARNER, Jack L. [1892-1978]; American film executive, who, with his brothers Harry, Sam and Albert, founded Warner Brothers Pictures in 1923. In 1927, the company produced the first feature film with spoken sound (*The Jazz Singer*).

THE THEATRE

LONG RUNS ON THE LONDON STAGE

* = revival   + = started before 1900
**Total as at 31 Dec., 1984. Still running at time of going to press

The Mousetrap	13,356**
No Sex Please, We're British	5647**
The Black and White Minstrel Show	4354
Oh! Calcutta!	3918
Jesus Christ Superstar	3357
Oliver!	2618
The Rocky Horror Show	2599
There's a Girl in My Soup	2547
Pyjama Tops	2498
Evita	2452**
The Sound of Music	2386
Sleuth	2359
Salad Days	2283
My Fair Lady	2282
Chu Chin Chow	2248
Charlie Girl	2202
The Boy Friend	2084
Canterbury Tales	2082
Boeing-Boeing	2036
Fiddler on the Roof	2030
Hair	1999
Blithe Spirit	1997
Ipi Tombi	1879
Murder at the Vicarage	1779
Dirty Linen	1667
*Worm's Eye View	1745
Me and My Girl	1646
Reluctant Heroes	1610
Together Again	1566
Seagulls Over Sorrento	1551
Oklahoma!	1543
The Business of Murder	1500**
Irma La Douce	1512
Annie	1493
Dry Rot	1475
+Charley's Aunt	1466
The Beggar's Opera	1463
The Secretary Bird	1463
Cats	1453**
Simple Spymen	1409
Arsenic and Old Lace	1396
+Our Boys	1362
Knights of Madness	1361
The Maid of the Mountains	1352
+The Farmer's Wife	1329
Annie Get Your Gun	1304
The Little Hut	1261
A Little Bit of Fluff	1241
Spring and Port Wine	1236
Sailor, Beware!	1231
One for the Pot	1223
Beyond the Fringe	1184
While the Sun Shines	1154
The Philanthropist	1138
Godspell	1128
A Chorus Line	1118
London Laughs	1113
A Severed Head	1111
Let's Get Laid	1095
A Chinese Honeymoon	1075
Quiet Weekend	1059
Romance	1049
The Magic of the Minstrels	1047
West Side Story	1040
French Without Tears	1039
Otherwise Engaged	1029
*The Man Most Likely To...	1023
Perchance to Dream	1022
Beyond the Fringe, 1964-6	1016
Roar Like a Dove	1007
The Wind and the Rain	1001

LONG RUNS ON THE NEW YORK STAGE

The Fantasticks	8175
A Chorus Line	3704
Oh! Calcutta (revival)	3349
Grease	3388
Fiddler on the Roof	3242
Life With Father	3224
Tobacco Road	3182
Hello, Dolly!	2844
My Fair Lady	2717
Godspell	2645
The Threepenny Opera	2611
Annie	2377
Man of La Mancha	2329
Abie's Irish Rose	2327
Oklahoma!	2212
Pippin	1994
South Pacific	1925
The Magic Show	1920
Jacques Brel Is Alive and Well and Living in Paris	1847
Deathtrap	1792
Gemini	1788
Harvey	1775
Dancin'	1774
Hair	1750
The Wiz	1672
Born Yesterday	1642
42nd Street	1604
Aint Misbehavin'	1604
You're a Good Man, Charlie Brown	1597

The Best Little Whorehouse in Texas	1584	Gemini	1303
Mary, Mary	1572	Angel Street	1295
Evita	1567	Lightnin'	1291
The Voice of the Turtle	1557	Promises, Promises	1281
Barefoot in the Park	1530	Let My People Come	1273
Mame	1508	The King and I	1246
The Premise	1490	Cactus Flower	1234
Same Time Next Year	1453	Sleuth	1222
Arsenic and Old Lace	1444	1776	1217
The Sound of Music	1443	This Was Burlesque	1200
How to Succeed in Business Without Really Trying	1417	Guys and Dolls	1194
The Blacks	1408	Cabaret	1165
*Hellzapoppin	1404	The Hot l Baltimore	1166
The Music Man	1375	Mister Roberts	1157
Funny Girl	1348	Annie Get Your Gun	1147
Mummenschanz	1316	Little Mary Sunshine	1143
Oh! Calcutta!	1316	The Seven Year Itch	1141
Vanities	1313	Teahouse of the August Moon	1129
		Butterflies are Free	1128

ACADEMY AWARDS

Year	Best Picture	Best Actor	Best Actress	Best Director
1927-28	Wings	Emil Jannings (The Way of All Flesh and The Last Command)	Janet Gaynor (Seventh Heaven; Street Angel; and Sunrise)	Frank Borzage (Seventh Heaven) Lewis Milestone (Two Arabian Nights)
1928-29	The Broadway Melody	Warner Baxter (In Old Arizona	Mary Pickford (Coquette)	Frank Lloyd (The Divine Lady)
1929-30	All Quiet on the Western Front	George Arliss (Disraeli)	Norma Shearer (The Divorcee)	Lewis Milestone (All Quiet on the Western Front)
1930-31	Cimarron	Lionel Barrymore (A Free Soul)	Marie Dressler (Min and Bill)	Norman Taurog (Skippy)
1931-32	Grand Hotel	Frederic March (Dr Jekyll and Mr Hyde) Wallace Beery (The Champ)	Helen Hayes (The Sin of Madelon Claudet)	Frank Borzage (Bad Girl)
1932-33	Cavalcade	Charles Laughton (The Private Life of Henry VIII)	Katharine Hepburn (Morning Glory)	Frank Lloyd (Cavalcade)
1934	It Happened One Night	Clark Gable (It Happened One Night)	Claudette Colbert (It Happened One Night)	Frank Capra (It Happened One Night)
1935	Mutiny on the Bounty	Victor McLaglen (The Informer)	Bette Davis (Dangerous)	John Ford (The Informer)
1936	The Great Ziegfeld	Paul Muni (The Story of Louis Pasteur)	Luise Rainer (The Great Ziegfeld)	Frank Capra (Mr Deeds Goes to Town)

Box office hits:
The Sound of
Music *(left) and*
The Godfather.

1937	*The Life of Emile Zola*	Spencer Tracy *(Captains Courageous)*	Luise Rainer *(The Good Earth)*	Leo McCarey *(The Awful Truth)*
1938	*You Can't Take It With You*	Spencer Tracy *(Boys' Town)*	Bette Davis *(Jezebel)*	Frank Capra *(You Can't Take It With You)*
1939	*Gone With the Wind*	Robert Donat *(Goodbye Mr Chips)*	Vivien Leigh *(Gone With the Wind)*	Victor Fleming *(Gone With the Wind)*
1940	*Rebecca*	James Stewart *(The Philadelphia Story)*	Ginger Rogers *(Kitty Foyle)*	John Ford *(The Grapes of Wrath)*
1941	*How Green Was My Valley*	Gary Cooper *(Sergeant York)*	Joan Fontaine *(Suspicion)*	John Ford *(How Green Was My Valley)*
1942	*Mrs Miniver*	James Cagney *(Yankee Doodle Dandy)*	Greer Garson *(Mrs Miniver)*	William Wyler *(Mrs Miniver)*
1943	*Casablanca*	Paul Lukas *(Watch on the Rhine)*	Jennifer Jones *(The Song of Bernadette)*	Michael Curtiz *(Casablanca)*
1944	*Going My Way*	Bing Crosby *(Going My Way)*	Ingrid Bergman *(Gaslight)*	Leo McCarey *(Going My Way)*
1945	*The Lost Weekend*	Ray Milland *(The Lost Weekend)*	Joan Crawford *(Mildred Pierce)*	Billy Wilder *(The Lost Weekend)*
1946	*The Best Years of Our Lives*	Frederic March *(The Best Years of Our Lives)*	Olivia de Havilland *(To Each His Own)*	William Wyler *(The Best Years our Lives)*
1947	*Gentleman's Agreement*	Ronald Colman *(A Double Life)*	Loretta Young *(The Farmer's Daughter)*	Elia Kazan *(Gentleman's Agreement)*
1948	*Hamlet*	Laurence Olivier *(Hamlet)*	Jane Wyman *(Johnny Belinda)*	John Huston *(Treasure of the Sierra Madre)*
1949	*All the King's Men*	Broderick Crawford *(All the King's Men)*	Olivia de Havilland *(The Heiress)*	Joseph L. Mankievicz *(A Letter to Three Wives)*
1950	*All About Eve*	Jose Ferrer *(Cyrano de Bergerac)*	Judy Holliday *(Born Yesterday)*	Joseph L. Mankievicz *(All About Eve)*

203

1951	An American in Paris	Humphrey Bogart (The African Queen)	Vivien Leigh (A Streetcar Named Desire)	George Stevens (A Place in the Sun)
1952	The Greatest Show on Earth	Gary Cooper (High Noon)	Shirley Booth (Come Back, Little Sheba)	John Ford (The Quiet Man)
1953	From Here to Eternity	William Holden (Stalag 17)	Audrey Hepburn (Roman Holiday)	Fred Zinnemann (From Here to Eternity)
1954	On the Waterfront	Marlon Brando (On the Waterfront)	Grace Kelly (The Country Girl)	Elia Kazan (On the Waterfront)
1955	Marty	Ernest Borgnine (Marty)	Anna Magnani (The Rose Tattoo)	Delbert Mann (Marty)
1956	Around the World in 80 Days	Yul Brynner (The King and I)	Ingrid Bergman (Anastasia)	George Stevens (Giant)
1957	The Bridge on the River Kwai	Alec Guinness (The Bridge on the River Kwai	Joanne Woodward (The Three Faces of Eve)	David Lean (The Bridge on the River Kwai)
1958	Gigi	David Niven (Separate Tables)	Susan Hayward (I Want to Live)	Vincente Minelli (Gigi)
1959	Ben-Hur	Charlton Heston (Ben-Hur)	Simone Signoret (Room at the Top)	William Wyler (Ben-Hur)
1960	The Apartment	Burt Lancaster (Elmer Gantry)	Elizabeth Taylor (Butterfield 8)	Billy Wilder (The Apartment)
1961	West Side Story	Maximilian Schell (Judgment at Nuremberg)	Sophia Loren (Two Women)	Robert Wise & Jerome Robbins (West Side Story)
1962	Lawrence of Arabia	Gregory Peck (To Kill a Mockingbird)	Anne Bancroft (The Miracle Worker)	David Lean (Lawrence of Arabia)
1963	Tom Jones	Sidney Poitier (Lilies of the Field)	Patricia Neal (Hud)	Tony Richardson (Tom Jones)
1964	My Fair Lady	Rex Harrison (My Fair Lady)	Julie Andrews (Mary Poppins)	George Cukor (My Fair Lady)
1965	The Sound of Music	Lee Marvin (Cat Ballou)	Julie Christie (Darling)	Robert Wise (The Sound of Music)
1966	A Man for All Seasons	Paul Schofield (A Man for All Seasons)	Elizabeth Taylor (Who's Afraid of Virginia Woolf?)	Fred Zinnemann (A Man for All Seasons)
1967	In the Heat of the Night	Rod Steiger (In the Heat of the Night)	Katharine Hepburn (Guess Who's Coming to Dinner)	Mike Nichols (The Graduate)
1968	Oliver	Cliff Robertson (Charly)	Katharine Hepburn (A Lion in Winter), Barbra Streisand (Funny Girl)	Sir Carol Reed (Oliver)

1969	Midnight Cowboy	John Wayne (True Grit)	Maggie Smith (The Prime of Miss Jean Brodie)	John Schlesinger (Midnight Cowboy)
1970	Patton	George C. Scott (Patton)	Glenda Jackson (Women in Love)	Franklin J. Schaffner (Patton)
1971	The French Connection	Gene Hackman (The French Connection)	Jane Fonda (Klute)	William Friedkin (The French Connection)
1972	The Godfather	Marlon Brando (The Godfather)	Liza Minnelli (Cabaret)	Robert Fosse (Cabaret)
1973	The Sting	Jack Lemmon (Save the Tiger)	Glenda Jackson (A Touch of Class)	George Roy Hill (The Sting)
1974	The Godfather Part II	Art Carney (Harry and Tonto)	Ellen Burstyn (Alice Doesn't Live Here Any More)	Francis Ford Coppola (The Godfather Part II)
1975	One Flew Over Over the Cuckoo's Nest	Jack Nicholson (One Flew Over the Cuckoo's Nest)	Louise Fletcher (One Flew Over the Cuckoo's Nest)	Milos Forman (One Flew Over the Cuckoo's Nest)
1976	Rocky	Peter Finch (Network)	Fay Dunaway (Network)	John G. Avildsen (Rocky)
1977	Annie Hall	Richard Dreyfus (Goodbye Girl)	Diane Keaton (Annie Hall)	Woody Allen (Annie Hall)
1978	The Deerhunter	John Voight (Coming Home)	Jane Fonda (Coming Home)	Michael Cimino (The Deerhunter)
1979	Kramer versus Kramer	Dustin Hoffman (Kramer versus Kramer)	Sally Field (Norma Rae)	Robert Benton (Kramer versus Kramer)
1980	Ordinary People	Robert De Niro (Raging Bull)	Sissy Spacek (Coalminer's Daughter)	Robert Redford (Ordinary People)
1981	Chariots of Fire	Henry Fonda (On Golden Pond)	Katharine Hepburn (On Golden Pond)	Warren Beatty (Reds)
1982	Gandhi	Ben Kingsley (Gandhi)	Meryl Streep (Sophie's Choice)	Sir Richard Attenborough (Gandhi)
1983	Terms of Endearment	Robert Duvall (Tender Mercies)	Shirley Maclaine (Terms of Endearment)	James L. Brooks (Terms of Endearment)
1984	Amadeus	F. Murray Abraham (Amadeus)	Sally Field (Places in the Heart)	Milos Forman (Amadeus)
1985	Out of Africa	William Hurt (Kiss of the Spider Woman)	Geraldine Page (The Trip to Bountiful)	Sydney Pollack (Out of Africa)
1986	Platoon	Paul Newman (The Color of Money)	Marlee Matlin (Children of a Lesser God)	Oliver Stone (Platoon)
1987	The Last Emperor	Michael Douglas (Wall Street)	Cher (Moonstruck)	Bernardo Bertolucci (The Last Supper)

The World of Sport

PERSONALITIES IN SPORT

AARON, Henry Louis [1934-]; American baseball player, Milwaukee/Atlanta Braves (1954-74), Milwaukee Brewers (1975-76).

ALI, Muhammad (Cassius Clay) [1942-]; American boxer, the first to hold the heavyweight title three times (1964-67, 1974-78, 1978-79).

ANQUETIL, Jacques [1934-]; French cyclist, who in 1964 won the 5000 kilometre (2,700 mile) race for the fifth time.

BALLESTEROS, Severiano [1957-]; Spanish golf champion, who won the British Open in 1979, 1984 and 1988; also the German Open, 1978, Spanish 1981, Netherlands 1976, 1980, French 1977, 1982, American Masters 1980, 1983.

BANNISTER, Sir Roger Gilbert [1929-]; British athlete; the first man to run the mile in under 4 minutes (1954).

BARNES, Sydney Francis [1873-1967]; British professional cricketer, and the most remarkable bowler of the century. He took a record 49 wickets in the 1913-14 Test series with South Africa.

BECKER, Boris [1967-]; German tennis player, the youngest man ever to win Wimbledon (17 years 228 days) in 1985. Won again in 1986.

BEST, George [1946-]; British soccer player, born in Northern Ireland. His brilliant career came to an end prematurely, in part because of too much too soon.

BLAIK, Earl Henry (Red) [1897-]; American college football coach, a player at Miami (Ohio) University (1914-17) and the US Military Academy (1918-19). Coached Dartmouth College and the US Military Academy.

BORG, Björn [1956-]; Swedish tennis player, who won the Wimbledon singles title five times running (1976-80).

BOTHAM, Ian [1955-]; British cricketer, famed as both batsman and bowler. Has achieved over 4000 runs and has taken more than 300 wickets in Test cricket. In 1984, he took 8 wickets in the Test against the West Indies.

BRABHAM, Jack [1926-] Australian motor-racing driver, the first to win the world championship in his own car. Retired in 1970.

BRADMAN, Sir Donald [1908-]; Australian cricketer, considered to be the most outstanding batsman of all time. Averaged 99.94 in 52 Tests (1928-48) and 95.14 in all matches.

BROWN, Paul E. [1908-]; American college and professional football coach, at Cleveland Browns (1946-62), Cincinnati Bengals (1968-76).

BRUNDAGE, Avery [1887-1975]; American sports personality, a dominant figure in the Olympic Games, being president of the International Committee for 17 years.

BUDGE, Donald [1915-]; American tennis player, the first to complete the Grand Slam of the four major titles in one year (1938).

BUSBY, Sir Matt [1909-]; Scottish international association footballer who became manager of Manchester United.

CAMPANELLA, Roy [1921-]; American baseball player, catcher for the Brooklyn Dodgers (1948-57).

CAMPBELL, Sir Malcolm [1885-1948]; British racing motorist, winner of over 400 trophies. Set up land-speed records, with over 300 mph (500 kph) in 1935, and the water-speed record of 141.74 mph (228.1 kph) in 1939.

CHADWICK, Florence [1918-]; American long distance swimmer, the first woman to swim the English Channel in both directions (1950 and 1951).

CHARLTON, Robert (Bobby) [1937-]; British association footballer, captain of Manchester United, who scored a record 49 goals in 106 internationals.

CLARK, Earl Harry (Dutch) [1906-]; American college and professional football player and coach, also a baseball player. A versatile player for the Detroit Lions (1934-38), and coach for the Cleveland Rams (1939-42).

CLARK, Jim [1936-1968]; Scottish racing driver, one of the greatest of all, who drove for Lotus. He won 25 grands prix. Killed at Hockenheim.

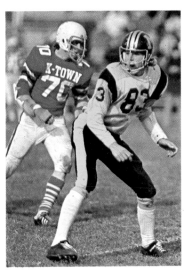

CLEMENTE, Roberto Walker [1934-72]; American (Puerto Rican) baseball player; an outfielder for the Pittsburgh Pirates, (1955-72). Killed in an aircraft crash.

COBB, John Rhodes [1899-1952]; British racing motorist, who set up world land speed records at Bonneville salt flats, USA in 1938, 1939 and 1947 (394.2 mph/634.4 kph). Killed while making water speed record in Loch Ness, Scotland.

COBB, Tyrus Raymond (**Ty**) [1886-1961]; American baseball player, an outfielder for Detroit Tigers (1905-26) and Philadelphia A's (1927-28).

COE, Sebastian Newbold [1956-]; British athlete who set three world records in 1981 (800 metres [1:41.73], 1000 metres [2:21.18] and mile [3:47.33]. He won gold and silver medals in the 1980 and 1984 Olympics in the 1500 metres and 800 events. Was not chosen for 1988 Olympics.

COMPTON, Denis [1918-]; British cricketer and association footballer. Cricket record of 3816 runs and 18 centuries in 1947 and fastest 300 (181 minutes). Played in 78 Tests.

CONNOLLY, Maureen ('Little Mo') [1934-1969]; American tennis player, who won the tennis Grand Slam in 1953. Her career ended after a horseriding accident in 1954.

CONNORS, Jimmy [1952-]; American tennis player; US singles champion 1974, 1976, 1978. Wimbledon champion 1974.

CONSTANTINE, Learie Nicholas (Baron) [1901-71]; West Indian cricketer, who played for the West Indies and Trinidad. An all-rounder; a fast bowler, fine batsman, and great fielder.

COURT, Margaret (b. Margaret Smith) [1942-]; Australian tennis player, the second woman (after Maureen CONNOLLY) to win the Grand Slam (1970). Won a record 22 major singles and 58 titles in all.

CRAPP, Lorraine [1938-]; Australian swimmer, who in 1956 was the first woman to break the 5 minutes 500 metres freestyle record.

CRUYFF, Johan [1947-]; Netherlands association footballer, and a leading goal-scorer for both the Ajax team and the national Netherlands side.

CULBERTSON, Ely [1891-1955]; American bridge authority, who invented a system of contract bridge, and helped establish it as an international game.

DAVIS, Joe [1901-78]; British billiards and

The West Indian Test cricketer Sir Learie Constantine (1902–1971)

snooker player, who was the only man to hold both world billiards and snooker titles simultaneously. He won the world professional title 15 times.

DAVIS, Steve [1957-]; British snooker player (unrelated to Joe DAVIS), who won his first world title in 1981, and became the most successful tournament winner in snooker history.

DEMPSEY, Jack [1895-1983]; American heavyweight boxer, a powerful puncher, who won the world title in 1919, losing it in 1926 to Gene TUNNEY.

DI STEFANO, Alfredo [1926-]; Argentinian association footballer, who played for Spain and Real Madrid as well as Argentina.

DIMAGGIO, Joe (Joseph Paul DiMaggio) [1914-]; American baseball player, outfielder (1936-51) with the New York Yankees team. Married to Marilyn MONROE 1954-55.

DROBNY, Jaroslav [1921-]; Czech lawn tennis player, who adopted British nationality. A former ice-hockey player, and a member of the Czech Olympic team at the age of 15. A left-hander, was famed for his strong service.

EUSEBIO, Ferreira da Silva [1943-]; Portuguese association footballer for Benfica and Portugal. In the Portuguese team, was the leading goal-scorer during the World Cup matches in 1966.

FANGIO, Juan Manuel [1911-]; Argentinian motor racing driver, who has been world champion five times.

FINNEY, Tom [1922-]; British association footballer; a brilliant winger for Preston and England. Record score of 30 goals in 76 games.

FRASER, Dawn [1937-]; Australian swimmer, who won Olympic gold medals in 1956, 1960 and 1964.

FRY, Charles Burgess [1872-1956]; British sportsman; a cricketer (Sussex, Hampshire and England); association footballer (England) and athlete. Greatest batsman of his time, making over 30,866 runs, with 94 centuries.

GEHRIG, Henry Louis (Lou) [1903-1941]; American baseball player, and a star of New York Yankees (1923-39). He died of a muscle-wasting disease.

GIBSON, Josh [1911-1947]; American baseball player (batter), excluded from major leagues because he was black.

GOOLAGONG, Evonne (Mrs Roger Cawley) [1951-]; Australian tennis player, champion at Wimbledon, 1971.

GRACE, Dr William Gilbert [1848-1915]; British physician and cricketer, an all-rounder who dominated the game at the end of the 19th century. Made 54,904 runs, with 126 centuries. His brother, Edward Mills Grace, was also a famed cricketer.

GRANGE, Harold Edward (Red) [1903-]; American college and professional football player. University of Illinois (1923-25), Chicago Bears (1925-35).

HAGEN, Walter [1892-1969]; American golfer, who was PGA champion 1921 and 1924-27, and British Open champion 1922, 1924, 1928 and 1929.

HENIE, Sonja [1912-1969]; Norwegian-born American ice-skater and Hollywood film star. Winner of 10 successive world titles (1927-36) and 3 Olympic gold medals (1928, 1932, 1936). Films: *One in a Million* (1936), *Sun Valley Serenade* (1941).

HERRERA, Helenio [1916-]; Association football manager, born in Spanish Morocco, later an Argentine citizen, finally French. A strong disciplinarian, has managed teams in France, Spain, Italy and Portugal.

HILL, Graham [1929-1975]; British motor-rac-

ing driver, who began as a mechanic. World champion 1962 (BRM) and 1968 (Lotus). Killed in an air crash.

HOBBS, Sir John Berry (Jack) ('the Master') [1882-1963]; British cricketer, and one of the century's leading world's batsmen. Scored 61,237 runs with 197 centuries.

HOGAN, William Benjamin (Ben) [1912-]; American golfer, winner of the US Open 1948, 1950, 1951, and 1953. Master's championship 1951 and 1953; PGA champion 1946 and 1948.

HUTSON, Donald [1913-]; American college and professional football player, at Alabama University (1932-34), Green Bay Packers (193545).

HUTTON, Sir Leonard [1916-]; British cricketer, who made the highest Test score against Australia, 364 (Oval, 1838) in 13 hours 17 minutes), the record lasting for 20 years.

IGLOI, Mihaly [1908-]; Hungarian-born American athletics coach. Successful trainees have been Sandor Iharos, Istvan Rozsavolgyi, Laszlo Tabori and Jim Beatty.

JAMES, Alex [1902-1953]; British association footballer, Scottish-born, but famed for his prowess with the English Preston and Arsenal teams.

JOHN, Barry [1945-]; Welsh rugby union fly-half (Llanelli, Cardiff, Wales and British Lions). Scored record 90 points for Wales in 25 games.

JOHNSON, Jack [1878-1946]; American heavyweight boxer, who was the first black fighter to win the championship (1908-1915). One of the greatest of heavyweights.

JOHNSON, Walter Perry [1887-1946]; American baseball player, a pitcher for the Washington Senators (1907-1927).

JONES, Bobby (Robert Tyre Jones) [1902-1971]; American golfer, and winner of the Grand Slam, 1930. Winner, US Opens 1923, 1926, 1929-30, and British Opens 1926-27 and 1930.

KILLY, Jean-Claude [1943-]; French ski-racer, and Olympic champion in downhill, slalom, and giant slalom, 1968. World Cup champion 1967, 1968.

KING, Billie Jean (Billie Jean Moffitt) [1943-]; American tennis player who won a record 20 Wimbledon titles, including six singles, and helped organize the women's professional circuit.

KNIEVEL, Evel (Robert Craig Knievel) [1938-]; American stunt motorcyclist.

KRAMER, Jack [1921-]; American tennis player and promoter. US singles champion 1946-47, Wimbledon champion 1947.

LAKER, James Charles (Jim) [1922-1986]; British cricketer (Surrey, Essex and England), a renowned right-arm off-spin bowler. World record 19 wickets for 90 in a Test against Australia, 1956.

LANDIS, Kenesaw Mountain [1866-1944]; American Federal judge and sports executive. The first baseball commissioner, (1920-44).

LAUDA, Niki [1949-]; Austrian motor-racing driver, and winner of the World Grand Prix 1977.

LAVER, Rodney George [1938-]; Australian tennis player, and the only man to achieve the Grand Slam of major singles titles twice, as an amateur and as a professional (1962 and 1969).

LENGLEN, Suzanne [1899-1938]; French tennis player, virtually unbeatable 1919-26. A professional from 1926 after winning 6 Wimbledon singles.

LEWIS, Carl [1961-]; American track star, Olympic medallist in 1984 and 1988 in 100 metres, 200 metres and long jump.

LILLEE, Dennis [1949-]; Australian cricketer, a devastatingly fast bowler, setting a new record after he took his 310th wicket in 1981.

LOMBARDI, Vincent [1913-1970]; American college and professional football player and coach. Head coach Green Bay Packers (1959-67).

LONGDEN, Johnny [1907-]; British jockey, who rode over 6032 winning horses, the first man to exceed 5000.

LONSDALE, 5th Earl (Hugh Cecil Lowther) [1857-1944]; British sportsman, with interests in hunting, racing, yacht-racing and boxing. Created the Lonsdale Belts in 1909 as awards to champion boxers winning titles at the National Sporting Club in London.

LOUIS, Joe (Joseph Louis Barrow), 'The Brown Bomber' [1914-1981]; American heavyweight boxer who won the world championship in 1937, defending his title successfully 25 times. Retired undefeated 1949. Was knocked out by Rocky MARCIANO in 1951 after unsuccessful comeback.

LUNN, Sir Arnold [1888-1974]; British pioneer in skiing and authority on mountaineering, son of Sir Henry Lunn, Methodist missionary and travel agent. Sir Arnold organized the first world skiing championships. *History of Ski-ing* (1953).

McBRIDE, Willie John [1940-]; Irish rugby second-row forward, who captained the British Lions to success in South Africa in 1974.

McENROE, John P. [1959-]; American tennis player, US and Wimbledon championship winner since 1979. A controversial player with a quick and caustic tongue.

MACK, Connie (Cornelius McGillicuddy) [1862-1956]; American baseball player, team manager and owner. Owned and managed Philadelphia A's (190150).

MANOLETE, (Manuel Rodriguez Sánchez) [1917-1947]; Spanish bullfighter, and innovator of the dangerous pass called *manoletina*. Died after being gored by a bull at Linares.

MARADONA, Diego [1960-]; Argentine soccer player, the outstanding player of the 1986 World Cup. In 1984 signed by Napoli for £7 million fee.

MARCIANO, Rocky (Rocco Francis Marchegiano) [1923-1969]; American heavyweight boxer, who won the world title in 1952, retiring unbeaten in 1956 after 49 fights. Killed in an aircraft crash.

MATHEWSON, Christopher (Christy) [1880-1925]; American baseball player, a pitcher for the New York Giants for 17 seasons (1900-16) and Cincinnati Reds (1916).

MATTHEWS, Sir Stanley [1915-]; British association footballer for Stoke City, Blackpool and England. A right winger, known as the 'Wizard of the Dribble' for his wonderful ball control.

MAYS, Willie Howard [1931-]; American baseball player, outfielder, batter and base runner for San Francisco Giants (formerly New York) and the New York Mets.

MEADS, Colin Earl [1936-]; Rugby union lock forward for New Zealand. Was sent off in 1967 while playing Scotland at Murrayfield. Retired 1972.

MOODY, Helen Newington Wills [1905-]; American tennis player, who dominated the game from 1922-38, winning 19 major singles.

MOORE, Robert Frederick (Bobby) [1941-]; British association footballer for West Ham United and England. Captained England to World Cup victory in 1966. Capped a record 108 times.

MOSS, Stirling [1929-]; British motor-racing driver who won 16 grands prix but never a world championship. Nearly died after a crash at Goodwood in 1962, ending his racing career.

Left: Rugby player, Willie John McBride of Ireland.

Left: Suzanne Lenglen of France.

Right: Stanley Matthews.

NAGURSKI, Bronislaw (Bronko) [1908-]; Canadian player in American football; a fullback and tackle with Chicago Bears.

NAISMITH, Dr James A. [1861-1939]; Canadian-born American physical educator, the originator of basketball in 1891.

NAMATH, Joe Willie (Joseph William Namath); [1943-]; American college and professional football player, with University of Alabama team, 1964, New York Jets (1965-77), Los Angeles Rams (1977-78).

NASTASE, Ilie [1946-]; Romanian tennis player, renowned for tennis court tantrums. US singles champion, 1972.

NAVRATILOVA, Martina [1956-]; Czechoslovakian-born American tennis player; Wimbledon champion 1978 and 1979; and for six years running, 1982-1987.

NEPIA, George [1905-]; New Zealand rugby union fullback player, a Maori. Visited England and France with the All-Blacks 1924-25, when the team won every one of 30 matches.

NICKLAUS, Jack William [1940-]; American golfer, considered by many to be the greatest golfer of all time. US amateur champion 1959, 1961; US Open champion 1962, 1967, 1972; Open champion 1966, 1970. Has won more titles than any other golfer in history.

NURMI, Paavo Johannes [1897-1973]; Finnish athlete and distance runner, who won nine Olympic gold medals and three silver (1920-28).

NUVOLARI, Tazio [1892-1953]; Italian motor-racing driver, who rivals Stirling MOSS, Juan FANGIO and Jim CLARK for the title of 'greatest motor-racing driver of all time'.

OVETT, Steven Michael James [1955-]; British athlete, who won the 800 metres title in the 1980 Olympics, was unsuccessful in the 1984 events. Set up a world record for 1500 metres in 1983 [3:30.77].

OWENS, Jesse (James Cleveland Owens) [1913-1980]; American athlete who set up five world records: the 100 yards (equal), long jump, 220 yards/200 metres, and 220 yards hurdles in one afternoon (25 May 1935). A black man, he embarrassed the Nazis at the 1936 Olympics by winning four gold medals.

PALMER, Arnold [1929-]; American golfer, winner of the Master's championship in 1958, 1960, 1962 and 1964, and the US Open championship in 1960.

PELÉ, (Edson Arantes do Nascimento) [1940-]; Brazilian association footballer, regarded by many as the world's greatest. He starred in two world cup championships, leading the Brazilian team in 1958 and 1970. With Santos team, and then with New York Cosmos soccer team 1975-77.

PERRY, Frederick John (Fred) [1909-]; British lawn tennis and table tennis player; the only man in the world to lead at both. World table tennis champion 1929. At Wimbledon, he won the men's singles for three years running (1934-36).

211

PIGGOT, Lester [1935-]; British jockey, who was champion 11 times and won 9 Derbys. Retired in 1985 to become a trainer.

PLAYER, Gary [1935-]; South African golfer; British Open champion 1959, 1968; US Open champion 1965; Master's champion 1961; US PGA champion 1962, 1972.

PUSKAS, Ferenc [1927-]; Hungarian association footballer for Kispest, Honved, Real Madrid and Hungary. Played for Real Madrid when they won the European Cup in 1960. Retired as a player, becoming a coach and manager.

RAMSEY, Sir Alfred E. (Alf) [1920-]; British association footballer for Southampton, Tottenham Hotspur and England. As manager, he masterminded the progress of the England team to victory in the World Cup in 1966.

RHODES, Wilfred [1877-1973]; British cricketer for Yorkshire and England, who took a record 4187 wickets (slow left arm), and scored 32,722 runs. Played in 58 Tests.

RICHARDS, Sir Gordon [1904-]; British champion jockey, who was champion in England 26 times 1925-53. Won a record 4870 races, including 269 in the year 1947. He rode 14 classic winners.

RICKEY, Wesley Branch [1881-1965]; American baseball administrator, who instituted the 'farm system' in 1919. Broke the baseball colour barrier by signing Jackie ROBINSON to the Brooklyn Dodgers team in 1946.

RIMET, Jules [1873-1956]; French association football administrator, who was president of the French Football League 1919-1949, and president of FIFA 1921-56. The World Cup trophy is named after him.

ROBINSON, Frank [1935-]; American baseball player and manager, with Cincinnati Reds (1956-65) and Baltimore Orioles (1966-71). The first black man to manage a major league team (Cleveland Indians).

ROBINSON, Jack Roosevelt (Jackie) [1919-72]; American baseball player; the first black man to enter major league baseball. With Brooklyn Dodgers 1947-56 as a leading batter.

ROBINSON, 'Sugar' Ray (Walker Smith) [1920-]; American welterweight boxing champion 1946-51. A middleweight champion five times 1951-60. Regarded by many as the greatest boxer of the past 40 years.

ROCKNE, Knute K. [1888-1931]; American college football player and coach at Notre Dame (1918-31), a team which he developed into a major force in American football.

RONO, Henry [1952-]; Kenyan athlete, who held world records for 5000 metres, 10,000 metres and the 3000 metres steeplechase.

ROSE, Pete [1941-]; American baseball player who broke Ty Cobb's record of 4,191 hits in 1985, playing for the Cincinnati Reds.

ROUS, Sir Stanley [1895-1986]; British association football referee and executive. President of FIFA 1961-74. Was secretary of the English Football Association 1934-1961.

ROZELLE, Alvin Ray [1926-]; American football executive; general manager of Los Angeles Rams 1957-60. Commissioner of the National Football League from 1960.

RUTH, Babe (George Herman Ruth) [1895-1948]; American baseball player for the Boston Red Sox, New York Yankees and Boston Braves. Famed mainly for his time (1920-34) with NY Yankees, setting up many hitting records, including 60 home runs in the 1927 season and 714 during his career. In 1919 he hit a home run of 587 feet (178.9 metres).

SCHMELING, Max [1905-]; German heavyweight boxer, who was world champion 1930-32. Knocked out Joe LOUIS in 1936, but was in turn knocked out by Louis in 1938.

SHOEMAKER, Willie [1931-]; American jockey, a national champion three times. Rode Kentucky Derby winner 1955, 1959, and 1965. Has ridder over 8000 winners.

SOBERS, Sir Garfield St Aubin (Gary) [1936-]; West Indian cricketer, who played for the West Indies, Barbados, South Australia and Nottinghamshire. One of the world's finest all-rounders, who scored a record 8032 runs in 93 Tests.

SPITZ, Mark Andrew [1950-]; American swimmer, who won 7 gold medals in the 1972 Olympics, and 2 in the 1980 Games.

STAGG, Amos Alonzo [1862-1965]; American football coach for the University of Chicago for the 41 years 1892-1932.

STEWART, John Young (Jackie) [1939-]; Scottish motor racing driver, who won three world championships and 27 grands prix before retiring in 1973.

SURTEES, John [1934-]; British racing motorcyclist and motor-racing driver, the only man to

212

win world championships in both fields.

THORPE, Jim (James Francis) [1888-1953]; American athlete, probably the most outstanding all-round sportsman of all time. He won the pentathlon and decathlon in the 1912 Olympics, but was denied the medals on the grounds he was not a true amateur. Half Indian, he played major league American football and professional baseball.

TILDEN, William Tatem ('Big Bill') [1893-1953]; American tennis player, who dominated men's tennis in the 1920s. Voted the greatest tennis player of the first half of the 20th century in 1950.

TRUEMAN, Frederick Sewards [1931-]; British cricketer for Yorkshire and England. A popular fast bowler, he took 307 Test wickets. Now a radio and TV commentator.

TUNNEY, Gene [1898-1978]; American heavyweight boxer, who was world champion 1926-28, and who twice defeated Jack DEMPSEY.

VARDON, Harry [1870-1937]; British golfer, who won a record six Open championships and one US Open championship. One of the century's outstanding golfers, he reigned supreme during the years before World War I.

WADE, Virginia [1945-]; British tennis player who was Wimbledon champion in 1977.

WAGNER, John Peter (**Honus**) [1874-1955]; American baseball player, an infielder with the Pittsburgh Pirates 1900-17. Made 3415 hits.

WARNER, Glenn Scorey (**Pop**) [1871-1954]; American college football player and coach, among them the Carlisle Indians.

WARNER, Sir Pelham Francis (**Plum**) [1873-1963]; British cricketer for England, Oxford University and Middlesex. Had a great victory in leading England in Australia 1903-4. Founded *The Cricketer* magazine, 1921.

WEISSMULLER, Peter John (**Johnny**) [1903-1984]; American swimmer and film star, famed for his portrayal of Tarzan in 19 films. Voted the greatest swimmer of the half-century.

WILKINSON, Charles B. (**Bud**) [1916-]; American college football coach, at the University of Oklahoma (1947-63), where his teams won 145 games.

YOUNG, Denton True (**Cy**) [1867-1955]; American baseball pitcher with major league teams for 22 years, achieving 511 victories.

ZAHARIAS, Babe (Mildred Ella Didrikson) [1914- 1956]; American all-round athlete, who won javelin and 80 metre hurdles at the 1932 Olympics; US Open golf championship, 1948, 1950, and 1954.

ZATOPEK, Emil [1922-]; Czechoslovak athlete and runner who achieved 18 world records and won 4 Olympic titles, including the 5000 metres, 10,000 metres and marathon in 1952.

Mark Spitz of the USA—winner of seven Olympic gold medals in 1972. Right: Virginia Wade—Wimbledon tennis champion in 1977.

Religion & Philosophy

AUSTIN, John Langshaw [1911-60]; British philosopher, who stressed the need for a clear and precise understanding of the language of thought.

BARTH, Karl [1886-1968]; Swiss Calvinist theologian, who taught that the sole source of religious truth is the word of God as revealed by Christ.

BENEDICT XV (Giacomo della Chiesa) [18541922]; Italian-born Pope 1914-22. He failed in his attempt to settle World War I by negotiation, but helped to alleviate the suffering of prisoners of war.

BERGSON, Henri [1859-1941]; French philosopher, who believed that evolution comes from a life force rather than being subject to physical laws.

BESANT, Annie (b. Wood) [1847-1933]; British theosophist and Socialist propagandist, fervent in the cause of Indian nationalism.

BONHOEFFER, Dietrich [1906-45]; German Protestant theologian, opposed to the Nazis, who executed him in Buchenwald concentration camp.

BUBER, Martin [1878-1965]; Jewish philosopher who considered that religious faith is a dialogue between God and Man.

BUCHMAN, Frank Nathaniel David [1878-1961]; American evangelist, founder of the Oxford Movement, and who in 1938 conducted the 'Moral Rearmament' Campaign.

CARNAP, Rudolf [1891-1970]; American philosopher, born in Germany, who developed logical positivism.

CROCE, Benedetto [1866-1952]; Italian philosopher and historian, for whom the only reality is the mind or spirit, especially as seen in aesthetics.

DEWEY, John [1859-1952]; American philosopher, an adherent of pragmatism, who regarded philosophy as relevant to practical problems: 'the truth is what works'.

EDDY, Mary Morse (b. Baker) [1821-1910]; American religious leader, and founder of the Christian Science movement.

FRAZER, Sir James George [1854-1941]; British anthropologist, and an authority on ritual beliefs around the world.

FREGE, (Friedrich Ludwig) Gottlob [1848-1925]; German mathematician and philosopher, and founder of modern mathematical logic.

GRAHAM, Billy (William Franklyn Graham) [1918-]; American evangelist, who has been amazingly successful in religious campaigns throughout the world.

HEIDEGGER, Martin [1889-1976]; German philosopher, considered to be a leading EXISTENTIALIST. *Sein und Zeit* (1962).

HUDDLESTON, Trevor [1913-]; British missionary in Africa, and an opponent of apartheid in South Africa. Anglican Bishop of Masasi, Tanzania, 1960. *Naught for Your Comfort*, (1956).

HUSSERL, Edmund Gustav Albrecht [1859-1938]; Austrian philosopher (born in Moravia). His system is known as phenomenology.

JOHN PAUL I (Luciani Albino) [1912-78]; Italian-born Pope, who held office in 1978 for only 34 days before his sudden death.

JOHN PAUL II (Karol Wojtyla) [1920-]; Pope since 1978. Born near Cracow, he is the first Polish Pope, and the first non-Italian Pope for over 450 years.

JOHN XXIII (Angelo Giuseppe Roncalli) [18811963]; Italian-born Pope (1958-63), the son of a peasant, admired for his simplicity and generosity.

KAUTSKY, Karl [1854-1938]; German socialist and associate of Marx and Engels, who failed in interpretation arguments with LENIN, disagreeing with his proletarian dictatorship.

KELLER, Helen Adams [1880-1968]; American writer and scholar, who became deaf and blind at the age of 19 months. Her struggle against handicap became an inspiration to others.

KING, Martin Luther [1929-68]; black American civil rights leader, and a Baptist minister. A proponent of non-violence, he was assassinated in Memphis, Tennessee.

KNOX, Ronald Arbuthnott [1888-1957]; British religious scholar and author, who converted to Roman Catholicism and became a priest. He made a new translation of the Vulgate into modern English. Brother of E.V. Knox, editor of *Punch* (1933-1949).

LASKI, Harold Joseph [1893-1950]; British Socialist intellectual, who influenced others of his kind in the British Labour Party.

MARITAIN, Jacques [1882-1973]; French philosopher, and an exponent of St. Thomas Aquinas.

MERLEAU-PONTY, Maurice [1908-1961]; Marxist philosopher, and a chief exponent of phenomenology.

MINDSZENTY, József [1892-1975]; Hungarian Roman Catholic priest, a Cardinal of the church, and opponent of both Fascism and of Communism, who was forced to take refuge in the US Embassy in Budapest for 15 years.

MONTESSORI, Maria [1870-1952]; Italian educationist, whose ideas led to schools in various countries. She taught that young children learned best with spontaneous activity, and as little restraint as possible.

MOORE, George Edward [1873-1958]; British philosopher and editor, much of whose work was in the field of ethics.

McLUHAN, (Herbert) Marshall [1911-81]; Canadian analyst of mass media, who argued that the 'medium is the message'.

NEILL, Alexander Sutherland [1883-1973]; British educationist of libertarian views, best known for his school, Summerhill, in Suffolk, England.

PARSONS, Talcott [1902-1979]; American sociologist, who formulated the theory of classification of societies and their parts.

PAUL VI (Giovanni Batista Montini) [1897-1978]; Italian-born Pope 1963-78. He made a number of pilgrimages, among them to Jerusalem in 1964 and to the United Nations in New York.

PIUS X (Giuseppe Melchiorre Sarto) [1835-1914]; Italian-born Pope 1903-14. He was declared a saint in 1954.

PIUS XI (Achille Ratti) [1857-1939]; Italian-born Pope 1922-39. During his reign, Italy recognized the sovereignty of the Vatican City state.

PIUS XII (Eugenio Pacelli) [1876-1958]; Italian-born Pope 1939-58. He was criticized for not denouncing Nazi atrocities.

POPPER, Sir Karl [1902-]; British philosopher, born in Austria, particularly interested in scientific and social progress.

RUSSELL, Bertrand Arthur William (3rd Earl)

Maria Montessori, the Italian educationist, visiting a school.

[1872-1970]; British philosopher and mathematician, who in his *Principia Mathematica* (1910-1913) attempted to show that mathematical truths are derivable from basic logical truths.

SKINNER, Burrhus Frederic [1904-]; American psychologist of the behaviourist school, believing all behaviour to be unconscious.

SOREL, Georges [1847-1922]; French syndicalist (trades union) philosopher, who believed in violent revolution. A champion of DREYFUS.

SPENGLER, Oswald [1880-1936]; German philosopher, famous for his idea that civilizations grow and decay like human beings. *Decline of the West* (1926-1928).

TARSKI, Alfred [1902-]; Polish logician and mathematician. Founder of the system called metamathematics, which investigates theories.

TILLICH, Paul Johannes [1886-1965]; American theologian and philosopher, born in Prussia. He attempted to synthesize traditional Christianity and modern culture in *Systematic Theology* (1951-63).

WASHINGTON, Booker Taliaferro [1856-1915]; black American social reformer and educator, who established Tuskegee Institute for coloured people, 1881.

WEBER, Max [1864-1920]; German sociologist, who was a prolific author on the subject of categorizing social groups. *The Protestant Ethic and the Spirit of Capitalism* (1920).

WITTGENSTEIN, Ludwig Josef Johann [1889-1951]; British philosopher, born in Austria, who was mainly concerned with the theory of language. *Tractatus Logico-Philosophicus* (1921).

215

The World of Business

LEADERS IN BUSINESS AND INDUSTRY

AGNELLI, Giovanni [1866-1945]; Italian car manufacturer who founded Fiat (Fabbrica Italiana Automobili Torino) in 1899.

ARDEN, Elizabeth (Florence Nightingale Graham) [1884-1966]; American businesswoman with luxury beauty salons and a line of cosmetics.

ATLAS, Charles (Angelo Siciliano) [1894-1972]; American body builder who developed a method of muscle building, and a mail-order business based upon it. He was declared the 'World's Most Perfectly Developed Man'.

AUSTIN, Herbert (1st Baron Austin) [1866-1941]; British car manufacturer, who founded the Austin Motor Company in 1905 to produce small motor-cars.

AVEDON, Richard [1923-]; American photographer, renowned for his work for *Harper's Bazaar* and *Vogue*.

BALENCIAGA, Cristóbal [1895-1972]; Spanish couturier, famed for elegant ball gowns, and with successes in Spain and Paris.

BALMAIN, Pierre Alexandre [1914-1982]; French fashion designer, who, with Christian DIOR and Cristóbal BALENCIAGA, launched the 'New Look' in the late 1940s.

BARTHOLOMEW, Guy [1885-1962]; British newspaper magnate, who was responsible for the development of the *Daily Mirror*, which he joined in 1904 as a picture engraver.

BEAVERBROOK, 1st Baron (William Maxwell Aitken). [1879-1964]; Canadian-born British newspaper proprietor, whose newspapers, particularly *The Daily Express*, were often used for political campaigns.

BENTON, William [1900-1973]; American businessman and publisher, who owned *Encyclopaedia Britannica*. He was co-founder of the advertising firm Benton and Bowles.

BIRDSEYE, Clarence [1886-1956]; American businessman who invented an efficient method of freezing food.

BOOT, Jesse (1st Baron Trent) [1850-1931]; British pharmacist and manufacturer, who devel-

oped a chain of chemist's shops.

BURTON, Sir Montague Maurice [1885-1952]; multiple tailor, born in Lithuania of Jewish parentage. He came to England in 1900, had hundreds of shops, and improved working conditions in the industry.

BUTLIN, Sir Billy (William Edmund Heygate Colbourne Butlin) [1899-1980]; South African-born British holiday camp promoter. He opened his first camp at Skegness, Lincolnshire, in 1936.

CHAMBERS, Sir Paul [1904-]; British civil servant and industrialist. Formerly with the Inland Revenue, he went into industry and became head of Imperial Chemical Industries and later of Royal Insurance.

CHRISTIANSEN, Arthur [1904-63]; British newspaper editor, who was responsible for making the *Daily Express* the best-selling British newspaper.

CHRYSLER, Walter Percy [1875-1940] American automobile manufacturer, who became head of several firms (Buick, Willys, Maxwell) forming the Chrysler Corporation in 1925.

COHEN, Sir John Edward [1898-1979]; British businessman and chairman of the Tesco group of grocery and allied stores.

CUDLIPP, Hugh (Baron) [1913-]; British newspaper editor and publisher.

DASSAULT, Marcel [1892-1986]; French aircraft manufacturer, engineer, journalist and publisher. Produced the Mirage jets.

DE HAVILLAND, Sir Geoffrey [1882-1965]; British aeronautical engineer, a pioneer of aircraft design. Forming his own company, he built the famous Moth aircraft. Later, he produced the Mosquito, Vampire and Comet.

DIOR, Christian Ernest [1905-1957]; French couturier, who, with Pierre BALMAIN and Cristóbal BALENCIAGA, launched the 'New Look' after World War II.

DOUBLEDAY, Frank Nelson [1862-1934]; American publisher, who founded, in 1897, Doubleday and Co., Inc., the world's largest book publishing organization.

ESCOFFIER, Georges-Auguste [1846-1935]

French chef, director of the kitchen of the Grand Hotel, Monte Carlo, and later of the Savoy, Carlton and Ritz hotels in London.

FERGUSON, Harry George [1884-1960]; British engineer, born in Ireland. In 1909, he made the first flight over Ireland in an aircraft designed and built by himself; and in 1935 he designed and built the Ferguson farm tractor.

FERRARI, Enzo [1898-1988]; Italian motor manufacturer, renowned for the racing cars which bear his name.

FIRESTONE, Harvey Samuel [1868-1938]; American tyre manufacturer; founder, in 1900, of the company which bears his name.

FLICK, Friedrich [1884-1972]; German industrialist, son of a farmer/timber merchant. Sentenced at Nuremberg for war crimes, but later became one of the richest men in Germany.

FOKKER, Anthony Herman Gerard [1890-1939]; American aircraft designer and builder, born in Java of Dutch parentage. Established aircraft factories in Germany, and produced warplanes in World War I.

FORD, Henry [1863-1947]; American automobile manufacturer, father of the mass-produced car. Introduced the famous Model T in 1903, and in 1913 produced a car selling at $500.

FRIEDMAN, Milton [1912-]; American economist, best known for his ideas in monetary and laissez-faire economics. A professor at Chicago University.

GALBRAITH, John Kenneth [1908-]; Canadian-born American economist, and professor at Harvard in 1949. US ambassador to India 1961.

GALLUP, George Horace [1901-1984]; American statistician, originator, in 1935, of the famous Gallup Poll.

GETTY, Jean Paul [1892-1976]; American oil magnate, who formed, with his father, George Franklin Getty, the Getty Oil Co. At his death, he left over $1,000,000,000.

GILLETTE, King Camp [1855-1932]; American inventor and manufacturer, who invented, about 1900, the safety razor and blade.

GLUCKSTEIN, Montague [1854-1922]; British businessman, a partner in the Salmon and Gluckstein tobacco retailers, and founder, with a relative, Joseph Lyons, of the chain of Lyons teashops in London.

HALEY, Sir William [1901-]; British journalist,

Paul Getty (1892–1976)—once reputed to be the richest man in the world.

editor of *The Times* (starting as a telephonist), who became Director General of the BBC.

HEARST, William Randolph [1863-1951]; American editor and publisher of the largest newspaper chain in the USA. Renowned for sensational journalism.

HEINZ, Henry John [1844-1919]; American food manufacturer, who founded the H.J. Heinz company in in 1876. The '57 varieties' were never defined.

HILTON, Conrad Nicholson [1887-1979]; American hotelier, who started his empire of Hilton hotels in 1918, and owned 125 hotels by the date of his death.

HONDA, Soichiro [1906-]; Japanese motor manufacturer, who started the world's largest motor-cycle firm after World War II. Later became a leading automobile manufacturer.

HOOVER, William Henry [1849-1932]; American industrialist, who bought the patents of an electric sweeper and formed his own company in 1908.

ISSIGONIS, Sir Alex Arnold Constantine [1905-1988]; British automobile engineer, born in Turkey, who in 1959, designed the Mini, Britain's most successful motor-car, and previously, in 1948, designed the Morris Minor.

IWASAKI, Koyota [1879-1945]; Japanese business leader, and head of the Mitsubishi company, founded in the 1870's by his grandfather, Yataro Iwasaki. He was a Cambridge graduate. The company originally controlled shipping, automobiles, aircraft, chemicals and electrical goods, but was broken up after World War II.

JOHNSON, Howard Deering [1898-1972]; American restaurant-owner, famed for his ice-cream, made in 28 flavours. The Howard Johnson chain includes over 1000 eating-houses.

KEARTON, Sir (Christopher) Frank (Baron) [1911-]; British industrialist who became chairman of Courtaulds, and later head of the British National Oil Corporation.

KELLOGG, Will Keith [1860-1951]; American food manufacturer, who founded his company in 1906, introducing cornflakes, after experiments made by his brother John Harvey Kellogg [1852-1943], a physician.

KEYNES, John Maynard (1st Baron) [1883-1946]; British economist, most influential of all in recent times, especially with regard to ideas on government intervention in the economy to deal with unemployment.

KRUPP, Alfred Alwin Felix [1907-67]; German arms manufacturer, grandson of the founder of Krupps. Sentenced to 12 years jail at Nuremberg for war crimes. The company is now a manufacturer of consumer goods.

LANE, Sir Allen (Allen Lane Williams) [1902-70]; British publisher, and founder of Penguin Books.

LEVER, William Hesketh (1st Viscount Leverhulme) [1851-1925]; British soap manufacturer, who started in Lancashire as a grocer, forming companies which eventually became the vast Unilever empire.

LIPPMANN, Walter [1889-1974]; American editor and author, famed as a syndicated political columnist. He coined the phrase 'the cold war'.

LIPTON, Sir Thomas Johnstone [1850-1931]; British merchant, born in Glasgow of Irish parents. Founder of a chain of grocers and tea merchants. Also a noted yachtsman.

LOEWY, Raymond [1893-1986]; French-born American industrial designer, famed for his ideas on 'streamlining', which influenced a wide variety of products from railway engines to razors.

LORANT, Stefan [1901-]; Hungarian-born American author and editor. In Berlin as editor of *Münchner Illustrierte*; in Britain, founded the magazines *Weekly Illustrated*, *Lilliput* and *Picture Post*.

LUCE, Henry Robinson [1898-1967]; American journalist and publisher; founder of the magazines *Time* and *Life*.

MARKS, Simon (1st Baron Marks of Broughton) [1888-1964]; businessman and retailer, son of a Jewish immigrant from Poland who founded the firm Marks and Spencer. Simon Marks, with his brother-in-law Lord Sieff, transformed a small business into a large retail chain.

MOORES, Sir John [1896-]; British businessman, who founded Littlewoods Football Pools in 1923. The organization now owns mail-order and high-street chain-stores.

MURDOCH, (Keith) Rupert [1931-] Australian-born newspaper publisher, US citizen since 1985. In Britain, he owns the *Sun* and *The Times*. Also owns papers in the USA, TV stations.

MURROW, Ed(ward) [formerly Egbert] Roscoe [1908-65]; American journalist and broadcaster. Made notable broadcasts from London during World War II, later head of the US Information Agency.

NIARCHOS, Stavros Spyros [1909-]; Greek shipping magnate, who founded a fleet of supertankers which eventually became the world's largest. Brother-in-law of Aristotle ONASSIS.

NORMAN, Montagu Collet (1st Baron Norman) [1871-1950]; British banker, who became governor of the Bank of England from 1920 to 1944.

NORTHCLIFFE, 1st Viscount (Alfred Charles William Harmsworth) [1865-1922]; British newspaper magnate and pioneer of popular journalism, born near Dublin. He founded popular magazines, and several newspapers: among them the *Daily Mail*, and the *Daily Mirror*.

NUFFIELD, 1st Viscount (William Richard Morris) [1877-1963]; British manufacturer and philanthropist. Began as a motor-cycle manufacturer, later made cars. Later mergers led to the formation of British Leyland.

OGILVY, David Mackenzie [1911-]; British-born American advertising executive, founder of large American agency, famed for several popular campaigns.

ONASSIS, Aristotle Socrates [1906-75]; Greek shipping magnate who formed a large fleet of passenger and cargo ships.

OPPENHEIMER, Sir Ernest [1880-1957]; South African mining magnate and politician. Became a leader in the diamond industry, and his company held a near-monopoly of diamond production.

PHILIPS, Anton [1874-1951]; Dutch industrialist, and from 1921 leader of the large electrical firm (founded by his brother, Gerard) which bears his name. Outside the USA it is the world's largest company of its kind.

PORSCHE, Ferdinand [1875-1951]; German motor engineer of Czech origin. Designer (1934) of the Volkswagen, he formed his own company after World War II to manufacture the sports car which bears his name.

PULITZER, Joseph [1847-1911]; American newspaper publisher. A former reporter and writer, he is regarded as the founder of modern American journalism. His sight failed, and he founded a School of Journalism, and endowed the Pulitzer Prizes for journalism and letters.

QUANT, Mary, OBE [1934-]; British fashion designer and hair-stylist, famed for the 'Chelsea Look' of the 1960s.

RATHENAU, Walther [1867-1922]; German industrialist of Jewish origin, son of Emil Rathenau, founder of the giant AEG (*Allgemeine Elektrizitäts-Gesellschaft*) electrical company. Entered politics, and was a minister in the Weimar Republic government in 1921. Assassinated by anti-Semitic extremists.

REEVES, Rosser [1910-1984]; American advertising executive and pioneer. Built up the Ted Bates agency to leading position, and helped to promote EISENHOWER in his presidential campaign.

REITH, 1st Baron (John Charles Walsham Reith) [1889-1971]; British administrator, the first general manager, later director-general of the British Broadcasting Corporation, and its most influential head. A man of great, if severe, integrity and zeal.

ROCKEFELLER, John Davison [1839-1937]; American financier, industrialist and philanthro-

The cover of the first issue of Time magazine, published on 3 March 1923. Founder of the magazine was Henry Robinson Luce (1898–1967).

pist. In 1870, founded the firm which became Standard Oil, and in 1913 set up the Rockefeller Foundation to further science and promote public health.

ROLLS, Charles Stewart [1877-1910]; British automobile manufacturer and aviator. With Frederick ROYCE, formed the Rolls-Royce firm. On 2 June, 1910, he was the first British airman to fly the English Channel; was killed a month later.

ROSS, Harold [1892-1951]; American journalist, and founder/editor of *The New Yorker* magazine. He started the one-line cartoon, and encouraged such contributors as James Thurber and and John O'Hara. Other famous names included Dorothy PARKER, Robert Benchley, Ogden Nash, Peter Arno and Charles Addams.

ROYCE, Sir Frederick Henry [1863-1933]; British automobile manufacturer, who in 1906, joined with C.S. ROLLS to form the Rolls-Royce firm.

RUBINSTEIN, Helena [1872-1965]; American

beauty and cosmetics executive, born in Poland.

SAINSBURY, Alan John (Baron) [1902-]; British retail executive, and head of the grocery and supermarkets chain which bears his name.

SAMUEL, Marcus (1st Viscount Bearsted) [1853-1927]; British oil magnate and banker. Son of an east-end London Jewish shell-dealer, he named his oil company from his father's business. Developed the Shell company.

SARNOFF, David [1891-1971]; American communications executive, born in Russia. Went to the USA, became a radio operator (being the first to pick up the *Titanic* distress signal). A pioneer in radio and TV, was head of RCA (Radio Corporation of America), and formed the National Broadcasting Co. in 1926.

SASSOON, Vidal [1928-]; British hairdresser who grew up in the east end of London, rising to be a leading exponent of hairdressing styles.

SELFRIDGE, Harry Gordon [1864-1947]; American-born British merchant. Formerly with the Marshall Field company in Chicago, he went to London in 1906 and in 1909 opened the department store which bears his name.

SLOAN, Alfred Pritchard [1875-1966]; American automobile executive, who became head of the General Motors firm, making it the world's largest business.

SPRINGER, Axel [1912-1985]; German newspaper and magazine proprietor. Starting from scratch after World War II, has formed the largest newspaper organization in Europe, which includes the dailies *Bild Zeitung* and *Der Welt*.

TATA, Sir Jamsetji [1839-1904]; Indian Parsee industrialist, who with his son, Dorabji Tata [1859-1932], founded a large cotton empire in Bombay. Discovering iron ore near Nagpur, Dorabji founded a steel town.

THOMPSON, James Walter [1847-1928]; American advertising executive who formed his own agency in 1878, which became a market leader by the early years of this century.

THOMSON OF FLEET, 1st Baron (Roy Herbert Thomson) [1894-1976]; Canadian-born newspaper proprietor, who started by running a small Ontario radio station. Set up the Thomson Organization, which controlled, among others, the British papers *The Scotsman* and *The Times*.

TRIPPE, Juan Terry [1899-1981]; American airlines executive, who in 1927 founded Pan American Airways.

ULLSTEIN, Rudolf [1874-1964]; German publisher, who with his four brothers (Hans [1859-1935], Franz [1868-1944], Rudolf [1874-1964], and Hermann [1875-1943], developed his father's publishing house until it became the largest private firm of its kind in the world. It controlled many newspapers and magazines. This was a Jewish business, and was taken over by the Nazis when they came to power, and the name of the firm was changed to *Deutsche Verlag*. The business was restored to the family after World War II, but is now part of the SPRINGER empire.

WALLACE, Dewitt (William Roy DeWitt) [1899-1981]; American editor and publisher, who with his wife, Lila Acheson Wallace, in 1921 founded the *Reader's Digest*, now the largest-circulation magazine in the world, selling over 30 million copies monthly in 16 languages.

WATSON, Thomas John [1874-1956]; American industrialist, who converted a poorly-run business-machine firm into an international giant which became IBM in 1924.

WELLCOME, Sir Henry Solomon [1853-1936]; British chemist and patron of science, born in Dakota, USA. He went to Britain in 1880, and set up the firm of Burroughs, Wellcome to sell drugs under the name of 'Tabloid'. Founded museums and laboratories, and the Wellcome Foundation, to which he left the whole of the business .

WILSON, Kemmons [1913-]; American hotelier, who began the Holiday Inn motel chain in 1952 in Memphis, Tennessee, USA.

WINCHELL, Walter [1897-1972]; American journalist, who wrote a famous syndicated gossip column, and who also had a similar programme on radio. He was originally in vaudeville (1909-20).

WOODRUFF, Robert [1890-1985]; American businessman who built the Coca-Cola concern into a huge empire after becoming president in 1923.

WOOLWORTH, Frank Winfield [1852-1919]; American merchant, who started his empire with a small store selling goods at only 5 cents, and then also at 10 cents. A chain of five-and-ten-cent stores spread throughout the USA, and to Britain in 1910 (with nothing over sixpence).

YERKES, Charles Tyson [1937-1905]; American railway financier, who went to Britain in 1900, where he organized, and helped to finance, the building of London's underground.

Nobel Prizewinners

THE NOBEL PRIZE FOR PHYSICS

Year	Winner	Country*
1901	Wilhelm Conrad RÖNTGEN	Germany
1902	Hendrik Antoon LORENTZ	Netherlands
	& Pieter ZEEMAN	Netherlands
1903	Antoine-Henri BECQUEREL	France
	Pierre CURIE	France
	& Marie CURIE	France (b. Poland)
1904	Lord RAYLEIGH (John William Strutt)	Great Britain
1905	Philipp Eduard Anton VON LENARD	Germany
1906	Sir Joseph John THOMSON	Great Britain
1907	Albert Abraham MICHELSON	USA (b. Germany)
1908	Gabriel LIPPMANN	France
1909	Guglielmo MARCONI	Italy
	& Carl Ferdinand BRAUN	Germany
1910	Johannes Diderik VAN DER WAALS	Netherlands
1911	Wilhelm WIEN	Germany
1912	Gustaf Nils DALÉN	Sweden
1913	Heike KAMERLINGH-ONNES	Netherlands
1914	Max VON LAUE	Germany
1915	Sir William Henry BRAGG	Great Britain
	& Sir William Lawrence BRAGG	Great Britain
1916	*Not awarded*	
1917	Charles Glover BARKLA	Great Britain
1918	Max Karl Ernst Ludwig PLANCK	Germany
1919	Johannes STARK	Germany
1920	Charles Édouard GUILLAUME	Switzerland
1921	Albert EINSTEIN	Germany
1922	Niels Henrik David BOHR	Denmark
1923	Robert Andrews MILLIKAN	USA
1924	Karl Manne Georg SIEGBAHN	Sweden
1925	James FRANCK	Germany
	& Gustav HERTZ	Germany
1926	Jean Baptiste PERRIN	France
1927	Arthur Holly COMPTON	USA
	Charles Thomson Rees WILSON	Great Britain
1928	Sir Owen Willans RICHARDSON	Great Britain
1929	Prince Louis-Victor DE BROGLIE	France
1930	Sir Chandrasekhara Venkata RAMAN	India
1931	*Not awarded*	
1932	Werner HEISENBERG	Germany
1933	Erwin SCHRÖDINGER	Austria
	& Paul Adrien Maurice DIRAC	Great Britain
1934	*Not awarded*	
1935	Sir James CHADWICK	Great Britain
1936	Victor Franz HESS	Austria[1]
1937	Clinton Joseph DAVISSON	USA
	& Sir George Paget THOMSON	Great Britain
1938	Enrico FERMI	Italy
1939	Ernest Orlando LAWRENCE	USA
1940	*Not awarded*	
1941	*Not awarded*	
1943	Otto STERN	USA (b. Germany)
1944	Isidor Isaac RABI	USA (b. Austria)
1945	Wolfgang PAULI	Austria[1]
1946	Percy Williams BRIDGMAN	USA
1947	Sir Edward Victor APPLETON	Great Britain
1948	Lord Patrick Maynard Stuart BLACKETT	Great Britain
1949	Hideki YUKAWA	Japan
1950	Cecil Frank POWELL	Great Britain
1951	Sir John Douglas COCKCROFT	Great Britain
	& Ernest Thomas Sinton WALTON	Ireland
1952	Felix BLOCH	USA (b. Switz.)
	& Edward Mills PURCELL	USA
1953	Frits (Frederik) ZERNIKE	Netherlands
1954	Max BORN	G.B. (b. Ger.)
	& Walther BOTHE	Germany
1955	Willis Eugene LAMB	USA
	& Polykarp KUSCH	USA (b. Germany)
1956	William Bradford SHOCKLEY	USA
	John BARDEEN	USA
	& Walter Houser BRATTAIN	USA
1957	Chen Ning YANG	China[1]
	Tsung-Dao LEE	China[1]
1958	Pavel Alekseyevich CHERENKOV	USSR
	Ilya Mikhailovich FRANK	USSR
	& Igor Yevgenevich TAMM	USSR
1959	Emilio Gino SEGRÈ	USA (b. Italy)
	& Owen CHAMBERLAIN	USA
1960	Donald Arthur GLASER	USA
1961	Robert HOFSTADTER	USA
	Rudolf Ludwig MÖSSBAUER	Germany
1962	Lev Davidovich LANDAU	USSR
1963	Eugene Paul WIGNER	USA (b. Hungary)
	Maria GOEPPERT-MAYER	USA (b. Germany)
	& Johannes Hans Daniel JENSEN	Germany
1964	Charles Hard TOWNES	USA
	Nikolai Gennadievich BASOV	USSR
	& Aleksander Mikhailovich PROKHOROV	USSR
1965	Sin-Itiro TOMONAGA	Japan
	Julian Seymour SCHWINGER	USA
	Richard Philips FEYNMAN	USA
1966	Alfred KASTLER	France
1967	Hans Albrecht BETHE	USA (b. Germany)
1968	Luis Walter ALVAREZ	USA
1969	Murray GELL-MANN	USA
1970	Hannes ALFVÉN	Sweden
	& Louis-Eugène NÉEL	France
1971	Dennis GABOR	G.B. (b. Hun.)
1972	John BARDEEN	USA
	Leon N. COOPER	USA
	& John Robert SCHRIEFFER	USA
1973	Leo ESAKI	Japan[1]
	Ivar GIAEVER	USA (b. Norway)
	& Brian D. JOSEPHSON	Great Britain
1974	Sir Martin RYLE	Great Britain
	& Antony HEWISH	Great Britain
1975	Aage Niels BOHR	Denmark
	Benjamin Ray MOTTELSON	Denmark
	& L. James RAINWATER	USA

1976	Burton RICHTER	USA
	& Samuel Chao Chung TING	USA
1977	Philip Warren ANDERSON	USA
	Sir Nevill Francis MOTT	Great Britain
	& John Hasbrouck VAN VLECK	USA
1978	Peter Leonidovich KAPITSA	USSR
	Arno Allan PENZIAS	USA
	& Robert W. WILSON	USA
1979	Sheldon L. GLASHOW	USA
	Abdus SALAM	Pakistan
	Steven WEINBERG	USA
1980	James W. CRONIN	USA
	& Val L. FITCH	USA
1981	Nicolaas BLOEMBERGEN	USA
	Arthur L. SCHAWLOW	USA
	Kai M. SIEGBAHN	Sweden
1982	Kenneth G. WILSON	USA
1983	Subrahmanyan CHANDRASEKHAR	USA (b. India)
	William A. FOWLER	Great Britain
1984	Carlo RUBBIA	Italy
	Simon VAN DER MEER	Netherlands
1985	Klaus VON KLITZING	Germany
1986	Ernst RUSKA	Germany
	Gerd BINNIG	Germany
	Heinrich ROHRER	Switzerland
1987	Karl MULLER	Switzerland
	Johannes BEDNORZ	Germany
1988	Leon LEDERMAN	USA
	Melvin SCHWARTZ	USA
	Jack STEINBERGER	USA

THE NOBEL PRIZE FOR CHEMISTRY

Year	Winner	Country*
1901	Jacobus Henricus VAN'T HOFF	Netherlands
1902	Hermann Emil FISCHER	Germany
1903	Svante August ARRHENIUS	Sweden
1904	Sir William RAMSAY	Great Britain
1905	Johann Friedrich Wilhelm Adolf VON BAEYER	Germany
1906	Ferdinand-Frédéric-Henri MOISSAN	France
1907	Eduard BUCHNER	Germany
1908	Lord Ernest RUTHERFORD	Great Britain
1909	Friedrich Wilhelm OSTWALD	Germany (b. Russia)
1910	Otto WALLACH	Germany
1911	Marie CURIE	France (b. Poland)
1912	François-Auguste-Victor GRIGNARD	France
	& Paul SABATIER	France
1913	Alfred WERNER	Switz. (b. Alsace)
1914	Theodore William RICHARDS	USA
1915	Richard Martin WILLSTÄTTER	Germany
1916	*Not awarded*	
1917	*Not awarded*	
1918	Fritz HABER	Germany
1919	*Not awarded*	
1920	Walther Hermann NERNST	Germany
1921	Frederick SODDY	Great Britain
1922	Frances William ASTON	Great Britain
1923	Fritz PREGL	Austria
1924	*Not awarded*	
1925	Richard Adolf ZSIGMONDY	Germany
1926	The (Theodor) SVEDBERG	Sweden
1927	Heinrich Otto WIELAND	Germany
1928	Adolf Otto Reinhold WINDAUS	Germany

1929	Sir Arthur HARDEN	Great Britain
	& Hans Karl August Simon VON EULER-CHELPIN	Sweden
1930	Hans FISCHER	Germany
1931	Carl BOSCH	Germany
	& Friedrich BERGIUS	Germany
1932	Irving LANGMUIR	USA
1933	*Not awarded*	
1934	Harold Clayton UREY	USA
1935	Abdus SALAM Frédéric CURIE	France
	Irène JOLIOT-CURIE	France
1936	Petrus (Peter) Josephus Wilhelmus DEBYE	Netherlands
1937	Sir Walter Norman HAWORTH	Great Britain
	& Paul KARRER	Switzerland
1938	Richard KUHN	Germany
1939	Adolf Friedrich Johann BUTENANDT	Germany[2]
	& Leopold RUZICKA	Switz. (b. Austria)
1940	*Not awarded*	
1941	*Not awarded*	
1942	*Not awarded*	
1943	George VON HEVESY	Hungary
1944	Otto HAHN	Germany
1945	Ilmari Artturi VIRTANEN	Finland
1946	James Batcheller SUMNER	USA
	John Howard NORTHROP	USA
	& Wendell Meredith STANLEY	USA
1947	Sir Robert ROBINSON	Great Britain
1948	Arne Wilhelm Kaurin TISELIUS	Sweden
1949	William Francis GIAUQUE	USA
1950	Otto Paul Hermann DIELS	Germany
	& Kurt ALDER	Germany
1951	Edwin Mattison McMILLAN	USA
	& Glenn Theodore SEABORG	USA
1952	Archer John Porter MARTIN	Great Britain
	& Richard Laurence Millington SYNGE	Great Britain
1953	Hermann STAUDINGER	Germany
1954	Linus Carl PAULING	USA
1955	Vincent DE VIGNEAUD	USA
1956	Sir Cyril Norman HINSHELWOOD	Great Britain
	& Nikolai Nikolayevich SEMENOV	USSR
1957	Lord Alexander Robertus TODD	Great Britain
1958	Frederick SANGER	Great Britain
1959	Jaroslav HEYROVSKY	Czechoslovaki
1960	Willard Frank LIBBY	USA
1961	Melvin CALVIN	USA
1962	Max Ferdinand PERUTZ	G.B. (b. Austria)
	& Sir John Cowdery KENDREW	Great Britain
1963	Karl ZIEGLER	Germany
	& Giulio NATTA	Italy
1964	Dorothy Crowfoot HODGKIN	Great Britain
1965	Robert Burns WOODWARD	USA
1966	Robert S. MULLIKEN	USA
1967	Manfred EIGEN	Germany
	Ronald George Wreyford NORRISH	Great Britain
	& Sir George PORTER	Great Britain
1968	Lars ONSLAGER	USA (b. Norway)
1969	Sir Derek Harold Richard BARTON	Great Britain
	& Odd HASSEL	Norway
1970	Luis F. LELOIR	Argentina
1971	Gerhard HERZBERG	Canada (b. Ger.)
1972	Christian Boehmer ANFINSEN	USA
	Stanford MOORE	USA
	& William Howard STEIN	USA
1973	Ernst Otto FISCHER	Germany
	& Sir Geoffrey WILKINSON	Great Britain
1974	Paul J. FLORY	USA

1975	Sir John Warcup CORNFORTH	Australia & G.B.
	& Vladimir PRELOG	Switz. (b. Bosnia)
1976	William N. LIPSCOMB	USA
1977	Ilya PRIGOGINE	Belgium (b. Russia)
1978	Peter MITCHELL	Great Britain
1979	Herbert C. BROWN	USA (b. G.B.)
	& Georg WITTIG	Germany
1980	Paul BERG	USA
	Walter GILBERT	USA
	& Frederick SANGER	Great Britain
1981	Kenichi FUKUI	Japan
	& Roald HOFFMANN	USA
1982	Aaron KLUG	Great Britain
1983	Henry TAUBE	USA (b. Canada)
1984	Bruce MERRIFIELD	USA
1985	Herbert HAUPTMAN	USA
	Jerome KARLE	USA
1986	Dudley HERSCHBACH	USA
	& YUAN LEE	USA
	John POLYANI	Canada
1987	Charles PEDERSEN	USA
	& Donald CRAM	USA
1988	Johann DEISENHOFER	Germany
	& Robert HUBER	Germany
	& Hartmut MICHEL	Germany

THE NOBEL PRIZE FOR PHYSIOLOGY OR MEDICINE

Year	Winner	Country*
1901	Emil Adolf VON BEHRING	Germany
1902	Sir Ronald ROSS	Great Britain
1903	Niels Ryberg FINSEN	Denmark
1904	Ivan Petrovich PAVLOV	Russia
1905	Robert KOCH	Germany
1906	Camillio GOLGI	Italy
	& Santiago RAMÓN Y CAJAL	Spain
1907	Charles-Luis-Alphonse LAVERAN	France
1908	Ilya Ilyich MECHNIKOV	Russia
	& Paul EHRLICH	Germany
1909	Emil Theodor KOCHER	Switzerland
1910	Albrecht KOSSEL	Germany
1911	Allvar GULLSTRAND	Sweden
1912	Alexis CARREL	France
1913	Charles Robert RICHET	France
1914	Robert BÁRÁNY	Hungary
1915	*Not awarded*	
1916	*Not awarded*	
1917	*Not awarded*	
1918	*Not awarded*	
1919	Jules-Jean-Baptiste-Vincent BORDET	Belgium
1920	Schack August Steenberger KROGH	Denmark
1921	*Not awarded*	
1922	Sir Archibald Vivian HILL	Great Britain
	Otto Fritz MEYERHOF	Germany
1923	Sir Frederick Grant BANTING	Canada
	& John James Richard MACLEOD	Canada (b. Scot.)
1924	Willem EINTHOVEN	Netherlands
1925	*Not awarded*	
1926	Johannes Andreas Grib FIBIGER	Denmark
1927	Julius WAGNER-JAUREGG	Austria
1928	Charles-Jules-Henri NICOLLE	France
1929	Christiaan EIJKMAN	Netherlands
	& Sir Frederick Gowland HOPKINS	Great Britain
1930	Karl LANDSTEINER	Austria

1931	Otto Heinrich WARBURG	Germany
1932	Sir Charles Scott SHERRINGTON	Great Britain
	& Lord Edgar Douglas ADRIAN	Great Britain
1933	Thomas Hunt MORGAN	USA
1934	George Hoyt WHIPPLE	USA
	George Richards MINOT	USA
	& William Parry MURPHY	USA
1935	Hans SPEMANN	Germany
1936	Sir Henry Hallett DALE	Great Britain
	& Otto LOEWI	Austria[1]
1937	Albert VON SZENT-GYÖRGI	Hungary[1]
1938	Corneille-Jean-François HEYMANS	Belgium
1939	Gerhard DOMAGK	Germany[2]
1940	*Not awarded*	
1941	*Not awarded*	
1942	*Not awarded*	
1943	Henrik Carl Peter DAM	Denmark
	& Edward Adelbert DOISY	USA
1944	Joseph ERLANGER	USA
	& Herbert Spencer GASSER	USA
1945	Sir Alexander FLEMING	Great Britain
	Sir Ernst Boris CHAIN	G.B. (b. Ger.)
	& Lord Howard Walter FLOREY	G.B. (b. Australia)
1946	Hermann Joseph MULLER	USA
1947	Carl Ferdinand CORI	USA (b. Austria)
	Gerty Theresa CORI	USA (b. Austria)
	& Bernardo Alberto HOUSSAY	Argentina
1948	Paul Hermann MÜLLER	Switzerland
1949	Walter Rudolf HESS	Switzerland
	& Antonio Caetano de Abreu Freire	
	Egas MONIZ	Portugal
1950	Edward Calvin KENDALL	USA
	Tadeus REICHSTEIN	Switz. (b. Poland)
	& Philip Showalter HENCH	USA
1951	Max THEILER	South Africa
1952	Selman Abraham WAKSMAN	USA (b. Russia)
1953	Sir Hans Adolf KREBS	G.B. (b. Ger.)
	& Fritz Albert LIPMANN	USA (b. Germany)
1954	John Franklin ENDERS	USA
	Thomas Huckle WELLER	USA
	& Frederick Chapman ROBBINS	USA
1955	Axel Hugo Theodor THEORELL	Sweden
1956	André Frédéric COURNAND	USA (b. France)
	Werner FORSSMANN	Germany
	& Dickinson Woodruff RICHARDS	USA
1957	Daniel BOVET	Italy
1958	George Wells BEADLE	USA
	Edward Lawrie TATUM	USA
	& Joshua LEDERBERG	USA
1959	Severo OCHOA	USA (b. Spain)
	& Arthur KORNBERG	USA
1960	Sir Frank Macfarlane BURNET	Australia
	& Sir Peter Brain MEDAWAR	Great Britain
1961	Georg VON BÉKÉSY	USA (b. Hungary)
1962	Francis Harry Compton CRICK	Great Britain
	James Dewey WATSON	USA
	& Maurice Hugh Frederick WILKINS	Great Britain
1963	Sir John Carew ECCLES	Australia
	Sir Alan Lloyd HODGKIN	Great Britain
	& Sir Andrew Fielding HUXLEY	Great Britain
1964	Konrad BLOCH	USA (b. Germany)
	& Feodor LYNEN	Germany
1965	François JACOB	France
	André-Michael LWOFF	France

	& Jacques-Lucien MONOD	France
1966	Peyton ROUS	USA
	& Charles Brenton HUGGINS	USA
1967	Ragnar GRANIT	Sweden
	Haldan Keffer HARTLINE	USA
	& George WALD	USA
1968	Robert William HOLLEY	USA
	Har Gobind KHORANA	USA (b. India)
	& Marshall NIRENBERG	USA
1969	Max DELBRÜCK	USA (b. Germany)
	Alfred Day HERSHEY	USA
	& Salvador Edward LURIA	USA (b. Italy)
1970	Sir Bernard KATZ	Great Britain
	Ulf VON EULER	Sweden
	& Julius AXELROD	USA
1971	Earl Wilbur SUTHERLAND	USA
1972	Gerald Maurice EDELMAN	USA
	& Rodney Robert PORTER	Great Britain
1973	Karl VON FRISCH	Ger. (b. Austria)
	Konrad LORENZ	Austria
	& Nikolaas TINBERGEN	G.B. (b. Nether.)
1974	Albert CLAUDE	Belgium
	Christian-René DE DUVE	Belgium
	& George Emil PALADE	USA (b. Romania)
1975	David BALTIMORE	USA
	Renato DULBECCO	USA (b. Italy)
	& Howard Martin TEMIN	USA
1976	Baruch S. BLUMBERG	USA
	& D. Carleton GAJDUSEK	USA
1977	Roger GUILLEMIN	USA (b. France)
	Andrew SCHALLY	USA (b. Poland)
	& Rosalyn YALOW	USA
1978	Werner ARBER	Switzerland
	Daniel NATHANS	USA
	& Hamilton O. SMITH	USA
1979	Allan M. CORMACK &	USA (b. S.Africa)
	Sir Godfrey Newbold HOUNSFIELD	Great Britain
1980	Baruj BENACERRAF	USA (b. Venezuela)
	Jean DAUSSET	France
	& George D. SNELL	USA
1981	Roger W. SPERRY	USA
	David H. HUBEL	USA
	& Torsten N. WIESEL	USA
1982	Sune BERGSTRÖM	Sweden
	Bengt I. SAMUELSSON	Sweden
	& John Robert VANE	Great Britain
1983	Barbara McCLINTOCK	USA
1984	César MILSTEIN	Great Britain
	Georges KOHLER	Germany
	& Niels JERNE	Denmark
1985	Michael BROWN	USA
	& Joseph GOLDSTEIN	USA
1986	Rita LEVI-MONTALCINI	USA (b. Italy)
	& Stanley COHEN	USA
1987	Susumu TONEGAWA	Japan
1988	Sir James BLACK	Great Britain
	Gertrude ELION	USA
	& George HITCHINGS	USA

THE NOBEL PRIZE FOR LITERATURE

Year	Winner	Country*
1901	SULLY-PRUDHOMME (René-François-Armand PRUDHOMME)	France
1902	Christian Matthias Theodor MOMMSEN	Germany
1903	Bjørnstjerne BJØRNSON	Norway
1904	Frédéric MISTRAL	France
	& José ECHEGARAY Y EIZAGUIRRE	Spain
1905	Henryk SIENKIEWICZ	Poland
1906	Giosuè CARDUCCI	Italy
1907	Rudyard KIPLING	Great Britain
1908	Rudolf Christoph EUCKEN	Germany
1909	Selma Ottoliana Lovisa LAGERLÖF	Sweden
1910	Paul Johann Ludwig HEYSE	Germany
1911	Count Maurice (Mooris) Polidore Marie Bernhard MAETERLINCK	Belgium
1912	Gerhard Johann Robert HAUPTMANN	Germany
1913	Rabindranath TAGORE	India
1914	*Not awarded*	
1915	Romain ROLLAND	France
1916	Carl Gustav Verner VON HEIDENSTAM	Sweden
1917	Karl Adolph GJELLERUP	Denmark
	& Henrik PONTOPPIDAN	Denmark
1918	*Not awarded*	
1919	Carl Friedrich Georg SPITTELER	Switzerland
1920	Knut Pedersen HAMSUN	Norway
1921	Anatole FRANCE (Jacques-Anatole THIBAULT)	France
1922	Jacinto BENAVENTE	Spain
1923	William Butler YEATS	Ireland
1924	Wladyslaw Stanislaw REYMONT (REYMENT)	Poland
1925	George Bernard SHAW	Great Britain
1926	Grazia DELEDDA (MADESANI)	Italy
1927	Henri BERGSON	France
1928	Sigrid UNDSET	Norway (b. Den.)
1929	Thomas MANN	Germany
1930	Sinclair LEWIS	USA
1931	Erik Axel KARLFELDT	Sweden
1932	John GALSWORTHY	Great Britain
1933	Ivan Alekseyevich BUNIN	France (b. Russia)
1934	Luigi PIRANDELLO	Italy
1935	*Not awarded*	
1936	Eugene Gladstone O'NEILL	USA
1937	Roger MARTIN DU GARD	France
1938	Pearl BUCK (Pearl WALSH)	USA
1939	Frans Eemil SILLANPÄÄ	Finland
1940	*Not awarded*	
1941	*Not awarded*	
1942	*Not awarded*	
1943	*Not awarded*	
1944	Johannes Vilhelm JENSEN	Denmark
1945	Gabriela MISTRAL (Lucila GODOY Y ALCAYAGA)	Chile
1946	Hermann HESSE	Switz. (b. Ger.)
1947	André-Paul-Guillaume GIDE	France
1948	Thomas Stearns ELIOT	G.B. (b. USA)
1949	William FAULKNER	USA
1950	Bertram Arthur William RUSSELL (Earl RUSSELL)	Great Britain
1951	Pär Fabian LAGERKVIST	Sweden
1952	François MAURIAC	France
1953	Sir Winston Leonard Spencer CHURCHILL	Great Britain
1954	Ernest Miller HEMINGWAY	USA
1955	Halldór Kiljan LAXNESS	Iceland
1956	Juan Ramón JIMÉNEZ	Spain
1957	Albert CAMUS	France
1958	Boris Leonidovich PASTERNAK	USSR

1959	Salvatore QUASIMODO	Italy
1960	Saint-John PERSE (Marie-René-Auguste Alexis LÉGER	France
1961	Ivo ANDRIĆ	Yugo. (b. Bosnia)
1962	John STEINBECK	USA
1963	Giorgos SEFERIS (SEFERIADIS)	Greece (b. Turkey)
1964	Jean-Paul SARTRE	France[3]
1965	Mikhail Aleksandrovich SHOLOKHOV	USSR
1966	Shmuel Yosef AGNON	Isr. (b. Au.-Hun.)
	& Nelly SACHS	Sweden (b. Ger.)
1967	Miguel Angel ASTURIAS	Guatemala
1968	Yasunari KAWABATA	Japan
1969	Samuel BECKETT	Ireland
1970	Aleksander Isaievich SOLZHENITSYN	USSR
1971	Pablo NERUDA (Neftali Ricardo Reyes BASOALTO)	Chile
1972	Heinrich BÖLL	Germany
1973	Patrick WHITE	Australia (b. Eng.)
1974	Eyvind JOHNSON	Sweden
	& Harry MARTINSON	Sweden
1975	Eugenio MONTALE	Italy
1976	Saul BELLOW	USA
1977	Vicente ALEIXANDRE	Spain
1978	Isaac Bashevis SINGER	USA (b. Poland)
1979	Odysseus ELYTIS (ALEPOUDHELIS)	Greece
1980	Czeslaw MILOSZ	USA & Pol. (b. Lithuania)
1981	Elias CANETTI	G.B. (b. Bulgaria)
1982	Gabriel GARCÍA MÁRQUEZ	Colombia
1983	William Gerald GOLDING	Great Britain
	*At time of award. [3]Declined prize.	
1984	Jaroslav SEIFERT	Czechoslovakia
1985	Claude SIMON	France
1986	Wole SOYINKA	Nigeria
1987	Joseph BRODSKY	USSR
1988	Naguib MAHFOUZ	Egypt

THE NOBEL PRIZE FOR PEACE

Year	Winner	Country*
1901	Jean Henri DUNANT	Switzerland
	& Frédéric PASSY	France
1902	Élie DUCOMMUN	Switzerland
	& Charles Albert GOBAT	Switzerland
1903	Sir William Randal CREMER	Great Britain
1904	Institute of International Law	Ghent, Belgium.
1905	Baroness (Bertha Sophie Felicita) VON SUTTNER	Austria
1906	Theodore ROOSEVELT	USA
1907	Ernesto Teodoro MONETA	Italy
	& Louis RENAULT	France
1908	Klas Pontus ARNOLDSON	Sweden
	& Fredrik BAJER	Denmark
1909	Auguste-Marie-François BEERNAERT	Belgium
	& Paul-Henri-Benjamin-Balluet D'ESTOURNELLES DE CONSTANT	France
1910	Permanent International Peace Bureau	Berne, Switzerland
1911	Tobias Michael Carel ASSER	Netherlands
	& Alfred Hermann FRIED	Austria
1912	Elihu ROOT	USA
1913	Henri LA FONTAINE	Belgium

1914	*Not awarded*	
1915	*Not awarded*	
1916	*Not awarded*	
1917	International Red Cross Committee	Geneva, Switzerland
1918	*Not awarded*	
1919	Thomas Woodrow WILSON	USA
1920	Léon-Victor-Auguste BOURGEOIS	France
1921	Karl Hjalmar BRANTING	Sweden
	& Christian Louis LANGE	Norway
1922	Fridtjof NANSEN	Norway
1923	*Not awarded*	
1924	*Not awarded*	
1925	Sir Austen Joseph CHAMBERLAIN	Great Britain
	& Charles Gates DAWES	USA
1926	Aristide BRIAND	France
	& Gustav STRESEMANN	Germany
1927	Ferdinand BUISSON	France
	Ludwig QUIDDE	Germany
1928	*Not awarded*	
1929	Frank Billings KELLOGG	USA
1930	Lars Olof Nathan Jonathan SÖDERBLOM	Sweden
1931	Jane ADDAMS	USA
	& Nicholas Murray BUTLER	USA
1932	*Not awarded*	
1933	Sir Norman Ralph Lane ANGELL	Great Britain
1934	Arthur HENDERSON	Great Britain
1935	Carl VON OSSIETZKY	Germany
1936	Carlos SAAVEDRA LAMAS	Argentina
1937	Viscount CECIL of Chelwood (Edgar Algernon Robert Gascoyne CECIL)	Great Britain
1938	Nansen International Office for Refugees (1921)	Geneva, Switzerland
1939	*Not awarded*	
1940	*Not awarded*	
1941	*Not awarded*	
1942	*Not awarded*	
1943	*Not awarded*	
1944	International Committee of the Red Cross (1863)	Geneva, Switzerland
1945	Cordell HULL	USA
1946	Emily Greene BALCH	USA
	& John Raleigh MOTT	USA
1947	The Friends Service Council [The Quakers] (1647)	London, England
	& The American Friends Service Committee [The Quakers] (1672)	Washington, USA
1948	*Not awarded*	
1949	Lord (John) BOYD ORR of Brechin	Great Britain
1950	Ralph BUNCHE	USA
1951	Léon JOUHAUX	France
1952	Albert SCHWEITZER	France (b. Alsace)
1953	George Catlett MARSHALL	USA
1954	Office of the United Nations High Commissioner for Refugees:	Geneva, Switzerland
1955	*Not awarded*	
1956	*Not awarded*	
1957	Lester Bowles PEARSON	Canada
1958	Father Dominique-Georges PIRE	Belgium
1959	Lord (Philip John) NOEL-BAKER	Great Britain
1960	Albert John LUTULI	South Africa
1961	Dag Hjalmar Agne Carl HAMMARSKJÖLD	Sweden
1962	Linus Carl PAULING	USA

1963	International Committee of the Red Cross	Geneva, Switzerland
	& League of Red Cross Societies	Geneva, Switzerland
1964	Martin Luther KING	USA
1965	United Nations Children's Fund (1946)	New York, USA
1966	Not awarded	
1967	Not awarded	
1968	René CASSIN	France
1969	International Labour Organization	Geneva, Switzerland
1970	Norman BORLAUG	USA
1971	Willy BRANDT	USA
1972	Not awarded	
1973	Henry Alfred KISSINGER	USA
	& LE DUC THO	Vietnam³
1974	Seán MacBRIDE	Ireland
	& Eisaku SATO	Japan
1975	Andrei Dmitrievich SAKHAROV	USSR
1976	Betty WILLIAMS	Northern Ireland
	& Mairead CORRIGAN	Northern Ireland
1977	Amnesty International	London, England
1978	Mohamed Anwar EL SADAT	Egypt
	& Menachem BEGIN	Israel (b. Poland)
1979	Mother TERESA	India (b. Yugo.)
1980	Adolfo PÉREZ ESQUIVEL	Argentina
1981	Office of the High Commissioner for	
	Refugees:	Geneva, Switzerland
1982	Alva MYRDAL	Sweden
	& Alfonso GARCÍA ROBLES	Mexico
1983	Lech WALESA	Poland
	*At time of award.	³Declined prize.
1984	Desmond TUTU	South Africa
1985	International Physicians for the	
	Prevention of Nuclear War	USA
1986	Elie WIESEL	USA
1987	Oscar ARIAS SANCHEZ	Costa Rica
1988	United Nations Peace-keeping Force	

THE NOBEL PRIZE FOR ECONOMIC SCIENCE

Year	Winner	Country*
1969	Ragnar FRISCH	Norway
	& Jan TINBERGEN	Netherlands
1970	Paul SAMUELSON	USA
1971	Simon KUZNETS	USA (b. Russia)
1972	Sir John Richard HICKS	Great Britain
	& Kenneth Joseph ARROW	USA
1973	Wassily LEONTIEF	USA (b. Russia)
1974	Gunnar MYRDAL	Sweden
	& Friedrich August VON HAYEK	G.B. (b. Austria)
1975	Leonid KANTOROVICH	USSR
	& Tjalling C. KOOPMANS	USA (b. Nether.)
1976	Milton FRIEDMAN	USA
1977	Bertil OHLIN	Sweden
	& James Edward MEADE	Great Britain
1978	Herbert Alexander SIMON	USA
1979	Theodore W. SCHULTZ	USA
	& Sir Arthur LEWIS	Great Britain
1980	Lawrence R. KLEIN	USA
1981	James TOBIN	USA
1982	George J. STIGLER	USA
1983	Gérard DEBREU	USA (b. France)
	*At time of award.	
1984	Sir Richard STONE	Great Britain
1985	Franco MODIGLIANI	USA
1986	James BUCHANAN	USA
1987	Robert SOLOW	USA
1988	Maurice ALLAIS	France

PHOTOGRAPHIC ACKNOWLEDGEMENTS

The Publisher wishes to thank the following photographers, agencies, galleries, museums and other establishments for their help in supplying photographs for this book.

George Allen & Unwin Ltd, "The Ra Expedition" by Thor Heyerdahl; Allsport; Atomic Energy Authority; Australia News & Information Bureau; British Aircraft Authority; British Museum; Richard Bryant; Camera Press; Cavendish Laboratory; C.O.I.; Collins Publishers; Colorsport; Cyprus High Commission; Frank Driggs; E.E.C; Mary Evans; Fox Rank; German Embassy; Henry Grant; Collection of Mrs V.W. Ganz, for Picasso; Stanley Gibbons Ltd; Sonia Halliday; Hamilton Studios; Robert Harding; Heinemann Ltd; Hulton; Imperial War Museum; India High Commission; Israel Embassy; Japanese Embassy; Kenya High Commission; Kobal Collection; Mansell Collection; Methuen Books Ltd; NASA; National Film Archive; National Hungarian Tourist Office; National Maritime Museum; National Portrait Gallery; Novosti; Jeu de Paume Musée, Paris; Penguin Books; P & O Lines; Photosource; Popperfoto; Rediffusion Computers; Syndication International; Tampa Chamber of Commerce; Tate Gallery; Time-Life; Topham; Trinidad Tourist Office; Ulstein; Unimate; Victoria and Albert Museum; Walt Disney Productions; Zefa; Zimbabwe Tourist Office.

Index

Page numbers in *italic* indicate
that the subject is illustrated

Aalto, H. Alvar 168
Aaron, Henry 206
Abbey Theatre 163
Abdullah Ibn Hussein, King of
    Jordan 30, 101, 120
Abel, Sir Frederick 123, 132
Abercrombie, Sir L. Patrick 168
Aberfan disaster 38, 96, 97
Abstract 163, 166, 168
Abstract Expressionism 163
Academy awards 202–5
Achebe, Chinua 168
Acheson, Dean G. 101
Action painting 163
Activism 163
Adenauer, Konrad 101
Adrian, Edgar Douglas, *1st
    Baron* 138, 224
Afghanistan 65, 67
Africa 35
Afrikaners 82
Agnelli, Giovanni 216
Ahmed Maher Pasha 119
Aiken, Howard Hathaway 128, 130
Aircraft, powered 122
Air events 143–50
Airship 122
Albania 65, 66; monarchs 115
Albee, Edward Franklin 168
Alcock, Sir John W. 17, 145, 161
Alder, Kurt 124, 130, 132, 223
Aldrin, Edwin E. 43, 153, 154, *155*,
    161
Alexander, Harold *1st Earl* 101
Alexander Kieland (oil rig
    platform) 99
Alexander, King of Yugoslavia 118
Algeria 65, 66; earthquakes 95, 99
Algerian War 85
Ali, Muhammad (Cassius
    Clay) 206
Allenby, Edmund Henry
    Hynman 101
Allende (Gossens), Salvador 101
Alps, avalanches in 96, 100
Amin Dada, Idi 44, 46, 56, 101
Amundsen, Roald 13, 161, 162
Andorra 65
Andropov, Yuri 63
Angola 65, 67
Anguilla 65
Anouilh, Jean 168
Anquetil, Jacques 206
Antigua and Barbuda 65
Antonioni, Michelangelo 188
ANZUS 80
Apartheid 82
Appollinaire, Guillaume 168–9
Apollo 2 *151*

Appleton, Sir Edward Victor 130,
    221
Aqualung 122, 128
Aquino, Benigno 121
Arab League 80
Arden, Elizabeth 216
Argentina 65, 66
Armstrong, Louis Daniel 188
Armstrong, Neil 41–2, 43, 153, 154,
    157, 161
Arp, H. Jean 167, 169
Arrhenius, Svante August 130, 223
Artaud, Antonin 188
Art Nouveau 163, 169
Ascension Island 65
Ashcroft, Dame Peggy 188
Ashton, Sir Frederic 188
Asquith, Herbert Henry 12, 15,
    101, 117
Assassinations 118–21
Association of South East Asian,
    Nations (ASEAN) 80
Astaire, Fred 188, *189*
Aston, Francis William 130, 223
Astor, Nancy, *Viscountess* 18, 101
Atatürk, Kemal 18, *19*, 101
Atlas, Charles 216
Attenborough, David Frederick 138
Attlee, Clement Richard 101, *117*
Auden, W. H. 169, 182
Austin, Herbert 216
Austin, John Langshaw 214
Australia 65, 67; disasters 97, 98,
    100
Austria 65, 66; Vienna hotel fire 99;
    avalanche 100
Austro-Hungarian
    Empire:monarchs 115
Autogiro 122, 128
Avalanches 96, 100
Avendon, Richard 216
Ayckbourn, Alan 169
Ayub Khan, Mohammad 101

Baade, Walter 130
Babel, Isaak Emmanvilovich 169
Bacharach, Burt 188
Bacon, Francis (artist) 169
Bacon, Francis (scientist) 124, 128
Baden-Powell, Robert 12, 161
Baekeland, L. H. 122, 128, 130–1
Bahamas 65, 66
Bahrain 65, 66
Baird, John Logie 20, 127, 129, 131
Bakst, Leon 169
Balanchine, George 188
Baldwin, Stanley 20, 101, 117
Balenciaga, Cristóbal 216
Balfour, Arthur James 101, 117
Balkan Wars 13–14, 85
Ballesteros, Severiano 206
Ball-point pen 122, 128
Balmain, Pierre 216
Bangladesh 65, 66; floods 98, 100;
    political murders 120, 121
Bannister, Sir Roger 32, 206
Banting, Sir Frederick Grant 125,
    138
Bara, Theda 188
Barbados 65, 67
Barbirolli, Sir John 169
Bardot, Brigitte 188

Barnard, Christiaan 138
Barnes, Sydney 206
Barnhill, Jack 120
Barr, Murray 138
Barrault, Jean-Louis 188
Barrie, Sir J. M. 169
Barth, Karl 214
Bartholomew, Guy 216
Barthou, Louis 118
Bartók, Béla 169, 173
Basie, Count 188
Bateson, Gregory 138
Bathyscaphe 122, *123*, 128
Batten, Jean 146, 161
Battersea fun fair, disaster at 97
Battery, solar 122, 128
Baugh, Samuel 206
Bauhaus 163
Bavaria: monarchs 115
Bawden, Sir Frederick 138
Bayliss, Lilian Mary 188
Beadle, George Wells 138, 141
Beatles, The 59, 188, *189*
Beaverbrook, William, *1st
    Baron* 216
Bebop (Bop) 163
Beckett, Samuel 164, 167, 169, 184,
    226
Beebe, W. 122
Beecham, Sir Thomas 169
Begin, Menachem 55, 56, 227
Behrens, Peter 169
Behring, Emil Adolf von 138
Beiderbecke, Bix 188
Belgium 65, 66; disasters 95, 96;
    monarchs 115
Belize 65, 67
Bell, Alexander Graham 131
Belloc, Hilaire 169, 180
Bellow, Saul 169, 184, 185, 186,
    187, 226
Benedict XV, Pope 14, 214
Benes, Eduard 101
Ben-Gurion, David *101*
Benin 65, 66
Bennett, Arnold 169, 180, 181
Benny, Jack 188
Benton, William 216
Benz, Karl Friedrich 131
Berg, Alban 169
Bergman, Ingmar 188
Bergman, Ingrid 188, 203, 204
Bergson, Henri 169, 214
Beria, Lavrenty Pavlovich 101
Berkeley, Busby 188
Berlin, Irving 188
Berlin Wall 36
Bermuda 65; murder of
    governor 120
Bernadotte, Count Folke 30, 101,
    120
Bernal, John Desmond 131
Berhnardt, Sarah *173*, 188
Bernstein, Leonard 169
Besant, Annie 214
Best, Charles H. 125, 138
Best, George 206
Betelgeuse (tanker), explosion of 99
Bethe, Hans Albrecht 131, 221
Betjeman, Sir John 46, 169
Bevan, Aneurin 101
Beveridge, William, *1st Baron* 102

Bevin, Ernest 102
Bhutan 65, 66
Bhutto, Zulfikar Ali 102
Biffen, Sir Rowland Harry 138
Big Bang theory 122
Binet, Alfred 138
Birdseye, Clarence 216
Birkenhead, Frederick Edwin Smith, 1st Earl 102
Biró, Láslo 24, 122, 128, 131
Bishop, Maurice 121
Blackett, Patrick Maynard Stuart, 1st Baron 131
Blaik, Earl Henry (Red) 206
Blaue Reiter 163
Blériot, Louis 13, 142, 143, 161
Blok, Aleksander 169
Blues 163
Blum, Léon 102
Blyton, Enid 169
Boccioni, Umberto 169
Boer War 10, 85, 161
Bogart, Humphrey 188, 204
Bohr, Niels Hendrik David 131, 221
Bolden, Buddy 188
Bolivia 66, 68
Bomb disasters 98, 100
Bomberg, David 169
Bondfield, Margaret Grace 102
Bondi, Hermann 127, 131
Bonhoeffer, Dietrich 214
Bonnard, Pierre 169
Boogie Woogie 163, 165
Books published 180-7
Boot, Jesse, 1st Baron Trent 216
Borg, Björn 206
Borges, Jorge Luis 169
Bosch, Carl 131
Botham, Ian 206
Botswana 67, 68
Boulez, Pierre 169
Boult, Sir Adrian 169
Bourguiba, Habib 102
Bovet, Daniel 138
Bow, Clara 188
Bowden, Sir Frederick 138, 141
Boyer, Charles 188
Brabham, Jack 206
Bracht, Baron Charles 121
Bradman, Sir Donald 206
Bragg, Sir W. Lawrence 131, 221
Bragg, Sir William Henry 131, 221
Brancusi, Constantin 169
Brandenberger, Jacques 123, 128
Brando, Marlon 188, 204, 205
Brandt, Willy 42, 101, 102, 227
Braque, Georges 169, 176
Braun, Wernher von 131
Brazil 66, 68; Amazon river boat disaster 99
Brecht, Bertolt 169
Brennan, Louis 124, 131
Breton, André 169
Breuer, Marcel Lajos 170
Brezhnev, Leonid 35, 37, 62, 102
Briand, Aristide 102
Britten, Benjamin 170, 173
Broadway 163, 168
Brode, Wallace Reed 131
Bromfield, Louis 170
Brook, Peter 188

Brooke, Rupert 15, 170, 181
Brown, Sir A. Whitten 17, 145, 161
Brown, Paul E. 206
Brundage, Avery 206
Brunei, 67, 68
Brutalism 163
Bryant, Sir Arthur 161
Buber, Martin 214
Buchan, John, 1st Baron Tweedsmuir 170, 180, 181
Buchman, Frank 214
Budapest 33, 71
Budge, Donald 206
"Buffalo Bill" (W. F. Cody) 15, 161
Bulganin, Nikolai Aleksandrovich 102
Bulgaria 67, 68; monarchs 115
Bunche, Ralph Johnson 102
Buñel, Luis 188
Burkina Faso 68
Burlesque 163
Burma 67, 68
Burnet, Sir F. Macfarlane 138, 224
Burton, Sir Montague 216
Burton, Richard 189
Burundi 67, 68
Busby, Sir Matt 206
Bush, Vannevar 131
Busoni, Ferruccio 170
Butler, Richard Austen 102
Butlin, Sir Billy 24, 216
Byrd, Richard E. 21, 145, 161

Cage, John 170
Cagney, James 189, 203
Calinescu, Armand 119
Callaghan, James 52, 102, 117
Callas, Maria 170
Calmette, Gaston 118
Calmette, Leon Charles Albert 138
Calvin, Melvin 131, 223
Cameroon 67, 68
Campanella, Roy 206
Campbell, Donald 38
Campbell, Sir Malcolm 206
Campbell, Mrs Patrick 189
Campbell-Bannerman, Sir Henry II, 117
Camus, Albert 170, 184, 185, 225
Canada 66, 68
Cannon, Walter Bradford 138
Cantor, Eddie 189
Capek, Karel 170
Cape Verde 66, 68
Capra, Frank 189, 202, 203
Caribbean Community and Common Market (CARICOM) 80
Carlson, Chester Floyd 29, 131
Carmichael, Hoagy 189
Carnap, Rudolf 214
Carne, Marcel 189
Caro, Anthony 170
Carothers, Wallace H. 24, 131
Carrell, Alexis 138
Carrero Blanco, Luis 120
Carrier, W. H. 122, 131
Carson, Edward Henry 102
Carter, Jimmy 53, 57, 58, 102-3, 114
Cartier-Bresson, Henri 170

Caruso, Enrico 170
Carver, George Washington 131
Casals, Pablo 170
Casson, Sir Hugh 170
Castro, Fidel 34, 36, 103
Cavell, Edith 15, 103
Cawley, Evonne (Goolagong) 209
Cayman Islands 68
Ceausescu, Nicholae 103
Central African Republic 67, 68
Ceylon, flood disaster in 96; see also Sri Lanka
Chad 67, 68
Chadwick, Florence 206
Chadwick, Sir James 131, 221
Chagall, Marc 170
Chain, Ernst Boriz 138, 139, 224
Chaliapin, Fyodor 170-1
Challenger space shuttle 160
Chamberlain, Sir J. Austen 103, 226
Chamberlain, Joseph 103
Chamberlain, Neville 24, 25, 25, 90, 92, 103, 104, 106, 117
Chambers, Sir Paul 216
Chandler, Raymond 171, 183
Chang, Samuel H. 119
Chaplin, Charlie 189
Chapman, Sydney 131
Charles, Prince of Wales 30, 34, 41, 60, 102, 103, 113
Charlton, Bobby 206
Chemistry: Nobel Prizewinners 223-4
Chernenko, Konstantin 64
Chesterton, G.K. 171, 180
Chevalier, Albert 189
Chevalier, Maurice 189, 196
Chiang Kai-Shek 20, 29, 103, 108
Chicago rail disaster 98
Childe, V. Gordon 161
Chile 66, 68; earthquakes 94, 95, 96
China: People's Republic of 67, 68; earthquake 94; floods 99
Chlorophyll 123
Chomsky, Noam 171
Chou En-Lai 52, 103
Christian Democrats 82
Christiansen, Arthur 216
Christie, Agatha 171
Christmas Island 68
Chrysler, Walter Percy 216
Churchill, Winston 25, 26, 27, 28, 29, 32, 37, 92, 93, 103, 105, 117
Cierva, Juan de la 122, 128, 131, 145
Clair, René 189
Clark, Earl Harry 206
Clark, Jim 206, 211
Clemenceau, Georges 103-4
Clemente, Roberto 208
Cobb, John 208
Cobb, Tyrus 208
Cobham, Sir Alan J. 145, 161
Cochran, Sir Charles Blake 189-90
Cockcroft, Sir John 131-2, 137, 221
Cockerell, Sir Christopher 125, 128, 132
Cocos (Keeling) Islands 68
Cocteau, Jean 171, 182

Cody, W.F. ("Buffalo Bill") 15, 161
Coe, Sebastian 208
Cohen, Sir John Edward 216
Cole, Nat 'King' 190
Colette 171, 181
Collins, Michael 118
Colombia 66, 68; disasters 94, 99
Columbia space shuttle 159–60
COMECON (Council for Mutual Economic Assistance) 30, 81
Common Market *see* EEC
Commonwealth of Nations 30, 79–80
Communism 82
Comoros 67, 69
Compton, Arthur Holly 132
Compton, Denis 208
Computers: analogue 123, 125; digital 123, *123*, 128
Concorde 149, 150
Congo 67, 69
Connolly, Maureen (Little Mo) 208
Connors, Jimmy 208
Conrad, Joseph 171, 180, 181
Conservative Party 82–3
Constantine, Learie, *Baron* 208, *208*
Continental drift 123, 137
Cook Islands 69
Coolidge, Calvin 114
Cooper, Gary 190, 203, 204
Copeau, Jacques 190
Cornell, Katharine 190
Cosmic rays 123
Costa Rica 67, 69
Council of Europe 30, 81
Country and Western 163
Court, Margaret 208
Cousteau, Jacques-Yves 122, 128, 161
Coward, Sir Noel 190
Crapp, Lorraine 208
Crawford, Joan 190, 203
Crick, Francis H.C. 138
Crippen, Hawley Harvey *12*, 13
Cristescu, Professor 119
Croce, Benedetto 214
Crookes, Sir William 132
Crosby, Bing 190, 194, 203
Cruyff, Johan 208
Cuba 66, 69
Cuban crisis 36–7
Cubism 163, 164, 169, 176
Cudlipp, Hugh, *Baron* 216
Culbertson, Ely 208
Cunningham, Merce 190
Curie, Marie 132, *133*, 221, 223
Curie, Pierre 133, 221
Curzon, George Nathaniel 104
Cybernetics 123, 137
Cyclotron 124, 128, 135
Cyprus 66, 69
Czechoslovakia 66, 69

Dacron *see* Terylene
Dadaism 163–4, 171
Dale, Sir Henry H. 138
Dali, Salvador 167, 171
d'Annunzio, Gabriele 17, 171, 190
Darlan, Jean François 27, 104, 119
Dart, Raymond A. 138

Dassault, Marcel 216
Davidson, Emily 93
Davis, Bette 190, 202, 203
Davis, Joe 208
Davis, Steve 208
Dayan, Moshe *103*, 104
Day Lewis, Cecil 171
DDT 124
de Broglie, Prince 132, 221
Debussy, Claude 171
de Forest, L. 124, 127, 128, 129, 132
de Gasperi, Alcide 104
de Gaulle, Charles *see* Gaulle, Charles de
de Havilland, Sir Geoffrey 216
de Havilland, Olivia 190, 203
de la Mare, Walter 171, 186
Delius, Frederick 171
de Mille, Cecil Blount 190
de Montherlant, Henri-Marie-Joseph 171
Dempsey, Jack 208, 213
Denmark 66, 69; monarchs 115
de Sica, Vittorio 190
de Valera, Eamon 22, 48, 104
de Valois, Dame Ninette 190
de Vries, Hugo M. 138
Dewar, Sir James 123, 132
Dewey, John 214
Diaghilev, Serge 190, 196
Dick-Read, Grantly 138
Dictatorship 83
Diels-Adler Reaction 124
Diels, Otto 124, 130, 132
Diesel, Rudolf 124, 132
Dietrich, Marlene 190
Dimaggio, Joe 208
Diode 124
Dior, Christian Ernest 216
Dirac, Paul Adrien Maurice 132
Director (theatre) 164, 166
Disasters 94–100
Disney, Walt 190, *191*
di Stefano, Alfredo 208
Djibouti 67, 69
Djilas, Milovan 104
DNA 124, 126, 137, 138, 142
Dobzhansky, Theodosius 138
Doenitz, Karl 104
Dollfuss, Engelbert 22, 23, 118
Domagk, Gerhard 138
Dominica 66, 69; hurricane 99
Dominican Republic 67, 69; hurricane 99
Dormoy, Marx 119
Dornberger, Walter Robert 132
Doubleday. Frank Nelson 216
Douglas, Kirk 190
Douglas, Norman 171
Douglas-Home, Sir Alex 117
Doumer, Paul 118
Dovzhenko, Alexander 190
Dowding, Hugh Tremenheere, *1st Baron* 104
Dreiser, Theodore 171, 180, 181, 182, 184
Dreyer, Carl 190
Dreyfus, Alfred 12, 103, 104, 215
Drobny, Jaroslav 208
Dubcek, Alexander 41, 104
Dubs, Adolph 121

Dufy, Raoul 164, 171
Dulles, John Foster 104
Duncan, Isadora 190
Durkheim, Emile 138
Durrell, Lawrence 171
Duse, Eleonora 190
Duvalier, François ('Papa Doc') 104
Dylan, Bob 190

Eames, Charles 171
Earhart, Amelia 146, 161, *161*
East Germany *see* German Democratic Republic
Eastman, George 132
Eccles, Sir John 138
Ecuador 66, 69; earthquake in 95
Eddy, Mary (Baker) 214
Eden, Anthony 24, 32, 33, 104, 117
Edison, Thomas Alva 124, 132
Edward VII of Gt Britain 10, 13, 104, 105, *113*
Edward VIII of Gt Britain 23, 24, 101, 104, 105–6, 113
EEC (European Economic Community) 47, 80; headquarters 47
EFTA (European Free Trade Association) 34–5, 81
Egypt 67, 69; Nile ferry fire 100
Ehrenburg, Ilya 171
Ehrlich, Paul 138
Eiffel, Alexandre-Gustave 132
Eijkman, Christiaan 138–9
Einstein, Albert 15, 132, *133*, 221
Einthoven, Willem 139
Eisenhower, Dwight D. 27, 28, 31, 33, 34, 41, 104, *105*, *114*
Eisenstein, Sergei 190
Electrons 122, 124, 126
Elgar, Sir Edward 171
Eliot, T.S. 171, *173*, 181, 225
Elizabeth II of Gt Britain 31, 34, 103, 105, 113, *113*; coronation *31*
Ellington, Edward ('Duke') 190
El Salvador 67, 69
Enders, John F. 139
Equatorial Guinea 67, 69
Ernst, Max 167, 171
Escoffier, Georges-Auguste 217
Ethiopia 67, 69
European Parliament 80
Eurydice (submarine), sinking of 96
Eusebio, Ferreira da Silva 208
Evans, Bergen 171
Evans, Dame Edith 190
Ewart-Biggs, Christopher 120–1
Existentialists 170, 172, 177, 214
Expressionism 163, 164, 173, 175, 176

Fabre, Jean-Henri Casimir 139
Fairbanks, Douglas 190–1
Faisal I (Ibn Hussein) 105
Falkland Islands 66, 69
Falklands War 60, 85–6
Falla, Manuel de 171
Fangio, Juan 209, 211
Farouk, King of Egypt 105
Fascism, 83

Faulkner, William 171, 182, 183, 184, 186, 225
Fauves 164
Ferguson, Harry George 217
Fermi, Enrico 132, *133*, 136, 221
Ferrari, Enzo 217
Fields, Gracie 191
Fields, W. C. 191
Fiji 67, 69
Film, sound 124, 128
Finland 67, 69
Finney, Tom 209
Firbank, Ronald 181, 182
Firestone, Harvey 217
First World War *see* World War I
Fischer, Hans 132
Fisher, John Arbuthnot, *1st Baron* 105
Fitzgerald, Ella 191
Fitzgerald, F. Scott 171–2, 181, 182, 184
Flagstad, Kirsten 172
Flaherty, Robert 191
F-layer (Appleton layer) 122, 130
Fleming, Sir Alexander 139, 224
Fleming, Sir J. Ambrose 124, 132
Flesche, Carl 172
Flick, Friedrich 217
Flixborough disaster 97
Florey, H.W. 138, 139
Flynn, Errol 191
Flynn, John 139–40
Foch, Ferdinand 105
Fokine, Mikhail 191
Fokker, Anthony 217
Fonda, Henry 191
Fonda, Jane 191, 205
Fontanne, Lynn 191, 195
Fonteyn, Dame Margot 191, *191*
Ford, Gerald 48, 50, 105, 114
Ford, Henry 13, 217
Ford, John 191, 202, 203, 204
Formosa (*later* Taiwan), earthquake at 94
Forssman, Werner Theodor Otto 140
Forster, E. M. 172, 180, 181, 186
Fox, Senator Billy 120
France 66, 69; disasters 94, 97, 98; motorway crash 100
France, Anatole 172, 180, 225
Franck, James 132
Franco, General Francisco 24–5, 51, 88, 105, 107
Frank E. Evans (destroyer) 41, 96
Franz Ferdinand, Archduke of Austria 118
Fraser, Dawn 209
Frazer, Sir James 214
Frege, Gottlob 214
French Guiana 69
French Polynesia 69
Freud, Sigmund *139*, 140
Friedman, Milton 217
Friese-Greene, William 132
Frost, Robert 172, 181
Fry, Charles 209
Fry, Christopher 172
Fuller, C. 122, 128
Fuller, R. Buckmaster 132
Furtwängler, Wilhelm 172
Futurism 164, 169

Gable, Clark 191–2, 202
Gabon 67, 69
Gabor, Dennis 125, 132
Gagarin, Yuri 36, 40, 151, 153, 162
Gagnan, E. 122
Gaitskell, Hugh 105
Galbraith, John Kenneth 217
Gallup, George 217
Galsworthy, John 172, 180, 181, 225
Galton, Sir Francis 140
Gambia 66, 69
Gandhi, Indira 64, *64*, 105, 109, 121
Gandhi, Mohandas Kamamchand (Mahatma) 21, 22, 29, 105, *119*
Garbo, Greta 192, *192*
Gardner, Ava 192
Garland, Judy 192
Gaulle, Charles de 30, 34, 39, 41, 44, 85, *103*, 104, 109
Gehrig, Henri Louis (Lou) 209
Geiger, J. H. W. 124, 128, 132
Gemayel, Bashir 121
Gemzell, Carl 140
General Assembly, United Nations 79
Genet, Jean 172
Geodesic structures 124
George I, King of Greece 118
George V of Gt Britain 13, 23, 105, 113, *113*
George VI of Gt Britain 24, 31, 105–6, 113, 145
German Democratic Republic 66, 69
German Empire: Monarchs 115
Germany, Federal Republic of 66, 69
Gershwin, George 192
Gershwin, Ira 192
Getty, Paul 217, *217*
Ghana 69
Giacometti, Alberto 172
Gibraltar 69
Gibson, Robert (Bob) 209
Gide, André 172, 181, 182, 225
Gielgud, Sir John 192
Gill, Eric 172
Gillespie, John Birks ('Dizzy') 192
Gillette, King Camp 217
Giscard d'Estaing, Valéry 106
Gish, Lilian 192
Glasgow: disasters 96, 97, 100
Glenn, John 152, 162
Gluckstein, Montague 217
Godard, Jean-Luc 192
Goddard, Robert Hutchings 133
Goebbels, Joseph 106
Goering, Hermann Wilhelm 29, 106
Golding, William 172, 185, 186, 187, 226
Goldmark, Peter Carl 133
Goldwyn, Samuel 192, 196
Gomez, J. C. 118
Goodman, Benny 192
Goolagong, Evonne 209
Gorbachev, Mikhail 64
Gorky, Maxim 172
Gouache 164

Grace, Dr William 209
Graham, Billy 214
Graham, Edgar 121
Graham, Martha 192
Grange, Harold Edward (Red) 209
Grant, Cary 192
Grass, Günter 172
Graves, Robert 172, 183
Gray, Sir James 140
Great Depression *21*
Greece 67, 69; earthquake 94; monarchs 115
Greene, Graham 172, 182, 183, 184, 185, 186
Greenland 66, 69–70
Grenada 70
Grey, Zane 172
Grierson, John 192
Griffith, D. W. 192, *193*
Grock (Charles Adrian Wettach) 192
Gromyko, Andrei Andreyevich 106
Gropius, Walter 163, 172
Guadeloupe 70
Guam 70
Guatemala 67, 70; earthquakes 94, 98
Guderian, Heinz Wilhelm 106
Guevara, Che 106
Guillaume, C. E. 124, 133–4
Guinea 66, 70
Guinea-Bissau 66, 70
Guinness, Sir Alec 193, 204
Gurney, Henry 120
Guthrie, Sir Tyrone 193
Guyana 67, 70

Haber, Fritz 134
Haemoglobin 121
Hagen, Walter 209
Hahn, Otto 134, 135
Haig, Douglas, *1st Earl* 106
Haile Selassie, King of Abyssinia 21, 50, *103*, 106
Haiti 67, 70
Hale, George Ellery 134
Haley, Bill 193
Haley, Sir William 217
Halifax, Edward Frederick Lindley Wood, *1st Earl* 106
Hall, Sir Peter 193
Hammarskjöld, Dag 31, 36, 106
Hammerstein, Oscar II 193
Hammond, John Hugo 140
Handley, Tommy 193
Hardie, James Keir 83, 106
Harding, Warren G. 106, 114
Hardy, Oliver 193, 194
Hardy, Thomas 172
Harlow, Jean 193
Harmsworth, Alfred 11
Harriman, William Averell 106
Harrison, Rex 193, 204
Hart, Lorenz Milton 193
Hauser, Gayelord 140
Hawks, Howard 193
Haworth, Sir W. Norman 134
Hayes, Helen 193, 202
Hayworth, Rita 193
Hearst, William Randolph 217
Heartfield, John 172
Heath, Edward 43, 48, 50, 106, 117

Heidegger, Martin 214
Heifetz, Jascha 172
Heinz, Henry John 217
Heisenberg, Werner Karl 134, 221
Helicopters 125, 128
Helpmann, Sir Robert 193
Hemingway, Ernest 172, 182, 183, 184, 225
Henderson, Arthur 106
Henie, Sonja 209
Hepburn, Katharine 193, 205
Hepworth, Dame Barbara 172
Heraklion (ferry), sinking of: 96
Herrera, Helenio 209
Hess, Rudolf 106
Hess, Victor Franz 134, 221
Heston, Charlton 193, 204
Heydrich, Reinhard 119
Heyerdahl, Thor 29, 43, *139*, 140
Hill, Graham 51–2, 149, 209
Hillary, Sir Edmund 31, *161*, 162
Hillier, James 134
Hilton, Conrad 217
Himmler, Heinrich 106
Hindemith, Paul 172
Hindenburg, Paul von 15, 20, 22, 23, 106, 108
Hinshelwood, Sir Cyril Norman 134
Hinton, Lord 134
Hitchcock, Alfred 193
Hitler, Adolf 19, 22, 24, *25*, 27, 28, 84, 88, 90, 103, 104, 106, *107*, 108, 109
Hobbs, Sir John Berry (Jack) 209
Ho Chi Minh 42, 88, 106
Hodgkin, Sir Alan Lloyd 140
Hodgkin, Dorothy Crowfoot 134
Hoffman, Dustin 193, 205
Hogan, William Benjamin (Ben) 209
Holiday, Billie 193
Holland, John Philip 134
Holloway, Stanley 194
Holography 125, 128
Holst, Gustav 172
Honda, Soichiro 217
Honduras 67, 70; floods 98, 100
Hong Kong 67, 70
Hoover, Herbert 20, 106, *114*
Hoover, John Edgar 106
Hoover, William Henry 217
Hope, Bob *192*, 194
Hopkins, Sir Frederick Gowland 140
Horthy, Miklos von Nagybanya 18, 106
Houdini, Harry 194
Hounsfield, Godfrey Newbold 140
Hovercraft 125, 128
Howard, Sir Ebenezer 172–3
Hoxha, Enver 107
Hoyle, Sir Fred 127, 131, 134
Hubble, Edwin Powell 134
Huddleston, Trevor 214
Huggins, Charles Brenton 140
Hughes, Howard Robard 194
Hughes, Richard 173, 183, 185
Hull, Cordell 107
Humbert I, King of Italy 118
Hungary, 66, 70; murder of prime minister 118

Hunt, Leamon 121
Hussein Ibn Talal, King of Jordan 31, 54, 107
Husserl, Edmund 214
Hutchinson, Sir W, Kenneth 134
Hutson, Donald 209
Hutton, Sir Leonard 209
Huxley, Aldous 173, 181, 182, 183
Huxley, Sir Julian Sorell 140
Hydrofoil 125, 128
Hydrogen bomb 125

Ibrox disaster 97
Iceland 66, 70
Igloi, Mihaly 209
Impressionism 164–5, 166, 175, 176
India 67, 70; disasters 94, 98, 99, 100
Indonesia 67, 70
Ingold, Sir Christopher Kelk 134
Insulin 125
International Court of Justice, United Nations 79
International organizations 79–81
Inventions 128–9
Ionosphere 122, 125
IRA (Irish Republican Army) 44, 52, 56, 61
Iran 67, 70; earthquakes 96, 98–9; political murders 121
Iraq 67, 70; political murders 120
Ireland, Republic of 67, 70; St Valentine's dance fire 99
Isaacs, Alick 140
Israel 66, 70
Israeli-Arab Wars 86
Issigonis, Sir Alec 218
Italy 67, 70; disasters 96, 100; earthquakes 94, 98, 99
Ito, prince of Japan 118
Ivory Coast 66, 70
Iwasaki, Koyota 218

Jacob, François 140
Jamaica 67, 70; earthquake 94
James, Alex 209
Jansky, Karl Guthe 134
Japan 67, 70; atomic bombs dropped 28, 29, 95; earthquakes 94, 95; mining disaster 99; Tokyo hotel fire 100; typhoon 96
Japanese theatre *167*
Jaurès, Jean 102, 107, 118
Jazz 165, 166
Jet engine 125, 128
Jinnah, Mohammed Ali 107
Jive 165
Joffre, Joseph Jacques Césaire 107
John, Augustus 173
John, Barry 209
John XXIII, Pope 34, 214
John Paul I, Pope 54, 55, 214
John Paul II, Pope 55, 57, 59, 61, 214
Johns, Jasper 166, 173
Johnson, Amy 21, 146, *147*, 162
Johnson, Celia 194
Johnson, Howard 218
Johnson, Jack 209
Johnson, Lyndon B. 37, 41, 107, *114*, 120

Johnson, Philip Cortelyou 173
Johnson, Walter Perry 209
Jolson, Al 194
Jones, Bobby 209
Jordan 66, 70; political murders 120
Joyce, James 173, 181, 183
Juan Carlos I, King of Spain 51, 107
Juliana, Queen of the Netherlands 30, 58
Jung, Carl 140
Junkers, Hugo 134
Jupiter, space mission to 158

Kafka, Franz 173, 183
Kahn, Louis 173
Kamerlingh Onnes, Heike 134
Kampuchea 66, 70
Kandinsky, Wassily 163, 173
Karajan, Herbert von 173
Karrer, Paul 134
Kautsky, Karl 214
Kaye, Danny 194
Kazan, Elia 194, 203, 204
Kearton, Sir C. Frank, *Baron* 218
Keaton, Buster 194
Keller, Helen 140, 180
Kellogg, Will 218
Kelly, Gene Curran 194
Kelly, Grace (Princess Grace of Monaco) 33, 61, 194, 204
Kendall, Edward Calvin 134
Kendrew, John Cowdery 140
Kennedy, John F. 35, 36, 37, *102*, 107, 114, 120
Kennedy, Robert F. 40, 107, 120
Kenya 67, 70
Kenyatta, Jomo 31, 54, 107, *108*
Kerensky, Alexander 16, 82, 107
Kern, Jerome 194
Kerst, Donald 122, 128
Kesselring, Albert 107
Keynes, John Maynard 218
Khatachaturian, Aram 173
Khomeini, Ruhollah, *Ayatollah* 56, 107
Khrushchev, Nikita 32, 33, 37, 107, 108
Killy, Jean-Claude 209
Kinescope 125, 137
King, Billie Jean 209
King, Martin Luther 40, *102*, 107, 120, 214, 227
King, W. L. Mackenzie 18, 107
Kinnock, Neil 63
Kipling, Rudyard 173, 180, 225
Kiribati 70
Kirov, Sergei 118
Kissinger, Henry 107, 227
Kitchener, Horatio Herbert, *1st Earl* 15, 107–8
Klee, Paul 163, 173, 175
Knievel, Evel (Robert Craig) 209
Koch, Robert 138, 140, 224
Kodaly, Zoltan 173
Kohler, Wolfgang 140
Kokoschka, Oscar 173
Kolff, Willem 140
Komisarjevsky, Theodore 194
Korda, Sir Alexander 194
Korea, North and South 67, 70

Korean War 30, 86
Kosygin, Alexei 37, 108
Kramer, Jack 210
Krebs, Sir Hans Adolf 140, 224
Kreisler, Fritz 173
Krupp, Alfred 218
Kubrick, Stanley 194
Kuhn, Richard 134
Ku Klux Klan 18, 19
Kurosawa, Akira 194
Kuwait 66, 70

Labour Party 10, 12, 83
LaGuardia, Fiorello Henry 108
Laker, James Charles (Jim) 210
Lancaster, Burt 194, 204
Land, Edwin Herbert 134
Landau, Lev Davidovitch 134, 221
Landis, Kenesaw 210
Landsteiner, Karl 140
Lane, Sir Allen 23, 218
Lang, Fritz 194
Langevin, Paul 135
Langmuir, Irving 135
Lansbury, George 108
Laos 67, 70
Larkin, Philip 173, 185
La Rocca, Nick 194
Laski, Harold 214–15
Las Vegas: hotel fires 99
Lauda, Niki 210
Laue, Max Theodor Felix von 135
Laughton, Charles 194
Laurel, Stan 193, 194
Laval, Pierre 108
Laver, Rodney 210
Law, Andrew Bonar 108, 117
Law, Denis 210
Lawrence, D. H. 173–4, 180, 181, 187
Lawrence, Gertrude 194
Lawrence, T. E. 173
League of Nations 83
Leakey, L. S. B. 35, 140
Lebanon 66, 70; bomb disaster 100
Le Corbusier 163, 171
Lederberg, Joshua 140
Leger, Fernand 174
Leigh, Vivien 194, 203, 204
Lemmon, Jack 194, 205
Le Neve, Ethel 12
Lenglen, Suzanne 210, 211
Lenin, Vladimir Ilyich 16, 19, 82, 108, 214
Lennon, John 59
Leoncavallo, Ruggiero 174
Lerner, Alan Jay 195
Lesotho 67, 70
Lever, William Hesketh 218
Levi-Strauss, Claude 140
Lewis, C. Day 171, 183
Lewis, Sinclair 174, 181, 182, 225
Liaquat Ali Khan 29, 30, 120
Libby, Willard Frank 123, 135, 223
Liberal Party 84
Liberia 67, 71
Libya 67, 71
Liddell Hart, Basil Henry 108
Lie, Trygve 29, 108
Liechtenstein 71; monarchs 116
Lifar, Serge 195

Lillee, Dennis 210
Lindbergh, Charles A. 20, 145–6, 162
Lindbergh baby, kidnapping of 22, 162
Lippmann, Walter 218
Lipton, Sir Thomas 218
Lister, Joseph, Lord 140
Literature: Nobel Prizewinners 225–6
Littlewood, Joan 195
Lloyd, Harold Clayton 195
Lloyd, Marie 195
Lloyd George, David 108, 117, 173
Lockwood, Margaret 195
Loewe, Frederick 195
Loewy, Raymond 218
Lombardi, Vincent 210
London, Jack 174, 180
London, Tom 195
London Group 165
London theatre: long runs 201
Long, Huey 119
Longden, Johnny 210
Lonsdale, Hugh Cecil Lowther, 5th Earl 210
Lorant, Stefan 218
Lorca, Frederico Garcia 174
Loren, Sophia 195, 204
Lorenz, Konrad 140–1, 225
Lorre, Peter 195
Louis, Joe 210
Lovell, Sir Bernard 135
Lubitsch, Ernst 195
Luce, Clare Booth 108
Luce, Henry Robinson 218, 219
Ludendorff, Erich Friedrich Wilhelm 108
Lunn, Sir Arnold 210
Lunt, Alfred 195
Lusitania, sinking of 15, 94
Lutyens, Sir Edwin Landseer 174, 177
Luxembourg 66, 71

Macao 71
Macarthur, Douglas 28, 30, 86, 108
McBride, Willie John 210, 211
McCarthy, Joseph R. 108
MacDonald, J. Ramsay 19, 21, 108, 117
McEnroe, John 210
McGraw, John Joseph 210
Mack, Connie (Cornelius McGillicuddy) 210
Mackenzie, Sir Compton 174, 181, 182, 183
McKinley, William 114, 118
McLuhan, Marshall 215
McMillan, Edwin Mattison 135
Macmillan, Harold 33, 108, 117
MacMurray, Fred 195
MacNeice, F. Louis 174
McQueen, Steve 195
McWhirter, Ross 120
Madagascar 67, 71
Maeterlinck, Maurice 174, 180, 225
Magritte, René François-Ghislain 174
Mahler, Gustav 174
Makarios III, Archbishop 33, 35, 50, 108, 108

Makarova, Natalia 195
Malamud, Bernard 174
Malawi 67, 71
Malaysia 67, 71
Malcolm X (Little) 37, 108, 120
Maldives 67, 71
Malenkov, Georgi 109
Mali 66, 71
Malinowski, Bronislaw 141
Malraux, André 174, 183, 184, 185
Malta 71
Manhattan 78
Mann, Thomas 174, 182, 184, 185, 225
Manolete (Manuel Sánchez) 210
Mao Tse-Tung (Mao Zedong) 29, 30, 53, 55, 108–9
Marceau, Marcel 167
March, Frederick 195, 202, 203
Marciano, Rocky 210
Marconi, Guglielmo 133, 135, 221
Maritain, Jacques 215
Markova, Dame Alicia 196
Marks, Simon 218
Mars, space mission to 152
Marshall, George C. 29, 109
Martin, Sir Leslie 174
Martinique 71; earthquake 94
Marx brothers 196, 197
Masaryk, Jan Garrigue 109
Masaryk, Tomas Garrigue 109
Mascagni, Pietro 174
Masefield, John 174, 180, 181
Maser 125, 128, 137
Mason, James 196
Massine, Leonide 196
Mata Hari 109
Mathewson, Christy 210
Matisse, Henri-Emile-Benoit 174
Mattei, Enrico 218
Matteotti, Giacomo 118
Matthew, Sir Robert 174
Matthews, Sir Stanley 210, 211
Maugham, William Somerset 174, 180, 181, 184
Mauriac, François 174, 182, 225
Mauritania 66, 71
Mauritius 67, 71
Maurois, André 174, 181
Maxim, Sir Hiram Stevens 135
Mayakovsky, Vladimir 174
Mayer, Louis Burt 196
Mayotte 71
Mays, Willie Howard 210
Mboya, Tom 120
Mead, Margaret 141
Meads, Colin Earl 210
Medawar, Sir Peter Brian 141
Medicine: Nobel Prizewinners 224–5
Meir, Golda 109
Meitner, Lise 135
Melba, Dame Nellie 174
Melbourne (aircraft carrier) 41, 96
Meldrum school 165
Melies, Georges 196
Mendes-France, Pierre 109
Menuhin, Yehudi 174
Menzies, Sir Robert Gordon 109
Merleau-Ponty, Maurice 215
Meson 126, 129
Messiaen, Olivier 174

Metaxas, Johannes 109
Mexico 66, 71; earthquake 98;
 political murders 118
Mhatre, Ravindara 121
Microscope, electron 126, 129
Midgley, Thomas 124, 135
Mies van der Rohe, Ludwig 163,
 175
Miller, Glenn 196
Miller, Henry 175, 183
Millikan, Robert Andrews 135
Mills, Sir John 196
Milne, A. A. 175, 182
Mindszenty, Jozsef 211
Minot, George Richards 141
Miró, Joan 163, 175
Mistinguett 196
Mitchell, Reginald Joseph 135
Mitterand, François 59, 109
Modigliani, Amadeo 175
Mellison, James Allan 146, 162
Molotov, Vyacheslav
 Mikhailovitch 109
Moltke, Helmut Johannes
 Ludwig 109
Monaco 71, monarchs 116
Monarchs: British 113;
 European 115, 115–17
Mondrian, Piet 175
Monet, Claude 165, 175
Mongolia 67, 71
Moniz, Antonio Caetano de Abreu
 Freire Egas 141
Monnet, Jean Omer Marie
 Gabriel 109
Monod, Jacques-Lucien 141
Monroe, Marilyn 196, 208
Montessori, Maria 215
Montgomery, Bernard Law, 1st
 Viscount 26, 93, 105, 109
Montgomery, Robert 196
Montserrat 71
Moody, Helen 210
Moon landings 43, 153–4, 155
Moore, George Edward 215
Moore, Henry 175
Moore, Robert Frederick
 (Bobby) 210
Moores, Sir John 218
Moorgate tube disaster 98
Morgan, Thomas Hunt 141
Moro, Aldo 54, 121
Morocco 66, 72; earthquake 96
Morton, 'Jelly Roll' 196
Moseley, Henry Gwyn Jeffreys 135
Mosley, Sir Oswald 22, 109
Moss, Stirling 210, 211
Mountbatten, Louis, 1st Earl, 56,
 109, 121
Mount St Helens volcano 99
Mozambique 67, 72
Mueller, Erwin Wilhelm 135
Mugabe, Robert 58, 60
Muller, Hermann Joseph 224, 141
Müller, Paul 124, 135
Murders, political 118–21
Murrow, Ed 37, 218
Musil, Robert Von 175
Mussolini, Benito 17, 18, 27, 28,
 83, 84, 88, 109, 119
Mustafa Kemel (Ataturk) 18, 19,
 101

Nabokov, Vladimir 175
Nadir Shah, King of
 Afghanistan, 118
Nagurski, Bronislaw (Bronko) 211
Nagy, Imre 109
Naipaul, Vidiadhar 175
Naismith, Dr James A. 211
Namath, Joe Willie 211
Namibia 67, 72
Namier, Sir Louis 162
Narutowicz, Gabriel 118
Nasser, Gamal Abdel 32, 33, 43, 86,
 105, 109
Nastase, Ilie 211
National Socialism 84
NATO 30, 32, 81; exercise
 disaster 99
Natta, Giulio 135
Nauru 72
Navratilova, Martina 211
Neave, Airey 121
Nehru, Jawaharlal 29, 105, 109
Neill, A. S. 215
Neo-Impressionism 165
Neo-Romanticism 165
Nepal 67, 72; earthquake 94
Nepia, George 211
Nervi, Pier Luigi 175
Netherlands 66, 72; monarchs 116
Netherlands Antilles 72
Nevins, Allan 162
Newman, Barnett 175
Newman, Paul 196
New Wave 165–6
New York: bomb explosion at La
 Guardia airport 98; long runs
 in theatre 201–2
New Zealand 67, 72;
 earthquake 94
Ngo Dinh Diem 120
Niarchos, Stavros 218
Nicaragua 67, 72; earthquakes 94,
 97; floods 100
Nicholas II, Tsar of Russia 118,
 119
Nicholson, Ben 175
Nicklaus, Jack 211
Niger 72
Nigeria 67, 72
'Night of the Long Knives' 118
Nijinsky, Vaslav Fomich 196, 197
Nimitz, Chester William 109
Niue 72
Niven, David 196, 204
Nixon, Richard 41, 42, 43, 47, 48,
 49, 50, 105, 109, 110, 114
Nkrumah, Kwame 47, 110
Nobel Prizewinners 221–7
Norfolk Island 72
Norman, Montagu Collet 218
Norris, Percy 121
Northcliffe, Alfred, 1st Viscount 218
Northern Ireland 44, 45, 46, 47, 48,
 51
Northrop, John Howard 141
Norway 67, 72; monarchs 116
Nuffield, William, 1st Viscount 218
Nureyev, Rudolf 191, 196
Nurmi, Paavo 211
Nuvolari, Tazio 211
Nyere, Julius 110
Nylon 126, 129

OAS (Organization of American
 States) 81
OAU (Organization of African
 Unity) 81
Oberth, Hermann 135
Obregon, Alvaro 118
O'Casey, Sean 163, 175
October Revolution (Russian
 Revolution) 16
OECD (Organization for Economic
 Co-operation and
 Development) 81
Ogilvy, David Mackenzie 219
O'Higgins, Kevin 118
Oistrakh, David 175
Olivier, Lawrence 194, 196, 196,
 203
Oman 67, 72
Onassis, Aristotle 218, 219
O'Neill, Eugene 175
Op Art (Optical art) 166, 176
OPEC (Organization of the
 Petroleum Exporting
 Countries) 81
Oppenheimer, Sir Ernest 219
Oppenheimer, J. Robert 135
Orwell, George 175, 184
Osborne, John James 175
Ostwald, Friedrich Wilhelm 135–6
Ottoman empire, monarchs of 117;
 see also Turkey
Ovett, Steve 211
Owens, Jesse 211

Pacific Islands Trust Territory 72
Paderewski, Ignace, Jan 110
Pakistan 67, 72; earthquakes 96,
 98; tidal wave disasters 95, 97
Palmer, Arnold 211
Paneth, Friedrich Adolf 136
Pankhurst, Emmeline 10, 93, 110
Papanicolaou, George Nicholas 141
Papua New Guinea 67, 72
Paraguay 66, 72
Pareto, Vilfredo 110
Paringaux, Yves 119
Parker, Charlie 196
Parker, Dorothy 175, 219
Parsons, Talcott 215
Partridge, Eric 176
Pasternak, Boris 176, 185, 225
Patton, George Smith 110
Paul VI, Pope 37, 38, 42, 44, 54,
 215
Pauli, Wolfgang 136, 221
Paulus, Frederick 110
Pauling, Linus Carl 136
Pavlov, Ivan Petrovich 141, 224
Pavlova, Anna 197
Peace: Nobel Prizewinners 226–7
Pearson, D. 122, 128
Pearson, G. 122, 128
Pearson, Lester Bowles 110
Peary, Robert 161
Peck, Gregory 197, 204
Pelé (Edson Arantes do
 Nascimento) 211
Penlee lifeboat disaster 60, 99–100
Perón, Eva 110
Perón, General Juan 48, 50, 110
Perry, Frederick John (Fred) 211
Pershing, John Joseph 110

234

Peru 66, 72: disasters 96;
  earthquake 96–7
Perutz, Max Ferdinand 141
Pétain, Marshal Henri 16, 92, 110
Petersen, William Earl 141
Petrie, Sir W. M. Flinders 162
Pevsner, Sir Nikolaus 176
Philip, Prince, Duke of
  Edinburgh 110
Philippines 67, 72; disasters 98
Philips, Anton 219
Physics: Nobel Prizewinners 221,
  223
Physiology: Nobel
  Prizewinners 224–5
Piaf, Edith 197
Picasso, Pablo Ruiz 163, 164, 169,
  176
Piccard, Auguste 162
Pickford, Mary 197
Piggott, Lester 212
Pinter, Harold 176
Pirandello, Luigi 176
Pirie, Norman Wingate 141
Piscator, Erwin 197
Pitcairn Island 72
Pius X, Pope 10, 14, 215
Pius XI, Pope 18, 215
Pius XII, Pope 215
Planck, Max 133, 136, 221
Player, Gary 212
Poincaré, Raymond 110
Poiter, Sidney 197, 204
Poland 67, 72
Pollock, Jackson 163, 176
Polyester 126
Pompidou, Georges 41, 50, 110
Pop art 166, 179
Pop music 166
Popper, Sir Karl 215
Porsche, Ferdinand 219
Porter, Cole 197
Portugal 66, 72; monarchs 116;
  murder of royal family 118
Positron 126
Post, Wiley 146, 162
Post-Impressionism 166, 169
Potter, Beatrix 176, 180
Poulenc, Francis 176
Poulsen, Valdemar 136
Pound, Ezra 176, 180
Powell, Cecil Frank 136
Powell, William 197
Presidents: United States 114
Presley, Elvis 197, 198
Priestly, J. B. 176, 182, 186
Prime Ministers: Britain 117
Primo de Rivera, Miguel 110
Prokofiev, Sergei 176
Protons 122, 124, 126
Proust, Marcel 176, 181
Puccini, Giacomo 176
Pudovkin, Vsevolod 197
Puerto Rico 66, 72
Pulitzer, Joseph 219
Punk rock 166, 166
Puskas, Ferenc 212

Qatar 72
Quant, Mary 219
Quantum theory 126, 136
Quisling, Vidkun 110

Rachmaninov, Sergei 176
Radar 125, 126, 129
Radio 126, 129
Radio-activity 126
Radio telescope 126, 135
Ragtime 166
Rail disasters 94, 98, 100
Raman, Sir Chandrasekhara 136,
  221
Rambert, Dame Marie 197
Ramsay, Sir Alfred E. (Alf) 212
Rasputin, Grigori 110
Rathenau, Walther 118, 219
Rattigan, Sir Terence 197
Ravel, Maurice 176
Reagan, Ronald 59, 63, 64, 110,
  114
Reber, Grote 136
Redford, Robert 197, 205
Redgrave, Sir Michael 198
Redgrave, Vanessa 198
Reed, Sir Carol 198
Reeves, Rosser 219
Reinhardt, Django 198
Reith, John, 1st Baron 219
Relativity, theory of 126
Renoir, Jean 198
Renoir, Pierre Auguste 165, 166,
  176
Resnais, Alain 198
Reunion 72
Rhodes, Cecil, John 110
Rhodes, Wilfred 212
Rhodesia: mining disaster 97; see
  also Zimbabwe
Ribbentrop, Joachim von 29, 110
Richards, Frank 176
Richards, Sir Gordon 212
Richardson, Sir Ralph 198
Richet, Charles-Robert 141
Rickey, Wesley Branch 212
Rickover, Hyman 110
Rilke, Rainer 176
Rimet, Jules 212
Robbe-Grillet, Alain 176
Robbins, Jerome 198
Robinson, Edward G. 198
Robinson, Frank 212
Robinson, Jackie 212
Robinson, Sir Robert 136
Robinson, 'Sugar Ray' 212
Rock and roll 166
Rockefeller, John D. 14, 219
Rockne, Knute K. 212
Rockwell, George 120
Rodgers, Richard 193, 198
Rodin, Auguste 177
Rogers, Ginger 188, 189, 198, 203
Rolls, C. S. 144, 219
Romania 67, 72; earthquake 98;
  monarchs 116
Romero, Oscar, Archbishop of San
  Salvador 121
Rommel, Erwin 109, 110
Rono, Henry 212
Roosevelt, Eleanor 110
Roosevelt, Franklin D. 22, 24, 26,
  27, 28, 93, 105, 110, 114
Roosevelt, Theodore 11, 110, 114,
  118, 226
Rorschach, Hermann 141
Ross, Harold 219

Rosselini, Roberto 198
Rothapfel, Samuel 198
Rothko, Mark 177
Rous, Sir Stanley 212
Royce, Sir Frederick 219
Rozelle, Alvin Ray 212
Rubinstein, Artur 177
Rubinstein, Helena 219
Russell, Bertrand 215, 225
Russia: monarchs 116; political
  murders 118; Royal
  Family 118, 119;
  Transcaucasian
  earthquake 94; see also USSR
Russian Revolution 16, 16
Russo-Japanese War 11, 11, 86–7
Ruth, George Herman
  ('Babe') 212
Rutherford, Ernest, 1st Baron 133,
  136, 223
Rutherford, Dame Margaret 198
Rwanda 67, 72–3
Ryle, Sir Martin 136

Saarinen, Eero 177
Sabin, Albert Bruce 141
Sadat, Anwar al- 44, 54, 55, 56, 60,
  110, 121, 227
Sainsbury, Alan John Baron 220
St Helena 73
St Kitts-Nevis 73
St Lucia 66, 73
St Pierre and Miquelon 73
Saint-Saëns, Camille 177
St Vincent: earthquake 94; volcanic
  eruption 99
St Vincent and the Grenadines 73
Salazar, Dr Oliveira 22, 41, 110
Salinger, J. D. 177, 184
Samoa, American 73
Samoa, Western 73
Samuel, Marcus 220
San Francisco, earthquake in 94
Sanchez Cerro, Luis 118
Sanders, George 198
Sanger, Frederick 136
San Marino 73
Santayana, George 177
São Tomé and Principe 73
Sargent, Sir Malcolm 177
Sarnoff, David 220
Sartre, Jean-Paul 170, 177, 184, 226
Sassoon, Vidal 220
Saudi Arabia 67, 73
Schmeling, Max 212
Schoenberg, Arnold 177
Scholl, William 141
Schrader, Gerhard 136
Schrödinger, Erwin 136
Schuman, Robert 110
Schweitzer, Albert 141
Science fiction 166
Scotland: disasters 96, 97, 98, 100
Scott, Robert F. 13, 161, 162
Scott, Sheila 148, 162
Scriabin, Alexander 109, 177
Seaborg, Glenn Theodore 136
Sea Gem (oil rig), sinking of 96
Second World War see World War II
Security Council, United
  Nations 79
Segovia, Andres 177

235

Selfridge, Harry Gordon 220
Selznick, David Oliver 195
Semenov, Nikolai
  Nikolayevitch 136
Senegal 66, 73
Senghor, Leopold Sedar 177
Sennet Mack 199
Serbia: monarchs 116; murder of
  royal family 118
Seychelles 73
Shackleton, Sir Ernest Henry 162
Sharif, Omar 199
Sharples, Sir Richard 120
Shaw, George Bernard 173, 177,
  189, 225
Shea, John 141
Shearer, Norma 195
Sherborne hospital fire 97
Shergar 62
Sherrington, Sir Charles 141
Shoemaker, Willie 212
Shoenberg, Sir Isaac 136
Sholokhov, Mikhail 177
Shostakovich, Dmitri 177
Sibelius, Jean 177
Sickert, Walter R. 165, 177
Sierra Leone 66, 73
Sikorsky, Igor 136, 144
Silicon chip 127
Simenon, Georges 177
Sinatra, Frank 198, 199
Sinclair, Upton 178, 180, 182, 183,
  184
Singapore 67, 73
Sino-Japanese War 88
Sitwell, Dame Edith 178, 185
Sitwell, Sir Francis Osbert, 5th
  Baronet 178
Skiffle 167
Skinner, Burrhus Frederic 215
Skinner, Dennis 121
Slim, William Joseph 110
Sloan, Alfred P. 220
Smith, Bessie 199
Smith, Sir Charles Kingsford 146,
  162
Smith, Ian Douglas 110
Smuts, Jan Christiaan 110, 110
Snow, Charles Percy, Baron 178
Sobers, Sir Garfield (Gary) 212
Socialism 84
Soddy, Frederick 136, 223
Soekarno, Achmad 110
Solidarity (trade union) 63
Solomon Islands 67, 73
Solzhenitsyn, Alexander 49, 178,
  183, 186, 187, 226
Somali Republic 67, 73
Sorel, Georges 215
Soul music 167
Sousa, John Philip 199
South Africa 67, 73, 74; mining
  disaster 99
South Dakota floods 97
Soviet Union see USSR
Soweto, riots in 53
Spaak, Paul Henri 110
Space exploration 151–60
Space shuttles 159–60
Spain 66, 73; disasters 96, 98, 99;
  monarchs 116
Spanish Civil War 88, 176

Spence, Sir Basil 178
Spencer, Sir Stanley 178
Spengler, Oswald 215
Spitfire (fighter plane) 142
Spitz, Mark 212, 213
Spock, Benjamin 141
Springer, Axel 220
Sri Lanka 67, 73
Stagg, Amos Alonzo 212
Stalin, Joseph 19, 23, 28, 31, 93,
  101, 105, 109, 110, 118
Stanislavsky, Konstantin 199
Stanley, Wendell 141
Stanwyck, Barbara 199
Staudinger, Hermann 136
Stein, Gertrude 178, 180, 182
Steinbeck, John 178, 182, 183, 184,
  226
Stephen, Sir Leslie 178
Stevens, Wallace 178, 181
Stevenson Adlai 110
Stewart, Jackie 212–13
Stewart, James 199
Stockhausen, Karlheinz 178
Stolypin, Piotr 118
Strasberg, Lee 199
Strauss, Richard 178
Stravinsky, Igor 178
Streisand, Barbara 199
Stroheim, Erich Von 199
Sturges, John 199
Sudan 67, 73
Suffragettes 10, 93, 93
Sumner, James B. 141
Sundback, Gideon 136
Sunshine Skyway Bridge,
  Florida 99
Sun Yat-Sen 13, 110
Surinam 67, 73
Surrealism 167, 169, 171, 173, 174
Surtees, John 212–13
Sutherland, Graham 178
Sutherland, Dame Joan 178, 179
Swanson, Gloria 199
Swaziland 67, 73
Sweden 67, 73; monarchs 116
Swing (music) 167
Switzerland 66, 73; train/bus
  crash 100
Sydney Opera House 48, 49
Sykes, Sir Richard 121
Synge, J. M. 163, 178
Syria 66, 73
Szent-Gyorgi, Albert von 141
Szilard, Leo 136

Taft, William Howard 114
Tagore, Sir Rabindranath 178
Taiwan 67, 73
Tanzania 67, 73
Tarski, Alfred 215
Tasmania: Tasman bridge
  disaster 99
Tata, Sir Jamsetji 220
Tati, Jacques 199
Tatum, Edward Lawrie 141, 224
Tawney, Richard H. 162
Taylor, A. J. P. 162
Taylor, Elizabeth 199
Tedder, Arthur William 110
Teilhard de Chardin, Pierre 142
Television 127, 129

Teller, Edward 136
Temple, Shirley 199
Templeman, William 142
Tereshkova, Valentina 152, 157,
  162
Terry, Dame Ellen
Terylene 127, 129
Tatrazzini, Luisa 178
Thailand 67, 73, 75
Thatcher, Margaret 56, 110, 117
Theatre: long runs 201–2; terms
  used in 163–8
Thomas, Dylan 178, 185
Thompson, Sir D'Arcy
  Wentworth 142
Thompson, James W. 220
Thomson, Sir Joseph John 136, 221
Thomson of Fleet, Roy Herbert, 1st
  Baron 220
Thorndike, Edward Lee 142
Thorndike, Dame Sybil
Thorpe, Jim 213
Thurber, James 178
Tilden, William Tatem ('Big
  Bill') 213
Tilley, Vesta 199
Tillich, Paul Johannes 215
Tinbergen, Nikolas 142
Tippett, Sir Michael 178
Tirpitz, Alfred von 112
Tiselius, Arne Wilhelm Kaurin 142
Tisza, Count Stephen 118
Titanic, sinking of 13, 94
Tito, Marshall 31, 58, 112
Tizard, Sir Henry Thomas 136–7
Tjio, Joe Hin 142
Todd, Sir Alexander 137, 223
Togliatti, Palmiro 112
Togo 67, 75
Togo, Count Heihachiro 112
Tojo, Hideki 112
Tokyo: hotel fire 100
Toland, Greg 199
Tolbert, William 121
Tolkien, J. R. R 178, 183, 185, 187
Tonga 75
Torrey Canyon (tanker) 96
Toscanini, Arturo 178
Townes, C. H. 125, 128, 137, 221
Toynbee, Arnold 162
Tracy, Spencer 193, 199, 203
Trad (traditional jazz) 165, 167,
  168
Transistor 127, 129
Tresca, Carlo 119
Tree, Sir Herbert 199
Trevelyan, George M. 162
Trinidad and Tobago 67, 75
Trippe, Juan Terry 220
Tristan de Cunha 75
Trotsky, Leon 20, 26, 112, 119
Trudeau, Pierre 40, 44, 112
Trueman, Frederick Sewards 213
Truman, Harry S. 28, 30, 108, 112,
  114
Trusteeship Council, United
  Nations 79
Tsiolkovsky, Konstantin
  Eduardovich 137
Tswett, Mikhail Semenovich 142
Tubman, William 112
Tucker, Sophie 200

236

Tunisia 66, 75
Tunney, Gene 213
Turkestan, earthquake in 94
Turkey 67, 75; coal pit
  explosion 100;
  earthquake 95, 96, 97, 98;
  monarchs 117; murder of
  prime minister 118
Turks and Caicos Islands 75
Tutankhamen 18, 19
Tuvalu 75

Uganda 67, 75
Ullstein, Rudolf 220
Undset, Sigrid 178
United Arab Emirates 66, 75
United Kingdom 66, 76; see also
  Britain
United Nations 79
United States of America 66, 76-7;
  disasters 96, 97, 98, 99, 100;
  presidents 114
Upper Volta see Burkina Faso
Uruguay 67, 76
USSR 67, 74, 75; soccer match
  disaster 100
Ustinov, Peter 200

Valentino, Rudolph 200
Valéry, Paul 178
Vanuatu 67, 76
Várdon, Harry 213
Vatican City 76-7
Vaughan Williams, Ralph 178
Venezuela 66, 77
Venizelos, Eleutherios 12
Ventris, Michael G. F. 162
Venus, space mission to 152
Verne, Jules 166, 178, 179
Verwoerd, Hendrik Frensch 112,
  120
Victory (tanker) 100
Vietnam 77
Vietnam Wars 39, 42, 47, 88
Vigo, Jean 200
Virgin Islands 77
Voroshilov, Kliment
  Yeiremovich 112
Vorovsky, Vaslav 118
Vorster, Balthazar Johannes 112
Vorticism 168

Wade, Virginia 213, 213
Wagner, John Peter (Honus) 213
Wahine (ferry), sinking of 96
Wainwright, Jonathan Mayhew 112
Waksman, Selman Abraham 142
Waldheim, Kurt 45, 60, 112
Wales: Aberfan disaster 38, 96, 97
Wallace, Alfred Russel 142
Wallace, Dewitt 220
Wallace, Edgar 179
Wallace, George Corley 112
Waller, Thomas Wright
  ('Fats') 200
Wallis, Sir Barnes Neville 137
Wallis and Futuna Islands 77
Walter, Bruno 179
Walton, Ernest T. S. 131, 137, 221
Walton, Sir William 179
Warhol, Andy 179
Warner, Glenn Scorey (Pop) 213

Warner, Jack L. 200
Warner, Sir Pelham Francis
  (Plum) 213
Wars 85-93
Warsaw Pact 81
Washington, Booker 215
Watergate affair 47, 49, 50-1
Watson, James Dewey 142
Watson-Watt, Sir Robert
  Alexander 137
Waugh, Evelyn 179, 182, 183, 184,
  185
Wavell, Archibald Percival, 1st
  Earl 112
Wayne, John 200, 205
Weaver, Warren 137
Weber, Max 215
Webern, Anton von 179
Wedgwood, Dame C. Veronica 162
Wegener, Alfred Lother 123, 137
Weill, Kurt 179
Weismann, August F. L. 142
Weissmuller, Peter John
  (Johnny) 213
Welch, Richard 120
Wellcome, Sir Henry 220
Welles, Orson 200
Wells, H. G. 166, 179, 180, 182,
  200
Wesker, Arnold 200
West, Mae 200
West, Dame Rebecca 179, 181, 184,
  185, 186, 187
Western Sahara 77
Western Samoa 77
West Germany see Germany, Federal
  Republic of
Wharton, Edith 181
Wheeler, Sir R. E. Mortimer 162
Whinfield, John Rex 137
White, Patrick 179
Whiteman, Paul Samuel 200
Whittle, Sir Frank 24, 125, 128,
  137, 137, 146, 147
Whitty, Kenneth 121
Wiener, Norbert 137
Wigglesworth, Sir Vincent
  Brian 142
Wilder, Billy 200, 203, 204
Wilhelm II, Kaiser 17, 112
Wilhelmina, Queen of the
  Netherlands 30, 112
Wilkins, Sir George H. 162
Wilkins, Maurice H. F. 142
Wilkinson, Charles B. (Bud) 213
Williams, Tennessee 179
Willstater, Richard Martin 137
Wilson, C. T. R. 123, 137, 221
Wilson, Edmund 179
Wilson, Harold 38, 50, 112, 117
Wilson, Sir Henry H. 118
Wilson, Kemmons 220
Wilson, Woodrow 13, 15, 83, 112,
  114, 226
Winchell, Walter 220
Wingate, Orde Charles 112
Wittgenstein, Ludwig 215
Wodehouse, P.G. 179, 180, 181,
  182
Women's Suffrage 93
Wood, Sir Henry 179
Woodruff, Robert 220

Woolf, Virginia 179, 182, 184
Woolworth, F. W. 220
World War I 14, 14-17, 87, 88-90,
  89; air events during 144-5
World War II 25-9, 27, 28, 89, 90,
  91, 92-3; air events during)
  147-7
Wright, Frank Lloyd 179
Wright brothers 10, 122, 137, 143

Yamamoto, Isoroku 112
Yeats, W. B. 163, 179, 185, 225
Yemen, North: earthquake 100
Yemen Arab Republic 66, 77
Yemen People's Democratic
  Republic 66, 77
Yerkes, Charles Tyson 220
Young, Denton True (Cy) 213
Yugoslavia 66, 77-8;
  earthquake 96;
  monarchs 117; rail
  disaster 98

Zaharias, Babe 213
Zaire 78
Zambia 67, 78
Zanuck, Darryl Francis 200
Zatopek, Emil 213
Zeeman, Pieter 127, 137
Zeffirelli, Franco 200
Zeppelin, Ferdinand, Graf von 137
Zhukov, Georgi 28, 112
Ziegfeld, Florenz 200
Ziegler, Karl Waldemar 137
Zimbabwe 58, 59, 67, 78; bus
  crash 100
Zuckerkandl, Emile 142
Zuckerman, Sir Solly 142
Zukor, Adolph 200
Zworykin, Vladimir 127, 129, 137